the whole woman

GERMAINE GREER

BLACK SWAN

TRANSWORLD PUBLISHERS
61–63 Uxbridge Road, London W5 5SA
a division of The Random House Group Ltd
www.booksattransworld.co.uk

THE WHOLE WOMAN
A BLACK SWAN BOOK: 9780552774345

First published in Great Britain
in 1999 by Doubleday
a division of Transworld Publishers
Anchor edition published 2000
Black Swan edition reissued 2007

This book is a work of non-fiction. The author has stated to the publishers
that the contents of this book are true.

A CIP catalogue record for this book
is available from the British Library

Addresses for Random House Group Ltd companies outside the UK
can be found at: www.randomhouse.co.uk
The Random House Group Ltd Reg. No. 954009

The Random House Group Limited makes every effort to ensure that the
papers used in our books are made from trees that have been legally
sourced from well-managed and credibly certified forests. Our paper
procurement policy can be found on www.randomhouse.co.uk

Typeset in Ehrhardt by Falcon Oast Graphic Art Ltd.
Printed and bound in Great Britain by
CPI Antony Rowe, Chippenham, Wiltshire.

6 8 10 9 7 5

This book is lovingly and respectfully dedicated to FLO *who taught me street lore and fed me soul food, who has seen more than I will ever see and understood more than I will ever understand, and has been called mad by the very people who most need to know the things she tells them as if they were jokes, hard facts made easy and memorable by Flo's ready wit, panhandling with a punch;*

BETH *whose life is the quintessential love-and-work, whose creativity and expertise are by now recognized by hundreds of thousands of people, if not by an establishment that is still exclusively interested in monuments, free-standing unchanging hardbodied things, when she works in living materials, in time and earth and air and water, Beth of the unswerving heart and clever workworn hands;*

JANET *who has endured every kind of professional insult and belittlement from men less talented than she is and, though she bitches them memorably from time to time, gets on with what she is good at, living and working, learning and laughing, always stylish, never apologetic;*

MIRIAM *who was born with none of Barbie's attributes and never let it worry her, becoming instead the avatar of real women, a galaxy of female characters, always eccentric and always beguiling, showing us all that the range of alternatives for unrepentant 'ams' is vastly richer than anything dreamed of by the wannabes;*

BEATRIX *who grows more beautiful as she ages, whose happiness is concerning herself for the happiness of others, who keeps the faith of her youth and her passion for social justice, unmocked by fashionable isms, as if she never doubted that gentle but firm persuasion would eventually liberate from his prejudices even the most hidebound.*

contents

the whole woman

GERMAINE GREER

recantation

This sequel to *The Female Eunuch* is the book I said I would never write. I believed that each generation should produce its own statement of problems and priorities, and that I had no special authority or vocation to speak on behalf of women of any but my own age, class, background and education. For thirty years I have done my best to champion all the styles of feminism that came to public attention because I wanted it to be clear that lipstick lesbianism and the prostitutes' union and La Leche and the Women's League for Peace and Freedom and pressure for the ordination of women were aspects of the same struggle towards awareness of oppression and triumph over it. Though I disagreed with some of the strategies and was as troubled as I should have been by some of the more fundamental conflicts, it was not until feminists of my own generation began to assert with apparent seriousness that feminism had gone too far that the fire flared up in my belly. When the lifestyle feminists chimed in that feminism had gone just far enough in giving them the right to 'have it all', i.e. money, sex and fashion, it would have been inexcusable to remain silent.

In 1970 the movement was called 'Women's Liberation' or, contemptuously, 'Women's Lib'. When the name 'Libbers' was dropped for 'Feminists' we were all relieved. What none of us noticed was that the ideal of liberation was fading out with the word. We were settling for equality. Liberation struggles are not about assimilation but about asserting difference, endowing that difference with dignity and prestige, and insisting on it as a condition of self-definition and self-determination. The aim of women's liberation is to do as much for female people as has been done for colonized nations. Women's liberation did not see the female's potential in terms of the male's actual; the visionary feminists of the late Sixties and early Seventies knew that women could never find freedom by agreeing to live the lives of unfree men. Seekers after equality clamoured to be admitted to smoke-filled male haunts. Liberationists sought the world over for clues to what women's lives could be like if they were free to define their own values, order their own priorities and decide their own fate.

The Female Eunuch was one feminist text that did not argue for equality. At a debate in Oxford one William J. Clinton heard me arguing that equality legislation could not give me the right to have broad hips or hairy thighs, to be at ease in my woman's body. Thirty years on femininity is still compulsory for women and has become an option for men, while genuine femaleness remains grotesque to the point of obscenity. Meanwhile the price of the small advances we have made towards sexual equality has been the denial of femaleness as any kind of a distinguishing character. If femaleness is not to be interpreted as inferiority, it is not to signify anything at all. Even the distinction between the vagina which only women have and the rectum which everybody has has been declared, as it were, unconstitutional. Non-consensual buggery, which can be inflicted on both sexes, has been nonsensically renamed 'male rape'. In June 1998 an overwhelming vote of the British House of Commons recognized the right of sixteen-year-old homosexual men 'to have sex', by which they meant, apparently, for it was never explained, the right to penetrate and be penetrated anally. This the MPs saw as granting homosexual men the same rights as heterosexuals. For them at least rectum and vagina were equivalent; in many cultures (and increasingly our own) the most desirable vagina is as tight and narrow as a rectum. Post-modernists are proud and pleased that gender now justifies fewer suppositions about an individual than ever before, but for women still wrestling with the same physical realities this new silence about their visceral experiences is the same old rapist's hand clamped across their mouths. Real women are being phased out; the first step, persuading them to deny their own existence, is almost complete.

> It is invariably the 'straightest' people who speak out against lowering the age of gay consent, paradoxically suggesting that buggery, for a young man, is so bloody enjoyable that just one taste and you're hooked, and women will forever seem to you like pretty small beer.
>
> Julie Burchill

In the last thirty years women have come a long, long way; our lives are nobler and richer than they were, but they are also fiendishly difficult. From the beginning feminists have been aware that the causes of female suffering can be grouped under the heading 'contradictory expectations'. The contradictions women face have never been more bruising than they are now. The career woman does not know if she is to do her job like a man or like herself. Is she supposed to change the organization or knuckle under to it? Is she supposed to endure harassment or kick ass and take names? Is motherhood a privilege or a punishment? Even if it had been real, equality would have been a poor substitute for liberation; fake equality is leading women into double jeopardy. The rhetoric of equality is being used in the name of political correctness to mask the hammering that women are taking. When *The Female Eunuch* was written our daughters were not cutting or starving themselves. On every side speechless women endure endless hardship, grief and pain, in a world system that creates billions of losers for every handful of winners.

It's time to get angry again.

warm-up

The woman question is answered. It is now understood that women can do anything that men can do. Anyone who tries to stop them will be breaking the law. Even the President of the United States, the most powerful person in the world, can be called to account by a female nobody who accuses him of asking her to fellate him. Power indeed! The future is female, we are told. Feminism has served its purpose and should now eff off. Feminism was long hair, dungarees and dangling earrings; post-feminism was business suits, big hair and lipstick; post-post-feminism was ostentatious sluttishness and disorderly behaviour. We all agree that women should have equal pay for equal work, be equal before the law, do no more housework than

Nothing is more empowering than towering over your boyfriend and your boss in shoes that double as an offensive weapon. Stilettos – not combat trousers and pierced tongues – are a real source of girl power.

Lesley Thomas, *Express*, February 1998

men do, spend no more time with children than men do – or do we? If the future is men and women dwelling as images of each other in a world unchanged, it is a nightmare.

In *The Female Eunuch* I argued that every girl child is conceived as a whole woman but from the time of her birth to her death she is progressively disabled. A woman's first duty to herself is to survive this process, then to recognize it, then to take measures to defend herself against it. For years after *The Female Eunuch* was written I travelled the earth to see if I could glimpse a surviving whole woman. She would be a woman who did not exist to embody male sexual fantasies or rely upon a man to endow her with identity and social status, a woman who did not have to be beautiful, who could be clever, who would grow in authority as she aged. I gazed at women in segregated societies and found them in many ways stronger than women who would not go into a theatre or a restaurant without a man. I learned the limitlessness of women's work from labourers, beggarwomen, tribeswomen. I learned about sexual pleasure from women who had been infibulated, about the goddess from great ladies whose hands were untouched by toil and from labouring grandmothers burnt black by the sun. Osage women in Oklahoma, Anmatyerre and Pitjantjatara women in Central Australia taught me about survival.

[Blokes] like you to wear really high heels – so keep stum about aching calf muscles and crippled toes.

Sun Woman, February 1998

No sooner had I caught sight of the whole woman than western marketing came blaring down upon her with its vast panoply of spectacular effects, strutting and trumpeting the highly seductive gospel of salvation according to hipless, wombless, hard-titted Barbie. My strong women thrust their muscular feet into high heels and learnt to totter; they stuffed their useful breasts into brassieres and instead of mothers' milk fed commercial formulae made up with dirty water to their children; they spent their tiny store of cash on lipstick and nail varnish, and were made modern. Even the hard-working women of China began curling their hair to prove that they too were real (i.e. phony) women. While western feminists were valiantly contending for a key to the executive washroom, the feminine stereotype was completing her conquest of the world.

This insidious process was floated on the lie of the sexual revolution. Along with spurious equality and flirty femininity we were sold sexual 'freedom'. One man's sexual freedom is another man's – or woman's or child's – sexual thraldom. The first tenet of sexual freedom is that any kind of bizarre behaviour is legitimate if the aim is orgasm. Men who nail each other's foreskins to breadboards are not to be criticized or ridiculed, still less humiliated or punished. An individual who gets his kicks by shoving live hamsters into his rectum must not be reviled, though he may be prosecuted for cruelty to animals. Political correctness forbids me to identify such a paraphiliac as male but if he turns out to be female I'll eat the hamster.

The sexuality that has been freed is male sexuality which is fixated on penetration. Penetration equals domination in the animal world and therefore in the unregenerate human world which is part of it. The penetree, regardless of sex, cannot rule, OK? Not in prison, not in the army, not in business, not in the suburbs. The person on the receiving end is – fucked, finished, unserviceable, degraded. Not actually, you understand, but figuratively, which, language being metaphor, is what counts. When a male soldier calls a female soldier a split, he identifies her as a fuckee and asserts his dominance over her. Penetration has but little to do with love and even less with esteem. In the last third of the twentieth century more women were penetrated deeper and more often than in any preceding era. The result in Britain is epidemic rates of chlamydia, genital warts and herpes, especially in women aged between sixteen and nineteen, together with a rate of teen pregnancy second only to that of the US. What the penis could not accomplish was done for it by the outsize dildo and the fist, the speculum and the cannula. If penetration was the point, it certainly got made.

> Why do we pretend we like giving head when we all know it's about as sexually exciting as stuffing a cold hot dog in your mouth?
>
> Julia Gaynor, *Company* magazine

The legitimization of the hunt for the perfect orgasm has greatly increased the extent and range of prostitution. Whole communities now live on immoral earnings. Czech women students 'choose' to give up their studies and work as prostitutes because they can earn in an hour what their professionally qualified mothers are paid in a month. Every day third-world women are smuggled into European countries to serve as sex slaves, with no papers, no identity and no rights. A person working as a prostitute to fund a drug habit is the least free individual on the planet.

If equality means entitlement to an equal share of the profits of economic tyranny, it is irreconcilable with liberation. Freedom in an unfree world is merely licence to exploit. Lip-service to feminism in the developed nations is a handy disguise for the masculinization of power and the feminization of poverty in the emerging nations. If you believe, as I do, that to be feminist is to understand that before you are of any race, nationality, religion, party or family, you are a woman, then the collapse in the prestige and economic power of the majority of women in the world as a direct consequence of western hegemony must concern you. And when you see women denounce cultural imperialism – the women who donned the chador and howled the Americans out of Iran, for example – you should recognize them and their struggle as your own.

> For women who are already a success in their field, working mothers, or just starting out on the career ladder, Tomorrow's Women offers an unmissable insight into what the future holds.
> Ticket prices (including VAT) are £176.25 (corporate rate), £129.95 (non-profit organisation rate) and £82.25 (individual rate) to include full-day event ticket, conference pack including copy of Demos report, morning refreshment and lunch.

The implosion of the Soviet regimes and the ensuing collapse of state capitalism caused great suffering to women. The women whose lives have been spent in hard labour in state-owned industries have lost their free health care and their state-subsidized housing just when they had most need of them. So-called 'free' economies are not kind to women who find they must sell whatever they have that is marketable in order to pay market rates for food and housing. 'User pays' is a fine principle, but not if you are ill or disabled or a child or responsible for a child. Women have historically been committed to caring; if they are now condemned to be uncaring, can this be a liberation? Or should feminists establish the female principle of caring as a political principle? To do that would be to become that most absurd and outmoded of beings, a socialist.

It is because feminism is not egotistic that its force has been dissipated among a flotilla of other concerns, the peace movement, the green movement, gay liberation, black liberation, anti-pornography, animal rights, the ordination of women, HIV and AIDS. In every street demonstration, direct action, picket, whatever, you will see feminists copping the flak in the front line, though they will seldom be identified as spokespersons.

The women at Greenham Common were all feminists but they were holding hands around the nuclear base as peace protesters. Women in Somalia have recently been publicly flogged for

> Cyclical amnesia seems to be a characteristic of feminism.
>
> Angela Phillips, 1998

daring to mount street protests against the sending of their menfolk into war zones. Should we accept altruism as part of the psychological make-up of the whole woman, or should we insist that she concentrate upon self-interest? Or should we politicize the principle of altruism on the grounds that it is no more than enlightened self-interest? We live in this world together and how we live together affects the way we live alone. We know the planet is in need of good housekeeping and that ecological measures have no impact unless they are co-ordinated and applied across regional, state and country boundaries, just as the childless among us know that we need good education for other people's children, if our lives are to be worth living. The question whether feminists have to be socialists is seldom asked. American feminists turn their faces away from Cuban feminists struggling to counteract the crippling effects of the American blockade.

It is a chokingly bitter irony that feminism accomplishes most within the confines of the superpower that grinds the life out of the world's women, makes war on them and starves their children. The identification of feminism with the United States has dishonoured it around the world. Half of the women soldiers in the world serve in the United States armed forces. Feminism can have little credibility with the women of Iraq who saw bare-legged women soldiers laughing with men as they made war on them and now watch their sick children die because of the trade embargo. Yet the women who work to raise finance and organize the buying and sending of medical aid to Iraq and Palestine are feminists.

As a political entity feminism had less clout than the merest lobby. It neither bought politicians nor fielded them. Feminism exists outside the realm of political instrumentality, as an idea. Feminist consciousness now leavens every relationship, every single social and professional encounter. This is not to say that feminism motivates social and political action; more often than not, courses of action are adopted that neutralize or pre-empt possible consequences of feminist awareness. There is no longer any free space where individuals might develop alternative cultural and social systems. Failure to enter into debt slavery equals social delinquency. In the 'free' world tax authorities, banks, building societies, credit card companies, the health service and the DSS exercise a degree of control over the individual undreamed of by the apostles of centralized economies. Changes in the law and the social security system force everyone, female, male, old, young, to capitulate. Marketing strategies, now adopted not only by manufacturers and suppliers of services, but by government, communications, churches, charities, schools and universities, obfuscate every issue. What they seek is not informed choice but compliance. Feminism being incompatible with consumerism, marketing co-opted

---

Helen Gurley Brown morphed into Naomi Wolf, seamlessly, girlishly, promiscuously. Now we have bimbo feminism, giving intellectual pretensions to a world where the highest ideal is to acknowledge your inner slut.

Maureen Dowd, *New York Times*, 7 July 1997

---

it as a fashion and then immediately declared it passé, only to co-opt it again and again under different designer labels.

In February 1997 a National Opinion Poll found that 'nearly

seven out of ten women feel political parties do not pay sufficient attention to issues of importance to women'. These women would not answer to the description of feminist, but if feminism is the consciousness of women's oppression, they were not afraid to display it. Three-quarters of *all* women aged between twenty-five and fifty-four were prepared to declare themselves dissatisfied with the politicians' record on issues such as childcare, low pay, part-time work and the under-representation of women in decision-making positions, and 55 per cent of men agreed with them. More than a third of the women polled had not decided how to vote. According to the psephologists it was the women's vote that returned Bill Clinton for a second term as US president. Hence Naomi Wolf's version of feminist triumphalism:

> The 'genderquake' started in America with the eruption of Oklahoma law professor Anita Hill's charges of sexual harass-ment, rocked through 1991–2's famous rape trials, flung into the light of day Senator Bob Packwood's sexual harassment of colleagues, and the sexual abuse of US Navy women at the Tailhook Convention; and provided the impetus for 52 new women legislators to take their seats in the House of Representatives and the Senate. From these beginnings, and with the election of pro-feminist President Clinton in the USA, the election of the first female Prime Minister of Canada, and the re-election – with the women's vote – of socialist Prime Minister Paul Keating in Australia, a train of events has been set in motion that leads to one conclusion: women have become the political ruling class.

Wolf's is an odd way of interpreting the prevalence of sexual harassment and assault throughout the American establish-ment, to be sure! *Fire with Fire* was published as recently as 1993; already many of the brave new initiatives Wolf identifies have withered away.

In the British election of May 1997 160 women stood for the Labour Party; 103 got in. When parliament opened there were so many Labour women running around in little red suits that the Palace of Westminster looked like a Butlin's holiday camp. None of the female candidates had cut any kind of a figure in press coverage of the election which generally treated it as a knock-down-drag-out fight between two men in suits. The media, which make news as well as carrying it, are the real sources of power in our pseudo-democracies. The most cursory examination of even the most progressive organs of information reveals a curious inability to recognize women as newsmakers, unless they are young or married to a head of state or naked or pregnant by some triumph of technology or perpetrators or victims of some hideous crime or any combination of the above. Women's issues are often disguised as people issues, unless they are relegated to women's pages which amazingly still survive. Senior figures are all male; even the few women who are deemed worthy of obituaries are shown in images from their youth, as if the last forty years or so of their lives have been without achievement of any kind. If you analyse the by-lines in your morning paper you will see that the senior editorial staff are all older men, supported by a rabble of junior females, the infinitely replaceable 'hackettes'. Twice a year the British government announces an honours list which is so sexist as to be laughable. The headline names on it are the new knights, who have to be male by definition and whose wives get to be called 'Lady'. The husband of the odd Dame (usually a performer of some kind) is still plain 'mister'. Women get few of the orders of the British Empire (*sic*) until we get to the MBE, called in the corridors of power 'the secretaries' award', where the proportion awarded to females goes up to 40 per cent.

Women may enter political institutions only after those institutions have formed them in the institutional mould; the more female politicians a parliament may boast, the less likely it

13

is to address women's issues. Prime Minister Blair has less trouble keeping his party under an unprecedented degree of central control because so many of the Labour MPs are inexperienced, young and female. A male Labour MP called them the Stepford Wives 'with a chip inserted in their brain to keep them on message'; the media call them 'Blair's babes'. One woman MP, slated to ask a question at the weekly Prime Minister's Questions, could not master the formula in which such questions have to be phrased and after two tries had to be coached by her colleagues. Few of the silly rituals of the house have been abolished nor has the parliamentary timetable been modified. After a year in the rowdy bear-garden that is the British House of Commons and many weeks without seeing their families for more than a few minutes at a time, the new women MPs were reporting levels of stress approaching the unbearable.

Though parliament is unconcerned about women's issues, universities appear obsessed by them. Every year brings forth thousands of academic publications on sex roles, the status of women, the history of gender, the politics of fertility, reproductive rights, women and power, women and war, women and peace, women and literature, women and illiteracy, women and Islam, women and violence, menstruation politics, menopause, gynaecophobia, the war of the sexes, segregation, woman power, the feminization of poverty, victimization, rape, anti-rape, heroines, amazons, motherhood, daughterhood, grandmothering, the bad mother, the madwoman in and out of the attic, written by old feminists, new feminists, radical feminists, cultural feminists, post-modernist feminists, post-structuralist feminists, gender feminists, feminist critics, feminist collectives, Jewish feminists, lesbian feminists, disabled feminists, feminist nuns, feminist sex workers, by sociologists, philosophers, geographers, psychologists. As far as the intellectual establishment is concerned there is still a profound and ramified women question, which has still to be correctly asked, let alone answered.

Reflecting on the advances made since 1977, when the NOW conference in Houston drew up the National Plan of Action, Susan J. Douglas says bitterly:

> They advocated government-funded battered women's shelters; national health insurance for all Americans with provisions for women's special needs; government funding for day-care centers; rape prevention programs and programs for victims of child abuse; and extension of Social Security benefits to housewives. Since as of this writing over fifteen years later America has three times as many animal shelters as it does battered women's shelters, no national health insurance plan, no federal funding for day-care centers, and a rape rate that is terrifying, any one of these provisions could be thought of as revolutionary.

The recommendations were in fact a wish-list and presupposed a commitment to social justice which has never characterized the US government at any time. Changes in British legislation have been slow and tentative, commitment to the economic enfranchisement of women more apparent than real. A woman is now slightly more likely to find a job than a man, entirely because of the restructuring of the job market in the employer's favour. As Larry Elliott put it:

> Britain has become not just a service economy, but a servant economy. This applies not only to the rapid increase in domestic servants – cleaners, nannies, window-cleaners, car valets and so on – but also to vast chunks of the workforce, which has seen the balance of power in the labour market shift massively in favour of employers.

The workers who will accept a zero-hours contract, which means that they are only called upon if business is brisk and then paid an hourly rate, who will carry pagers and mobile phones and be at the employer's beck and call twenty-four hours a day, who take work home every night, who are not unionized and have no job protection or guarantee of safe and hygienic conditions or insurance against work-related injury,

Gynocentric feminism defines women's oppression as the devaluation and repression of women's experience by a masculine culture that exalts violence and individualism.

Iris Marion Young, *Throwing Like a Girl*

are women. Now that the labour movement has been brought to its knees by job shortage, so that workers can no longer bargain for decent wages and conditions, women come to preponderate in the squalid and uncertain workplace, without insurance, without security, without safety, without representation, without contracts. Women have not willed this; they have come to outnumber men in paid employment because when male labour unions had power they did not use it to enfranchise the women who worked in cheaper sectors. They allowed a vast pool of cheap female labour to exist alongside them until their elite was eventually overwhelmed by it. Put simply it goes like this: women always did the shit work; now that the only work there is is shit work men are unemployed. Non-shit work will become shit work if women in any numbers get to do it. Prestige and power have seeped out of professions as women joined them. Teaching is already rockbottom; medicine is sliding fast.

Though they are close to parity in numbers, the total earned by British women is only 60 per cent of what men earn; their pay hour by hour is 79 pence for every pound earned by a man. The terms of the Equal Pay Act stipulate equal pay for work of equal value, as if work had an intrinsic value and was not simply worth what the worker could force the employer to pay or, more often these days, the least that the employer could get the worker to accept. The differential between women's pay and men's pay has now been enshrined. A woman who brings a case before an employment tribunal will wait for years before a decision will be reached; a decision in a single case is simply that. British equal pay legislation is legislation meant to be ineffective, designed to be ineffective. The Equal Opportunities Commission sent the recommendations for making the Equal Pay Act effective to the Tory government in 1990; they waited three years for the reply which rejected any need for major change. In the interim the government had abolished the Wages Councils that had previously offered some protection to low-paid workers, most of whom are women. The Equal Opportunities Commission has now taken its case to the European Commission, whose recommendations when they finally emerge will doubtless be ignored.

> In Britain in 1997 more than twice as many women as men set up new businesses; three out of four new businesses will fail but only one of the three will be headed by a woman.

Women are discriminated against by building societies who treat maternity leave as long-term sick leave and will not lend to couples with both partners in work if the woman is pregnant. Women pay 50 per cent more for medical insurance. Women are the stomping ground of medical technology, routinely monitored, screened and tortured, to no purpose except the enactment of control. They have been punished for their acquisition of a modicum of economic independence by being left with virtually total responsibility for the welfare of children, while gangs of professionals perpetually assess and record their inadequacies. Idealization of the mother has been driven out by criminalization of the mother. The most consistently misquoted sentence from *The Female Eunuch* is 'Women have very little idea of how much men hate them.' Some men hate all women all of the time; all men hate some women some of the time. I reckon that in the year 2000 more men hate more women more bitterly than in 1970. Our culture is far more masculinist than it was thirty years ago. Movies deal with male obsessions. Football is Britain's most significant cultural activity. Computer use is spreading into every home but more than 80 per cent of Internet users are male. Women are ignored by manufacturers of video games, which are mostly war games of one sort or another. Popular music is split as never before; the consumers of commercial pop are female; the rock music that appeals to men is deliberately, unbelievably and outrageously misogynist. While women were struggling to live as responsible dignified adults, men have retreated into extravagantly masculinist fantasies and behaviours.

> If we are sincerely concerned with ending the subordination of *all* women, feminists cannot afford unquestioned assumptions, orthodoxies or dogmatic commitments to positions alleged to be 'politically correct'.
>
> Alison Jaggar, 1994

Every day terrible revenges are enacted on women who have dared to use their new privileges. Female military recruits are sexually abused and harassed, young policewomen subjected to degrading ordeals, and hideous brutality inflicted on women apparently simply because they are female. What confounds women reading of the tortures inflicted on women by men is how elaborately constructed they are; such cutting, burning and maiming is the beginning of the continuum that culminates in the stupendous elaboration of the applied art of killing that is modern military technology. Wars nowadays are fought against civilians; the bulk of military casualties these days are women and children.

On every side we see women troubled, exhausted, mutilated, lonely, guilty, mocked by the headlined success of the few. The reality of women's lives is work, most of it unpaid and, what is worse, unappreciated. Every day we hear of women abused; every day we hear of new kinds of atrocities perpetrated on the minds and bodies of women; yet every day we are told that there is nothing left to fight for. We have come a long way, but the way has got steeper, rockier, more dangerous, and we have taken many casualties. We have reached a point where the way ahead seems to have petered out. The old enemies, undefeated, have devised new strategies; new assailants lie in ambush. We have no choice but to turn and fight.

body

beauty

Every woman knows that, regardless of all her other achievements, she is a failure if she is not beautiful. She also knows
that whatever beauty she has is leaving her, stealthily, day by
day. Even if she is as freakishly beautiful as the supermodels
whose images she sees replicated all around her until they are

> I learned fairly early on that a beautiful woman doesn't consider
> herself beautiful at all. She's often crippled by lack of confidence.
> Every woman has something they dislike about themselves: if
> they're blonde, they want to be dark, if they're tall, they want to
> be short. If they have big breasts, they want to be flat-chested.
> The list is endless.
>
> Ed Burns, 1998

more familiar than the features of her own mother, she cannot
be beautiful enough. There must be bits of her that will not do,
her knees, her feet, her buttocks, her breasts. Even if all these

are fine and flawless, she knows that within she has guts full of decomposing food; she has a vagina that smells and bleeds. She is human, not a goddess or an angel. However much body hair she has, it is too much. However little and sweetly she sweats, it is too much. Left to her own devices she is sure to smell bad. If her body is thin enough, her breasts are sad. If her breasts are full, her arse is surely too big.

Scientists call abnormal preoccupation with a perceived defect in one's appearance Body Dysmorphic Disorder or BDD. In July 1996 the annual meeting of the Royal College of Psychiatrists was told by David Veale of the Royal Free Hospital:

> These [BDD] individuals are very socially handicapped. There is a high rate of depression and 25 per cent have attempted suicide . . . Michael Jackson seems to be a clear case of BDD. He has had over 30 cosmetic surgery operations and his ex-wife Lisa Presley has said he would never take off his make-up, even in bed.

What is pathological behaviour in a man is required of a woman. A bald man who wears a wig is a ridiculous figure; a bald woman who refuses to wear a wig is being stroppy and confrontational. Women with 'too much' (i.e. any) body hair are expected to struggle daily with depilatories of all kinds in order to appear hairless. Bleaching moustaches, waxing legs and plucking eyebrows absorb hundreds of womanhours. A woman who disported herself in a bikini out of which a bush of pubic hair sprouted would be regarded as a walking obscenity. No-one would say that the woman who puts herself through the agonizing ordeal of hot-waxing her bikini-line must be suffering from BDD. One of my girlfriends is forever stroking the under-side of her chin with the backs of her fingers, unconsciously feeling for the emergence of a bristle, and can be seen doing it even in her daughter's wedding video. Such insecurity has been instilled into women over generations; we have made not the least headway in the struggle to dispel it. Every issue of every woman's magazine exploits women's anxiety about 'unwanted hair'. Readers are not counselled to love their hairiness but to resort to depilatories or electrolysis and even to check that they don't suffer from the very rare thyroid disorder that causes hirsutism.

> You're born naked, and the rest is drag.
>
> RuPaul, gender illusionist

Even if you escape hairiness, you will fall foul of cellulite. When *The Female Eunuch* was written 'cellulite' was a French disease. The English word should by rights be 'cellulitis' but, as British pharmaceutical companies jumped onto a bandwagon set off by sales campaigns for French products, they adopted the French word. Cellulite is subcutaneous fat, pure and simple. It keeps women warm and softens the contours of their bodies and, if it builds up, it often dimples. Whether or not your fat dimples is a matter of genetic endowment; some women have tight smooth fat and some women have softer fat, which droops and dimples, even on their knees, invariably on their bottoms. The characteristic orange-peel appearance can be seen even in the bottoms of babies who have not eaten chocolate, drunk coffee or alcohol or smoked, or committed any other of the sins that are punishable by cellulite. Once upon a time men and women both admired dimply fat; it took twentieth-century marketing to render it disgusting. Most of what is written about 'globular fat cells', 'poor lymphatic drainage' and 'toxins that have solidifed' is cynical tosh. Dimply fat will only disappear if it is starved off; no amount of pounding or vibrating or massaging will have any effect on it whatsoever. No cream whether made of placenta or the brains of aborted foetuses or ground glass will break down cellulite. Your cellulite is you and will be with you till death or liposuction, which is expensive and extremely painful and sometimes more

In the UK 47% of women take a size sixteen or above.

Diet Breakers, 1993

disfiguring than the dimply fat itself. As fat distribution is hormonally regulated the fat will probably build up again gradually after liposuction. As cellulite will neither kill you nor go away it is a goldmine for doctors, nutritionists, naturopaths, aromatherapists, fitness experts and lifestyle managers. The manufacturers of creams, exercise equipment, skin brushes and dietary supplements all make a bundle out of women's carefully cultivated disgust with their own bodies, scarfed about as they are by 'unsightly fat cells'. Criminalizing cellulite is just another way of demonizing fat, any fat, anywhere.

As a way of inducing them to buy products of no use or value, women have been deliberately infected with BDD. Conditions that practically all women 'suffer from' are spoken of as unsightly and abnormal, to make women feel that parts of their bodies, perhaps their whole bodies, are defective and should be worked on, even surgically altered. Most women think that their hair is not good enough and dye it or bleach it or perm it. Most women feel that their legs are not long enough, that their thighs are too heavy or not firm enough. Most women are unhappy about their bottoms which are either too flat, too low-slung, too fat or too broad. Preoccupation about her appearance goes some way towards ruining some part of every woman's day. Multi-million-dollar industries exploit both her need for reassurance and her need to do something about the way she looks.

Thirty years ago it was enough to *look* beautiful; now a

woman has to have a tight, toned body, including her buttocks and thighs, so that she is good to touch, all over. 'Remember,' she will be told, 'beauty starts from within,' so she keeps her bowels open with plenty of fibre and her kidneys flushed with lots of pure water. She might also take Perfectil, 'just . . . one capsule a day, every day, for care that is more than skin deep', which will cost her £7.95 for a month's supply, even though the capsules can do little more than 'safeguard' her 'supply of essential factors – like magnesium, zinc and Vitamin B complex', worth a few pence, if that. If she has another £24 to invest she might try 'Firm Believer Body Toning Treatment' by Clinique, which aims to eliminate cellulite 'by building up collagen and elastin and preventing fat from infiltrating the skin', thus transforming the orange-peel effect into the peach-skin effect. Being beautiful from within takes even more time than slapping beauty on from without. Demi Moore is said to work out for four hours a day, beginning with a cardiovascular aerobic workout, then working her legs and buttocks with pliés, standing lunges and thigh lifts, her upper body with shoulder and punching exercises, and toning her abdominal muscles. She also eats only non-processed, pesticide-free, totally vegetarian foods. The result, taut abs, a rock-hard butt and twanging musculature, was still not enough to save her marriage.

Says Dr Fenton, dermatologist, 'Avoid wasting money on expensive top-of-the-range creams offering tiny amounts in elaborate packaging.'
Products to try: *Guerlain Odélys Perfect Care* (£29.50), *Estée Lauder Vérité Moisture Relief Cream* (£36), *Prescriptives All You Need + for Drier Skins* (£32).

Whatever a woman does, she must not look her age. The fitness regime is lifelong, to go with the lifelong sexual activity that is nowadays obligatory. 'Today's granny, rather than being a white-haired old lady in a shawl, will probably wear trainers and a track suit and arrive for babysitting duties straight from the gym or still in her business suit, fresh from her job.'

The UK beauty industry takes £8.9 billion a year out of women's pockets. Magazines financed by the beauty industry teach little girls that they need make-up and train them to use it, so establishing their lifelong reliance on beauty products. Not content with showing pre-teens how to use foundations, powders, concealers, blushers, eye-shadows, eye-liners, lip-liners, lipstick and lip gloss, the magazines identify problems of dryness, flakiness, blackheads, shininess, dullness, blemishes, puffiness, oiliness, spots, greasiness, that little girls are meant to treat with moisturizers, fresheners, masks, packs, washes, lotions, cleansers, toners, scrubs, astringents, none of which will make the slightest difference and all of which would cost money the child does not have. Pre-teen cosmetics are relatively cheap but within a few years more sophisticated marketing will have persuaded the most level-headed young woman to throw money away on alchemical preparations containing anything from silk to cashmere, pearls, proteins, royal jelly, placenta extracts, ceramides, biotin, collagen, 'phyto-tensers', bisabolol, jojoba, 'hydra-captors', serine, fruit hydroxy-acids, oleospheres, corneospheres, nanovectors, glycerol, anything real or phony that might fend off her imminent collapse into hideous decrepitude.

I don't know how many more times I can beat this face into submission.

Cher, November 1987

Women are exhorted to fight and deny their age by every means in their power. Consumer research regularly reports that nothing applied to the surface of the skin can affect the underlying structures or prevent ageing, and still the anti-ageing products sell. Every day hospitals put placenta into special freezers to be collected once a week by unmarked vans and sold on to face-cream manufacturers. So desperate are some women to stave off ageing that they are prepared to submit to injections of botulin toxin to freeze their facial muscles and prevent wrinkles. It must be a sad world when what *every* mother wants for Mother's Day is 'younger-looking skin'. That is one thing she is never going to have, not even if she endures all the agonies of a face-lift.

What is truly depressing about the false dawn of feminism is that, as we have been congratulating ourselves on largely imaginary victories, BDD has become a global pandemic. Women who were unselfconscious and unmade-up thirty years ago, who walked at a natural pace and worked alongside men in the fields and the factories, are now infected. In provincial cities in China hanging up over shop doorways you can see boards with padded brassieres pinned all over them, and trays of cheap lacquer and lipstick under fly-spotted glass, so that women who are naturally small-breasted can assume the 'new shape'. Beauty salons crimp and curl shining hair with a fall like silk into shapeless frizz. The two billion people worldwide who regularly view *Baywatch* are all recognizing a single, tawdry, synthetic kind of skinnied-down, pumped-up, bleached and depilated female beauty. Real girls tell me that when they run

---

Vichy LiftActiv, £15, is the first anti-ageing cream to incorporate aminokine, made from a derivative of soya protein, which helps stimulate the production of glycans in your skin.

---

along the beach, their male companions make fun of their real breasts that bounce up and down unlike the rigid half-tennis-ball boobs of the *Baywatch* babes. Who cares that Pamela Lee Anderson who has been put together out of all the movable parts of male and female fetishism has been abused by her husband? We are selling fantasy here. When German supermodel Claudia Schiffer visited Argentina the president accorded her an hour of his undivided attention. Two-thirds of Argentinian girls want to be Teutonic blonde models, just like Claudia. Barbie is an Aryan.

It seemed a quarter of a century ago that the days of the Barbie doll were numbered. Barbie was descended from a swimsuit-clad German porno-toy called Lilli, a twelve-inch peroxided nymph with a sidelong glance, designed to be sold to men in tobacconists' shops. At her American debut in the spring of 1959 Barbie was the first toy to be directly marketed to three- to eleven-year-old girls on Saturday morning TV. American girls now own eight Barbies apiece, British girls six. With her non-functional body, boasting a nipple-free bosom more than twice the circumference of her minute waist, legs twice as long as her torso, and feet so tiny that she cannot stand on them, Barbie is unlikely to have been very effective in her career roles as astronaut, vet or stewardess. Realistic-minded little girls ought to be given the option of recognizing her as disabled and supplying her with a wheelchair, but Barbie fans prefer to promote her as an unattached career girl, women's liberation in effigy. At the end of 1996 the Barbie Newsdesk at Mattel UK could report that every two seconds a Barbie is sold somewhere in the world. Though she may come in black or Hispanic or Oriental models, her bodily proportions remain roughly the same. Every year Barbie gets 120 new outfits, including a range of sexy underwear, and a new career. She has thirty-five pets, as well as a kitchen, a bathroom and a patio. She is currently put together by 11,000 Chinese peasant women in two factories in Guangdong Province; 23p of the total price of a Barbie doll is payment for their labour. Sales last year topped $1.2 billion. More than one billion Barbies have been sold since 1959; she is brand leader in every one of the 140 countries where she is sold. 'Her hair is from Japan, her colouring from America and the oil that makes up the plastic resins is imported from Taiwan, with most of the oil originating in Saudi Arabia.'

In 1998 a makeover was announced; the millennial Barbie is to stand on flat feet, her bosom and hips are to be slightly reduced and her waist slightly enlarged, but she will still be a far cry from Action Woman. Even so, a US columnist objected, 'Why not just give her a moustache, cellulite and varicose veins too?' The further from the natural a female form, the more attractive it becomes. The further from the natural a female form, the more feminine it is.

Thirty years ago it seemed that the beauty contest would soon be a thing of the past, yet this year in the United States more than 2,000 beauty pageants will be staged. The pageant of pageants, Miss World, was first broadcast on the BBC in 1951; it was then staged in the Lyceum Ballroom to the strains of the Joe Loss Orchestra, and later at the Royal Albert Hall where the feminist protests were mounted in 1969. In 1977 and 1984 the telecast of the contest pulled in 18 million viewers; even so it was dropped by ITV in 1988. Though cool Britain might have declared Miss World passé, the world did not agree. In the 1990s when the contest was held at Sun City in South

---

Kate Shapland, host of *The Big Breakfast*'s beauty slot, swears by Guerlain Divinaura, £39.50, a skin-priming gel containing real gold flakes.

New Woman, February 1997

Africa it was watched on TV by two billion or so viewers around the world. In 1996 promoter Amitabh Bachchan decided to stage the Miss World pageant in the South Indian city of Bangalore, on a stage built to look like a Bollywood version of an ancient Hindu temple, with hundreds of dancers, two elephants, eighty-eight contestants. The cheapest seats at the spectacle cost 2,000 rupees, the most expensive more than ten times that. Outside stood untold thousands of protesters and 10,000 state troops to quell them. An alternative pageant featured the crowning of Miss Poverty and Miss Illiteracy. Bachchan was burned in effigy. In the neighbouring city of Madurai a protester burned himself to death. The right-wing Hindu Bharata Janata Party organized a twenty-four-hour strike, and blockaded the stadium. Schools and colleges were closed. A suicide squad was formed of women ready to immolate themselves if the pageant went ahead. The Indian Tigers had 400 commandos assembled ready to trash the event, which went ahead just the same.

What to do? The Miss World contest costs £6 million to put on; it raises vast quantities of money for children's charities (we are told) and a lot of lovely girls are made to look ridiculous trying to answer questions put to them by men speaking idiomatic English which they do not understand. As the carcasses are neither for sale nor suitable for human consumption, the Miss World contest is neither a cattle market nor a meat market; it is worse than that. The Miss World contest reinforces Anglo-capitalist values and imposes Anglo-capitalist norms by recognizing only one physical type as having any pretensions whatsoever to beauty. Mattel now have so much control over the market that its juggernaut can roll over any toy that threatens to compete with Barbie. Barbie has been instrumental in teaching broad-shouldered women, short-legged women, wide-bodied women, real women the world over to despise their bodies as we do, so that they pay out money that could be put towards the cost of books or computers or bicycles, for cheaply produced, expensively packaged 'beauty' products. After the implosion of the USSR the first western shops to open in the old Soviet cities were cosmetic franchises; before a Russian woman could buy an orange or a banana she could buy a lipstick by Dior or Revlon.

manmade women

Women are illusionists. They fake light-heartedness, girlishness and orgasm; they also fake the roses in their cheeks, the thickness, colour and curliness of their hair, the tininess of their waists, the longness of their legs and the size and shape of their breasts. Men do not seem to have demanded this of them; rather women seem to have bedizened themselves in an all-out last-ditch attempt to grab the attention of otherwise uninterested males. Even in countries where women are naked the limited opportunity for fantastic elaboration has been taken, to the point of inserting plates in the lower lip, rings in

> We want women to be beautiful, to be capable, to be able to compete with men.
>
> Wu Qing, Municipal People's Congress, Beijing

the ears and nose, elongating the neck, covering the skin with decorative scarifications. A naked woman can hardly pretend that her breasts are other than they are or elongate her legs by wearing high heels but as soon as she modernizes and covers her nakedness, she will also get into the high heels and brassiere, the lipstick and mascara.

Though dressing and painting, be-wigging and padding are things a woman can do for herself, she has always been at the mercy of the manufacturers and purveyors of her beauty products. She has always known as much, that is to say as little, as the supplier needed her to know. When all unknowing she painted her face with preparations of white lead and died as a consequence, she was both the perpetrator of the crime and the victim. Nobody forced her to apply the fatal compound to her face; nobody cared if it was dangerous because a good, modest, inconspicuous woman would not have been using it in the first place. Blaming the victim for the crime is a pattern of injustice very familiar to feminists, who see it repeated every time a raped woman is asked what she was wearing or what she was doing in the place where, at the time when a man assaulted her. Nowadays beauty products are known to be safe only because they have been tested on animals, which is also women's fault. So they are led a silly dance to find products that have not been tested on animals, and cynically misinformed by the manufac- turers who know only too well that, though tests might not have been carried out by them or recently, everything they sell has been tested on animals at some stage.

In a culture that reserves the right to humiliate women who are considered plain, a desperate longing for beauty is insep- arable from the dread that such beauty as one has is already on the wane. One way of exorcizing such fear and longing is to submit to the ghastly ritual of plastic surgery. More women are now undergoing cosmetic surgery more and more often. In millennial Britain there are 65,000 cosmetic operations a year. At first the procedures were relatively simple, nose-jobs and tit-jobs. Now surgeons can remould entire bodies by shifting adipose tissue. The Surgical Advisory Service reported in September 1996 that its most popular procedure was 'breast enlargement, followed by endoscopic brow lift, face lift, laser skin smoothing, nose jobs, liposuction on thighs and legs, breast reduction, uplift and nipple correction'. Dr Takowsky of Hollywood siphons fat from women's thighs, syringes it into the vulvae (to make them plump) and 'squishes' it up into the walls of the vagina (to make it tight). The way Takowsky tells it you'd think his patients invented this procedure themselves: 'The girls have told me that when they go to the gym they love the definition in their leotard,' he said.

Nowadays none of the varieties of natural is good enough. As the Swiss cosmetic surgeon Dr Maja Ruetschi told *Cosmopolitan* in August 1996: 'We can make better breasts than God. Women grow up with a Barbie doll – her long legs, tiny waist and huge breasts – it's no wonder they want to look like that.' One in forty US women has silicone breast implants. In November 1997 Santa Monica cosmetic surgeon Mark Berman advised the male readers of *Maxim* that they could identify implants because of their symmetry, a 'fundamental giveaway'. 'If the top half is as full and round as the bottom, they're probably implants. The scars fade from red to white but if she's tan or dark-skinned, you may notice lighter areas where she's lost pigment.' Women who are worried that their scars might show can have them tattooed skin-colour. Fake breasts stand up and out all the time. As Berman remarked, 'Even if she's a DD, real breasts will flatten out across her chest when she's on her back.' The truth is that we all have 'falling away breasts' until they are pumped up.

Implants go wrong. Christine Williamson had implants for cosmetic reasons in 1979. A few years later they began to harden and she underwent a number of corrective procedures. By 1992 her marriage was foundering. Her husband said she was not the woman he had married. An operation to soften one of the implants ruptured it, spilling silicone into the breast tissue. In April 1993 a woman surgeon operated on the ruptured breast which was full of silicone granules and fibrous lumps and removed both the breast and the underlying muscle, an outcome which Mrs Williamson had not been told to expect and to which she had not consented. She was awarded £20,636 in damages.

One girl's blouse fell wide open while she was modelling it. She had no idea she was exposing her breasts because implants meant she'd lost all sensitivity.

Lowri Turner on catwalk models, 1993

Women have not always been keen on exaggerating the form of their breasts; for centuries the women of the elite flattened their breasts under stomachers and agonized about a 'neck' that was too full, perhaps to distinguish themselves from women of the lactating classes. Breasts were first pushed up and out with corsetry and padding, until some surgeon realized that he could easily pull up the skin and tighten it over the breast mass to give the unsupported breast as 'good' an outline as the breast in a brassiere. The race was soon joined to find ways of pumping the breast up to something more pneumatic than nature intended. In the 1940s the breasts of the Japanese prostitutes who served the US military were injected with industrial-grade liquid silicone. Then Dow Corning developed Silastic® implants. In April 1992 the US Food and Drug Administration banned them. In the two years that followed 20,000 lawsuits were filed against Dow Corning who in 1998, faced with 200,000 claims world wide, negotiated an out-of-court settlement for the US of $3.1 billion to be divided among 170,000 women. The 60,000 British women complaining of fatigue, headaches, memory loss and nausea caused by silicone leaking from ruptured implants stand to get rather less.

In Britain Silastic implants are still being used on 8,000 women a year. Within forty-eight hours of the announcement of the Dow Corning settlement an independent review group set up by the British government reassured women that they could accept silicone implants; 'providing the risks and benefits are explained to them, they can make their own decision,' said Professor David Sturrock, chair of the review body. The learned gentlemen of the all-male review body did not question the justification for their own practices but used the occasion to condemn commercial clinics for adopting tactics 'more attuned to double-glazing salesmen', and failing to employ specialist cosmetic surgeons, even though, in the words of Professor David Sharpe, President of the British Association of Cosmetic Plastic Surgeons, 'A trained chimpanzee could put in a breast implant.'

In the US, where millions of dollars have been made out of women having their implants removed or changed, surgeons now understand how the implants and surrounding tissue behave. The literature makes sickening reading as it lists bacteria found inside implants, silicone found in other parts of the body, and the difficulties of detaching some kinds of implants, in particular the ones covered with polyurethane foam, from the surrounding tissue. Saline implants appear if anything worse, capable for example of absorbing fluid from surrounding tissues and ballooning hugely, and of incubating an astonishing variety of bacteria. The media campaign against silicone made vast amounts of money for surgeons and lawyers, but the jury is still out as to the role played by silicone in disorders of the immune system, principally because nobody bothered to find out how much environmental silicone was already distributed through women's bodies and what its effects might be before adding more in the form of silicone oils and implants.

It is difficult to find any kind of consensus in the now vast literature, but the suspicion is that silicone migrating from implants stimulates the immune system, causing human adjuvant disease which presents in a variety of ways. The effects of possible silicone ingestion on infants breast-fed by mothers with implants are also not known. We do know that after twelve years 63 per cent of implants will no longer be intact but it is thought that the effects, granulomatous inflammation, capsular contraction and infection, are local and not systemic. Nevertheless a silent decision has been taken by many health authorities in the US and elsewhere not to use blood or organs donated by acceptors of silicone implants.

I was embarrassingly flat-chested and promised myself at sixteen that if I didn't have a decent chest by the time I was twenty-one, I'd have surgery. I did and I don't regret it. It's amazing – I feel so feminine that for the first time in my life I've started carrying a handbag!

Karen Watson, London

As usual women are portrayed in the medical literature as both the perpetrators and the victims of the silicone scare; women demanded implants, doctors gave in to their demands and now women have become irrationally terrified of those same implants so the harassed doctors have to take them out again. It does not take a feminist to see that initially women were manipulated by a sexual culture that demanded bigger and better breasts, then by a medical establishment that encouraged unrealistic expectations, by the media that make money out of orchestrating female panic and lastly by the lawyers for whom these cases are a bonanza. The only losers on this extremely lucrative merry-go-round are the women.

Time was when feminists were considered to be *sui generis* against all cosmetic procedures. Whenever a famous person showed off a new face or bosom feminists were expected to howl their scorn and derision, yet no feminists who could afford it would refuse the most important cosmetic procedure of all, namely, cosmetic dentistry. Having a new set of capped and shining teeth will do more to slow down the changes that age brings to the face than any kind of fiddling with skin and soft tissue. The woman whose teeth become worn down and broken and finally have to be removed will have collapsed and pouchy cheeks and the tip of her nose will drop down towards her chin in the classic witch profile. Of course feminists and everyone else can say that we need teeth to eat with and that crumbling teeth compromise the health of the whole person, but if good choppers were made of aluminium we would be rather less willing to equip ourselves with them. Restoration of battered teeth produces miraculous rejuvenation partly because the new teeth have the clear and unstained colour of young teeth, and none of us would have it otherwise. Once teeth have been done the cosmetic procedure of self-betterment is already far advanced. Clearing away a wattle or two is minor by comparison.

If you were disfigured in an accident, scarred by scalding or burning for example, you would accept cosmetic surgery to minimize the damage, no? Breast implants were first used to correct disfiguring anomalies of breast development, such as failure of one breast to develop at all. We would not object to evening breasts up in such a case, but the criteria of unsatis-factoriness keep shifting until naturally small breasts are perceived by everyone as a defect. A memo from the American Association of Plastic Reconstructive Surgeons to the FDA stated quite firmly, 'There is a substantial and enlarging body

---

It costs a lot of money to look as cheap as I do.

Dolly Parton

---

of medical opinion that these deformities are really a disease.' No-one has ever said that outsize breasts are a disease, though women who have to carry them about and to lift them when they turn over in bed refer bitterly to the brassieres that cut their shoulders as 'boulder-holders'. Feminists, unwilling to accept that breasts outsize or flat are any kind of a disease, must also consider the implications of the fact that US insurers get out of paying for breast reconstruction after mastectomy or lumpectomy by arguing that reconstruction is elective and not an intrinsic part of the life-saving procedure.

Once a woman has begun surgically improving her body, she need never stop. A cosmetic surgeon described his mother: 'She's 75, swims every day and doesn't ever want to look her age. I've done liposuction on her back, her inner thighs, her triceps and a little on her abdomen. She's on her third face-lift.' Time and money spent on tinkering with an old face and body are not available for other things, be they trips around the world or relieving the sufferings of the poor. To be so involved with the soul-case is the abomination of desolation, like a life spent in front of the mirror. It would be so even if cosmetic surgery were painless, which it most definitely is not. The more a procedure hurts, the more reason the victim has to convince herself that she has been miraculously transformed. To a dispassionate observer the best cosmetic surgery is the surgery that makes the least perceptible difference; faces that really have been lifted tend to look more or less ghastly because the skin and adhering tissue have had to be separated from the underlying structures to be pulled up and tightened. The new face may look fine in the mirror but other people are aware that it is far less expressive and mobile than the old.

Sarah Dunant interprets the year-by-year increase in the number of cosmetic operations as yet more evidence that feminism has failed: 'Is it not in some way an admission that another major cultural force over the last twenty-five years has failed, which is feminism? Because feminism set out to say women do not need to feel a tyranny upon them as to what they should look like, they should be able to be who they are without conforming to a version of beauty.' What feminism actually said was that the demand that a woman be beautiful was and is a tyranny, not that women did not 'need' to feel it for what it was. Many times more women would pay good money for the agony of cosmetic surgery, and the bruises and the stitches and the scars, if they could only afford it; some British women are so desperate that they make cut-price package trips to Poland for cheaper surgery. 'Even old-school feminists would go to the mat for a woman's right to do what she wants with her body,' said Jan Breslauer, erstwhile teacher of feminist theory at Yale, now famous as the post-post-feminist who bought herself a great pair of bazongas. Women blessed with a great pair of natural bazongas have been less aware of empowerment than the fact that most men were too busy looking at their chests to attend to a word they said. Tit-power does not add up to much, all said and done.

> I'm a 36D and find it bizarre that some women risk an op to have breasts my size. Large breasts cause problems: clothes don't fit well, they're a nuisance when you exercise and they attract some dodgy men.
>
> Laura Horbury, Somerset

The feminist is the person who is entirely unsurprised by both the fact that virtually all cosmetic operations are performed on women and the fact that virtually all the people carving women into acceptable shapes are men. The battered face of the French artist Orlan after surgery, with her stitched and swollen lips and her blood-suffused eyes, is a feminist ikon. We may wring our hands at the knowledge that '*Il faut souffrir pour être belle*' but we should not forget that to be ugly, as every woman privately feels herself to be, is to suffer in a different way. Before women can feel that their looks are uniquely their looks and better (realer, more authentic, more interesting) than anything they could buy in their place, they will have to feel at least as confident as men. Men will have to give up their right to judge, to give points out of ten, to reward the extravagantly lovely and humiliate the usual, and begin listening to women rather than watching them when they speak. Women will have to stop caring whether men find them attractive because, even if they decide to tart themselves up, they cannot win. The violinist who diets, bleaches and teases her hair, has collagen injected into her lips and her boobs pumped up, and plays her concerts in a bikini, certainly gets attention but no-one takes her musicianship seriously. If the woman-made woman is never good enough, the man-made woman is no better than a toy, built to be played with, knocked about and ultimately thrown away.

womb

When a woman is born her sex will be decided on the outward appearance of her genitalia. No-one will bother to verify whether womb and ovaries are actually present. Our culture is virtually unaware of the womb as an intrinsic part of the female body let alone the ovaries already carrying their vast store of genetic instructions at the time of birth. Men must make endless copies of their genetic programme all day and every day throughout their lives; women have the information ready stored in the archive of the ovaries. Nowadays, when essentialism is heresy, we may not affirm that this contrast between

> The obscenity of the female sex is that of everything that gapes open.
>
> Jean-Paul Sartre, *Being and Nothingness*

men and women means anything, let alone much. Male genitals are drawn on every wall, female genitals only on doctors' blotters.

While the entire man thinks he has the proof of his maleness before his eyes the entire woman is given to believe that she has a lack, a hole inside her. When Courtney Love was asked why she called her band 'Hole' she is supposed to have replied, 'It's about the abyss inside.'

The degree of ovarian activity in the little girl is not understood, though every mother who watches her three-year-old rolling on the floor displaying her labia knows that she is responding to a hormonal stimulus and everyone who bathes a little girl knows her female smell. Anyone who has had to fish out the beads and coins that a little girl has secreted in her vagina knows that she is aware of her hidden place and proud of it. What the little girl knows at three she is destined very soon to forget. When only seeing is believing the unseen reproductive anatomy of the female cannot be an article of faith. The internal genitalia of the female fade out of mind long before the menarche, as feminine identity is written over female nature and soul-deep modesty casts its pall over little girls' joys and desires.

Though Freud makes much of the fact that boys' genitalia are visible and little girls' are not, mere invisibility cannot account for the absence of any imagery of the womb from our general culture. The heart is no less invisible yet we refer to it constantly. The heart exists to pump blood around the body not to generate feelings, which are in fact mental events, yet we are intensely conscious of it as the centre of our selves. When D. H. Lawrence tells us in *Lady Chatterley's Lover* that Connie felt things 'in her womb' the expression seems odd, even slightly shocking. Even when women visit their doctors seeking help with menstrual cramping, they will not say that they feel the pain in their womb. As far as they are aware they feel nothing in their wombs. Their wombs are out of sight and out of mind.

The womb rudely awakens the growing girl to its presence by causing her to shed blood through her vagina. The more difficult the process, the more bloated and bilious she feels, the more dragging the pain, the more negative the idea of a womb will seem to her. As she has heard the womb spoken of as a space inside her, like a room she did not know she had, her menstruation appears like a troublesome tenant after whom she

> Because of the omnipotence of the uterus it begets life and it belongs to woman, man has attempted to take control and even replace it and its offspring with medicine, laws of property, marriage, inheritance, by attacking the uterus directly with accusations of hysteria, taboos on menstruation and blood. The act of pulling in the uterus into the computer . . . completes the creative union between woman and machine . . .
>
> Josepha Grieve, 'In my Gash'

has to clean up. She might even give the tenant a name. Italian girls make him a man and call him *il marchese*, as German girls used to call him *der rote König*. Both are names for a tyrant but they are less resentful than the commonest English name for menstruation, 'the curse'. Though feminists have argued that we should celebrate the menarche as a young woman's coming of age, with a visible rise in status to compensate her for the inconvenience of menstruation and ward off any attempt on her part to cancel the whole process by remaining a skinny child, nothing has happened to endow the cycle with glamour or respect. We call the napkins used to soak up menstrual discharge 'sanitary protection' as if the blood was both dirty and dangerous. Sanitary protection may now be advertised on television, not because women's functions are no longer considered shameful or disgusting but because the potential earnings are enormous. High profit margins on napkins that women have no choice but to buy are used to subsidize marketing campaigns for luxury products.

Neither women nor men have a positive attitude to menstruation. In *The Female Eunuch* I wrote: 'If you think you are emancipated, you might consider the idea of tasting your menstrual blood – if it makes you sick, you've a long way to go, baby.' In 1997 *Guardian* columnist and feminist of sorts Linda Grant rendered this as: 'Thirty years ago Germaine Greer told women that they weren't feminists until they had tasted their own menstrual blood, missing the point as so often she does, trying to construct a ritual where a law is needed.' The 'law' that Grant thinks is needed is the lifting of VAT on sanitary protection – not something I could have argued for thirty years ago when there was no such thing as VAT. The question of the exorbitant cost of napkins and tampons has been raised regularly by feminists; feminists were the first to point out the dangers of asbestos in tampons and of Toxic Shock Syndrome. My point, as distinct from Grant's point, was that if women regard their own menstrual fluid as 'googoomuck' we are a long way from taking the pride in our femaleness that is a necessary condition of liberation. Hundreds of feminists have tried all kinds of strategies for filling the idea of menstruation with positive significance but it remains a kind of excretion, the liquefaction of abjection. Advertising of sanitary protection can no more mention blood than advertising of toilet paper can mention shit. When we come to recognize the taste of our menstrual blood on the lips or fingers or penis of a lover, perhaps then we will realize that it is not putrid, not dangerous, not in the least disgusting. One of the latest explanations of the real function of the uniquely human process of menstruation holds that the shedding of blood is not an excretion but protection of the sloughing womb from infection.

For thirty years feminists have struggled to develop a positive imagery of the womb and ovaries. Feminist artists have painted, modelled, woven, potted, photographed, filmed, videoed and embroidered sumptuous images of the female genitalia to absolutely no purpose. As far as mainstream culture was concerned cunt-art was no more than a sub-branch of gynae-cology. Though much of the most influential art of the 1990s was focused upon the body as the locus of gender and the modality of socialization, no girl drifted off to sleep at night and dreamed of her mysterious innards under any shape that she could recognize. Though women artists devised myriad fabulous boxes, purses lined with satin or fur and glimmering bottomless caves, ordinary women derived little comfort from a new awareness of themselves as buried treasure. It would take more than a trip through the vagina of sculptor Niki de St Phalle's ninety-feet-long female figure 'Hon' to awaken the consciousness of womb. More memorable perhaps were the artistic experiences of the womb dramatized as bruising encounters with obstetric technology.

Using a huge magnifying glass to show my vagina (the pubic hairs on one half were painted blue) during my period, a video screen showed the head of the man or woman who was about to see, another showed the head of the men and women who were looking, and at the exit, Freud's text on the head of Medusa was distributed. It read: 'At the sight of the vulva the devil himself flees.'

Orlan

Perhaps womb-pride was too much to expect. The word 'womb' originally meant any hollow space and by extension came to mean 'belly' or 'abdomen'. The use of the word in modern times exclusively to signify the organ of gestation demonstrates our inability to think of the womb as anything but a passive receptacle, a pocket inside a person rather than the person herself. The ideal body is imperforate; the wombed body is grotesque and gaping, like Luna Park. Women's 'inner space' implies a negative, an unsoundness, a hollowness, a harbour for otherness. But the term is misleading; there is no more a void inside a woman than there is inside a man. The unpregnant womb is not a space, but closed upon itself. The womb is not a sinus or a sac. The image of the uterus as a void waiting to be filled is an artefact derived from billions of lying diagrams that represent the fabulous baroque biochemistry of the womb as if it were the pocket of a billiard table. Women artists have done their best to counteract this by introducing fibre-optics into their own bodies, to show the quivering liveliness of the cervix's puppy-muzzle and the surging pulse of the fallopian tube amid its dancing fimbriae. Very few are watching and for those who are there can be no shock of recognition. Consciousness is made of language and we have no language for this. Cock and balls have a thousand names but uterus and ovaries have only their medical labels.

There was a time when human beings imagined the womb as a powerful, positive something rather than a nothing. Hippocrates saw female reproductive physiology as energetic and active, and the womb as a voracious, questing creature, capable of invading other body parts. Hippocrates's idea of the aggressive womb persisted until comparatively recently. Women's history has focused on the misogynist content of the idea of hysteria; certainly the galaxy of maladies thought to be caused by the wandering womb were cited as irrefutable evidence of women's unfitness for authority and even independence, but little or nothing is known about the effect of such consciousness on women themselves. To interpret the ownership of a womb as a licence to misbehave, sufficient in itself to account for rebellious and destructive behaviour as well as for sexual self-interest, may be both oppressive and liberating, as current versions of a Pre-Menstrual Syndrome have proved to be. If women of the fourth century BC inherited from women of millennia before them concepts of their inward bodies as active and the sexes as equally aggressive in their search for pleasure, evolving patriarchy made short work of interpreting both notions negatively, so as to criminalize female libido.

In *The Female Eunuch* I attempted to provide a different version of female receptivity by speaking of the vagina as if it were active, as if it sucked on the penis and emptied it out rather than simply receiving the ejaculate. This was mischievously rendered by hacks hunting for outrageousness, and then mindlessly repeated by lifestyle hackettes, to be an exhortation to get laid more often by more men. Cunt-power as I defined it has still to manifest itself; what we got instead was its opposite, penetration mania, the outsize dildo and the fist, the world split open. The sanitized, deodorized, sterilized, always accessible vagina and womb are more, not less, passive than they ever were. There are many, and more and more each day, who think a rectum has more character and that buggery is more intimate than coitus. It is the rectum not the vagina that leads to the heart of a person, male or female. Remember Lady Chatterley and weep.

> She would have thought a woman would have died of shame. Instead of which, the shame died. Shame, which is fear: the deep organic shame, the old, old fear which crouches in the bodily roots of us, and can only be chased away by the sensual fire, at last it was roused up and routed by the phallic hunt of the man, and she came to the very heart of the jungle of herself. She felt, now, she had come to the real bed-rock of her nature, and was essentially shameless . . . But it took some getting at, the core of the physical jungle, the last and deepest recess of organic shame.

The heart of the jungle of Connie's self is not the blind alley where she conceives but the lower extremity of her alimentary canal. Unconscious substitution of the alimentary canal for women's reproductive organs is so common in ordinary speech that we hardly think of it as representing a somatization disorder.

After the birth of her second child Fiona Shaw entered into a severe depression of which she has written a recently published account entitled *Out of Me*, in which she repeatedly refers to her womb as her stomach: 'For nine months I lived with a child in my stomach,' she tells us. When her first child quickened she declares, 'I felt its movements in my stomach.' Her first labour is described as her 'stomach's clutches' and 'pain in my stomach'. She was pregnant again within a year and 'didn't know it'. She says of her little daughter: 'She knew what was in my stomach, as well as you can when you're only a year and a half out of it.' When the post-natal depression strikes it turns her stomach. We are not surprised to learn that she has a history of eating disorders or that during the worst of her depressive illness she cannot eat at all. 'Ten days earlier, I had gathered toothbrush, nightclothes, babygros and books, my stomach taut with anticipation. Now, my stomach was slack, empty and I had a very different bag to pack.' Within days she was talking of wanting 'another baby quickly'.

In her own account of the genesis of her illness, Shaw begins with baggage:

> When I was a little girl I always had my suitcase packed, so my mother told me . . . The best present I ever had from my dad was a floppy blue suitcase with green piping . . . Though my bags have changed since then, their imaginary baggage hasn't.

Shaw means by baggage here her history, but the mechanism also works in reverse. Her history is spelt out in bags, not least the bag of her 'stomach' out of which babies come. Why do women always carry bags, and why are those bags so often heavy? Why is it that most women will not go out of the house without bags loaded with objects of no immediate use? Is the tote bag an exterior uterus, the outward sign of the unmentionable burden? The cause of Shaw's illness was never identified, least of all by herself. Towards the end of her account she describes seeing a woman whose bag has been snatched: the thief jogged past 'self-contained, silent and with little sense of urgency', while the woman was 'untucked', with flailing arms, bereaved and violated. It would be the height of arrogance to suggest that Shaw's ordeal began and will continue with imaging of her body and perhaps even her self as all stomach, because such distortion of body image is ubiquitous, but then so is menstrual distress. If menstrual distress was caused by denial of the womb it would be another expression of the Body Dysmorphic Disorder that afflicts all women in our culture. One gallant band of feminists struggles to disseminate a view of peri-menstrual tension and menstrual discomfort as positive and life-enhancing, without conspicuous success. Far more women want to assert that they are who they are despite their wombs, not because of them.

The stripping of all sacredness and mystery from the female genitalia has taken as long as civilization itself. The mandorla of Christian iconography, in which saints on a visit from heaven are enclosed as if in a pod of paradisal bliss, is a womb emblem. The Garden of Eden is usually represented as a *hortus conclusus*, an enclosed garden, another womb analogue. The character of the womb must have been understood differently in medieval culture where adult women were usually pregnant and the womb therefore conspicuous. Some women's fashions in other epochs have been meant to mimic ebullient pregnancy rather than flat-bellied virginity. In his formidably learned *History of Women's Bodies* Edward Shorter lists examples from European popular culture of the comparatively recent past, derived from imposing German studies of *Volksmedizin*, of women's apostrophizing the womb as a mischief-making alien inside their own bodies. Women uttered incantations to keep the womb in its place much as they apostrophized Matthew, Mark, Luke and John to bless the bed that they lay on, in a garbled recollection of the culture of the ruling elite, in one case medical in the other clerical. Still, it is important that in women's somatization, that is, their identification of various states of mind and health with parts of the body, they characterized the uterus as a source of trouble. Men's fear of the uterus and menstruation may be problematic but more devastating by far are women's own negative attitudes.

Once again, we are faced with the essentialist feminist paradox: do we liberate women by freeing them from the tyranny of the womb or is the attack on 'the undifferentiated gloop of the womb' an attack on women? Should a feminist rehabilitate the womb or should she argue that it is anti-feminist to think of women as wombed creatures? The question is not merely academic. Women are suffering in and through their wombs. Though psychoanalysts set themselves to cure women's 'psychic emptiness and pain' they never ask themselves or their patients about their patients' attitude to their wombs.

Psychoanalyst Dinora Pines, in *A Woman's Unconscious Use of Her Body*, describes the coming to consciousness of a patient: 'What she could no longer deny was that her body contained a void, and bad and dangerous faeces and urine. Now began a time of mourning for her lost penis.' The grammar of this suggests that, for this patient, psychoanalysis consisted of pressure to admit a falsehood, namely, that she had a 'void' inside her that was of the same order of reality as her faeces and urine. Pines also writes: 'A boy may impregnate a girl and a girl may fill her internal body space with a living and growing foetus.' Pines apparently believes that to be healthy a woman has to be aware that she has a void in her body but should not feel that she has any void in her self, in much the same way that a man with a bullet-hole in him could still know that he was a whole person. This would be feasible if the 'void' inside female bodies was an anatomical fact rather than an idea existing in the mind, and thus part of the consciousness of self. Predictably, feeling empty is given by Pines as a cause of chronic over-eating. Pines tells us too that after delivery a mother passes through 'a period of adjustment to a feeling of void and emptiness where the baby once was . . . The mother's body image has to change again, in order to feel whole and not empty, before there can be a reconciliation with the actual birth and the recognition of the baby as a separate individual . . .' Yet Pines has shown by her own semantics that she believes the unpregnant female body to be constructed around an internal space, and therefore empty rather than whole.

Our everyday language reinforces the conception of the womb as a permanent space, an empty lodging waiting for a tenant. Descriptions of surrogacy often use expressions like 'wombs to let' or 'wombs for rent', as if the woman who agrees to act as a surrogate was running a kind of fleshly boarding-house. Any society that can regard asking one woman to act as a surrogate mother, by allowing the fertilized ovum of another to be implanted in her uterus and gestation to continue there until the child is born and handed over, as both feasible and tolerable can attach little importance to the process or the mother's role in it. The woman who thinks that her own conceptus is a stranger taking over her body is supposed to be in deep psychic trouble but, if preparing a womb to harbour the progeny of strangers is morally acceptable to us, we must have to some extent accepted the idea of the womb's being an impersonal container. If bodily proximity has anything whatever to do with intimacy, there can be no relationship closer than that of a woman to the child developing inside her own body, yet we expect a surrogate mother to go through labour and give the child away without a pang. In Britain commercial surrogacy was outlawed by the Surrogacy Arrangements Act of 1985 but shortage of women prepared to act as surrogates is bringing pressure for change. The Human Fertilization and Embryology Authority is of the opinion that not more than £10,000 is due to a surrogate mother for 'loss of earnings, maternity clothes, travelling and the like'. To accept surrogacy at any price is to deny that any bond need exist between a woman and the child she carried beneath her heart for nine months, whether it has her genes or not. The blood that ran in its veins was her blood but, if someone can produce her signature on a legal document, that is a matter of no consequence.

In putting their wombs to use much as they would a handbag or any other useful receptacle women are simply taking over the attitude of the obstetricians whose text-books often refer to the uterus as if it were a public utility. More and more it seems that women themselves are coming to regard their wombs as a burden they have been lumbered with on behalf of the race. Every year vast numbers of women have their wombs removed, even though the operation is expensive, difficult and the recovery period long. More worrying than the gynaecologists who despise the womb, and tell women that once they have completed their family size their wombs will give them nothing but trouble and might as well come out, are the women who will not accept that their womb is not the cause of their woes and will seek high and low until they find a practitioner who will agree to spay them. If men flee the female, we will survive, but if women themselves treat femaleness as a disease we are lost indeed.

breasts

All mammals have nipples. Not all mammals have breasts; to have breasts you have to be both female and human. Human females are unique in that the flesh containing the mammary glands is always more or less distended as if they were permanently lactating. Explanations of this human peculiarity are necessarily speculative; some say that when humans came to feel so secure that they could give up the dog-fashion position and copulate face to face, the breast had to mimic the buttocks which had been the original visual stimulus to intercourse. This curious line of argument raises more questions than it answers. If human beings, like other anthropoids, attracted each other by displays of oestrus – their bums turning scarlet and blue and swelling out spectacularly, say – why did they ever stop? Why did human oestrus fade almost entirely away so that human beings copulate when one partner is not fertile? The usual explanation for this development in *Homo sapiens sapiens* is that with the increasing brain size and correspondingly longer period of relative helplessness in human young, copulation became primarily a bonding mechanism. The human mother had to keep on having sex with her male mate in order to keep him from straying, because she needed him to protect her and her children, so she developed buttock-like breasts. Most female mammals do not welcome the attentions of the male when they are not in season; the human female cannot manage without them – or so the thinking goes.

If this account is true, it would seem that the primary purpose of human breasts is not to feed infants but to attract and keep a mate. Nipples that give milk can function perfectly adequately on the flattest bosom, with little or no attendant fat. Fat breasts often function less well. If it were true that breasts are for men to play with, we would expect intense interest in breasts to be a universal trait of the male human. Very little is actually known about the anthropology of breast fetishism. Among races whose mammary development is seldom spectacular, the Chinese and Japanese for example, the breast is not the focus of erotic imagery. Caucasian women who have never lactated often exhibit pronounced breast development, sometimes even when the distribution of subcutaneous fat over the rest of the body is below average. The latter, extremely rare, combination of characteristics made Brigitte Bardot the most admired woman of her day. The supermodels of today are

My boyfriend is a 'breast man' and, as I am a 34E, I felt I had plenty to offer him. That was until I saw the pin-ups on his bedroom wall. I can't compete with women like Pandora Peaks, who has freakishly huge breasts. I don't know what angers me more – the men who lust after these bimbos or the women who pander to their fantasies.

Laura, Cardiff

much taller and skinnier than Bardot ever was, and far less likely to have been endowed with ebullient breasts by nature.

Every little girl hopes that one day she will grow good

breasts, but what constitutes a good breast? *Playboy* magazine invented the pencil test; if a pencil slid under the breast of a standing woman stayed put, her breasts were saggy. A good breast, by definition, does not sag. A good breast is not small either. Breasts are not balloons. A large breast that does not sag defies gravity; there is no muscle in a breast that can be honed and toned to tighten it up. The pectoral muscle which is overdeveloped in female bodybuilders is not part of the breast proper; the breast overlies it and will jump if the muscle is flexed, but the muscle does not support it. A woman who has good breasts then is one who has sizeable breasts that do not sag. To demand so much is already to demand too much, but a good pair of breasts is also supposed to consist of breasts of exactly the same size. The symmetry of the human body is only apparent; just as eyes and ears are very seldom of exactly the same size and symmetrical shape, breasts are usually unequal. About 50 per cent of women have the left breast larger than the right, about 45 per cent of women have the right larger than the left, and about 5 per cent have exactly equal breasts. Even breasts that are equal in size do not necessarily sit at the same angle on the rib cage. None of this is important, except to women who, when they see in the mirror that their breasts are not perfectly symmetrical, feel that they are deformed. The straitjacket of the brassiere equalizes, uplifts, pads out and separates breasts into rigidified pairs. In mid-1995 Dr Cathy Read remarked:

Two decades after feminists sought to destroy its symbolism with flames, the brassiere is back. As a spokeswoman for Wonderbra told me at its recent US launch: 'The bra is now a fashion accessory, women have whole wardrobes of bras: a jog bra to work out in, a bra for work and a more glamorous bra for special occasions.'

Brassieres impose an international norm on the staggering varieties of breast shapes found on human females the world over. Some breasts have a broad spreading base with the nipple held close to the underlying muscle (fried-egg-shape), others are narrow based and comparatively long (sweet-potato-shape). Almost none are the standard shape, which seems to be perfectly hemispherical with the nipple exactly at the centre-point. The proportion of the nipple to the breast is also highly variable. Some nipples are actually larger and more protuberant than the breast mound; others are tiny and so flat as to seem indented. Anthropologists classified the interesting protuber-ances on native women's chests as globuliform, conical, piriform, à tête de brioche, en galette, hemispherical or elongated. They noted that the aureole could be flat, cup-shaped or raised from the breast like a bottle gourd, and vary in colour from pale cream to blue black. The deciding factors in natural breast configuration are mostly genetic and therefore we find certain breast formations more common in some races than in others. The more-or-less hemispherical breast is typically Aryan. The imposition of a standard variety of 'good' breast is as racist as it is sexist.

> Both my husbands had grey smiles
> And were transvestites.
> I thought that stupid
> (so what if my breasts
> are like two fried eggs?)
> They haven't any.
>
> Leland Bardwell, 'Husbands'

The breast as perky plaything must be dense and full. Generations of women have regularly splashed their breasts with cold water to stimulate the blood flow, supposing that this would tighten them up. Dozens of creams made billions of dollars because women thought that they would firm their breasts when actually the constitution of the breast can only match the fat in the rest of the body regardless of how much icewater is sprayed at it or how much royal jelly or seaweed extract is rubbed into it. After genes the most potent influence upon the breasts is the menstrual cycle; the effects of the cycle upon the breasts can be virtually imperceptible or clearly marked. In some women, after ovulation the breasts become full and tender, with marked veins. It is one of life's little ironies that breasts are never fuller or more tense than when their owner is pregnant. The woman who had spent her youth grieving that her breasts had not been a touch more ebullient may now find them altogether too much of a good thing. As the nipples spread and darken, even a lover may find a woman's breasts less attractive and be less disposed to toy with them, supposing that she could bear it if he did.

Did men first fall in love with the breast when it was a source of nourishment and a connection with the mother, when the nipple filled their mouths and squashed their noses? No research has ever been done on breast-centred eroticism in bottle-fed as opposed to breast-fed individuals. No sub-group of fetishists is turned on by bottle-shaped breasts, as far as we know. The baby girl fell in love with the breast too. Women are at least as concerned about breasts and interested in breasts as men are. Womb and ovaries can be and are jettisoned on relatively slight pretexts but breasts are held onto at the risk of the owner's life. No attempt has ever been made to discover why women are so attached to their breasts, or why they consider the breast the defining sexual characteristic of the female. If it is hard to explain grown men's fascination with tits, jugs, boobs, norks, bazookas, bazooms, knockers, bristols, paps, dugs, titties, bubbies, etc., and their readiness to slobber them and suck them like giant stubbly babies, women's attitudes to men's caressing their breasts are no less mysterious. Some women derive intense pleasure from it, others less and some none at all. The nipple is partly constructed of erectile tissue and can become engorged; stimulation and manipulation of the nipple can of themselves lead to orgasm. Suckling is said to provoke contractions and speed the return of the uterus to its non-pregnant dimensions. Despite incessant interest in the breasts as triggers of erotic action, there has been no systematic investigation of the female breast as an erogenous zone. E. Helsing and F. Savage King are quite clear about the pleasurability of breast-feeding:

> The milk-ejection reflex is closely connected with the sexual reflexes. Sexual stimulation may cause oxytocin to be secreted from the posterior pituitary, and so make milk flow. The connection works in the opposite direction too, and many women have sexual sensations while they nurse. This makes some women feel guilty and anxious instead of accepting the sensation for what it is: nature's way of making breast-feeding pleasant, and of helping the survival of the species.

We have not the faintest idea how many women find suckling pleasurable to the point of orgasm; the phenomenon, though common, is never discussed. Women who have never heard that such a response is not only possible but normal feel guilty and frightened. One woman, asked if she enjoyed breast-feeding,

When in the darkness
Behind closed lids I perceive
The blind, furled fist
And the questing
Mouth, hungry as a kiss
For the place where she alone exists –
I think with infinite compassion
Of all the breast–
Starved lovers of our world undressing
You to drink at this
Soft inverted cup of maternal bliss
In gratitude, and less
Than ignorance of what they miss.

Elizabeth Garrett, 'Mother, Baby, Lover'

replied, 'Yes, I did. It was pleasurable, yes, pleasurable. Am I a pervert, do you think?' She was so guilty about her pleasure that she gave up breast-feeding after just one week. There is nothing perverted or unnatural about erotic feelings during breast-feeding. If mammals found suckling less than pleasant infant mammals would be at constant risk of abandonment. Breast erogenicity is clearly adaptive, though many human females say that they feel no pleasure or excitement when their breasts are handled. The taboo on sexual intercourse during lactation which is found so often in human societies may be a tacit recognition that the mother is involved in a pleasurable interchange with the infant, which precludes her taking, as it were, another lover.

Fathers are jealous of the mother's new lover. Examples of male humans who prevented their spouses from breast-feeding their own children can be found throughout history, culminating in the large-scale twentieth-century campaign against breast-feeding which health authorities are still struggling to reverse. In some cases, because breast-feeding was thought to delay the next conception, it was left off because fathers wanted more offspring, or offspring of a different sex, without delay. Mostly however the motivation seems to have been a combination of jealousy of the physical intimacy between mother and child and simple revulsion. Display of their breasts by topless waitresses earns them better tips; bouncing one's breasts in the face of a complete stranger is a fun way of making a living as a lap-dancer but breast-feeding is considered obscene. Every week British newspapers carry stories of women moved on from park benches and seats in malls and department stores and thrown out of public meetings because they dared to give their infant the breast.

As breast shape is largely determined by fat, dieting women can expect to have flaccid breasts; Cher admitted that, though she could keep the rest of her body in shape by exercise, there was nothing she could do for her breasts but have implants to take up the slack. As Cher's body is an intrinsic part of the show that is her business, the work she did on her breasts was no more than necessary maintenance of her stock in trade. When a woman whose breasts are not public decides upon implants her motives are more difficult to understand. A married woman who thought her breasts looked sad and empty after feeding three children decided that she would have them 'pumped up', as she put it. Her husband, a famous rock musician, was less than appreciative, saying that he liked them as they were. 'But I didn't,' she said. Certainly women find pleasure and excitement in exposing their breasts to advantage, otherwise the Wonderbra would never have earned a nickel. Throughout human history breasts have been pushed about, lengthened, pulled and tied down, scarified, pushed up, pushed apart, shaped into shelves and *balcons* without apparent cleavage, and pushed together to exaggerate cleavage.

Dr Cathy Read summed up the vicissitudes of the twentieth-century breast:

> While the brassiere market has been busy lifting, separating and expanding, plastic surgeons have 'enhanced' the breasts of millions of women with silicone implants. Cosmetically, breasts have been systematically worked over from the inside out. It is unfortunate that breast health has not received an equal amount of attention. The breast cancer statistics are the marker of just how unhealthy our breasts are beneath the gloss.

A healthy breast may not be a sexy breast; a breast is healthier if it has lactated before the age of thirty or so, and it is healthier the longer it has lactated. Lactation caused breasts to discolour, the nipples to grow nodose and dark, and after lactation the breast is often slack and empty-looking. Contrariwise, a recon-structed breast is seldom a healthy breast. The history of breast reduction mammoplasty is full of accounts of women whose breasts did not heal properly and became infected, resulting in scarring and disfigurement. Tanya Hatherall was sixteen when she had her breast size surgically reduced: 'The surgeon had cut a vertical line from my nipple to the bottom of each breast and taken out the excess fat. Then he'd taken my nipples off and repositioned them on my new smaller breasts. I had 260 stitches and couldn't bear to walk because of the pain.' Photographs showed her reconstructed breasts as not only much smaller but also less symmetrical than the originals and perceptibly scarred. A substantially reduced breast is usually incapable of lactation.

The lifting of sagging breasts is a difficult matter; the patient has to be operated on in a sitting position so that the hang of the breast can be correctly assessed; the breast must be lifted off the rib cage and cut around, the excess skin drawn down and cut off and the breast mass sewn into the reduced area of skin. Often the nipple must be removed and repositioned at the apex point. The history of implants has been equally painful; implants can shift or turn themselves upside down. In a few cases, agonizing even to read about, the implants wore through the skin and had to be removed. Such cavalier treatment of breast tissue goes against folklore which imagines the breast to be made of especially vulnerable tissue that should not be knocked or bruised.

Women hardly need to be exhorted to 'be breast aware'; worry about breasts has expanded until it hangs like a pall over women's lives. If they examine their own breasts for signs of cancer they are never sure that they have done it properly; if they put themselves through the ordeal of screening they have to worry about the interval before the next examination and the effects of soft tissue irradiation itself. The extreme unpleasantness of the mammogram is systematically and deliberately underplayed by the proponents of mass screening. To make matters worse, newspapers take a delight in publishing unnerving reports. 'US study links abortion with breast cancer' was the headline the *Guardian* gave to a report of the findings of a

City University of New York team published in the *Journal of Epidemiology and Public Health* in October 1996. Research linking an elevated risk of breast cancer with abortion has been around for forty years and is still unsatisfactory in that no physiological connection can be demonstrated and other lifestyle factors remain to be taken into account, but most readers of the article would have had only the haziest idea of the actual increase in likelihood as against other factors (which was not explained) or that the research was questionable (as emerged in the last paragraph or two). Three buzz-words in one headline makes a story too good to play down. In January 1997 when a Danish study proved that there was no correlation between induced abortion and elevated breast cancer risk the story was not reported, even in the quality dailies.

Breast self-examination is not as reassuring as it should be because nobody seems to know what breasts should feel like. Up to 70 per cent of women have fibrocystic breasts, which is just another way of saying that their breasts have palpable strings and lumps in them, and are apt to become engorged and sore as menstruation approaches; 40 to 70 per cent of women will complain to their doctors of painful nodular breasts at some time in their lives. Other women, although they will have as much pain, will not consider it a medical matter. When breast pain or 'mastalgia' becomes unbearable the only treatment is mastectomy. What causes this condition is not known; what is known is that eliminating coffee, chocolate and saturated fats from the sufferer's diet can alleviate the symptoms. It is also advisable to give up smoking. Environmental oestrogens are also suspected, and avoiding recycled tap-water and cow's milk and meats that have been treated with steroids is also worth trying. Some researchers have found a link between benign breast disease and constipation. The treatment of choice is gammalinoleic acid, present in evening primrose oil.

One of the few privileges of British women turning fifty is that they may enter the free breast-screening programme. They will be invited to turn up at a hospital – or a Portakabin in the hospital car park – to undergo ordeal by mammogram, in which each breast is squashed between polished steel plates to the thickness of an English ham sandwich, i.e. about three-quarters of an inch, and exposed to soft-tissue X-ray, as the owner, in unspeakable discomfort, holds her breath. If nothing shows up, you get three years off before the next ordeal. For all the capital invested in and careers made by the campaign for mass mammographic screening, 90 per cent of all breast lumps are detected by women themselves. There is an obvious case for taking two views of the breast, as is done elsewhere, but the British programme remains the exception in only taking one. The increase in the number of lumps detected has led to an increase in the number of painful and stressful investigations. While the sum total of trauma and anxiety has soared, the number of deaths from breast cancer has only slightly fallen. In Britain there were 15,180 deaths from breast cancer in 1990; by 1995, after five years of mass screening, the number had fallen no further than 14,080, a decline of less than 3 per cent a year, while the number of diagnoses had sky-rocketed. This was not news; as long ago as 1991, the US General Accounting Office audited the results of the investment of more than a billion dollars in breast-screening programmes and found that the incidence of the disease was rising much faster than survival rates were improving. Early diagnosis, especially of a disease with no reliable treatment regime, actually extends the known incidence of disease. Early detection means more treatment, and more pain and anxiety, though the afflicted woman lives no longer than she would have without it. All of this means that the cost of breast cancer (that is, the money to be made out of breast cancer treatment) rises steadily and steeply. Between 1982 and 1992 the cost of treating a detected cancer quad-rupled. The screening of women under fifty in the US, with no detected benefit in mortality statistics, costs $3 billion a year.

In 1995 Professor Michael Baum, consultant surgeon at the

Royal Marsden Hospital, resigned as adviser to the NHS breast-screening programme, amid a good deal of shrill controversy. He subsequently endeavoured to explain that he simply wanted to question the cost-effectiveness of the programme in terms of lives saved. In the case of a disease with such variable progress as breast cancer 'lives saved' is a curious criterion. A woman with breast cancer will probably live five years after the diagnosis; she is less likely to live ten years. The huge disparity between the numbers of cancers diagnosed and the small improvement in survival rates suggests that the wrong cancers are being diagnosed and women who are not in danger of death are being treated while women who are in immediate danger are being missed. Breast cancer of itself does not kill; what kills is cancer in a different site that has metastasized from the original cancer in the breast. More depends on establishing whether or not a cancer has metastasized than on verifying its presence in the breast. Instead of cutting breasts off or carving out lumps, grubbing out lymph nodes and hoping for the best, we should be developing techniques of tracing sentinel nodes as effective as those used in treating testicular cancer, where survival rates have improved dramatically.

Though women are terrorized by the constant evocation of the spectre of breast cancer they are never put in possession of the facts. Newspaper handling of evidence about the effectiveness of tamoxifen is a perfect example of how issues are wantonly obfuscated to produce an immediate reaction from frightened women. The cessation of the US tamoxifen trials in early 1998 was presented in such a way that British women of all ages began demanding tamoxifen; within a few weeks contrary findings from much smaller British trials were published, so that the 'controversy' could rage for a few more weeks. No attempt was made to set out the differences between the populations involved in the US and British trials so that individual women could get a glimpse of where they stood in relation to the new information. So different are the careers of pre-menopausal and post-menopausal cancer that they should be treated as different diseases. Pre-menopausal breast cancer is an aggressive disease, which develops rapidly and is extremely invasive. A new Swedish study of 11,000 Swedish women aged between thirty-nine and forty-nine has showed that routine screening of this group had halved the death rate; in Britain only women over fifty and under sixty-four are included in the free breast cancer screening programme. Pre-menopausal women must find their lumps by self-examination, and then ask their GPs to refer them for a mammogram. For a young woman with dense breasts the mammogram is exquisite torture. Women who show signs of breast lesions in a mammogram are then examined by ultrasound, which seems to be the wrong way round. Great hopes have been placed in improved techniques of magnetic resonance imaging (MRI) but so far this method, which is still scandalously expensive, results in an unacceptably high number of false positives. Doctors know that unless a more user-friendly diagnostic procedure is found the battle against breast cancer will continue to be lost.

Once a cancer is detected there is no consensus as to what should be done with it. The options vary from radiation without surgery, radiation and chemotherapy without surgery, lumpectomy with or without radiation, with or without chemotherapy, simple mastectomy with or without radiation, with or without chemotherapy, radical mastectomy with or without radiation, with or without chemotherapy, bilateral mastectomy with or without radiation, with or without chemotherapy. Within these kinds there are further refinements of procedure, including varieties of reconstruction from repairing dents with exported fatty tissue to growing muscle for implantation to the immediate insertion of silicone prostheses, which in England is still considered best practice. British breast cancer survival rates are still the worst in Europe because many of the detected cancers are not treated by oncologists or breast surgery specialists. In July 1998 a British surgeon was suspended for failing to carry out the proper investigations to verify the presence of malignancy before performing lumpectomies; other surgeons are performing lumpectomies justified by biopsies that reveal 'pre-cancerous' cells. There is no surer way to an optimum outcome than to treat patients for cancers they haven't got.

In 1989 Johanna Johenson was found to have cancer in her left breast. After her mastectomy at a hospital in Rochester, Kent, she was referred for possible post-operative treatment to a consultant radiotherapist who told her she had widespread bone cancer, which had not been detected on a skeletal scan. She then underwent five months of intensive radiotherapy and chemotherapy which made her so ill that she had to be hospitalized. She subsequently learned from a consultant at a London hospital that she had no bone cancer. At first she was delighted, but shortly afterwards her spine collapsed and she had to spend another four and a half months in hospital. The health authorities involved admitted that the post-operative treatment had been inappropriate but denied the 'the treatment had caused further illnesses'. The damages Johenson ultimately settled for did not cover the costs of the action she brought against the health authorities. In Britain in 1998 127 women attempted to bring a class action against sixty hospitals for overdosing them with radiation, which damaged the nerves in their arms causing loss of function and pain, in some cases necessitating amputation. The hospitals' defence is that their practice was justifiable in terms of what was understood about the sequelae of radiotherapy at the time. The women, who were on legal aid, were offered an out-of-court settlement which would have barely covered their legal fees.

It was inevitable that problems would arise within the mass screening programme itself. In November 1997 the British health minister announced an overhaul of all breast cancer screening units after an audit of 1,920 mammograms commissioned by the Royal Devon and Exeter NHS Trust found that

229 women who should have been called for further assessment had been missed. In January 1998 a routine inspection of 16,000 mammograms showed that some were 'not up to standard'; a thousand women screened between April 1995 and March 1996 were recalled to take their mammograms again. Meanwhile radiographers were fleeing the programme because they could not cope with the pain that they were forced to inflict on healthy women; staff shortages exacerbated the problem; by July 1998 the programme was in crisis. Mass screening based on mammography could only have been instituted by a health establishment that regarded women's anguish as an insignificant factor in the drive to reduce mortality. The story of the mass screening programme is one of mistaken priorities and misplaced faith in the wrong technology.

For years the familial element in susceptibility to breast cancer was loudly denied, until the case was more than obvious. Now mass screening of post-menopausal women only is unjustified and unjustifiable, especially when we can identify a younger at-risk population who are being ignored. Meanwhile the incidence of breast cancer around the world continues to rise steeply until researchers are talking about an epidemic; American women are now twice as likely to develop breast cancer as they were thirty years ago. The rates are highest in the industrialized world, for reasons that we can only speculate about. Environmental chemicals targeting oestrogen receptors, perhaps? Too many menstrual cycles? Too little lactation? Women continue to die, and they are dying younger. In the United States breast cancer research is funded to the tune of $550 million, having grown from $91 million in 1991. In Britain the research budget is a paltry £2–3 million which, taken together with the failure to identify at-risk women, and to set up appropriate treatment regimes for confirmed cases, shows us the downside of treating the breast as a plaything. A plaything that ceases to be amusing is bound for the trash-can. It's time we stopped fooling about with breasts, time to take them seriously.

food

Food is a feminist issue. Women are providers of food. Part of
the contrast between male and female is that the egg the female
brings to maturity is a complete feeding mechanism concocted
out of her own bodily substance. Take the nucleus out of a
sperm and there is nothing there; take the nucleus out of an
ovum and you can grow another in its place. While the child
develops in the womb the mother feeds it from her own body;
when it is born she lactates and could, if she chose, provide a
significant part of its nourishment for years. All over the world
the preparation of food for men and children is women's work.
Not all women are good at preparing food, not all women want
to put food on the table three times a day. Millions of women
would be transported with bliss if they *could* put food on the
table three times a day. Many a labouring peasant woman
worries about the children left unfed until her long day's work
is done, grieving that her drudgery does not earn enough to buy
her children adequate food. Looking at the shining clean advertisements for Nestlé baby milk, she is only too easily persuaded
that what comes from her toil-racked body is inferior. Feminists

have always been involved in the fight against the marketing of powdered baby milks to poor women and they have also seen that the devaluation of the milk that has no price tag is part of a generalized devaluation of women's contribution to the nourishment of the race, a devaluation that is now reaching its nadir in a distorted attitude to food on the part of women themselves. In March 1997 BBC foodies interviewing women who confessed that they don't cook, cook rarely or cook badly remarked on the fear and loathing of food that they all seemed to share.

For thousands of years men hunted and women gathered. What the men brought home was ceremonial food, feasting food, not the food of every day. What hunter-gatherer groups actually survived on was what was gathered by the women: roots, seeds, fruits, larvae, shellfish, reptiles, eggs, honey – not to mention the back-breaking weight of water that women had to carry, sometimes for miles, every day. The food the men brought was easily prepared, roasted or grilled. When the women weren't searching, digging, picking or lugging, they were threshing, cleaning, husking, peeling, grinding, pounding and kneading. Their food-production was labour-intensive and undervalued; the men's food-gathering was sport and ceremonial. The pattern of devaluing women's contribution is as old as human civilization. Clearly food production and consumption have changed vastly since industrialization but the devaluation of women's contribution remains a constant. Though their part in food preparation has been to a large extent usurped by industry, women are still held responsible and hold themselves responsible for what the family eats. In the matter of nutrition, as in so much else, they are confronted with the typical female dilemma of lack of control combined with total responsibility. The media play upon the female food-provider's helplessness by exaggerating the risks of listeria and salmonella, of CJD and *Escherichia coli* 0157. The food-provider is told that food additives may cause her child's hyperactivity, but not what foods contain what and what additives are responsible for what. Worst of all, sophisticated marketing techniques prompt her family to demand certain processed foods, and excesses of sugar and flavourings in those foods get her kids hooked.

> Soon, I will take you and feed you
> My stew. It will be thick, reddish-brown,
> And rich as the beginning of the world.
>
> Connie Bensley, 'Cookery'

When the family was required to gather around the table for meals at least once a day, and snack foods were unknown, the food-provider was directly responsible for her family's quality of life. She could display both authority and skill and express her love for her family by the effort that she put into the dishes that she brought to the table. That female role has now disappeared. It could only last as long as there was not a shop on the corner selling things more delicious than mother could ever make. The rule used to be that if you ate between meals you spoiled your appetite and disappointed the person who tried so hard to make the pastry light and the gravy tasty. Marketing soon demolished all such foolish piety; the merest twinge of hunger is represented by the food-vendors as intolerable. The minute 'hunger strikes' you are supposed to eat something. The food-provider shopping for her family has no idea whether they will eat what she buys or not, or how much or what they have been eating all day. Practically all of the foodstuffs she can find in the supermarket represent added value of one kind or another, in packaging and presentation, if not in actual pre-preparation. If she insists on buying grains and pulses rather than ready-cooked dishes, she will pay ludicrously high prices for them. On the grounds of economy as well as convenience she might as well buy ready-made ham and pea soup as try to find a ham knuckle and split peas. More and more women are finding that they cannot compete with the food technicians who pre-cook dishes for the supermarkets, or with the take-away, if only because the people they are feeding will no longer all consent to eat the same thing. Home-cooking is expressly sneered at in TV commercials; Dad confesses to his toddler son that he is not worried about Grandma's dreadful cooking because he has already eaten a delicious Big Mac. The clever cook is the woman who dishes up convenience food as if it were her own unaided effort.

The commercialization of food preparation has not relieved women of their obsession with food because, although they cannot control what goes into commercially produced foods or what their familes eat, they are still responsible for 'getting the food in'. The refrigerator and the freezer must be well stocked with food that has not passed its sell-by date, and people must be got to eat it. Eating behaviour being now impulse-led and chaotic, women are being asked to control the uncontrollable. Obese children are their mothers' fault. Mothers are meant to sort the kids out, though many grossly obese people eat very daintily when family members or friends are looking on, saving their gorging for the privacy of their own room or the anonymity of the street. Gluttony is often a solitary vice, having very little to do with actual enjoyment of food and rather more to do with pushing things into the body, in this case through the mouth. Psychiatrists are aware of fetishistic use of food, but they are less aware of the way our culture encourages various kinds of food fetishism. The marketing of chocolate bars as phallic shapes that induce states rather like orgasm is an obvious case, made more obvious by the current emphasis on chocolate as a euphoria-inducing drug. Food scientists in Britain, ostensibly concerned to get children to eat vegetables, have devised peas that taste like baked beans and carrots that taste like chocolate, which seems as good a way as any of getting kids hooked on real baked beans and real chocolate.

Manufacturers who produce novelty foods to make meal-times more entertaining are doing their bit to encourage children to play with food rather than eat it up. Though men more often than women impose all kinds of rules about what

> She mourned the long ears
> Hung in the pantry, his shot fur
> Softly dishevelled. She smoothed that,
> Before gutting – yet she would rather
> Sicken herself, than cheat my father
> Of his jugged hare.
>
> Jean Earle, 'Jugged Hare'

they will and will not put into their mouths, it is women who become obsessed by their alimentary canals, following in imagination every morsel that is introduced and waiting anxiously for it to reappear as excrement. What sets sufferers from eating disorders apart is their consciousness of food as a presence in their bodies, their primary characterization of themselves as eaters-and-shitters. Anorexia is usually understood as a somatization disorder of a fairly obvious kind. The anorexic does not eat, it is said, because she wants to be as thin as a supermodel and cannot see that she is already thinner than a supermodel. She is simply wrong about her body shape and needs to be re-educated. Another kind of anorexia involves a different kind of somatization disorder, in that the sufferer thinks of herself as nothing but an alimentary canal, like some large gastropod, constantly taking in and pushing out, needing to be sure that she is maintaining some equilibrium, by pushing out as much as she is taking in. If what comes out is not sufficient she feels that she is bloating and poisoning herself. Many women of this persuasion treat their hunger pangs by drinking water, secure in the belief that they are flushing their systems and achieving purity. Youth culture tells them that this is OK; their role models can be seen everywhere, even at movie premières, clutching their plastic half-litre bottles of water. In all these cases what we have is not so much disorderly eating as a protest against disorderly eating, a desperate attempt to get an uncontrollable situation under control.

> I have days, now, when I don't think much about my weight. I have days, at least, when I see properly, when I look in the mirror and see myself as I am – a woman – instead of as a piece of unwanted flesh, forever verging on excess.
>
> Marya Hornbacher, *Wasted*

Most anorexics, 90 per cent, are young women. All kinds of theories are advanced as to why women abuse food. The psychoanalytic school holds that self-starvation is caused by inability to cope with the developmental crisis of adolescence, possibly because of an unresolved Oedipal conflict. Those who argue that the anorexic is fleeing from maturity interpret the failure to menstruate that results from self-starvation as a causal factor, which seems the wrong way round. Others blame a disordered mother–child relationship, dating from the pre-Oedipal stage. Others posit a sense of inadequacy as the mainspring of eating disorder, though anorexics are typically model children who give great satisfaction to their parents and superiors – until their secret vice becomes manifest. Others look for the cause in the family, seeking to identify a typical anorexia family as one that does not allow the child sufficient freedom or privacy. Most take the usual course of blaming the mother. All such explanations assume that the self-starver is sick, damaged or deviant. The emaciated young woman may very well not care what they think; every time she looks into a girls' magazine she will find approbation of her self-destructive behaviour. A survey carried out in 1997 by the British Schools' Health Education Unit found that one in five schoolgirls aged between fourteen and fifteen had nothing for breakfast, and as many again had only a drink. One in seven did not eat lunch. Six out of ten thought they needed to lose weight.

There is besides a clearly visible youth culture of disorderly eating, in which young women boast of bizarre eating exploits in much the same way as boys will boast of grotesque extremes of drunken behaviour. Wherever young women are gathered one may hear confessions: 'I once ate a whole Sara Lee chocolate cake at a sitting,' capped by 'Well, I ate a whole kilo of pickled beetroot in less than an hour,' and so on. Such boasts are mostly lies and the girls who make them perfectly healthy, but they do suggest that anorexia is a variety of conformism. Anorexia, like hysteria, is catching.

Anorexia and its related disorders are intrinsic to the kind of 'girlpower' that is expressed in being conspicuously out of control. Girlpower presupposes 'bad behaviour' but the kinds of bad behaviour available to teenage girls are limited. Their exploits begin with shouting and screaming in public places and progress to shop-lifting, brawling, drunkenness, drug use, body piercing, sexual aggression and – especially for those who would shrink from such hoydenish transgressions – bizarre eating habits. Extreme anorexics come to emaciation by different routes; there is no single aetiology of eating disorders. We can all agree only that eating disorders are epidemic; one in twenty-five fifteen-year-old girls is already anorexic. The specialized unit set up at Great Ormond Street Hospital thirteen years ago to treat children with eating disorders now sees four new cases a week. Some of these children are so ill that they need immediate hospitalization. Some have been starved by their anorexic mothers; in one case reported in the medical press an anorexic mother had bought two bananas to feed the family for a week.

All discussions of eating disorders focus upon the disorderly eater rather than chaotic food. No attempt is made to treat the food or the representation of food in our culture, though it is obvious that eating disorders are unlikely to arise in conditions where food is relatively scarce and hunger familiar. They are much more likely to arise when there is abundant food available on demand, where binge-eating is possible, and where pickiness and lack of appetite cause concern in others and the build-up of accumulated tensions and resentments. The giving and withholding of food is a powerful controlling mechanism in human affairs; children who are rewarded or pacified with food can hardly be blamed for becoming confused about the point of eating. Many children develop garbled eating habits at a very early age, refusing to eat a vast range of nourishing foods, insisting on eating exactly the same foods at every meal. A good deal has been written about the role of the mother in causing feeding difficulties but more attention could be given to what the child feels when she refuses to eat, causing members of the family to take turns in sailing her food into her mouth as if the spoon was an aeroplane, and all the rest of it, dragging meal-times out for hours. Refusing food is power, the only power the girl child knows. As she sits in her high chair, shying food all over the kitchen, she has everybody's fascinated attention. No mother these days would dare to up-end a child's food bowl on her head and leave her to scream. Instead the food drama is intensified. Each plateful becomes a mini battle-ground; the person with the spoon has to resist the impulse to ram it down the kid's throat. The kid clenches her teeth.

Thirty years ago we did not hear of eating disorders, which is not to say that they did not exist, but that there was little awareness of them. Now that we know that women do bizarre things with their food, we are aware of self-starvation as a his-toric problem. It seems that women have always been prone to distorted ingestion- and elimination-behaviour. Green-sickness probably involved disordered eating, as did the 'consumption' and 'decline' that killed so many young women in the late eighteenth and early nineteenth centuries. The girls who pined and died for love would nowadays be thought anorexic. When a woman didn't eat it was assumed that she couldn't eat, when the truth was that she was refusing to eat. Elizabeth Barrett Browning explained her own self-starvation in her verse novel *Aurora Leigh*.

When imprisoned members of the Women's Social and Political Union refused to eat they made public use of a secret weapon that women had been using undetected for centuries. Self-starvation is so merciless to the self that it is hardly conceivable that any woman would use it. Because no legitimate grounds for protest could be acknowledged, the angry woman's self-immolation had to be interpreted as illness and hence beyond anybody's control. Once the hunger-strike had been used politically it was hardly available for home use any more and we hear much less of consumptions and declines in the twentieth century, until the emergence into notoriety of the anorexics and the bulimarexics, the starvers and gorgers, in the last quarter of the century. The political history of self-starvation offers us a clue to the function of disorderly eating as protest; the protest of the powerless, dependent as they are on the approval of others, must take a secret form. Given the universal awareness of young women as bodies rather than people, it is inevitable that their impotent rage be turned against those bodies, which they are wilfully destroying, even as they are most admired. Disorderly eating is closely related to other kinds of self-mutilation and blood-draining, all behaviours that are similarly secret and apt to be found in the same highly narcissistic and over-achieving population.

If food is a weapon it is also a source of power. In April 1998 a survey conducted by the BBC *Good Food* magazine came to the entirely unsurprising conclusion that the nation's cooking was still being done by women; more than 90 per cent of the women questioned said that they prepared supper every night for their husbands or partners. This was generally interpreted as bad news for feminism. Most of these women will have already done a day's work; many of them surely resent having to put food on the table night after night, and feminists must

> Your pantry stocked with sweet cooked fish,
>   pink herring, Polish cucumbers
> in newspaper, and on the gas
>   a bristly hen still boiling into soup:
> most gentle sloven, how I honour now
>   all your enormous, unfastidious welcome.
>
> Elaine Feinstein, 'Rose'

support them in their demand to be freed from this burden. But what is to be done for the women who find giving food to the ones they love the only potentially satisfying part of their day? We do not know what proportion of the 90 per cent were defending their control of the domestic environment. Running a house is a complex task requiring high levels of management skills; if men did it, the domestic sphere would be invested with prestige and value. The same BBC *Good Food* magazine report informed us that the rise and rise of food snobbery in our time has so undermined the confidence of all the women putting food before their families every day that they would not risk cooking for guests. Not all feminists have regarded women's traditional skills with contempt; there are feminists who see the home as a creative opportunity, who bake bread and cakes, who knit and sew, who grow fruit and vegetables and make pickles and preserves, in the forlorn hope that someone will value the work of their hands above the work of machines. These are the earth mother feminists, flat-footed, broad-hipped figures of fun. The reinvestment of women's traditional fields of expertise with prestige and value is one more feminist cause that is being lost.

pantomime dames

The only way a man can get rid of healthy genitals is to say that he is convinced that he is a woman. Then another man will remove them and gladly. In order to justify sex-change surgery a new disorder called gender dysphoria has come into being. The disease has no biological marker; its presence is discerned by a history of inappropriately gendered behaviour, social disability and affective disorder. Though there is some research linking gender dysphoria with other affective disorders, trans-

As a consequence of the toxic action of tributylin in anti-fouling paints used on ships' hulls, female dog-whelks are growing huge penises, which block their oviducts so that the pressure of their growing eggs eventually bursts them apart.

sexuals themselves emphatically insist that they do not suffer from any mental disease.

Governments that consist of very few women have hurried

to recognize as women men who believe that they are women and have had themselves castrated to prove it, because they see women not as another sex but as a non-sex. No so-called sex-change has ever begged for a uterus-and-ovaries transplant; if uterus-and-ovaries transplants were made mandatory for wannabe women they would disappear overnight. The insistence that manmade women be accepted as women is the institutional expression of the mistaken conviction that women are defective males. The biological truth is the opposite; all biologists know that males are defective females. Though external genitalia are the expression of the chromosomal defect, their removal will not alter the chromosomal fact, any more than removal of the tails of puppies will produce a tailless breed. 'Sex-change operations' can only be carried out in Swift's Laputa. As Dwight D. Billings and Robert Urban argued in 1982:

> transsexualism is a relational process sustained in medical practice and marketed in public testimony . . . The legitimization, rationalization and commodification of sex-change operations have produced an identity category – transsexual – for a diverse group of sexual deviants and victims of severe gender role distress.

As sufferers from gender role distress themselves women must sympathize with transsexuals but a feminist must argue that the treatment for gender role distress is not mutilation of the sufferer but radical change of gender roles. Throughout their history women who could not carry out their prescribed gender roles have suffered all kinds of ghastly gynaecological procedures and, like transsexuals, they have been grateful to their abusers. Women could hardly now condone the elaborate mutilations practised on individuals of both sexes, even though the victims argue that such mutilations are their right.

Sex-change surgery is profoundly conservative in that it reinforces sharply contrasting gender roles by shaping individuals to fit them. Not all transsexuals opt for mutilation. In Spain and Latin America transsexual prostitutes, who are expected both to display a spectacularly feminine appearance and to bugger their clients, will have breast implants and silicone oil injections in their hips and buttocks, but retain their penises and testicles. The literature on transsexualism rather undermines its own respectability by failing to distinguish between pre-operative transsexuals, post-operative transsexuals and cross-dressers who are merely 'hiding their candy'. The far greater numbers of men requesting sex-change surgery compared to women has been explained by the failure of practitioners to weed out effeminate homosexuals, transvestites and diagnostically uncertain cases; it seems as likely that surgeons and their cohorts have simply not understood the cultural context of transsexualism or the symbolic significance of the long and elaborate procedures themselves.

Men who opt for the mutilation option are first heavily dosed with oestrogens; then the testicles are cut off and the penis slit and scraped out, so that its skin can be used to line the surgical cleft that will do duty as a vagina. The first vaginas were clumsy affairs; in some the urethral opening was partly obscured by the remains of the scrotal sack, the so-called 'Kangaroo Pouch' vulvovaginoplasty. Pseudo-vaginas have been constructed from non-genital skin grafts, penile skin grafts, penile skin flaps and pedicled intestinal implants. Nowadays the most expensive operations mimic the labia, and construct a vaginoid orifice of 12 cm depth in the right plane, using inverted penile skin, and exposing some part of the glans penis to function as a clitoris. The new-made woman then has the option of continuing to remake herself in woman's image. In this process a nose-job may be as important as her penectomy. She may also opt to have her chin or jaw-bone trimmed, her cheeks rounded, her hairline lowered, her breasts pumped up, and the framework of her larynx altered to give her a voice of higher pitch. She will need hundreds of sessions of electrolysis to control her facial hair.

The few follow-up studies show that post-operative trans-sexuals have no higher rates of suicide or psychosis after surgery than before. Concern about breast cancer has waned since the oestrogen regimes were rationalized, but venous thrombo-embolism is common. Concealed in such studies is the fact that many transsexuals work in the sex industry because, they say, discrimination prevents them from finding other employment. In some countries the number of transsexuals working as prostitutes equals the number of women; rates of HIV, hepatitis B and C and active syphilis tend to be higher among transsexual prostitutes than amongst women. It has been suggested that the high cost of sex-change operations may itself drive many post-operative transsexuals to prostitution; in the 1970s the average cost of the basic operation was around $10,000; to this must be added the cost of lifelong oestrogen maintenance. The first sex-change procedure not infrequently results in a need for others. Grafts fail, tissue necrotizes, the pseudo-vagina narrows or closes up. In 1977 the Stanford University gender clinic reported that their two-stage sex-change procedure actually required an average of 3.5

Transvestites and transsexuals do not challenge the social construction of gender. Their goal is to be masculine men and feminine women.

Judith Lorber

---

operations and fully half their cases involved complications of one sort or another. The acceptor of a surgical sex-change enters into a lifelong relationship with the medical establishment in which her mutilation is regularly dramatized; though she demands acceptance as a woman, she is never unaware of her special status. Though she imposes a silence upon others when it comes to referring to her ambiguous gender status, she reserves the right to draw attention to it herself. There is in this dual posture more than a suspicion of hostility towards the intact.

In the sacred Indian city of Varanasi one may see quite often veiled and skirted men with their hair dressed and their faces painted like women. These men too have lost their genitalia but they make not the slightest attempt to pass as women. Their female dress is garish and parodic, their behaviour loud and aggressive, even frightening. They are hijras, agents of the mother goddess who receive offerings in return for dancing at weddings and child-namings. Their offering to the goddess was their genitalia, bloodily and painfully removed, sometimes by the hijras themselves. Their clients may demand proof that the sacrifice has been made, clutching at them through their skirts or demanding that they raise them.

> In narratives of this sort, the castration is social (proof to the heckling crowd), symbolic (giving up the position of having 'just as a man has, everything'), and often physiological. Castration is necessary physically to change internal gender. Through the bleeding, maleness flows out, female flows in; mixture results. Hijras from Baroda explain . . . that 'maximum blood should be poured out of the body during the castration ceremony . . .'

Lawrence Cohen, who studied hijras in Varanasi in the late 1980s and again in 1993, came to the conclusion that they desired the violence of self-mutilation and they didn't mind who knew it. In our own culture too sex-change surgery seems to be an aim in itself, presented as a reward for meticulous playing out of a female role. In India, where a third sex can be both acknowledged and created, there is no obligation on a born intersexual to have him/herself sorted out one way or the other. As in India marriage is universal and the point of marriage is children, intersexuals who are sterile will not succeed in imitating one or other sex. As a childless wife can only suffer, there would be no point in passing an intersexual off as a woman. In our own society cases of genital ambiguity tend to be classified as women of one sort or another, which seems unfair to both women and intersexuals.

Male-to-female (MTF) transsexuals in Europe and America may now draw attention to their special status as part of the campaign to achieve full civil rights, that is to be accepted as women. Transsexuals who have undergone 'full reconstructive surgery' may contract valid marriages with persons of their born sex in New Zealand, Australia, Sweden, Germany, Italy, the Netherlands and some US states. No-one ever asked women if they recognized sex-change males as belonging to their sex or considered whether being obliged to accept MTF transsexuals as women was at all damaging to their identity or self-esteem. As far as anyone could tell, women did not mind calling sex-change males 'she'. Perhaps this development should have been resisted, because it was part of the definition of the female as 'other', as simply the 'not-male'. Femaleness is not the other side of the Rorschach blot of maleness, but a sex of its own, with a sexuality of its own and a whole spectrum of possible expressions, many of which take no account of maleness at all.

No man can have the history of being born and located in this culture as a woman. He can have the history of *wishing* to be a woman and of *acting* like a woman, but this gender experience is that of a transsexual, not of a woman. Surgery may confer the artefacts of outward and inward female organs but it cannot confer the history of being born a woman in this society.

Janice Raymond

Woman is not placed on earth for the use of man any more than men are placed on earth for the use of women. Both could do without each other if it were not for the pesky business of sexual reproduction. Though they stress their role in 'the sex act', MTF transsexuals have so far shown no more interest in reproduction than most men do.

There is nothing new in using the catch-all category 'female' to describe incomplete males. In August 1996 the British media were alerted to the existence of individuals who had become women despite their Y chromosome because they were not and had never been responsive to testosterone. Their condition is called Androgen Insensitivity Syndrome (AIS). Male foetuses that are completely unresponsive to androgens in utero and do not develop external genitals at all are said to demonstrate Complete Androgen Insensitivity Syndrome (CAIS), male foetuses that respond weakly to androgens and develop inadequate or ambiguous external genitalia Partial Androgen Insensitivity Syndrome (PAIS). CAIS babies are usually assumed to actually be female until investigation in later life reveals that they lack a female reproductive system; PAIS babies are usually surgically castrated, their undescended testicles and defective penis removed, and thus made 'female'. The journalists' way of explaining these anomalies was to say that the male foetuses developed 'along female lines'.

'Biologically they are male; in every other way they are female' ran the sub-head to a piece by Beverley D'Silva in the *Guardian*. *Cosmopolitan* too ran the story of AIS as the story of women with men's genes. Christine was operated on to remove undescended testicles at the age of two; after puberty she found that her vagina was only a centimetre long; a gynaecologist told her, 'Come back when you want to get married, and we'll operate. There's no reason why you shouldn't regard yourself as a normal woman.' The operation was performed when she was in her forties but her artificial vagina closed up again. According to Simone Cave in *Cosmopolitan*, 'doctors insist there is no ambiguity over the gender of AIS babies, they are always female'. Cases of genuine ambiguity were taken to be those where the penis had developed sufficiently to be noticed. Cave became confused:

The sex of a newborn baby is questioned if its penis is shorter than about 2.5 cm or its clitoris longer than 0.9 cm. If a baby has a very large clitoris, it can function well as a girl, as it will just need a vagina constructed.

But AIS individuals have neither womb nor ovaries; XX women are almost always born with both. What is more XX females do respond to testosterone. What the CAIS babies are is not female but feminine, more feminine in truth than XX women because they have no body hair whatsoever. Letters sent to me by AIS individuals boast that if they and I were standing naked side by side passers by would have no doubt who was the more feminine. I don't doubt it. The indubitable femininity of sleek-bodied AIS females proves as nothing else could that femininity has nothing to do with sex. Men can do femininity better than women can, because femaleness conflicts with femininity as maleness does not.

Doctors are hardly less confused than Cave: they judge according to impressionistic criteria whether the genital they are looking at is a clitoris or a penis and apportion sex arbitrarily on the basis of this visual assessment. Evidently they choose not to establish chromosomal sex. As we know that a mother treats a baby very differently according to her understanding of what its sex is, we need hardly be surprised that babies brought up as girls believe that they are girls whether they are or not and

> We can surgically and chemically alter people to such an incredible extent that their own mothers may not recognize them.
>
> Tracie O'Keefe

behave accordingly. In the past chromosally male children who were classified at birth as male could not be re-registered as female even in cases where it had subsequently been decided to raise them as female. The case of Joella Holliday set an important precedent when it was decided in December 1998 that her birth registration should be changed and that she should be re-christened. From now on chromosomal sex is irrelevant.

Helen Mather, though male by this criterion, stated categorically, 'It would be grotesque to suggest I'm anything other than female. I wouldn't know how to be a man.' The possibility that men know as little about how to be a man as she does is worth exploring; more interesting to a feminist is what Mather thinks being a man involves and how she knows that she is 'being' a woman.

It was a woman doctor who said to an AIS patient, 'You can consider yourself female if you like.' An eminent man, Howard Jacobs, Professor of Reproductive Endocrinology at Middlesex Hospital, is reported as telling the same patient that 'she' was 'completely female' though 'her' 'genes were male'. 'That,' she went on gratefully, 'was the first time my condition had been explained to me.' Professor Jacobs is directly quoted as saying, 'Revealment, not concealment, is the way to go. Euphemism is out. Full-frontal honesty is in.' 'Full-frontal honesty' (the term is revealing) would have informed this patient that she was not a woman but a failed male who may pass for a female and even marry her long-term boyfriend because she was wrongly identified at birth as a female. AIS 'females' have no female organs and not a female cell in their bodies. We need to be sure that their being classified as female is not a reflection of a refusal on the part of entire males to recognize these damaged males as belonging to their sex. Cruel and unsympathetic though it may seem, women should not automatically accept all those who do not wish to be male as being *ex gratia* females.

The same article told the story of an AIS baby who was correctly identified as male. From the age of three he was subjected to surgical procedures meant to enhance his undersized external genitalia. He explained: 'My schooldays were hell. At primary school I was the weirdo in the corner with the funny little thingy. Come secondary school, with PE and changing rooms, you can't avoid being seen naked. With me it was once seen, never forgotten.' Schoolboys are here enacting in an obvious and tribal way what grown-up endocrinologists do in a devious and respectable fashion – they are rejecting an AIS male as any kind of a male. When this patient was in his mid-twenties he accepted the inevitable and began to live as a woman. 'She' consulted a psychiatrist, had surgery to tidy up 'her' ambiguous equipment, had a vagina constructed out of a section of bowel and 'hormone replacement therapy' which, I presume, means that she was dosed with oestrogens. Accounts of the procedures inflicted on AIS males are shocking; no two cases are treated in the same way. Most but not all have their male gonads removed – without explanation. Many but not all have vaginas surgically constructed for them so that they can function as normal, i.e. heterosexual females. This implies a curious attitude to females as simply bodies with clefts in for the accommodation of a penis. Even so, more and more sex-change males now feel free to come out as lesbians, as Tracie O'Keefe has done. Tracie O'Keefe is a Harley Street psycho-

> Rave culture, like its speed freak ancestors, mod and Northern Soul, is remarkable for its asexuality; dancers frug and twirl for the self-pleasuring narcissistic bliss of it, not to attract a potential mate. This 'androgyny' may really be a subconscious attempt to usurp female potencies and pleasures, in order to dispense with real women altogether.
>
> Simon Reynolds and Joy Press, *The Sex Revolts*

therapist who at the age of twenty-two had vaginoplasty, breast augmentation and rhinoplasty, and married twice before setting up house with Katrina Fox. O'Keefe thinks 'perhaps it is time to jettison the bipolar elitist model of human behaviour', though it would be hard to see how her life would have made sense without a bipolar model to react against.

AIS males appear in some cases to have made a free choice to live as spurious females. One patient is quoted as saying, 'I sit between AIS and transsexualism because I was brought up male and changed to female. But being reared male was determined by society, not by me. Given the choice I would have grown up female.' No baby is given the choice; every baby is endowed with a sex at birth by 'society'. That identification can prove to be wrong. On the one hand we have intersexual children who cannot grow into the gender role chosen for them by their parents and revert to their chromosomal sex, to the huge delight of the genes-dictate-everything school, and on the other fully developed normal males with active testicles and no shortage of testosterone who decide that they are locked into the wrong body. If no-one saw anything odd or unconvincing in the case brought against the Gloucestershire health authority for refusing to fund a sex-change operation for a person known simply as 'W', a 'former labourer in her mid-thirties who has lived as a woman for four years' and 'has suffered psychological trauma through believing she was in the wrong body, became an alcoholic and was unable to work', the story would hardly have made the newspapers. Various NHS authorities in England had imposed a blanket ban on sex-change operations; in the case of W it was argued that such bans were 'irrational and unreasonable' and in breach of both the Sex Discrimination Act and EC law. The health authority was ordered to pay £7,000 for W's surgery. W's solicitor Madeleine Rees commented, 'Informed medical opinion says transsexualism is a medical condition. The only treatment is surgery.' In Holland, where the Free University Hospital in Amsterdam has performed more than a thousand MTF sex changes, youngsters are considered eligible for treatment and may begin pre-operative oestrogen therapy as young as sixteen.

Female to male (FTM) transsexuals are rarer than male to female and very much less conspicuous. Evaluation of women seeking sex-change treatment shows a variety of pre-existing conditions leading to masculinization, in particular non-classical adrenal hyperplasia, polycystic ovarian syndrome and other hyperandrogenic disorders. If this is the case, FTM transsexuals are very different from their male counterparts, who seldom display endocrine derangement. They behave very differently too; there is no possibility of a career in the sex industry for an FTM transsexual, many of whom are sexually inactive. Cosmetic surgeons are enormously intrigued by the challenge of fabricating a functional penis, but they have so far failed to meet it. Only a small minority, around 10 per cent, of FTM transsexuals have any kind of phalloplasty; those who do may be told that they will never have an orgasm again. Being able to pee standing up seems more important to wannabe men than erectile function; MTF transsexuals on the other hand regard enjoyment of penetrative sex in the pseudo-vagina as crucial. FTM transsexuals do not have the opportunity for the kind of exhibitionism that MTF transsexuals go in for. No FTM transsexual has posed for photographs on the steps of the Garrick Club or the MCC or a men's toilet as part of a heroic campaign against discrimination. An article for the *Guardian* by Louisa Young produced three examples, Gene, Alex and Mark. All three had had bi-lateral mastectomies. Gene said, 'On paper I'm still a woman . . . I haven't been abroad for years because in my passport I'm Jeanette. I'll get that sorted.' Gene followed her bi-lateral mastectomy with a hysterectomy. Forty-year-old Alex began dosing herself with male hormones at nineteen, and had her breasts removed four years later, but she was still not accepted as a man. 'People assume we have civil rights the same as men and tend to be shocked when they realize we don't. We can't marry, for instance.' 'Mark' was the well-known FTM transsexual Mark Rees whose autobiography *Dear Sir or Madam* was published in 1996. As a consequence he was persecuted:

'Last summer the kids were dreadful, throwing things, obscenities'. Though Rees has no breasts, womb or ovaries, he still has a vagina. Though his clitoris is outsized, it has not been enhanced by surgery, which is one of the available options. Rees's attempts to have his identity documents changed and to secure the right to marry have so far failed. In August 1996 an FTM transsexual came before the court of Strasbourg pleading for the right to be registered as the legal father of the children his partner had had by donor insemination. He was refused.

Norman Horton enjoyed his new hobby of line dancing so much that he decided to go twice a week – once as a man and once as a woman. But now he has been forced to hang up his cowboy boots and stetson because one of his instructors took offence and banned him from dancing as a man.

Guardian, 17 April 1998

In the meantime women will probably continue to accept as women all those who wish to be regarded as female, including AIS males and surgically altered males and XXY androgynes and single-X individuals. A good-hearted woman is not supposed to mind that her sex is the catch-all for all cases of gender ambiguity, but her tolerance of spurious femaleness, her consent to treat it as if it is the same as her own gender identity weakens her claim to have a sex of her own and tacitly supports the Freudian stereotype of women as incomplete beings defined by their lack of a penis. Women's lack of choosiness about who may be called a woman strengthens the impression that women do not see their sex as quite real, and suggests that perhaps they too identify themselves as the not-male, the other, any other. Yet we know that women feel anxiety about being 'real' women. A woman who is faced with mastectomy may say that she feels that her womanhood is being removed, that she is being de-sexed.

Menopausal women sometimes complain that with the cessation of ovarian function their femaleness is being stripped from them. We are told that irresponsible women get pregnant solely to reinforce their gender identity. Gender reassignment is usually justified as a harmonization of self-image and gender image, as if such harmony was a human right. Born women are all too aware of a disharmony between who they are and what their gender role requires of them; some of them too will undergo surgery designed to bring them into line with the Teutonic round-breasted, short-nosed stereotype. Gender identification is never more than approximate. All women as they age are compelled to watch the feminine veils wearing through until only the bedrock of their femaleness is left. A thousand years from now the archaeologists who dig up their bones will know that they were women, and they will come to the same conclusion about the FTM transsexuals as well.

The transsexual is identified as such solely on his/her own script, which can be as learned as any sex-typed behaviour and as editorialized as autobiographies usually are. The lack of insight that MTF transsexuals usually show about the extent of their acceptance as females should be an indication that their behaviour is less rational than it seems. There is a witness to the transsexual's script, a witness who is never consulted. She is the person who built the transsexual's body of her own flesh and brought it up as her son or daughter, the transsexual's worst enemy, his/her mother. Whatever else it is gender reassignment is an exorcism of the mother. When a man decides to spend his life impersonating his mother (like Norman Bates in *Psycho*) it is as if he murders her and gets away with it, proving at a stroke that there was nothing to her. His intentions are no more honourable than any female impersonator's; his achievement is to gag all those who would call his bluff. When he forces his way into the few private spaces women may enjoy and shouts down their objections, and bombards the women who will not accept him with threats and hate mail, he does as rapists have always done.

manmade mothers

Until our own day the only way patriarchal authorities could control human reproduction was by owning and exchanging women much as they did other breeding animals. Even then they could not be sure that women had not deceived them and connived with their enemies. Male interference with conception and birth dates back at least as far as the seventeenth century, when the first male health practitioners invaded the private female realm of the birthplace. Long before he had developed anything useful in the way of instruments and techniques the man-midwife used calumny and cunning to drive out his female rivals. We know from historians that the immediate results for the health of infant and mother were seldom good and sometimes catastrophic. From the first the man-midwife saw the labouring woman as coming between him and his object, a new improved baby, that would be his product rather than hers. It was a couple of centuries before the mother could be tipped on her back with her feet in stirrups, and rendered completely passive by anaesthesia, which was seen by all as a great improvement on the old struggles on the birthing stool. Caesareans were practised since ancient times, when the mother always died. It was not until the late nineteenth century that obstetricians succeeded in extracting infants by Caesarean section without killing their mothers. The healthiest women who have ever lived on earth now have more Caesareans than any others, not simply because they are rich enough to pay for them, or because birth by Caesarean section is less likely to deliver a damaged child and a subsequent malpractice suit, but because patriarchal authority is relentlessly driven towards controlling the unpredictability of pregnancy and birth.

The first tenets of the gospel of manmade motherhood are, one, that female fertility must be managed and, two, that women themselves cannot be trusted to manage it. Doctors are needed to manage female fertility which becomes a medical problem. The initial treatment is pharmaceutical contraception. The acceptor of modern contraception becomes a manmade non-mother. When pharmaceutical contraception first became possible there was a good deal of embarrassment about allowing women not involved in stable heterosexual unions to use it; within months this squeamishness had evaporated. At the end of the millennium, it is the bounden duty of any woman with any prospect however remote of being involved in heterosexual activity either to allow a manmade device to be installed in her uterus or to take by mouth every day a steroid concoction about which she knows nothing, not even its correct name. An unusually stroppy woman might insist on using condoms; even then she has to have faith in the condom manufacturer as well as faith in the male participant in her sexual activity. Women who rely on the pharmaceutical industry to deliver usable methods of birth control would, if the law changed and the sale of such products was prohibited, find controlling their fertility impossible. Yet fertility was controlled before commercial products were available to control it. Human beings are not so unimaginative that they cannot think of ways to orgasm that do not involve the exposure of the cervix to sperm; what happened in the late twentieth century is that they gave up using them. Oral sex, from being a way to pleasure one's wife, became a service performed by women for men they might hardly know, by interns for presidents of the United States, for example.

Most manmade non-mothers choose sooner or later to become mothers, these days later rather than sooner. In Britain, births to women over forty increased from 6,872 in 1983 to 10,525 in 1993. According to Robert, Lord Winston, Professor of Fertility Studies at Hammersmith Hospital, 'By the age of forty-two at least 50 per cent of women are biologically sterile.' Unable to become a mother by her own efforts, the forty-plus-year-old can only be made a mother by the efforts of others who take control of her. In the event of male factor infertility the mother-makers may recommend artificial insemination by donor, in which case they choose the donor. Mostly their female patients do not know that they could collect a spoonful or two of sperm from a man known to them and impregnate themselves with a turkey baster. Women have little choice but to attend fertility clinics in deep humility, and accept whatever puzzlement and torture the mother-makers may inflict. To be sure there is counselling but the patient is too needy and ignorant to invent reasons why she should not put herself through the extended trauma of IVF treatment. Women seeking access to reproductive technology are quizzed, but the questions all relate to the baby they will probably not have, not to their preparedness for the grief and trauma of unsuccessful treatment, or the effect it might have on their relationship with their partner or their financial well-being.

The counsellors are all subscribers to the belief that a strong desire to have a baby accompanied by inability to have a baby is a disease in crucial need of treatment. The only treatment is recourse to reproductive technology. You could remove a desperate desire to have a baby by other means. Hypnosis would be the cheapest and perhaps the most effective way to relieve the suffering of the child-desiring infertile woman. If the infertile woman in question were seventy years old, there would be no question but that her desire for a child was inappropriate, and steps would be taken to suppress or obliterate her desire. If the child-desirer already had three or four children, she could expect to be talked out of her craving for another one, though it must be at least as genuine as the craving of the childless woman. If you consider that she already knows just what having a child is and does not need to prove her womanhood by exercising her fertility, you might conclude that another child for her is a better outcome than a child for someone who has no experience of motherhood. If the woman seeking help is a gifted mother who derives huge contentment from being with children and conveys that deep satisfaction to the small people in question, secondary infertility that would prevent her from achieving her desired family size could be a great loss to us all, happy children being something of a rarity nowadays.

Women seeking treatment for infertility are not granted that treatment on the strength of their fitness to perform the role of mother for the ensuing sixteen years or so. Evaluation of clients for IVF has always been arbitrary, impressionistic and inept. Indeed, there seems to be a competition between the fertility nabobs to choose the least promising subjects so that they can stun us all with their remarkable prowess in getting a perfect baby out of any old thing. In the beginning clinics imposed their own limits; women over thirty-nine went to the bottom of the waiting list; women over forty could have no more than three cycles of treatment, and so on. Even these self-denying ordinances are now in abeyance. In 1997 a sixty-year-old British grandmother, who smoked and suffered from emphysema, lied about her age, was accepted for fertility treatment and bore a son. The lie about her age would have been easily detected; a request to see a birth certificate would be a routine part of the assessment of a case as suitable for treatment – if anyone cared. The hard fact is that anyone can have infertility treatment who has or can get the money to pay for it. All of it, even Artificial Insemination by Donor Sperm, is expensive. The success rate quoted by US sperm banks for AIDS is about 19 per cent; it takes two shots a month for six to nine months for a pregnancy to result, and the cost will be between $50 and $100 a shot.

About a quarter of British national health authorities refuse to finance any fertility treatments whatsoever, because they do not buy the fertility establishment's account of involuntary infertility as an illness, or of IVF, which is mostly unsuccessful, as the treatment for that illness. Other health authorities will pay for IVF treatment but only for a limited number of cycles per woman. Most IVF treatment is paid for by women themselves. The runaway development of reproductive technology did not happen in response to needs articulated by women; it happened because scientists needed to know more about human conception, and they were driven to test what they found out by trying to replicate the process in the laboratory. When the first test-tube baby was born in 1978 Steptoe and Edwards did not know what they had done right; only three babies were produced by the method in the next three years. IVF procedures are still anything but reliable but they are being sold as a triumph of human ingenuity, and the beginning of a revolution in the production of new human beings. The manmade mother is already on earth; right now she is constructed out of living women but it is only a matter of time before somewhere in the world a human child is born of a pig or an incubator. To be born *inter faecem et urinam* may one day seem as bestial as eating live animals would seem to us today. To understand whether such changes will be in women's interest, we need to consider in whose interest the technology is now operating. Reproductive technology is accepted because it brings to some of the women who endure its procedures the supreme joy of the birth of a desperately wanted child, but is that actually why it exists?

Fertility treatment causes far more suffering than it does joy.

The first part of the treatment is the infertility work-up as both the would-be father and the would-be mother are evaluated, a process that can be long, embarrassing and stressful. In women infertility can result from failure to ovulate, tubal damage that prevents the ovum from reaching the uterus, or problems of the uterine environment. Failure to conceive can also be utterly inexplicable. The female acceptor of IVF will have her hormonal status assessed, and she will be tested for rubella immunity, HIV and hepatitis B antigens. Then she may undergo exploratory laparoscopy. Laparoscopy is an invasive procedure; the laparoscope must be inserted through an incision in the abdomen which is inflated and the patient inverted to give a clear view of the ovaries. If it is found that the ovaries do not function the would-be mother will need an egg from another woman; a woman with tubal damage may have her eggs harvested, fertilized in a petri dish and implanted in her uterus; a woman without a uterus will have to find another woman who is prepared to gestate an embryo for her. In order to impregnate a woman by the *in vitro* method it is necessary to cause her to superovulate, so that eggs can be harvested from her ovaries; this itself is a risky procedure which can result in multiple pregnancy. The harvesting of the eggs is an invasive procedure and the reimplantation of the embryo another. In order to produce ova for reimplanting in herself or in somebody else a woman must be injected with a sequence of drug cocktails to stimulate the ovary.

Ovarian hyperstimulation comprises a syndrome ranging from an increase in oestradiol and progesterone secretion in the absence of clinical symptoms, through varying degrees of ovarian enlargement and associated discomfort, with the most severe cases experiencing increases in blood viscosity, electrolyte imbalances and hypovolaemic shock. Excessive ovarian hyperstimulation can cause death.

One in five women will be discharged from treatment before oocyte recovery, for all kinds of reasons, including that ovulation took place outside office hours. When ovulation is occurring the eggs will be harvested by any one of a variety of methods including 'ultrasound guided percutaneous follicular puncture' or passing a needle through an ultrasonic transducer inserted through the vagina, or whatever. New methods are being devised and tried out on unsuspecting patients every month or so. All have so far involved discomfort described by clinicians as 'limited'. Unlimited discomfort would of course be indescribable. The literature of IVF gives more attention to 'quality control' than to patient perception.

In some fertility clinics a woman under thirty-five whose oocytes are being collected will be asked if she will make some of them available for other patients who produce no eggs of their own, and she may be offered her procedure for free as an inducement. If she accepts she may be given even higher doses of the hormones that stimulate ovulation and therefore run a greater risk of hyperstimulation. The director of a British clinic quoted in the *Guardian* in August 1997 explained his practice in chillingly pragmatic terms:

> We try hard to suit the dosage of drugs to the individual, yet for the sake of those receiving eggs, we want to get a good response. If a donor produces two or three eggs and a woman is paying £2–3,000 for the treatment, she is getting a less good deal than if she receives ten eggs.

The British Human Fertilization and Embryology Agency takes a dim view of such 'egg-sharing' and proposes to ban it. Current egg-sharing agreements require that a woman supplying eggs for another woman remain unknown to her. A woman who persuades a friend to donate oocytes will not get them herself. The genetic mother is not allowed to know which children carry her genes in case she should interfere with the gestational mother's control of the child. So is motherhood dismembered by the technology. A nominal £15 payment is all the HFEA will allow an egg donor, though it does accept that the donor can be paid 'expenses'. Payments of up to £10,000 as expenses are now under investigation. In Britain by 1998 there was such a shortage of human eggs that it had even been suggested that clinics should pay women to provide them. That such a suggestion could be made indicates how much public sensibilities about the traffic in human body parts have changed in the twenty years since the first IVF baby was born. As the sacredness of the body wanes and it is increasingly seen not as an unalterable part of the self but as raw material out of which a customized self can be manufactured, the idea of producing gametes for sale grows ever less repugnant. I suspect that even if fertility clinics offer significant sums for oocytes, women will not respond, not simply because being farmed for oocytes is painful and dangerous but because women do not regard their seminal material as light-heartedly as men do, and have no ambition to spread their genes through the ecosphere. It may in the long run be in women's interest to starve reproductive technology of its oocytes so that the exploitation of childless women grinds to a halt.

> When you give an egg, it's only the beginning of the story. If it implants successfully and a baby is born, you know out there is a living, breathing child . . . All sorts of people talk about their right to have a child, like single people, and old people. This may be so, but not with my egg.
>
> Mara Lane, egg donor

At 1998 prices IVF costs £2,500 per cycle; the odds of a pregnancy increase with each cycle to about evens at the fifth cycle. Nothing is more difficult than calculating the probability that IVF treatment will result in a live birth. The pregnancy rate per transfer is still rather less than 20 per cent and stubbornly refuses to improve; a study in *The Lancet* in November 1996 of 37,000 cycles of IVF carried out between 1991 and 1994 revealed that women of twenty-five to thirty stood a 16 per cent chance of becoming pregnant from each cycle, while a woman of forty had no better than a 7 per cent chance. As we have seen, about 20 per cent of patients will have already dropped out before oocyte collection, and only two-thirds or so of the 20 per cent who are found to be pregnant will go on to give birth. More than half of all IVF births are by Caesarean section. The risk of miscarriage, ectopic pregnancy, breech presentation, multiple birth and stillbirth are all much higher in IVF cases. Peri-natal mortality is twice to four times as common in IVF infants, pre-term delivery three times as common and low birth weight five times as common. It should be clear from these figures that IVF is not in any sense a substitute for natural pregnancy and birth, and that IVF patients are relatively unlikely to achieve the much desired outcome of the natural birth of a healthy baby. Some of the risk factors are associated with the procedures and some with the patients, in particular their age. Acceptors over forty have a 50 per cent chance of miscarriage. All adverse outcomes are more common in older acceptors.

The IVF baby has been studied with great care but the IVF mother and non-mother have not been studied at all. Nobody has asked whether IVF treatment is good for women. The reproductive wizards want us all to believe that infertility is practically unbearable but they do not want us to ask what becomes of the infertile woman who puts herself through repeated ordeals in a desperate quest for a pregnancy only to suffer a miscarriage. Is she better or worse off than she was before treatment? She or her local health authority is certain to be much poorer. Although the HFEA is funded out of the huge amounts paid by women for IVF treatment it concerns itself not a whit about their fate. Treatment cycles are usually about three months apart; after months of upheaval to daily life and high levels of pain and stress the relationship of a couple is often severely distorted, which is not an optimum time for even an uneventful pregnancy to begin. As usually no pregnancy does begin, we must wonder how infertile couples manage to repair the damage. No-one is interested in measuring the quantum of misery among IVF acceptors who remain childless, but nobody cares about the new IVF parents either. Despite the sentimental rhetoric of the male fertility magnates whose only expressed desire is to make women happy, the women who undergo hormonal stimulation, egg harvest and reimplantation seem to matter very little more than any other laboratory animals. When fertility treatments consisted of little more than artificial insemination in the case of male factor infertility, the doctor quite often popped out of the room and produced a sample of his own fresh sperm. The chief donors to sperm banks were medical students. Some male fertility experts call the babies that result from IVF treatment 'their' babies and boast that they have made thousands of women pregnant (with other men's sperm, understood). Professor Ian Craft and Lord Winston both display hundreds of photographs of their IVF successes on the walls of their consulting-rooms.

Developments in reproductive technology have followed each other so fast that there has been no time for the ethical conundrums posed by the several stages to be addressed. In Britain the first attempt to regulate the creation and destruction of human life in the laboratory was the Human Fertilization and Embryology Act of 1990, which placed no limit on the number of embryos that might be created in the course of any single fertility work-up and allowed for frozen storage of embryos not used at the time, but only for five years. In the United States, Canada, the Netherlands and Belgium no such limit had been imposed. In Germany the storage of frozen embryos was banned. In Western Australia embryos may be stored for three years only. The British law was subsequently amended; embryos could be stored for ten years with further extensions at the request of both parents until the mother reached the age of fifty-five. By 1996, according to Ruth Deech, chairwoman of the HFEA, about 300,000 embryos had been created since storage began in the late 1980s. Only a minute percentage of this huge figure had gone on to become live babies and only about 9,000 were suspended in frozen nitrogen. If IVF begins human lives only arbitrarily to end the huge majority of them in the quest for a single successful outcome it is in essence an unethical procedure.

As reproductive technology pursues its headlong career, the mother dwindles from being essential to the survival of her child to becoming an obstacle to efficient quality control, best out of the way. As she has no indispensable function she might as well be totally inert. In the United States a woman who has been brain-dead for two months has been successfully delivered. In Rome in 1995 Pasquale Bilotta announced the birth of a child to a woman two years dead. In Britain when pregnant Karen Battenbough suffered devastating brain-damage in a car crash she was placed on life-support until her daughter could be safely delivered by Caesarean section. Nineteen months later Karen died of kidney failure and pneumonia, never knowing that she was a mother. When her child was laid on her breast she did not react, which makes her much easier to manage than the mother who has her own ideas about whether she wants a Caesarean or not, and when she wants the cord cut and whether she wants to breast-feed or feed on demand. In the 1950s the pressure to get all birthing women into hospitals sprang directly from fear and distrust of the mother, symbolized by demands that she wear a mask when in proximity to her child, and that she wash her breast before and after giving suck and that the child was only to be left to her tender mercies for twenty minutes before being removed to the nursery. The survival rate for the babies was the same as it had been with home births; the important aspect of the hospital confinement was that it got mothers into line and under control, their pubes shaved and their bowels washed out and their waters manually broken. Then it was that episiotomy came to be routinely practised and the number of Caesarean sections inexorably to rise. The message was and still is, despite years of feminist agitation for the rights of mothers, that actual women are no good at mothering and can't get to first base without massive intervention.

The way to sell off a public service is to run it down so drastically that its users come to despise it, and then to fragment it. Motherhood, after being deprived of all privilege and prestige, was further dilapidated by ostracism and neglect. The relentless advance of reproductive technology has now split motherhood into three compartments, genetic motherhood, gestational motherhood and parental motherhood. The genetic mother supplies the egg that is fertilized. The gestational mother is the owner-manager of the womb in which the embryo implants and grows. The parental mother is the person who raises and feeds the child. The law when asked to distinguish between the rights of these three kinds of mothers has succeeded only in pitting them against each other. Nobody really knows whether a genetic mother has more entitlement to claim a child than the woman who grew and nourished it in her womb or the woman who rears and nourishes it outside the womb; when motherhoods collide, the patriarchal reproductive establishment is easily persuaded to consider doing without them altogether. Every time an elderly woman or child abuser is given fertility treatment, every time an irresponsible woman deliberately incurs a multiple pregnancy as a way of making herself rich and famous, women's grip on motherhood is loosened a little more. Already the genetic mother's children may be unknown to her; the gestational mother could be superseded by an electronically controlled and monitored 'ideal' gestational environment; the parental mother can now be male or female. Shulamith Firestone looked forward to a time when women would not be defined as wombed creatures, when gestation would be an out-of-body experience and pregnancy a thing of the past. Only then she thought would women be truly free. I think it rather more likely that, if women should be found to be unnecessary for the continuation of the species, they would cease to exist at all. In Rome in 1992–3 a black woman married to a white man underwent IVF in order to bear a white child with none of her own genes so that it would not suffer racial discrimination. In Asia huge numbers of foetuses are aborted simply because they are female. If women come to believe that technology will deliver better children than they can, they may breed themselves out of existence so that no-one need suffer sexual discrimination. If state-of-the-art gestation cabinets could manufacture children and virtual female fetishes could furnish sexual services, men would not regret the passing of real, smelly, bloody, noisy, hairy women.

abortion

Feminism is supposed to be pro-abortion. There are some who fancy that feminists used to march shouting, 'What do we want? Abortion! When do we want it? We want it now!' Those same people think that for once marching and shouting were effective. Reluctant authorities gave in to the women's screaming and allowed a tide of foeticide to sweep the world. This is not what happened. In the United States the crucial factor was a decision in the Supreme Court in the case of 'Roe' vs Wade, which upheld the principle that, as the law had no part to play in what passed between a woman and her doctor, intervention by the state to prevent an abortion was a breach of the patient's privacy. 'Jane Roe' or Norma McCorvey, a sometime carnival barker and druggie who was pregnant for the third time, was the stooge selected by a young Texas lawyer called Sarah Weddington; the decision was written by Harry Blackmun, a Nixon appointee to the Supreme Court. McCorvey has subsequently been born again and now repudiates her part in the decision that 'legalized' abortion in the US. The decision in 'Roe' vs Wade did nothing to confront let alone resolve the deep moral conflicts surrounding the issue of abortion. Subsequent decisions, such as the outlawing of the use of federal funds to finance abortion and withholding by the US Senate of payments of more than a billion dollars' worth of overdue UN dues on the grounds that UNFPA finances abortion, reveal that the issue is far from settled. It would take no more than concerted action on the part of people other than the mother who might have an interest in a particular foetus to establish that pregnancy is unlike other patient–doctor relations in that there are two more interested individuals involved, the father-to-be and the child-to-be. Every time a foetus is recognized as a party to other litigation, the safety of the decision in the case of 'Roe' vs Wade is called in question.

The real powers in the case were the masculine medical establishment and the masculine judiciary. The law regarding abortion was being massively broken; there were fortunes to be made in pregnancy termination at a time when advances in the technology were making a risky procedure foolproof. In the US before legalization, abortion clinics were run by organized crime which raked money off the top in rentals cum protection; organized crime did not give up the lucrative abortion business just because it became legal but retained its property and a good deal of its control. Many clinics were obliged to keep up a rapid rate of patient turnaround with a required number of procedures per operator per hour, so that often cervical blocks were not given time to work. What is worse, some of the women who were scheduled for abortion and paid for abortion were not even pregnant. As attacks on abortionists and their clients become more common, the role of organized crime in protecting the abortion industry will become more significant; the prices of the procedures will rise and women will shoulder the increased cost. What women 'won' was the 'right' to undergo invasive procedures in order to terminate unwanted pregnancies, unwanted not just by them but by their parents, their sexual partners, the governments who would not support mothers, the employers who would not employ mothers, the landlords who would not accept tenants with children, the schools that would not accept students with children. Historically the only thing pro-abortion agitation achieved was to make an illiberal establishment look far more feminist than it was.

The abortionists who went to prison in the run-up to legalization for 'helping girls in trouble' were all male. All saw themselves as champions of women and defenders of women's rights. They were repaid with the love and loyalty of women, who were grateful for the right to expiate their sexual activity in pain and grief. The goal was 'every child a wanted child'; it should also have been 'every abortion a wanted abortion', but the two sides of the phony debate were never to meet. Any feminist who saw abortion as an assault on women and agitated for a concomitant right to bear children without being condemned to poverty, misery and failure was suspected of being a crypto-right-to-lifer. In 1997 Cardinal Winning took the first step in the direction of providing a genuine alternative to abortion by offering support in the form of an unspecified lump sum of money to women who would otherwise have an abortion because they could not afford to have a baby. The outcry was immediate; the money was called a bribe that would lure women away from what was best for them, i.e. childlessness. Nevertheless donations poured in to Cardinal Winning's fund until at the time of writing £180,000 had been donated, half of which had been paid out. Two hundred women had applied for assistance, fifty of whom had borne children, with fifty more on the way. Cardinal Winning no doubt hopes that government will take over his responsibility and offer support to every child conceived. Feminists should share his hope but the media have locked feminists into a position which they define as 'pro-abortion'. Feminism is pro-woman rather than pro-abortion; we have always argued for freedom of reproductive choice. A choice is only possible if there are genuine alternatives.

As the demographic crisis worsens, and the highly developed countries one by one come to regard their collapsing birth-rates with dismay, we may expect access to abortion to be limited.

Go carefully angels, I miss you. The others are lovely. You would have been lovely too.

Pamela Pickton
Letter to two babies who never were

The German Bundestag passed a federal abortion law in 1995 requiring that all candidates for abortion 'receive counselling', i.e. face interrogation, and secure a certificate before an abortion is allowed; 264 of the 1,685 centres that provide the counselling and issue the certificates are run by Catholic charities. A law passed in August 1996 in Catholic Bavaria demands that women identify a reason for the termination during counselling and forbids practitioners to earn more than 25 per cent of their income from abortion. In Britain the anti-abortion lobby in the House of Commons brings private members' bills year after year, apparently unaware that the medical establishment has no intention of allowing any curb on its right to dispose of blastocysts, foetuses and embryos as, when and how it sees fit. Feminists react to each successive attack on the availability of abortion with grave concern and an investment of scarce resources, fighting a battle on behalf of the richest and most powerful organizations in the world. The pharmaceutical multi-nationals will not allow any wholesale revision of abortion rights, in case the mode of operation of their so-called contraceptives should be called in question.

Though women still do not have access to abortion technology as of right, though even the morning-after pill can only be obtained by a woman after recourse to the medical establishment, though governments still keep tabs on abortion statistics and still license beds, and thereby exercise a *de facto* control on numbers, though organized crime still gets a rake-off from some American abortion clinics, the anti-abortion lobby is still

Western feminists have scored an own goal in lobbying for abortion rights rather than for ongoing research for new, safer and cheap contraceptive methods and securing access and availability of contraceptive services, including emergency contraception.

Letter to the *Lancet*, August 1996

on the offensive. In the British elections of 1997, the 'pro-Life' alliance hoped to field fifty candidates, thus qualifying as a political party and for a party political broadcast in which to alert the unconscious public to the horrors of pregnancy termination, but they were fighting a rearguard action. A poll conducted by the *Mail on Sunday* found that, even after a series of pregnancy-related scandals, 81 per cent of people still thought that a woman had the right to choose whether or not to continue a pregnancy. In the House of Commons the proportion was much lower; only 298 MPs supported a woman's right to choose as against 254 opposing. Another poll carried out by MORI on behalf of the British Birth Control Trust and the British Pregnancy Advisory Service showed that abortion was no longer a minority issue; 45 per cent of the sample knew close friends or members of the family who had had abortions, whereas in a similar poll in 1980, only 27 per cent had such knowledge of the actual situation. The people polled were asked if they thought that abortion should be available for 'all who wanted it' and 64 per cent answered in the affirmative; of the 11 per cent of the people polled who were Catholics, half agreed with what thirty years ago would have been considered an extreme position. As more and more people have personal knowledge of how and when abortion is the only solution they realize that the only feasible principle is 'the woman's right to choose'. These same people showed the beginnings of a retreat from the notion of eugenic abortion in cases where mental or physical handicap was suspected, which was supported by 84 per cent of people in 1980 and by only 66 per cent in 1997. In the contest between the doctor's right to choose versus the woman's right to choose whether to deliver a handicapped baby, the woman appears to be gaining ground.

There can be no gainsaying that women cannot manage their own lives if access to abortion is to be denied, but the need for abortion is itself the consequence of oppression. The whole woman of reproductive age produces an ovum a month, representing a single shot at a pregnancy every twenty-eight days. A man is constantly engaged in spermatogenesis, every hour of every day and night, and can release 400 million sperm at every ejaculation. A woman who maximized her reproductive potential could, if all her pregnancies proceeded to term, produce no more than thirty children. A (young) man who had intercourse as often as possible with a different fertile woman each time could sire three or four children a day. A man whose sperm was donated as often as he could manage to a sperm bank could be the genetic father of literally thousands of children. It can hardly be rational for a woman who does not desire pregnancy to expose her cervix to hyperfertile seminal fluid when what she is seeking is not pregnancy but sexual pleasure. A woman's pleasure is not dependent upon the presence of a penis in the vagina; neither is a man's. We must ask therefore why intromission is still, perhaps more than ever, described as normal or full intercourse. We have accepted that lesbians and gays who choose not to pleasure each other in this way have natural and normal relations. Only heterosexuals are required to perform sex in an orthodox fashion, as if they were imitating the founding fathers and seeking to people the earth, when that is the last thing on their minds. The explanation seems to lie in the symbolic nature of intercourse as an act of domination.

Half of all pregnancies in Britain are unplanned.
One in five will end in termination.

Statement issued by an alliance of FPA, BCT, Brook
Advisory Centres and the Health Education Authority, 1998

If we accept every instance of abortion as the outcome of unwanted and easily avoided pregnancy, we have to ask ourselves how it is that women are still exposing themselves to this risk. A woman who is unable to protect her cervix from exposure to male hyperfertility, who cannot suggest another way of making love or ask for a condom to be used, is certainly not calling the shots. The man is most likely to have initiated the episode of intercourse, to have chosen the place and the time; the woman is probably still dancing backwards. Because he ejaculates when and where he ejaculates, she conceives against her will. If the child is unwanted, whether by her or her partner or her parents, it will be her duty to undergo an invasive procedure and an emotional trauma and so sort the situation out. The crowning insult is that this ordeal is represented to her as some kind of a privilege. Her sad and onerous duty is garbed in the rhetoric of a civil right.

Where other people decide that a woman's baby should not be born she will be pressured to carry out her duty to herself, to the foetus, to other people, to the health establishment, to the state by undergoing abortion. Her autonomy is the least important consideration. In both cases she is confronted with other people who know better than she what she ought to do. She will be required to undergo investigations of her pregnancy for which there is no treatment but termination, whether she would countenance a termination or not. If she undergoes the tests, say for Down's Syndrome, and refuses the termination she will be asked why she had the test in the first place. And she will probably be talked into the termination. Her agony of mind is increased by the regular publication of results of research to establish whether and when human foetuses become aware, feel pain, can learn. In March 1998 we learnt that foetuses are alert and can learn at twenty weeks gestation, before the formation of a cerebral cortex. The evidence was unconvincing, in that reaction was being construed as consciousness, but it had the desired effect, which was to worry women. Feminists have argued that delaying abortion is immoral, but all measures to put in place speedy and non-traumatic abortion procedures, which would be embryologically identical with what passes for contraception, have been blocked by the same authorities who regularly produce evidence about the developing sensibilities of the foetus.

> I don't suppose Jack ever gave a thought
> To such ideas. Men are so wasteful,
> Careless of their seed. I often guess
> What lives those might have had
> Given some luck.
>
> The colours of their eyes . . .
>
> Jean Earle, 'Menopause'

No woman who approaches the medical establishment for access to abortion technology will be encouraged to think of herself as claiming a right. A right would be available to her on demand. If she is seeking abortion on the National Health Service she is likely to find that it is not enough that she has decided that it would be wrong for her to continue with the pregnancy; she has to convince other people who have no interest in the outcome or responsibility for it, that she has made the right decision. In January 1997 a study undertaken for the British Abortion Law Reform Association found that among 108 health authorities in England and Wales, some funded virtually all abortions and others as few as 40 per cent. Women who were deemed able to pay were steered towards the private sector by their GPs or openly denied free treatment.

A woman who is granted an abortion does not get to choose between abortions. Abortion, like HRT and the pill, is presented to her as a single entity, when as with HRT and the pill there is a bewildering array of options. Abortion can be surgical, part-surgical or entirely non-surgical. Non-surgical do-it-yourself abortion has been possible for twenty years or more but the health establishment rations and controls access to it. In the United States RU–486, the so-called 'morning-after' pill manufactured by the French firm Roussel–Uclaf, is unavailable. In Britain the 'morning-after pill' is usually a double dose of 'contraceptive' steroids and not usually made available until the client has endured a sermon on reliable contraception. One of the best-kept secrets in gynaecology is the use of methotrexate and other cytotoxics for non-surgical abortion. In the United States surgical abortion is usually a ten-minute procedure, vacuum aspiration with local anaesthetic; in Canada, a cumbersome two-stage procedure, involving the insertion of a laminaria tent and dilatation and curettage (D and C) under general anaesthetic twenty-four hours later, is preferred; in Russia, which has the highest abortion rate in the world, no anaesthesia is used; in Britain vacuum aspiration under general anaesthetic is usual. Recently the use of better pregnancy testing and smaller cannulas has made possible the surgical removal of the fertilized ovum as early as eight to ten days after conception, when it is no bigger than a pinhead, at much the same point that it would be shed by the woman using the 'contraceptive' pill or an intra-uterine device. Whether women will have access to the procedure will depend on whether clinics tool up for it. At the time of writing only about twenty of the clinics affiliated to Planned Parenthood are using the method and only in the United States.

To be pregnant against your will is to see your life swerve out of control. The urgent task is to stop it crashing altogether. If a woman is to be an adult, she cannot also be a person whose life decisions will be made by other people. To become a mother without wanting to is to live like a slave or a domestic animal. Like any other adult, a woman would wish to be infertile and fertile when appropriate: she is led to believe that contraception is her duty and that the available techniques are easy to use and completely effective. If she were totally in control of the manner in which she is sexually active, she might insist that her male partner control his excessive fertility rather than delegating to her the responsibility for inhibiting his power to fecundate. Though vasectomy is available, it is culturally invisible. Men don't get pregnant, therefore men don't bother about contraception. Men do get sexually transmitted diseases so they do use condoms, sometimes, but nowhere near as often as they should.

> There seem to be two images of women who have an abortion; cold-hearted bitches who have the operation as easily as having a tooth out, regarding it as just another form of contraception, or victims racked by depression, guilt and regret. The truth lies somewhere in between. It's not an easy decision to make. It's somewhat more complex than having a tooth out. Yet you do get over it.
>
> Anne Marie, *Girl Frenzy* No 6

These days contraception is abortion, because the third-generation pills cannot be shown to prevent sperm fertilizing an ovum. A lobby exists to push for the prescription of 'contraceptive' steroids to young women under the age of fourteen, who should not in any case be having unprotected sex. In 1996 a National Opinion Poll commissioned by Schering Healthcare showed that the proportion of women who don't use the pill because of side-effects has risen from one in four to one in three. Schering wisely did not ask whether women would reject contraceptives if they thought they were abortifacients. No-one feels so strongly against abortion at any stage that they picket the factories where birth control pills are produced. IUDs are clearly abortifacient but the case made against them is not brought under the Trades Descriptions Act but on the same old ground of side-effects; so successful have these actions been that women who want an intra-uterine 'contraceptive' device must sign a twenty-page indemnity form. The latest device to become the subject of litigation is the Copper 7 or Graviguard, launched by G. D. Searle in 1972 as a safer alternative to orally ingested steroids. For ten years a hundred British women have been seeking compensation and damages from the manufacturers, a subsidiary of the giant conglomerate Monsanto; £750,000 has been spent preparing their case which has now been dropped by the Legal Aid Board. Ten of the women are still trying to pursue the action. Hundreds of women in Australia, New Zealand and Canada await the outcome of an Australian case; in the US Searle has faced twenty-five court trials, of which it has won nineteen and lost five. Others have been settled out of court. Intra-uterine devices, medicated or not, work by creating inflammation of the uterus, often accompanied by infection; women who accepted them as contraceptive devices were actually being equipped with a DIY abortionist's tool. The outcome was frequent occult abortion, heavy bleeding and pelvic inflammatory disease, with the accompanying elevated risk of ectopic pregnancy.

All this suffering, all this mess, is the direct consequence of the insistence upon the accessibility of the cervix to the ejaculating penis. Whether you feel that the creation and wastage of so many embryos is an important issue or not, you must see that the cynical deception of millions of women by selling abortifacients as if they were contraceptives is incompatible with the respect due to women as human beings. You must also see that expecting women to be grateful for the opportunity to have inserted into their bodies instruments for sucking and scraping out the products of avoidable conception shows them as much contempt. Fake contraceptive technology manipulates women in ways that we are coming to condemn when they are practised on members of other species. What women don't know does hurt them. If we ask ourselves whether we would have any hope of imposing upon men the duty to protect women's fertility and their health, and avoid the abortions that occur in their uncounted millions every day, we will see in a blinding light how unfree women are. Women from the youngest to the oldest are aware that to impose conditions on intimacy would be to be accorded even less of it than they get already. The woman who refuses to enter the gynaecological abattoir, which extends into every bathroom in the country, must be prepared to do without male approval and attention. We know that condom use among heterosexuals is a fraction of what it should be if women's health and fertility are to be safeguarded, but women are afraid to insist in case they should speed men even faster on their flight from true companionship and intimacy into the realms of virtual sex.

mutilation

The word 'mutilation' suggests savage initiation customs surviving in darkest Africa, as in January 1997 when the women's secret Bondo society entered the Grafton camp for displaced persons in the eastern suburbs of Freetown, Sierra Leone, and removed the clitorises from 600 women, without anaesthetic or antiseptics. About a hundred girls aged between eight and fifteen were reported to have suffered severe complications. The American Academy of Pediatrics recommends that clitorises of more than three-eighths of an inch in length should be removed from baby girls before they are fifteen months old. Five such procedures are performed every day in the United States; such 'reconstructive surgery' is not included in world statistics which estimate that 120 million women alive today have suffered genital mutilation. Female genital mutilation (FGM) has been condemned as a violation of human rights by the International Conference on Population and Development, the Fourth World Conference on Women in Beijing, the World Health Organisation, UNICEF, and the United Nations Family Planning Authority. Male genital mutilation is seldom condemned. Men mutilate the genitals of other men; usually women mutilate the genitals of other women, except where the procedure is carried out by a male professional. In England a doctor will be struck off the medical register if it is found that he has carried out a female circumcision of any kind. He will not be struck off for splitting a penis down the middle so that its owner can insert rings in it fore and aft for the gratification of himself and partners. He will not be struck off but rather encouraged to 'tidy up' the ambiguous genitalia of intersexual newborns, usually by removing the inadequate penis and creating an opening that will pass for a vagina, so that the child becomes a girl, regardless of actual chromosomal make-up. And he may massively mutilate both men and women seeking gender reassignment. But he may not carry out any form of female circumcision at the request of a patient or her parents.

A surgeon is allowed to whittle away female genitalia if the operation is understood to be cosmetic. A thirty-nine-year-old woman wrote to the doctor at *Woman* magazine: 'My problem is my vagina – the inner lips stick out a bit. My mother says it's normal and my doctor says the same, but I keep worrying about what it looks like. Is there an operation I can have?' The *Woman* doctor reassured her, and added: 'There is a simple gynaecological operation to trim the inner labia so that they don't protrude. But you may have trouble having this done on the NHS and will probably have to seek private treatment. It's usually carried out under local anaesthetic and costs £200–£300.'

Human beings have always modified the external appearance of their bodies in one way or another; one man's beautification is another man's mutilation. Looked at in its full context the criminalization of FGM can be seen to be what African nationalists since Jomo Kenyatta have been calling it, an attack on cultural identity. Any suggestion that male genital mutilation should be outlawed would be understood to be a frontal attack on the cultural identity of Jews and Muslims. Notwithstanding, the opinion that male circumcision might be bad for babies, bad for sex and bad for men is steadily gaining ground. In Denmark only 2 per cent of non-Jewish and non-Muslim men are circumcised on strictly medical grounds; in Britain the proportion rises to between 6 per cent and 7 per cent, but in the US between 60 per cent and 70 per cent of male babies will have their foreskins surgically removed. No UN agency has uttered a protocol condemning the widespread practice of male genital mutilation, which will not be challenged until doctors start to be sued in large numbers by men they mutilated as infants. Silence on the question of male circumcision is evidence of the political power both of the communities where a circumcised penis is considered an essential identifying mark and of the practitioners who continue to do it for no good reason. Silence about male mutilation in our own countries combines nicely with noisiness on female mutilation in other countries to reinforce our notions of cultural superiority.

To be sure there are influential feminists who are fighting to eliminate FGM in their own countries and their struggle must be supported but not to the point of refusing to consider the different priorities and cultural norms by which other women live. When I explained to Sudanese women that western women sometimes have their breasts cut and trimmed, they were every bit as mystified and horrified as we are by Pharaonic circumcision and infibulation. Stephanie Welsh, who won a Pulitzer Prize in 1996 for her photographs of the ceremonies surrounding female circumcision in rural Kenya, described it as 'a wonderful ritual that unifies the tribe. It's very beautiful – except for the circumcision itself.' Welsh's prize-winning photostory traces the lead-up to the climactic ritual: first the girl's mother builds the house where she will live as a woman; then the girl has her head shaved; circumcised women from surrounding villages gather to paint her with red ochre and assure her that she will have no pain; then they hold her down and stifle her cries as her own mother cuts her with a razor and plasters goat fat on the wound.

Male genital mutilation is considered trivial; female genital mutilation is considered devastating even if it involves nothing more than nicking the prepuce of the clitoris to provoke ritual bleeding. FGM takes so many forms that it is doubtful whether it represents a single phenomenon with a single cultural significance. The WHO recognizes degrees of severity of mutilation, one, in which the hood of the clitoris and surrounding tissue are removed, two, in which the clitoris and the labia minora are removed and three, infibulation, widespread in Somalia, Northern Sudan and Djibouti, in which the clitoris and labia minora are removed and raw surfaces created on the labia majora so that they can be stitched together to form a seal over the urethra and most of the introitus of the vagina. The accepted view of what these practices mean can be summed up as follows:

> Beliefs and practices regarding Female Genital Mutilation seem to show a desire to control women's sexual experience and reinforce established gender roles. They support a priority of male over female sexual satisfaction (often at reproductive risk to women) and give evidence of profound ambivalence among men regarding the sexual needs and concerns of women.

This is indeed a curious explanation of something that women do to women, because it suggests that they are simply carrying out the desires of men, desires which in these cultures men would never have discussed with them. In Ethiopia circumcision is common but not universal among both Christian and Muslim women; when I asked Ethiopian men whether they preferred sex with circumcised or uncircumcised women they appeared not to know. They could not say for certain whether the women in their own families were circumcised or not. Circumcised women in Sudan told me that it was 'no problem for the sex' but 'a big problem with the childbirth'. They thought they might not have it done for their daughters, because it was going out of fashion, but when their mothers became agitated and said that their granddaughters would be considered ugly and unmarriageable, they said maybe they would do it anyway. These Sudanese women were very sensual and up front about their erotic interests; it is impossible to think of them as having no notion of their own sexual pleasure. Certainly in many of these cultures tightness in the vagina is prized by both men and women; the susceptibility of African women to HIV and AIDS is greatly increased by the almost universal use of astringent herbs to tighten the vagina. Penetration of a tight dry vagina causes pain but pain can become indistinguishable from pleasure in a state of high sexual arousal.

There is also a pronounced cosmetic element in the way women talk of their own circumcision. Many women who are circumcised or infibulated also remove absolutely all their body hair; the depilated, infibulated genitalia become virtually invisible – as they were in all western painting and sculpture until very recently. Certainly FGM represents a significant health risk but it must also be a procedure with considerable cultural value because it has survived fifty years of criminalization and concerted propaganda campaigns. The fact that it is both painful and dangerous adds to its undeniable function as ordeal in the rite of passage from child to woman. As UN workers in Eastern Uganda found, women would not abandon female circumcision until some similarly significant procedure could take its place.

Though I was among the feminists at Mexico City in 1985 who first raised the problem of FGM in an international forum, I am loath now to pronounce upon its significance as a cultural phenomenon given the occult attachment to self-mutilation that can be discerned in our own culture. This can perhaps be explained as partly an angered response to being defined as our bodies. The woman who cuts her body asserts undeniably and emphatically that there is a self that has power over that body. Time and again we are told by young women who cut themselves that they find release in watching their own blood flow. Claire Keighley-Bray told *Bliss* magazine, 'It sounds weird, but cutting myself made me feel better. There's a sense of relief and I felt so numb – drawing blood proved I was alive.' For more than two years she cut herself, as often as four times a week. Self-harming of this kind is not a cry for help nor is it clamouring for attention, because it is secret. It is a genuine attack by the self upon the body, by which mental anguish is swapped for bodily pain. Self-harming is older than Christendom, embedded in contrition, penance and expiation and rotten with guilt.

When Erica published her own girl zine in 1995–6 she called it *Scars and Bruises*; her readers understood both her rage and why she took it out on herself:

> The sorrys, the supposed warmth.
> None of it means anything. And
> I'm still afraid of losing you even
> Though I'm not sure I want you
> anymore because this hurts like
> fuck, it hurts too much.
> So I'll come back and I won't say
> shit because I can release my pain.
> I can release my pain. I can release
> my pain another way.
> And I'm hurting myself and I'm
> laughing and my body is yours.

It will be objected that Erica is a quintessential victim, perpetuating the self-defeating and anti-feminist genre of the abandoned woman's lament, but she is also an artist of no mean order. Her tiny photocopied zine, price 50p, is built up of layer upon layer of cries, type-written, torn up, photographed, enlarged, rewritten, reduced, relettered, until it takes on the endlessly proliferating shape of women's futile obsessing about events that they did not choose and cannot change.

> Sometimes when you can't feel anything, you'd rather feel pain than nothing.
>
> Lydia Lunch

Piercing is no less mysterious to a non-piercer than cutting, but the underlying dynamic is similar. In *fucktooth* 19 jen angel explained why she had piercings:

> Before I was pierced myself, I read a lot about men and women who pierced themselves as a way of reclaiming their body, of making their body their own. I always thought that sounded a little hokey. Then one day . . . I saw the picture of Genesis P'Orridge's wife's genital piercings. I thought it made her genitals look so beautiful, and I had never really thought of my own genitals being particularly beautiful. In fact, I never really liked them much. So my piercings have taken on that kind of meaning. I love the way they look, and in a way, it's my slap in the face to everyone who in any way made me feel ashamed about my body. I haven't felt that way in a long time, but I was a young girl once, and I know what it's like to think that not only my genitals, but my whole body, are gross (because it's not model perfect) and not to be talked about and just kind of ignored.

To hear jen angel tell it genital piercing is simply body adornment. Stripper Jane Shag Stamp explains her interest in piercing and tattooing as reminding her of her physicality and her body, forcing her to take time to let it heal, causing her to forget depression and concentrate on her physical pain.

> I get off on the initial pain, admit it. It's not often you really feel physically, such an acute and temporary (this being the key-word) pain . . . And I come home high and treat myself to taking it easy . . . Some folk seem to think by stripping I'm offering up my body to all these men, well I like to think tattooing/piercing helps me to feel like it is my own.

Perhaps we should be considering the possibility that FGM acts in a similar way to assert the individual woman's control over her genitals and to customize them to her specification, which may also be the hallmark of the group to which she wishes to signify her allegiance. If an Ohio punk has the right to have her genitalia operated on, why has not the Somali woman the same right? Infibulation and clitoridectomy could well be as gratifying to the Somali woman as jen angel's dangling hardware. Jen angel would be incensed if anyone assumed that she had had her pudenda encrusted with niobium or titanium in order to please a man. She insists, 'Do it for yourself, and no-one else.' We ought at least to entertain the notion that the African woman is having FGM done for herself and allow her the same access to professional assistance as jen angel can expect. Instead of prescribing improved operating techniques and antisepsis, westernized governments have criminalized FGM and driven it underground, so that the painfulness of the procedure and the attendant health hazards are much magnified. In our own culture girls too young to qualify for professional piercings have been known to do it themselves. I used to teach at a school where bad girls carved their own tattoos with steel pen-nibs and coloured them with school-issue ink.

Thirty years ago parents were not fighting with their sons and daughters over piercings and tattoos. No teeny-bopper heroine sported a stud through her tongue as Scary Spice does and sticks her tongue out ostentatiously to prove it. The tongue stud is supposed to have an erotic function in stimulating the underside of the penis during fellatio. What the Spice Girls' eight-year-old girl fans make of this is anybody's guess. Mothers know that their daughters' insistence on having a nose stud or a navel piercing or a bracelet of barbed wire tattooed around an arm is an act of hostility towards them. The child is asserting her right to alter irrevocably, even to damage and destroy, the body that her mother grew for her out of her own substance. The child thinks she is claiming her own body, exerting her autonomy; the mother sees it as mindless tribal behaviour, pretty much as the 'first' world sees FGM. The mother wants the tattoo parlours closed down, and piercing banned. The law capitulates only so far as to impose an age limit, thus presenting the mutilation even more effectively as a privilege, a goal to be fought for, a sign of adulthood, a rite of passage. Though we might suspect that the child who thinks she needs a nose-ring might be afraid that her face is a blank in need of illustration, that she becomes a piercer and tattooer because rings and tattoos make her visible to herself, we have got to see that this is no more than a continuation of the incessantly stimulated desire in the little girl to bedizen herself,

---

Makeover of thirteen-year-old:
New Look Make-up: Deep purple eyeshadow along top lashes, pink over eyelids, pink blusher and lipstick, brown eyebrow pencil.

Shout magazine, 13–26 March, 1998

---

to change her hair colour, to paint her face, and her nails. All these are ways of making herself visible. Or invisible, depending how she sees it.

Genital mutilation of western women is only rarely consciously and deliberately undergone for their own gratification; usually it is inflicted on them by medical practitioners. If it were true that episiotomy, Caesarean section and hysterectomy were never performed except when genuinely necessary, we would not expect to see such an enormous range of variation in the numbers of operations carried out in countries with much the same standards of living and health care. Though the women who underwent the procedures may well have thought that in having them they were doing the minimum necessary to safeguard their lives and health, no epidemiologist or analyst of health care costs would agree. The wombs of American women are not four times as unhealthy as those of Swedish women, but American women have four times as many hysterectomies.

Ob–gyn consultants, 85 per cent of whom are male, routinely mutilate women for no good reason, as when for example they perform episiotomies, which Sheila Kitzinger calls 'our western way of female genital mutilation'. Episiotomies are usually justified on the grounds cited by one Dr Wetherall (BM ChB Manchester 1978) in a letter to the editor of the *Independent Magazine* in 1991: 'Episiotomy is performed during childbirth to prevent the baby's head splitting the birth canal in an uncontrolled manner, with the risk of damage to the mother's anal sphincter and of subsequent incontinence.' Wetherall appears to believe that women's vaginas have such a dreadful tendency to split from stem to stern while doing the job they were designed for that they have to be surgically opened in advance to avoid a very nasty mess. In fact ano-vaginal tears are very rare, while episiotomy is common practice. Virtually none of the cut women was likely to experience a third- or fourth-degree tear involving bladder or anus.

Dr Wetherall was understandably vague about when the cut is made, 'during childbirth' is all he says. He must have been aware of the famous skirmish in 1981 between the adherents of the scissors school and the old gentlemen of the scalpel persuasion. According to the grand master of the scalpel school, Charles Flood, scissors, which merely 'gnawed' at the perineum when it was already stretched paper thin and all the tearing in the vagina proper had already happened, were worse than useless. He believed in a good deep cut early in second-stage labour, *before* the child's head began to put pressure on the perineum, followed by a generous number of tight sutures. In an article in *World Medicine* called 'The Real Reason for Episiotomy', he maintained that the true purpose of the cut was to ensure restoration of muscle tone. How these august personages measured pelvic muscle tone is best left to the imagination, for imagination was all they had to go on. Their hypothesis does not survive even the most cursory consideration of the anatomy involved.

For 'improved pelvic muscle tone' read 'tight vagina' and Flood's argument begins to make a kind of sense. The consideration is important, especially in the United States, where a relaxed vagina after childbirth could lead to a malpractice suit. If the real purpose of episiotomy is as Flood suggests it really does not matter whether it is done before or after delivery: several women who have written to me complaining of doctors who talked of 'tidying them up down below' were convinced that they had come through labour intact. One woman who wrote of the medic who talked of making her 'nice and tight for her husband' was in fact unmarried.

The practice of episiotomy was introduced by the man-midwife, who sneered at those female midwives who regarded a successful delivery as one that left the woman intact. Obstetricians persuaded themselves that the area they sliced into, either medio-laterally or along the midline (for on an irrational procedure who can agree?), was insensitive, another notion which does not survive even an elementary understanding of the anatomy of the nervous system. As the men did not do the post-natal nursing, they did not care that the wounds swelled and the stitches hurt so that it was very difficult to make new mothers comfortable. It may be too much to expect that a senior surgical registrar concern himself with the quality of a new mother's life and her ability to delight in her baby, but

> Unlike most obstetricians who prefer to make an episiotomy for a variety of rationalizations, midwives take great pride in maintaining an intact perineum. This is the hallmark of a real midwife and is genuine proof of her patience and loving touch.
>
> John A. Walsh

he has a moral responsibility to make the best use of limited resources, including nurses' time. Even in America, where a cut in time earns money and avoids a malpractice suit because everything possible will be seen to have been done, the routine practice of episiotomy has been under review. J. M. Thorpe and W. A. Bowes summed up the case for and against in a review article, 'Episiotomy: can its routine use be defended?' published in the *American Journal of Obstetrics and Gynecology* in May 1989. A few years earlier P. Luekens, R. Lagasse, M. Dramaix and E. Wollast reported in the *British Medical Journal* in 'Episiotomy and third degree tears' that they found third-degree tears in 1.4 per cent of deliveries with episiotomy and 0.9 per cent without; when the other factors were equalized the authors had to come to the conclusion that episiotomy does not prevent trauma to the anal sphincter or rectum. The West Berkshire Perineal Management Trial, reported in the *BMJ* in 1987, came to the conclusion that episiotomy played no part in preventing post-partum urinary incontinence either. The suspicion that episiotomy is useless having become a certainty, researchers are now investigating whether serious tears are not *more* likely *after* episiotomy.

In England episiotomy support groups have been formed to help women whose doctors have been so callous as to tell them to drink a bottle of wine before having sex, so as to be less aware of the pain from episiotomy scars. One woman's husband was given an analgesic spray to 'numb the bottom half of [his]

In a two-hour performance, 'The Lips of Thomas', Abramovic ate a kilo of honey, drank a litre of red wine, cut a five-point star on her stomach with a razor blade, whipped herself for as long as she could, then lay naked slowly freezing on an ice cross until the audience removed her.

wife's body' so that their sexual relationship could resume. The figures are depressing: 15 per cent of women will suffer perineal pain for up to three years after giving birth. One unnecessary procedure leads to another:

Wendy Cox, a music teacher, suffered nearly a year of misery when an episiotomy carried out during the birth of her first child failed to heal properly, leaving her with scar tissue which made her unable to sit comfortably.

When she became pregnant for a second time, Cox was quite clear that she did not wish to go through the same thing again: 'I jumped at the chance of a Caesarean section.'

One way of avoiding mutilation by episiotomy is to have one's belly cut open instead. More and more healthy women who have prepared carefully for childbirth will be told that they have to undergo a Caesarean. More and more, despite all their pre-natal exercises, will have their babies lifted from them as they lie inert. Many of these women will have opted for active birth only to be convinced by their attendants that the baby is struggling, that they are incompetent after all. In Brazil 38 per cent of women giving birth in public hospitals are delivered by Caesarean section; in private clinics the proportion is 75 per cent. In Italy the rate of Caesarean delivery has more than doubled since 1980 and now stands at about a quarter of all births. In Britain in 1996 one in seven babies was delivered by Caesarean section; only twenty years ago the figure was one in twenty-eight. Childbirth has not got riskier in those twenty years. Caesareans are still about four times more dangerous than vaginal deliveries.

One in three female obstetricians would choose a Caesarean delivery for herself, even in a perfectly normal pregnancy.

Lancet, 1996

Alongside the rise and rise of the Caesarean section we have the epidemic of hysterectomy. In the United States a third of all women will have had their wombs removed by the time they are sixty. One-fifth of women in England and Wales will have had a hysterectomy by age sixty-five. Of the women now alive in California, only half will be buried with their wombs. In 1992–3, 73,000 hysterectomies were carried out in England. Two-thirds of them were for nothing more serious than heavy periods; when analysed the blood loss was found to be within the range of normal. Non-surgical treatments for heavy periodic bleeding do exist, but general practitioners seem not to know of the most effective, which is tranexamic acid which reduces blood flow by 45 to 60 per cent. Mefenamic acid will reduce blood flow by between 30 and 45 per cent. Instead GPs prescribe norethistine which is much less effective and may even increase blood flow. Before resorting to hysterectomy there is also endometrial ablation to consider, which is the modern version of the old D and C for heavy bleeding. According to a survey reported in April 1997, one in thirteen GPs thinks that hysterectomy should be considered the routine treatment for heavy bleeding in women who have completed their family size. Of more interest to a feminist considering the female predilection for self-mutilation is the fact that one in seven of the 30 per cent of women of childbearing age who report heavy periods will ask her GP to refer her for a hysterectomy. Some, perhaps most, of the pressure for extirpation of the uterus comes from women themselves.

Hysterectomies are of two basic types: abdominal, in which the womb is removed through an incision in the abdomen, and vaginal, in which there is no visible scar, the incision being made through the upper wall of the vagina. Neither procedure is without risk. Vaginal hysterectomy is attended by a lower rate of post-operative infection (36 per cent as against 58 per cent), but a higher requirement for transfusion (15 per cent as against 8 per cent) and of incidence of complications (43 per cent as against 25 per cent). Recently in the United States efforts have been made by medical insurers Medicare and Medicaid to reduce the number of hysterectomies by insisting on a second opinion; nearly half the cases scheduled, 49.3 per cent, were rejected. A Swiss study found that women doctors were the least likely subjects for hysterectomy while the most coveted were the least educated and best insured. Female gynaecologists refer an average of eighteen patients a year for hysterectomy, male gynaecologists thirty-four. The Campaign against Hysterectomy and Unnecessary Operations on Women maintains that 90 per cent of referrals for hysterectomy cannot be justified. Between 10 per cent and 13 per cent of hysterectomy is performed to eliminate chronic pelvic pain; in about half the women reporting pelvic pain laparoscopy revealed no abnormality, in which case the pain might be thought to result from a somatization disorder or some other psychological cause. In about a quarter of women hysterectomized for chronic pelvic pain, the pain will be found to persist after hysterectomy, especially if performed by the vaginal route. Hysterectomy itself is a significant cause of pelvic pain. Nevertheless, though it is a major operation, with a significant complication and mortality rate, hysterectomy grows ever more popular. A prominent British gynaecologist has suggested that it will not be long before all women will be routinely hysterectomized once their family size is complete and dosed with oestrogens for the rest of their lives.

Unnecessary episiotomies, Caesarean sections and hysterectomies all represent assaults on femaleness, assaults that are the more difficult to recognize for what they are because of the patient's enforced posture of isolation and submission. Some doctors make the female patient's abdication of all responsibility a condition of treatment; more do not have to, because the women believe that their bodies are so mysterious that only a person in a white coat could unravel them, and so defective that there was never any hope of their functioning properly in the first place. Obstetrics and gynaecology, being relatively uncomplicated, are the least prestigious specialities in medicine; an obstetrician compares to a neurologist as a plumber compares to an aeronautical engineer. If we are to raise young women to be confident about knowing how their bodies work and how to get optimum performance from them we would have to start teaching them body-management as schoolgirls. We would soon discover that we had no answers to the most obvious questions about how healthy women function. Three hundred years of male professionals' lancing women's bodies as if they were abcesses is not easily undone.

our bodies, our selves

A woman's body is the battlefield where she fights for liberation. It is through her body that oppression works, reifying her, sexualizing her, victimizing her, disabling her. Her physicality is a medium for others to work on; her job is to act as their viceroy, presenting her body for their ministrations, and applying to her body the treatments that have been ordained. If she fails to present herself, if she refuses to accept the treatments, she is behaving badly. In some future epoch intelligent beings from another galaxy will hold seminars to discuss possible explanations of why a whole generation of female earthlings had their bellies cut open. They will probably interpret the phenomenon as some kind of superstitious ritual, there being none of us alive to say that we were all one by one convinced that these massive disruptions of our bodies were absolutely necessary. If the beings had a time-travel capacity they might use it to ask us how we can have been so stupid. And we will have to reply that, being ignorant, we were obliged to rely upon the priestly caste of doctors to operate on our bodies in our own best interests. Our interplanetary visitors might well be amazed at such foolish credulity.

Intellectual feminists have written millions of words on the ways in which men have colonized and controlled women but still the process rolls on, aided by better techniques for exploration and analysis and storage of data. All the time women have been agitating for freedom and self-determination they have been coming more and more under a kind of control that they cannot even protest against. Feminists used to demand the right to control our own bodies; what we got was the duty to submit our bodies to control by others. Much of what is done to women in the name of health has no rationale beyond control.

> Censor the body and you censor breath and speech at the same time . . . Write yourself. Your body must be heard. Only then will the immense resources of the unconscious spring forth.
>
> Helene Cixous

As soon as the possibility of looking inside the pregnant woman came into being ultrasound was applied by every agency with the money to do it. Peering at the conceptus in itself has no effect whatever on its viability or pregnancy outcome, but it is now routine. The pregnant woman who refuses to present herself for her regular scans is delinquent in her duty to herself and her baby. Knowing more about her pregnancy should have empowered her, but in fact it did the opposite. Her womb is transparent to the technician, not to her. Today's mother first meets her child on a TV monitor and cannot recognize it. Even the most gung-ho womb-gazers are now beginning to suspect that there are more negative effects of ultrasound than positive ones. The shock of the sound wave to the developing brain of the foetus may be destructive, particularly if real time techniques are used. A suspicion that ultrasound scanning is responsible for a vast increase in left-handedness coupled with dyslexia is now being entertained in many quarters. But it is too late to turn the clock back. Now the clients too are anxious to 'see' their baby. As human beings in the developed world become more and more blind to the signals sent out by the body, they become more and more dependent upon the silver screen. As TV soaps are more familiar to most British people than the life on their own street, their baby is only real to them when they see it on TV. The viewers can recognize characters in soaps not only as human beings but also as male and female. The pregnant woman gazing at the monitor has to be told which bits of her baby are which and will not be told of the child's sex unless she wants to be. Otherwise she will consent to let the technician know more about her baby than she does. She willingly abrogates the power that knowledge gives in order to remain in ignorance.

Health professionals want to look into the womb simply because they can. In their eagerness to ward off the disasters that might ensue if the woman is left to her own devices they have over-diagnosed congenital defects and turned unproblematic pregnancies into nightmares of anxiety. For the mother whose foetus has died in the womb the ultrasound scan can only verify what she already knows. It cannot tell her what she needs to know, that is, why her baby's life ended before it began. All the controllers can tell a woman whose pregnancy is ending before their very eyes is that it is not unusual, when what she wants to know is 'Why me? Why now?' While the professionals are looking in at everything going right, when there is really no need, women are begging for answers to questions about why things went wrong and being denied. Try again, the disappointed woman is told. The situation is not under control; she is.

By the time she is trying for a baby a woman is well used to being 'under the doctor'. If she has been practising contraception she has been obediently taking concentrations and combinations of drugs she knows nothing about. As a condition

137

of being allowed these she must be willing upon demand to climb up on an examination couch, lie on her back, and position her feet in high stirrups so that a doctor can insert a

> I am, a lady with infections
> Bladder kidney vaginal yeast
> I am a beast
> PMS wench sore back and headache
> Cysts on ovaries tubes uterus cervix
> Breast cancer scare
> Pap smear fear
>
> Anonymous poem,
> *Anarcha-feminist hag mag* No. 4

speculum to hold the vagina open and contemplate a part of her body that she has never seen. In the early days of the women's health co-operatives a great deal of effort went into giving women the right to see as much of themselves as doctors saw, by teaching techniques of self-examination. 'Our bodies, our selves,' the women chanted. The feminist health collectives struggled to develop workable ways of terminating pregnancies without recourse to punitive patriarchal authority and had some small success before prosecutions and scandals closed them down. At the same time more and more women were choosing to train as doctors; a minority of them are now exerting pro-feminist pressure from within the establishment against the massive institutional forces concentrated on bringing women under lifelong control.

To justify the dragooning and torturing of women the public health establishment uses the rhetoric of feminism. Screening for cervical cancer was hailed as a woman's right; the tax-payer willingly stumped up for it, convinced that if women just had this itty-bitty test every now and then they would stop dying of cervical cancer. But they didn't. Deaths from cervical cancer, which were already falling, continued to fall, at a rate of about 7 per cent a year. Meanwhile the one in six tested women called for retesting suffered agonies of fear and bewilderment, as well as all kinds of surgical interventions from colposcopy to hysterectomy. Women were practised on with an inefficient diagnostic tool because they were not the point; control was the point. The test was oversold as an insurance against developing cervical and uterine cancer when it was no such thing. In case this sounds incredible, let me explain.

The current state of our understanding of cervical cancer is that it is in whole or in part a sexually transmitted disease, caused by the human papilloma virus (HPV) which causes genital warts and is carried by male and female. Before 1976 only warty-looking forms of cervical HPV were identified; what doctors examining for signs of incipient cervical cancer were looking for was cervical intraepithelial neoplasia, CIN for short, that is, changes in the structure of connecting cells. Some of these manifestations were eventually discovered to be different kinds of HPV. Between 1960 and 1980 the incidence of cervical cancer in women under the age of thirty-five trebled and the number of deaths from the disease in this age group rose by 72 per cent. In the Nineties 15 per cent of cases occur in this age group. The disease appears to progress slowly, taking about ten years to become manifest, but in general its career is not well understood.

The national cervical cancer screening programme is based on the Papanicolaou smear which has a false-negative rate estimated in 1979 as anywhere between 25 and 40 per cent; where invasive cervical cancer is concerned the rate may be as high as 50 per cent. Abnormal Pap smears will also result from common infections. The remains of blood, or sperm, or contraceptive creams and jellies, vaginal douches and deodorants in the vagina will affect the quality of the sample. Contraceptive pills and medications of other kinds can also distort the cell profile. If the test is not taken twelve to sixteen days after a period, and forty-eight hours or more after the last intercourse, its reliability may be compromised. As the supposedly pre-malignant changes in cell conformation are quite subtle, the job of evaluating cervical smears is both immensely boring and unremittingly stressful, even without the constant pressure for greater productivity. The *Wall Street Journal* reported in 1988 that a large proportion of US smear tests were read in high-volume cut-rate laboratories where technicians were sometimes given financial incentives to up the number of slides they read in a day to as many as 300, four times the maximum recommended if the human error rate were to be kept to a minimum. Some laboratories paid screeners on a piecework basis, sometimes as little as 45 cents a slide. Comparisons of false-negative and false-positive rates between laboratories show wide differences; the rule was for doctors to 'know their lab' and the side it was likely to err on. The British cervical screening programme was set up before the necessary infrastructure of laboratories was in place, with catastrophic results both for the costing and efficiency of the programme and for the women who were screwed around by it.

The adoption of a simple positive–negative classification conceals seven categories, from minor and almost certainly insignificant changes in the cell structure to changes considered definitely pre-cancerous to actual *in situ* carcinoma. The difficulty of assessing smears correctly is clearly illustrated by the wide variations in practice between one region and another; in 1994 the British National Co-ordinating Network reported that in one region, North-East Thames, 7 per cent of smears were interpreted as positive as against 3.5 per cent in neighbouring North-West Thames. In November 1996 the Imperial Cancer Research Fund reported in the *British Medical Journal* that one in twelve cervical smear tests is 'inadequate' and needs to be repeated, costing the National Health Service 'an extra £4 million a year'. Out of 4–5 million tests in 1994–5, 350,000 were found to be inadequate; 183 reporting laboratories reported inadequacy ranges from 0.02 to 35.5 per cent. The average was about 8.3 per cent; the Royal Albert Edward Infirmary in Wigan explained that 35 per cent of its smears were difficult to read because of the high rate of vaginal infection in its client population! In Britain 5.5 million women a year are given smear tests; an average of seven in every hundred of their smears will be considered positive, giving a total of 385,000 smears. In fact no more than 4,500 women will develop cervical cancer in any year, so 380,500 will have been frightened needlessly. Abnormal cervical cells, which can be caused by all kinds of conditions, usually clear up spontaneously. In 1987 58 of 236 women examined were found to have CIN; when they were tested again after a mean interval of 4.7 months only ten produced positive smears. Few health authorities are prepared to risk doing nothing in the case of a diagnosis of CIN. In June 1995 an article in *The Lancet* reported that 'Staff live in fear of being blamed for failing to prevent invasive cases of cancer. The desire to avoid over-diagnosis, which in the past kept the detection rates low, has now been outweighed by the need to avoid any possibility of being held responsible for missing a case.' The result is an epidemic of terror.

In Bristol between 1988 and 1993 15,000 smears were classified as abnormal; more than 5,500 women were referred for further work-up and treatment for a disease they did not have and were not likely to get. Moreover, they were 'left with problems that include lasting worries about cancer, difficulties in obtaining life insurance and worries concerning the effect of their treatment on their subsequent reproductive ability'. To be recalled for a second Pap smear is to catch the disease of fear. The test having been oversold in the first place, the woman is sure that there is something terribly wrong. After all, if it is true that atypical cells usually clear up spontaneously, what was the point of going through all the humiliating palaver of the test in the first place? The woman who is recalled may be given the all-clear after another sampling or two, but will she quite believe it? If she keeps being called back, every three months, or every month, she is very likely to make sure that she hasn't got cervical cancer by opting for and actively seeking a hysterectomy. A hysterectomy is a major operation with a long recovery period. The hysterectomized woman will need hormone replacement therapy and be 'under the doctor' for a very long time, perhaps for the rest of her life.

The woman whose smear is classified as positive will not get to choose what happens afterwards. She may be offered colposcopy, that is, microscopic examination of the cervix using a colposcope, or speculoscopy, a newer kind of examination using light-producing chemicals. If an area of abnormality is identified a punch biopsy may be taken. A cone biopsy, which removes rather more tissue, requires a general anaesthetic. The practitioner might suggest loop diathermy, in which a hot wire cuts off abnormal tissue, or laser therapy to vaporize affected cells; both these procedures require local anaesthetic. Cryosurgery, freezing out the abnormal cells, does not require any anaesthesia. Electrodiathermy to cauterize the cervix requires a general anaesthetic and is falling into disuse. All these procedures have been over-used. After £100 million spent on the screening programme 1,500 women will still die each year of cervical cancer.

Strangely, what may happen at the taking of the sample itself seems to be anybody's guess. An American study of 1980 showed that only 16 per cent of doctors taking smears were careful to sample the endo-cervical canal, probably because probing into the mouth of the cervix hurts. A furore broke out in Gateshead in November 1993 when 'A doctor who bungled hundreds of cervical smear tests was allowed to continue using an unorthodox method because he had the backing of a world-renowned cancer specialist', or so the regional newspaper had it. Dr Felix Lustman was allowed to continue 'testing women with his finger' without using a speculum. The leading cancer specialist had said of Dr Lustman that his smears were 'of an excellent quality' and that 'his ability to recognize abnormalities of the cervix and to pick up cancers can only be described as excellent'. Dr Lustman may be that rare doctor who is good at bi-manual pelvic examination and can feel more with his fingertips than others can see through a microscope, but further opprobrium was heaped upon him when the leading cancer specialist went on to explain that Lustman did not routinely use a speculum because he found 'that many of his patients, being lower socio-economic groups, objected'. There are good grounds for objecting to the use of the speculum, which is usually cold, extremely hard edged and hurts, even if it does not pinch the tissues of the vaginal introitus. What hurts physically can also hurt psychologically; women whose modesty is offended by being spreadeagled and held open for a good view may accept manual investigation with less trauma. In the event more than 700 of Lustman's patients were recalled for retesting; a hundred of them ignored the recall, and seven of the more than 600 who were retested were classified as positive and further investigation scheduled.

There is no agreement about how to test, about how often to test or even about whom to test. In Britain health service policy requires the screening of all women between the ages of twenty and sixty-four 'at least every five years'. In 1988 the American College of Obstetrics and Gynecology and the American Cancer Society together arrived at the conclusion that a woman should have three annual Pap tests, starting at age eighteen or younger if she has already been sexually active. If all three are clear, she may then opt to be tested less often but the ACOG still recommends an annual test for women who have had more than one sexual partner or a partner who has had more than one sexual partner or were sexually active before eighteen or were exposed *in utero* to diethylstilboestrol or have ever suffered from genital warts or any other sexually transmitted disease – which seems to be just about everybody.

At Ninewells Hospital in Dundee doctors reported, 'We have long suspected that CIN is a condition which develops predominantly in young women. Our data show that it is extremely uncommon for CIN to develop *de novo* in older women.' This discovery was not one of the things that a mass screening programme was meant to achieve and it may be one of the few unalloyed benefits that it will turn out to offer. The benefits of the discovery were principally estimated in financial terms; if women over fifty were not screened the size and the cost of the mass screening programme could be reduced by 18 per cent. What the Dundee doctors thought was that the resources freed by excluding the women over fifty could be redeployed in reducing the screening interval from five years to three or by allowing more laboratory time for each test screened. In fact their discovery seems to have had no consequences at all. Women over fifty are still being screened.

In April 1993 the British government launched an independent inquiry into serious discrepancies in the cervical screening programme in Strathclyde. Random sampling by the Argyll and Clyde health board had reinforced the impression that too many of the smears were being classified as negative; suspicion had been triggered originally by the appearance of cervical cancer in a patient whose smear had been classified as clear. It was found that tests had been systematically misread since 1987. Shortcomings had also been detected in the cross-checking system. The professionals involved were only too aware that in recalling women for further testing they were likely to cause a panic. Again and again they said that the problems with the smears were technical and that most of the women who would be rescreened would have no sign of abnormality at all. Politics leapt into the fray. Dr Norman Godman, opposition Labour MP for Greenock and Port Glasgow, demanded a full inquiry 'led by a woman judge, to restore confidence in the cervical smear service'. In June the same year a local hospital in Norfolk announced that its managers had sacked a laboratory technician and had arranged for the rescreening of 3,000 Pap smears.

Every time the newspapers report that a health authority has had to recall screened women because a second examination of their slides has led to different conclusions about their status, fear stalks the land. In November 1997 a spot check of 500 smears taken by the Warwickshire health authority between January 1995 and April 1997 revealed sixteen that had been wrongly classified as clear; a review of 18,000 smears was ordered. In December 1998, as a result of re-examination of 3,930 smears screened at the Royal Berkshire Hospital between 1992 and 1994, six women were recalled for colposcopy and sixty-five were advised to have a repeat smear. In January 1998 Kent health authority reported that 91,000 slides had been reassessed; thirty women had had to have hysterectomies and eight women had died of cervical cancer after their smears had been misdiagnosed as clear. More than a thousand women had not been cleared; 114 women had moved and could not be traced. Seven of these had smears that showed serious abnormalities. Within a week Lincoln health authority had to announce that it too was recalling women because 180 out of 317 smears had been wrongly diagnosed as negative.

Though Baroness Jay, Labour Health Minister, announced her government's determination 'to restore public confidence in the screening process', it was by now undeniable that such confidence was misplaced. Public health consultant Dr Angela Raffle dared to tell the truth, that cervical screening is 'actually expensive, complicated and relatively ineffective. Only about 50 per cent of cases are picked up and there is huge and escalating over-detection and over-treatment.' Raffle went on, 'Screening has become something of a feminist ikon and it is very hard to explain that cervical cancer was a rare and diminishing cause of death before we even began screening.' Male-dominated governments are remarkably unaware of 'feminist ikons' and don't often, if ever, invest huge amounts of money in them. If the American government now spends $4.5 billion dollars on Pap smears every year, it is not because they are being pushed around by a bunch of noisy feminists but because of the power and priorities of the medical establishment.

Even though costly problems generated by cervical screening programmes continue to ramify, enthusiasm for screening entire populations of women does not waver. Breast screening is in almost as much trouble as cervical screening, yet it has now been suggested that all British women be screened for ovarian cancer by testing for the protein CA125 in the blood. Every year 6,000 women are diagnosed with ovarian cancer and 4,000 die. If the clinicians can show over the next seven years or so that the tests save lives, women can expect to have to undergo a third round of tests alongside their mammograms and Pap smears. The results will be fifty false positives for every genuine case detected, and a very slight improvement in the death rate, if any, because the protein does not appear in the blood until the cancer is fairly well developed. Which does not mean that screening will not be instituted. By the time a British survivor of ovarian cancer had appeared at a press conference to state emphatically that 'Of course everyone should be screened', a nationwide screening programme had already been piloted at St Bartholomew's Hospital, involving both 120,000 women from the general population and 3,000 from a high-risk family group.

No pressure group within the medical profession is lobbying for the right to save men's lives by regularly examining the prostate. Occasionally we hear that clinicians regret men's unwillingness to be routinely poked and prodded and X-rayed, but the temptation to set up a screening service for men has so far been successfully resisted, on the same sorts of considerations that should have prevented the setting up of women's screening programmes. There is a strong impression that men are no more likely to submit their testicles to official care and attention than they are to wear their muffler when it is cold and keep their feet dry. The service exists for them to avail themselves of if they want to, and that is deemed to be sufficient. Men have the right to take care of themselves, or not, as they see fit, but women are to be taken care of whether they like it or not. Screening is many times more likely to destroy a woman's peace of mind than it is to save her life. Women are driven through the health system like sheep through a dip. The disease they are being treated for is womanhood.

mind

work

As women do all the work in human reproduction, so they have always done most of the work required for human survival. While the male hunter-gatherer strolled along burdened with no more than his spear and throwing stick, his female mate trudged along after him carrying their infant, their shelter, their food supplies and her digging stick. She collected firewood and carried water. She prepared their food. The universal 'division of labour' between the sexes was in fact the apportioning of daily drudgery to the female, so that the male could indulge his appetite for sport, play, dreaming, ritual, religion and artistic expression. When beasts were domesticated, men drove them. If the beast died the woman pulled the plough and the man directed her. Even today, in many agricultural households, the valuable beasts are treated with more consideration than the replaceable women. The heaviness of work has never been a reason for women's not doing it; rather women were not admitted to jobs that required brain-power or management skills, even when the only thing being managed was a donkey. In some parts of the world you may still see the male peasant riding his donkey as his wife walks alongside. In the rich world the equivalent is the husband who drives a car with a wife who walks or catches the bus. All over the world women do the heavy, mindless, repetitive labour. Women gather scarce firewood over many miles and carry it home on their backs or on their heads. Water is heavy but men will not carry it. As soon as a source of energy is found that makes work lighter, men take it over. When cultivation is done with mattocks and hoes women do it; when a tractor comes along, men drive it. When a UN project made bicycles available to women traders in Asia, men took them for their own use and their wives walked to the market as they had always done, carrying their heavy produce on their heads.

> All scholars agree that even in studies suggesting that husbands of employed wives do statistically more [housework], the increase is small in absolute magnitude and employed wives continue to do the bulk of the family work.
>
> Joseph H. Pleck, sociologist

Women are the labouring sex. From the time girls are very small they learn that work is what time is for. Comparison of women's work-load with men's is difficult because a good deal of women's effort is not even recognized as work. Time spent with the children is not classified as work, although the mother does not use it to read the paper while the kid crawls between her legs, but to teach her child to speak, to advance its social skills, to answer its questions, to deal with its preoccupations, to prepare it for school activities. A woman who bears a child does so knowing that any leisure time she might have had in the past is effectively cancelled for the next sixteen years yet, if she is not earning pay of any kind, she will appear in statistics as idle, economically inactive. Conventional economic analyses, being based upon the 'gross national product' or 'gross domestic product', can take account only of activities that involve cash flow. In 1995 the UN Development Program published a Human Development Report which for the first time attempted to provide a picture of women's unpaid contribution, estimating its value worldwide as $11 trillion; men's unpaid work was valued at $5 trillion, less than half. Much of women's work remains as invisible to conventional data collection methods as the work of animals; recent attempts to compile comparisons of contrasting kinds of activity in widely varying economic circumstances, in response to feminist pressure to acknowledge women's contribution, have not been entirely successful. In *The World's Women 1995* UN analysts attempted to provide a picture of women's time-use rather than labour-force participation but the raw data emanating from the different countries were difficult to interpret. A French study came to the odd conclusion that employed men do two hours housework a day throughout the life cycle, while women's unpaid work takes up 3.4 hours a day rising to 4.5 hours a day at ages fifty-five to sixty-four. Equally baffling were statistics about women's work week which appears as longer than men's in all the developed countries except the USA. When we read that a Spanish woman's working week is twenty-three hours longer than a man's while a British woman's is only six hours longer, we have to conclude that different notions of 'working week' are being applied. Unpaid work the world over is starkly gendered; in the developed world women do three-quarters of all meal preparation and clean-up; in some countries the proportion rises to 90 per cent. According to a recent Canadian study, 52 per cent of Canadian women working full-time got no help with housework, and 28 per cent did most of it; only 10 per cent had partners who took equal responsibility, which seems about par.

All studies show that leisure is a masculine privilege. What is more, men are permitted to alienate money coming into the household to spend on their leisure pursuits; when recent floods in Cambridgeshire swept away the angling gear of a father, his friend and their sons camped on the bank of a river, the replacement cost was estimated at £7,000. All the attempts of record companies to get women to invest in their products fail because women, even if they consider themselves entitled to spend so much money on themselves, do not have the time to listen to CDs. The contrast between male and female patterns of spending is not limited to the developed world. In November 1996 Leena Kirjavainen, director of the women and population division of the Food and Agricultural Organisation (FAO), pointed out that 'If [aid] money is given to women, it is generally used for better nutrition, better clothing, and for the welfare of the household. If it's given to men, it tends to be spent on electronic goods, a new bicycle maybe, or – if we're to be really frank – on prostitution, alcohol and other forms of consumption that don't help the family.'

Excluding students the number of unemployed men who are not seeking work rose from 800,000 in 1979 to 2.3 million in 1997.

Employment Policy Institute

Men regard weekends as time off, when they play sport in a more or less serious way, or watch it, or not, as they please. Working women use weekends to catch up with the tasks left over from an exhausting week. They are grateful if their partner takes the kids out with him, so they can get on with their work, but if he does it is not for long.

Women have been conditioned to believe that men's work is harder and more stressful than theirs, which is a con. The truth seems to be that men resent having to work and harbour a positive ambition to do nothing, which women do not share. A love of idleness is another characteristic that male *Homo sapiens* has inherited from his anthropoid ancestors; an animal behaviour researcher observed 'that she would find it exceedingly difficult to observe a lone male gorilla for eight hours because he does so little'. Females, be they gorillas or worker bees, are naturally busy, which suggests another cause of men's irritability with women who penetrate their territories. They do not want the myth of male energy and purposiveness to be exploded. They might find themselves having to do some serious work, with concomitant loss of status among the other alpha males. In male hierarchies idleness is associated with status. Angling is the most popular sport in Britain because it is an excuse to do absolutely nothing for days on end.

When I was a little girl, little girls were kept in to do the housework while little boys were sent out to play. Half a century later boys aren't sent out to play because the outdoors is thought unsafe for children of either sex. Even so boys are not sharing the work around the house; they are playing in their rooms with their boys' toys (which is why they are so much further into computers than girls are). Conscientious mothers might try to teach their boys not to expect women to do their chores for them, but they are notably unsuccessful. When women were admitted to King's College, Cambridge, a cynical don was heard to remark, 'Now the men will get their laundry done free.' The men say that they don't mind if their digs are filthy and smell of unwashed clothes; the women who share those digs end up doing the housework out of self-defence. 'I'm not bothered about the state of the kitchen. You want the kitchen clean – you clean it,' goes the masculine script. Little girls are still expected to be tidy and keep themselves clean and big girls continue the tradition. A good deal of the unpaid work younger women do is maintenance of a hairless, odourless, band-box self. The boys are under no such obligation. In March 1998 little girls' mag *Mizz* ran a story on 'Super Slobs'. Slob No. 1 boasted, 'I never clean up my mess,' Slob No. 2,

'Some days I don't get up!' Slob No. 2's 'fave slobby outfit' was 'A tracksuit I wear when I go fishing – it's covered in holes and has dried fish slime all over it. I also own a pair of very smelly trainers.' Slob No. 3 liked to 'hog the couch and lay (*sic*) there for hours with the remote control, channel surfing'.

International surveys tell us the proportion of unpaid work done by men in the developed world is rising but it remains low, even though in these calculations no attempt is made to differentiate between gardening and DIY, both hobbies, and the unavoidable repetitive daily tasks that fall to women. Recent British surveys that tell us that 26 per cent of women *never* wash their own clothes contrasted with 57 per cent of men, and 7 per cent of women *never* wash dishes as against 21 per cent of men, give a very distorted impression of the difference in men's and women's contributions. Women may spend up to sixty-two hours a week on housework, men a third of that time. Though equal pay legislation has been in operation in all the developed countries for thirty years, women continue to earn less than men because the kinds of work that women do are considered to be of less value. Women are not only paid less, they are also disadvantaged in pensions, sickness benefits, conditions, in-service training and opportunities for promotion. The 1995 New Earning Survey showed that women were 70 per cent of the lowest earners and only 10 per cent of the highest. The age-old spectacle of women supplying the hard graft and men directing their efforts can be seen as clearly in universities, schools and hospitals as it can in the case of Um Sara photographed for the *National Geographic* in 1993 as she pulled the heavy oars of her husband's boat, with her baby asleep under the thwart, for eight hours a day, as he did the lighter work of casting his net into the Nile and pulling it up again.

In December 1997 consultants Towers Perrin reported back to the Universities and Colleges Employers Association, a consortium of 110 organizations that feared it might be vulnerable on the grounds of consistently paying women less than men, that, across all types of work in higher education, academic, administrative, manual and technical, 62 per cent of the jobs done by women were consistently undervalued as against 37 per cent of the jobs done by men. The skills and knowledge deployed by women, whether as nursery co-ordinators, secretaries or cleaning supervisors, were worth less than the skills and knowledge of security guards, building managers and mechanics. Other studies have shown that over a lifetime a woman's earnings will be significantly lower than those of men in the same professions; a female nurse, for example, will earn £50,000 less in her working life than a male nurse. The difference is not only the consequence of different rates of pay, but also of restrictions on access to overtime and promotion. Women have no spare time to devote to the employer. Women don't allow themselves any spare time. Lots of women don't give themselves time for sufficient sleep. Women rushing to catch up with the day's complement of tasks are usually anxious and guilty, afraid that they are spreading themselves too thin, maybe skimping this or fudging that, not giving a child or a husband or a project enough attention.

Women carry their worry about the quality of their contribution into negotiations with the employer, where it places them at a definite disadvantage. Employment analysts say that a job advertised with a salary of £40,000 a year will get no female applicants but women will gladly apply for the same job if it is advertised at £20,000. Successful entrepreneur Jane Wellesley was quoted as saying, 'I think women are less concerned with perks and getting up the ladder than with job satisfaction. Men are, by and large, better at promoting themselves.' Who would want a mere salary when she could have job satisfaction? Many women behave as if they feel a real sense of gratitude to their employer and act delighted as more and more work is heaped upon them, never pausing to ask if their male colleagues are doing anywhere near as much. If women themselves put a lower value on their own contribution than on that of men, personnel managers will seize the cue to employ them as low in the pay scale as they can.

'Your work is important but not valuable'
For this and other examples of employer bloodiness see
http://www.disgruntled.com/and
http://www.myboss.com/

Job evaluation is a subtle business, because work has no intrinsic value. Work is worth what the worker can force the employer to pay for it, no more and no less. Women's occupations have never developed effective collective strategies to protect pay and conditions, let alone to force up wages, which is why women are more welcome than men in the deconstructed workforce of the Nineties. Job evaluation plus legal action might have the effect of equalizing the perceived value of men's and women's jobs; the employer meanwhile uses an array of strategies to keep workers' pay and power at the lowest level possible. The traditional trades unions insisted on recognition for self-defining elites within the work force and overvalued the work of their male members by contrast with the ancillary female workers in their own administrations. In the 1980s labour was 'emasculated'; in the 1990s the sex-change procedure continued as the workforce became more than 50 per cent female. The trades unions had only themselves to blame. Their defeat was only possible because they never recognized the necessity of organizing all workers, women included, to fight for decent pay and conditions or of defending the right of all workers to a living wage and fair conditions of employment. Women who downed tools in protest against inhuman treatment picketed for years without any sign of solidarity from the labour hierarchy. In the most recent case fifty-three women cleaners of Hillingdon Hospital who refused to sign new contracts for reduced rates of pay and were sacked were originally supported by their union which then negotiated a settlement without securing the women's agreement. As the settlement did not include reinstatement most of the women rejected it. The union withdrew its support; the women lost their case for unfair dismissal as a consequence. At the time of writing their picket outside Hillingdon Hospital was still in place.

In understanding male power it is important to understand that masculine oligarchies exclude not only all women but most men. Male elites are as interested in exercising sway over other males in the same organization as they are in defending the organization as a whole. The labour movement, engrossed in the 'dick thing' of jockeying for power within its own organizations and at the same time resisting any erosion of its own elite status, allowed a huge pool of workers to remain unrepresented. Capital had only to hold off the organized onslaughts on its embedded power long enough to undermine old systems of collective bargaining, when it would find itself in a position to replace unionized labour with a biddable work-force recruited largely from undemanding female workers. The vast mass of female workers in modern industry, which is mostly service industry, have no job security, few privileges and little or no insurance. In Britain more than six million women workers, half the female workforce, are paid less than what is defined by the Council of Europe as the 'decency threshold'. The new Labour government, committed by its election manifesto to bringing in a national minimum wage, has set it at a level well below decency, having accepted the Tory argument that if employers were to be forced to pay a living wage they would sack vast numbers of workers. Thirty years ago a working man could keep his family on what he earned; now it takes two working people to afford a decent standard of living for a household with children. Higher paid workers in Britain might be able to support a household from their own earnings alone, but the penalty is the longest working week in Europe. They might be able to pay the bills, but paying the bills is all they can do. There is no time for anything else.

It is difficult to reconcile the powerlessness of the workforce of the twenty-first century with the triumphalism of 'the future is female' lobby.

Women are doing better than ever in the workplace where, finally, sexist attitudes appear to be on the decline – in 1995 more men than women complained to the Equal Opportunities Commission about job advertisements.

Women may be doing better in the workplace, but the workplace is not what it was. The fact that more men than women complained to the Equal Opportunities Commission in 1995 has less to do with the actual amount of sex discrimination in the job market than it does with men's readiness to use the existing instruments for redress of grievance, their readiness to fight. Men's lives are still organized in such a way that they have the time and energy to fight; women's lives, by and large, are not. Practically all the half-million British outworkers, nowadays as often called home workers, are female. Outworkers are employed by manufacturers to work in their own homes for piecework rates. The average outworker has children, works over thirty hours a week and can earn as little as £56 for her week's toil. Now that part-time workers are assured the same entitlements as full-time workers an outworker is quite likely to be forced by her employer to register herself as self-employed, which means that, instead of using factory equipment and being on the factory pay-roll, she must lease-hire her equipment and pay her own expenses before she can earn a penny.

Full acceptance of women in the workplace has been hampered by the rise and rise of male unemployment. Though a 1996 Cambridge University study found that support for the belief that it was the man's role to earn money fell from 65 per cent in 1984 to 43 per cent in 1994, men still objected to mothers working outside the home. Both men and women believe that women's family responsibilities, especially if young children are involved, must come first. Relatively few men or women agreed that a woman and her family would all be happier if she went out to work. One wonders how they would answer if they were asked how happy they would be to do without the central heating or the VCR or the computer games or the holiday that the working mother's money helps to pay for. One thing is certain: very little of the money that a working mother earns will be spent on herself, and none of it on any form of recreation. Most of the 45 per cent of British mothers who are in paid work do not actually have the choice of staying home; they must earn money to help service the family debt. If their children suffer it is because working mothers do not have access to affordable childcare. Nearly half of them have to rely on unpaid help from friends or family members. Only a quarter of British working mothers pay for childcare, professional or informal. In Britain, with six million children under eight years of age, there are only 700,000 regulated childcare places; the cost of such care is in the region of £3,000 per child per year. Only 2 per cent of care for children aged between three and five and 5 per cent of care for children between six and eleven is publicly funded. Only 2 per cent of employers offer workplace crèches; another 2 per cent offer childcare vouchers. Four out of five mothers told BSA researchers in 1996 that they would work and a quarter of mothers working part-time said they would work longer hours, if they could get the right childcare arrangements. The Labour government is offering credits to working mothers to pay for childcare but at a level which would pay only a fraction of the cost of professional, properly monitored care, supposing that it were available.

When a woman without other responsibilities is not earning her living she is working on her body, her appearance, her clothes. Staying in to wash her hair means staying in to work on her appearance. If she works out, she is still working. When she has a house to run she will work long hours on that. When she is in a relationship she will work much harder on that than her male partner will; when she has a child the work of raising it will devolve on her. If she has an older dependent relative she will work to care for her or him. Only a tiny fraction of the work that women do produces an income. The rest is done because somebody has to do it, if life is to be liveable. Women's industriousness need not be seen as oppression as long as they enjoy what they are doing while they are doing it. Work and play are manifestations of the same basic human urge to activity. Very few women can sit without something in their hands to work on; all men can sit for hours relaxing. Women cannot go out without something to carry; men keep their hands free and move about unburdened as much as possible. Women are busy; men are idle. Men have dispensed with any necessity to work on their appearance, beyond the choice of shaving or not. Their hair is low maintenance; their clothes are durable and suitable for cleaning by others; their domestic arrangements are of the simplest.

Women are worker bees; males are drones. Lionesses do the hunting to feed their cubs and their father; apesses do all the child-rearing. Male animals are conspicuously less busy than females, yet somehow the human male has convinced the human female that he not she is the worker. His work is real work; her work is vicarious leisure. Just how much work men actually do when they are 'at work' is an interesting and inscrutable question. How much of men's long work-days is spent in the pub, in the bar on the train, playing squash or golf, lunching? Despite all the media hype about working women, the lunchers in London restaurants who sit over their snifters well into the afternoon are still men. Men have still not realized that letting women do so much of the work for so little reward makes a man in the house an expensive luxury rather than a necessity. Many of the women who will this year shed a husband who thinks that he has behaved as well as could be expected will do so because he is just too much trouble. The cost in human terms of feeding him, grooming him, humouring him and financing his recreation is way out of proportion to the contribution that he makes in return, even if he is an attentive and sensitive lover. As things stand at the end of the century women are clear that they are doing all the work without having a fair share of the reward. Less work for the same reward must become an irresistible option. If men want the pleasure of living with women and children they are going to have to shape up. All work and no play may have made Jill too dull to understand a football game but all play and no work will make Jack that most vulnerable of creatures, a redundant male.

housework

By the millennium housework should have been abolished. In a sane world meaningless repetition of non-productive activity would be seen to be a variety of obsessive-compulsive disorder. People who said that they enjoyed doing housework or needed to do it or that doing it made them feel good would be known as addicts. Once the word got out that a person was cleaning her toilet every day, therapists would come to her house and reclaim her for rationality and the pleasure principle. Controls would be set up at supermarket checkouts, and anyone buying too many cleaning compounds would be suspected of substance abuse. Advertisers luring people into heavier and heavier reliance on cleansing products would be prosecuted and their bank accounts confiscated. Instead we have Professor Jean-Claude Kaufman of the Sorbonne telling us that housework is a deeply sensual experience – for women, that is, not for himself. Women do menial work because it turns them on; it doesn't turn men on, therefore they should not be expected to do it. Strange, isn't it, how much men know about sensations they have never had? Kaufman knows a woman in whom dish-washing produces explosions of joy. According to him rhythmic, repetitive, mindless tasks function as sexual antici-pation, building up pleasurable tension until it climaxes in conjugal relations. Faking it in bed has clearly not been enough; now women are having to fake sexual arousal even when they are cleaning the toilet.

In the world as ruled by Lever Brothers and Procter & Gamble housework has elaborated itself into a ravening tyrant whose demands have driven many families into debt and despair. These days housework doesn't just use people; it requires a gang of machines: vacuum cleaners, washing machines, dishwashers, driers, food processors, microwave ovens, refrigerators and freezers, immense quantities of water, power and detergent to feed into them and an army of tech-nicians who treat them when they malfunction and charge more than doctors do for a home visit. 'Domestic appliances' are costly, noisy, bulky and unreliable, compared to the industrial appliances that do the same job. When they wear out, as they are meant to do, they are impossible to dispose of. The effects of unbridled housework can be seen in every sudsy river and at every waste disposal site, but there is no chance that it will be made illegal. It is rather the people who live in caravans and huts and tents where chrome and formica are never seen who are driven across the land like criminals because they refuse to fall in with the merciless demands of housework.

Men spend 21 hours a week on sport, 9 hours playing, 8 hours watching, & 4 hours 'drinking with their sports friends'.
Total Sport magazine, April 1998

Though the houseworker doesn't now scrub and polish floors or pound clothes on a washboard or put aside an evening for ironing, she is equally busy hoovering, spraying-and-wiping and stuffing clothes in washing machines. As more and more home appliances have appeared in more and more homes, they have brought anything but increased leisure for the house-worker (who probably also has to earn the money to pay for them). Changing standards and notions of cleanliness have made cleaning more time-consuming than ever before. Kitchen worktops need to be constantly wiped; kitchen floors need to be mopped whenever a footprint or a pawprint appears; the bath has to be cleaned between baths; once a day is not often enough for the toilet. Every few minutes a television commercial illus-trates the standard and shows a way of achieving it, tightening the headlock on the 'housewife' – an expression that should be considered as shocking as 'yard nigger'. A recent television commercial for Bold laundry detergent opened with a mid-shot of a slender, good-looking, but not too good-looking, woman. A door opens behind her and a schoolboy rushes in. 'Hi, Darren,' she says. He does not answer. She answers herself, 'Hi, Mum.' Darren enters bedroom, looks surprised. She says, 'Thanks for tidying my room, Mum.' He rips off his school-shirt, grabs a fresh shirt from neatly folded pile (the inference being that he is immediately going out again). As the neatly ironed shirt billows out a special effect signifies the effects of Bold. Mum says, 'Thanks for washing my shirt, Mum.' No response. Then she says, 'I know you appreciate me really.' Darren smirks at himself in mirror, like any snotnose git with a doormat mother. This commercial would have been shown to a focus group of 'housewives' at the story-board stage and again before it was transmitted. They must have responded positively to this version of doting motherhood as the training of a tyrant or the commercial would never have gone to air. The financier George Soros suspects that the attitudes of the people viewing such a commercial have already been formed by marketing:

As the market mechanism has extended its sway, the fiction that people act on a basis of non-market values has become progressively more difficult to maintain. Advertising, marketing, even packaging, aim at shaping people's preferences rather than, as laissez-faire theory holds, merely responding to them.

Even as feminism is trying to transform attitudes, marketing is obliterating its traces. In commercial after commercial the performer of mindless routine tasks is an inanely smiling woman, unless some inanely smiling man pops up to demonstrate a new and better way of using even more of the product by dint of making her look a complete fool.

The first vacuum cleaners may have been a blessing for those who had carpets to clean. Their appearance on the market coincided with the rise and rise of the fitted carpet as seen in the movies so that 'hoovering' became a daily necessity. Carpet consciousness grew and grew until whole stores developed that sold nothing but carpets and sold them more and more often. Nowadays you can carpet your whole house and pay nothing for six months. In six months those carpets could be worn out with cleaning. Carpets that were hoovered every day are now shampooed regularly as well. Not long ago a pastel carpet was considered totally impractical and very few were made; now you may have the palest carpet imaginable, even pure white, in any of a dozen weights and qualities. All kinds of advertising, from cat food to toilet paper, subliminally pushes the message: pale carpet = cleanliness, comfort, luxury.

A mythical battle has to be waged by the houseworker against germs, depicted as intelligent beings of deviant appearance lurking under the rim of the toilet ready to infect helpless kiddies if the houseworker should be so remiss as to allow a single one to survive. There are more 'germs' in her mouth and under her fingernails and in her hair than there are under the rim of the toilet, but the houseworker is not told this. Her vocation is to rid the world of germs with the aid of a knight in shining armour, a genie in a bottle, a white tornado. This is housework as heroic exploit. The houseworker can only know that she has done her duty when she has squirted bleach-based agents into every nook and cranny of her house, even down the drains. Houses no longer smell of cooking; they smell of cleaning. As a consequence the houseworker stands indicted as the worst enemy the environment has. In the familiar distortion of the feminist ideal, we are told that the spray-and-wipe regime frees women from drudgery by saving on elbow grease and time. Sometimes we see a man gently removing the scrubbing brush from the housewife's clutch, and demonstrating in masterful and phallic fashion the penetrating power of the spray. Kitchens are not operating theatres and in kitchens antisepsis is as undesirable as it is impossible because it can only be achieved by huge overuse of powerful chemicals. Increasing reliance on convenience food means that no matter how diligently and often we spray and wipe, there are more, and more unusual, bacteria in our kitchens and our guts than ever before.

Cooking too has changed. The war on germs does not allow time for digging up vegetables, scrubbing them and peeling them and then cooking them from scratch, supposing mud was allowed in today's kitchen. Home cooks don't beg scraps and bones from the butcher to make stock; they don't cream sugar and butter, and eggs and flour to bake a cake. They don't go shopping every day to buy fresh vegetables and meat; they go to the supermarket once a week and select from a vast array of prepared foods which can be kept in the freezer until it's time to defrost, heat and serve them. They don't peel potatoes, chip them and then deep-fry them; they buy frozen oven chips instead. Most have never plucked and dressed a chicken or cleaned and filleted a fish in their lives. Many have never shelled a pea. Salad vegetables come cleaned, chopped and bagged; ready-made salads can be bought in plastic tubs. There is no need to build up a sauce from fresh ingredients when there is a cook-in sauce for everything. The real skills involved in food preparation have been professionalized. In 1975 when Shirley Conran's *Superwoman* was published, it bore the motto,

'Life's too short to stuff a mushroom.' Now ready-stuffed mushrooms can be found on the supermarket shelf. Life has always been too short to make consommé; bouillon was one of the first foodstuffs to be commercially produced.

Millennial food preparation takes less time than the old methods; the time spent getting food on and off the table has shrunk by a third, but it must not be thought the houseworker has more leisure time as a result. Housework expands to fill the time available. Time not spent doing one task will be taken up by another. Washing used to be done on a single day of the week, usually Monday. When washing machines became cheap enough to be owned by the majority, washing came gradually to be done on any day of the week, and then on every day of the week. Laundry is nowadays done several times a day. Television commercials show beaming women snatching a single soiled garment from the back of husband or child and producing it blazing clean minutes later, having been through the whole washing and drying process aided by a horde of sophisticated bio-digesters, enzymes and whitening agents as well as immense amounts of power and water, all squandered on a single garment. Kids won't wear their jeans and T-shirts for more than a few hours each before into the machine they go.

The person who does all this work is usually female. Advertisers and market researchers who tried to buck the stereotype and show men spraying Harpic under the rim of the toilet very soon realized their mistake. Nowadays it is always a woman who pops the meal in the microwave, whips off her apron, uncorks the wine, lights the candles and waits. There is no magazine called *Man and Home*. The 23 per cent of men who will consent to cook when they have a woman in the house do so on special occasions with great song and dance, leaving the clearing-up to be done by her. Men who clean and wash are presumed to have a wife in hospital. The few men who do a hand's turn around the house expect gratitude and recognition, so sure are they that, though it is their dirt, it is not their job.

Even though the number of women working outside the house has multiplied in the last thirty years, women still look after the house. Men are supposed to take care of repairs and improvements, DIY being still largely a male preserve. Work around the house is as gendered as ever it was. In March 1991, the Legal and General Insurance Company assessed the value to a husband of the unpaid work of his wife at £24,000 per year.

> The reality of trying to brow-beat an old-style man into doing his share can be more exasperating and time-consuming than simply doing it yourself.
>
> Sharon Maxwell Magnus

Men have not agreed to do a share, let alone a fair share, of domestic work because they have never agreed on the amount of work that needs to be done. It is difficult to know how they could because most of the work done in the home does not need to be done. The best reason for employing someone else to do your housework is that she/he will work rationally, getting as much done in the time as possible, not duplicating effort in foolish repetition of meaningless chores. Nothing is ever perfectly clean or germ-free; clean enough is good enough.

What men can and do say to the women they share houses with is that they do not see the need to wash dishes after every meal or to clean the toilets every day. The woman who is strong-minded enough to endure relative squalor may succeed in not doing most of the cleaning and cooking, but if the man or men in the household are determined to do nothing of the kind, as they usually are, she will soon find life unbearable unless she knuckles under and cleans up. The men who leave ziggurats of dirty dishes festering in the sink are actually involved in a power play which they have no intention of losing. All they need to do is to exploit inertia and wait it out.

Sooner or later the woman will give in, because the squalor is not held against the menfolk but against her. A man who is slovenly and untidy is considered normal; the woman who is either is a slut or a slommack or a sloven or a slag. A woman who is dirty is dirt. The external attribute becomes a moral quality, as it does not for a man. This works both ways; a house-proud woman equates her spotless house with her virtuous self and derives her sense of self-worth from the orderliness of her cupboards rather than qualities of her mind or soul.

The disregard for neatness and hygiene that characterizes the young male seldom survives into marriage. A man who marries expects his house to be kept clean, whether he says so or not. Many a woman is harassed by her husband's expectations of order. The wife of a commercial diver explained to *Woman and Home*: 'When Ron phones, my first reaction is: "Oh, my God, what does the house look like?" I'm not particularly tidy but he likes everything to be neat when he comes home.'

When Margaret Thatcher initiated the sale of council houses in the 1970s she greatly increased the ratio of housework to time available. Rented accommodation had to be maintained by the landlord, so the tenants did not have to concern themselves with it. Maintenance costs were calculated by the professional landlord as part of an investment that had to bring in a return, and so the costs of improvements to the property were kept to rational levels. The new race of owner-occupiers came into being because they wanted to transform their dwellings into the houses of their dreams and so a new and insidious kind of housework took over. The initial acquisition of the house sucked most people into debt, often more debt than they could service. They then went further into debt to refurbish those houses at a level that the old landlord would have known to be uneconomical. The first thing many of them did was to build an 'extension'; in pubs all over the country men discussed the relative sizes of their extensions. Once they became owner-occupiers men who had successfully resisted pressure to work *in* the house had no choice but to work *on* the house. Where once the house worked for the owner, the owner worked for the house, endlessly tarting it up, even when the value of the property was steadily declining. The importance of this mechanism in greatly increasing the vulnerability of the work-force can hardly be overstated. Because the indebted worker cannot afford industrial action, the power of the great trade unions was broken, the labour market was restructured, and many members of the brand-new property-owning democracy became unemployed, their houses voracious white elephants. Debt and DIY became a way of life.

The house of the millennium is still a temple of vicarious leisure, that is, pointless activity that serves no purpose but to demonstrate the status of the people who perform it. The amount of human work and attention that the house can absorb is and will remain limitless. The only way to escape this tyranny is to abandon the house. Some women do it by retreating into a single room and refusing to clean even that, living like a hamster in a cage full of litter. The punishment for this der-eliction of duty is to be incarcerated for the rest of one's life as incapable of taking care of oneself – rather than unwilling to spend what remains of one's energy in lavishing care on a house. The other way out is to pack what you really really need into a few plastic bags and move out to live on a park bench. Many an apple-cheeked bag lady has done her share of servi-tude to four or five rooms and figures that a cold day in the park is worth living by comparison. There are other, less dangerous and difficult ways to shed the cluttered carapace of house. You can live with nomads or hunter-gatherers, maybe, or become a nun with nothing but a cell to distract you from the day-long excitement of prayer. Or maybe you can make a vow that no more than an hour in any day may be spent on housework – and keep it. This really would be the end of civilization as we know it.

shopping

When a woman is not working at her job or working in her home or with her children she is working at shopping. A woman is always equipped for shopping, in case some window of opportunity should open up in her busy day. The 47 per cent of women who were described as 'economically inactive' in 1994 were actually anything but, because no woman can evade her duty as a consumer. Women are estimated to buy 80 per cent of everything that is sold. Modern economies depend at least as much upon women's consumption of goods and services as upon production of any kind. When economic growth depends upon spending before saving, shopping must be the primary function of the female in the consumer economy. Every time any woman, employed or unemployed, goes out of her dwelling she will buy something, usually for somebody else or 'for the house' and deliver it free of charge. No matter where she is going or why, she carries a shopping bag as a symbol of her primary function in the economy. The less money she has the more time and energy she has to devote to this function; there is absolutely no way she can get out of it.

Whether her money comes from social security payments or wages or an executive salary or borrowing, it is her job to get out and spend it. Even flat on her back in hospital she will be expected to shop. Immobilized on her couch by agoraphobia or disablement or laziness, she will surf the TV shopping channels. Though a woman may make an economic contribution in other ways, it is as nothing compared to the contribution she makes as a shopper.

Men don't shop, even for their own underpants. They buy stuff, in as little time as it can possibly take, but they don't shop. They buy newspapers and petrol for their cars, but they don't shop for them. Going shopping, looking through the selection of merchandise, hunting out the best value, finding bargains true and false, prowling the sale rails, is women's work. Men are brand loyal; women much less so. Men buy cars, computers, records, photographic, sound and sports equipment. Practically everything else is sold to women. Nobody knows why women do not buy information technology or recorded music. All explanations are merely speculative. Perhaps it is just that they have no money left after having had to buy everything else that men consume. Women undergraduates find themselves buying instant coffee, breakfast cereals, soap, toilet paper, detergent, bread and butter for the communal digs, while the men are buying CDs. The goods that the women buy are multifarious, cheap and bulky; these they lug back to their lodgings. The men can slip their CDs into a pocket. Though most men are physically stronger than most women, it is women who are expected routinely to carry heavy loads. The cars that are marketed to women are not high-performance roadsters but small cheap hatchbacks. Though they are sold as if they provided a passport to freedom and independence, getting you away from suburbia into the mountains and the desert and adventure, they are cars for shopping. Feminist ideals are called in to pitch for vehicles designed to take you no further than the parking lots around the mall. When straight-talking Ruby Wax sells a car to other women, she sells it as a glorified shopping trolley.

> For when I ask him if this necklace is
> alright he replies, 'Yes, if no means
> looking at three others.'
>
> Wendy Cope, 'My Lover'

The Demos report, *Tomorrow's Women*, is of the opinion that 'As consumers women may have more power than they realize.' What this seems to mean is that they could have more power than they exercise, which must be true, seeing as they could hardly have less. As evidence Demos produced a graph showing that about 60 per cent of women agree that 'companies who say things that might not be true make [them] very angry'. Angry and all as they might be, when a television documentary showed workers in Asian sweatshops machining 'Made in England' labels into clothing destined for a British high street chain store not a single store window was smashed and sales figures showed no tremor. The only power a consumer has resides in the power to refuse to buy, a version of withdrawal of labour. She says, 'I will not go to your shop, collect goods, fork out my money and deliver said goods' and acts upon her word. If the product is Californian iceberg lettuce, she may decide to do without it altogether, because the conditions of its production are incompatible with the most basic respect for other human beings. Otherwise she shops for less bloodstained goods elsewhere, putting in more trouble, more time and more money in order to exert an imperceptible minimum of influence on the vendor. Boycott is the most laborious and least effective form of political action. There is nothing a minority of angry shoppers can do to push the vending institution in the direction in which they want it to go. If the vendor decides that only a minority of people is buying a particular line and it is not moving off the shelf fast enough, it will be deleted. If he decides that the profit margin on one brand is less favourable than the margin on another, he may delete that too. The individual shopper has no recourse.

> I've just done the weekly shop for six hungry people – and yet again I feel shattered. Yet again the stock had been changed around, so I needed to do several circuits to find everything. Yet again I bent double getting goods out of my trolley, and yet again I couldn't keep up, as the cashier whizzed my items through the scanner. Yet again while I'm still grappling with carrier bags that won't open, and family size packs that won't go in them, the cashier says calmly 'That will be £109.50, please.' . . . How much longer will I put up with being made to feel they're doing ME a big favour?
>
> Loreto Keech, Stockport

Nowhere is the shopper's impotence more spectacularly displayed than in the supermarket. Customers in supermarkets are required to work extremely hard; they have to drive to the supermarket, park in a designated area, find a trolley, hunt for the commodities they want, load them into the trolley, unload them at the check-out, pay for them, reload them and wheel them back to the car, unload them again, load them in the car, drive them home, unload them again and transfer them to refrigerator, freezer, pantry or cupboard. A whole evening a week, say three or four hours, is added to the shopper's workload by the trip to the supermarket. The Demos report tells us that women will lead us into the era of electronic shopping from home via telephone or digital television; if it were down to women we would have at-home shopping already but the vending organizations will not tool up for it. Instead, every week brings new applications for development of supermarkets on new greenfield sites. And all over the country elderly citizens, of whom most are female, are losing their neighbourhood shops. There can be no question but that they would love to be able to shop from home for their weekly necessities. The likelihood is, even when this becomes possible, they will not be able to afford the service or permitted to buy in quantities small enough for their modest needs.

The only decision the shopper gets to make is the choice of supermarket; once that choice is made she is at the mercy of the company. If she should fall for the incessant promises of all kinds of benefits that will accrue to her and hers, and join a retail loyalty scheme, she will virtually belong to the company and carry a card to prove it. The supermarket computer may even send her an e-mail to remind her what she needs to buy that week, basing its recommendation on its knowledge of what she has bought every other week. Of women with children at home, 60 per cent are members of supermarket loyalty schemes. One-stop shopping enables the supermarket to dictate what the shopper can acquire. If she wants something the company has decided not to carry she will be intimidated into buying something it does carry. The techniques by which this is done are anything but subtle. Suppose she is looking for a jar of pimentos. She looks among the tinned vegetables and cannot find it. She looks in the Tex-Mex section. No luck. She looks among the pickles. Foiled again, she asks a man in a suit with a company pin in his lapel. 'Never heard of them.' The implications are plain: there is no such thing and the customer is mad. The customer is challenged to describe them: she shows him fresh red peppers and explains she wants skinned, seeded peppers in brine. 'No such product.' But there is (of course). He says that the store carries 13,000 lines and has never stocked such a thing. He is actually poising the authority of the company, which may even have a celebrity cook to prepare its products on prime-time TV, against the individual client, who is a creature of no importance. Supposing the store were to get a shipment of bottled pimentos at a price that permitted a huge mark-up, the celebrity cook would be sticking bottled pimentos in every other recipe. Witness the vogue for lime juice and lime zest. If I had asked ten years ago for sun-dried tomatoes, I would have been told that they did not exist. Now I can buy sun-dried tomato concentrate in a tube. The perennial optimists would say that this is because of consumer demand. It is rather because the vendors could see a huge profit in a product so cheap, produced by the cheapest labour abroad, provided they could associate it with style and affluence at home.

Tomorrow's Women also told us that women bring environmental concerns and concerns about the ethics of companies into their choices as consumers, citing the importance of the adoption of the Trade Fair campaign as an important factor in the emergence of Tesco as market leader among British supermarkets. This is in fact a vivid example of the helplessness of the consumer, for whom the adoption of fair trading rhetoric has to stand for adoption of fair trade practices. It is impossible for Tesco or any other supermarket to reverse either the rule that a merchant is one who buys cheap and sells dear or the rule that a salesman tries hardest to sell the product with the highest profit margin. Tesco did not banish instant coffee from its shelves, though any fool knows that the production of coffee is labour intensive and that if the best coffee in the world were not sold for hard currency at prices way below those charged in the country of origin, it would not be feasible to process it into cheap instant coffee. The numbers of products in the supermarkets that are stained with the hearts' blood of the labouring poor are legion; they include all tropical and semi-tropical fruit and the products made from them, all coffee, cocoa and chocolate, all imported vegetables. The female consumer may have passionate concerns about the environment and social justice; in the conditions of the marketplace these will be used to manipulate her for someone else's profit. Otherwise they are irrelevant.

Women's environmental concerns have had little impact on the manufacture of detergents and household cleaning agents beyond the appearance of various 'green' brands that were much more costly and startlingly less efficient than conventional brands. The chemical multi-nationals would have been best advised to manufacture such 'green' products themselves under an alias, so effective were they in showing women just how effective conventional products were. Meanwhile conventional products made their own claims of greenness, usually expressed in meaningless pseudo-chemical jargon. Sales of 'green' goods are said to have increased 40 per cent since 1990, which might sound impressive until the low level achieved by 1990 is taken into account. Likewise sales of goods supplied direct from third-world producers should have multiplied, but have only increased bit by bit. The aim is always and everywhere the same – to sell more and more of everything, including detergents. Hence the rise and rise of the household spray cleaner, which uses litres of detergents where once the same kinds of cleaning used millilitres diluted in hot water.

The sharpness of the contrast between the genders when it comes to shopping can be seen in the marketing of clothing. By and large men's clothing is constructed to last; women's clothing though not at all inexpensive is instantly obsolete. Menswear represents very much better value for money than womenswear. What is more, the clothes are expected or altered to fit the man; women have somehow to try to fit the clothes. There are a few male fashion victims; all women are victims of fashion. Men will not buy cosmetics; in the US women spend more than $10 billion a year on make-up and beauty aids.

For all the trudging that they do back and forth from the shops, up and down the supermarket aisles, women expect no recompense. Though chefs expect their employers to pay them for doing their marketing and bloodstock buyers get commissions, and buyers for stores are amongst the best-paid employees, home-makers pay to go shopping. They have been programmed to believe that shopping is recreation and that there is no greater female festival than a whole day's shopping. In provincial towns bus tours are organized to take women to the most famous 'outlet centres' for the day, the homeworkers' works outing as it were. Women are supposed to be possessed by a lust that can only be satisfied by shopping; left to their own devices they will shop till they drop. Shopping is actually exhausting work for which women are trained from infancy. Girls begin shopping long before they actually have any money to spend. The magazines that sell to little girls are glorified sales catalogues over which they are meant to pore in the privacy of their bedrooms, even as they take in the message of the television advertising directed straight at them. After school, girls repair to the mall to window-shop, handling and comparing the wares they have no money to buy. They watch other women shopping and learn how it is done. Goaded beyond endurance they may even shop-lift.

Advertising is usually justified as the only way of making customers aware that they have a choice; competition, we are told, forces up quality at the same time that it forces down price. The supermarket shopper's choices have already been made for her; goods that she knows and wants will have been deleted without reference to her wishes and preferences; goods that she does not know and cannot want will be forced on her instead. In these days of one-stop shopping, the shopper must place herself in the power of a particular merchandiser, who can then dictate what pasta, what bread, what canned goods, what frozen food she can buy. So minutely does the supermarket chain control its shoppers that it offers the same goods for different prices in its various stores, knowing that its captive shoppers will not be in a position to find them out. The shopper exists to be educated as a consumer, to be told what she wants. What she needs is of no consequence, because anything she does actually need, such as bread or toilet paper, she will not have to be sold, unless she is to be persuaded to pay more for some superior or more stylish variety. There will always be 'better' bread and toilet paper than what she thinks she can afford. There will always be 'better' shops than the ones she can afford to go to. Her job is to find the best value, the best quality for the least price, when in fact there can be no such thing. She cannot, as any peasant woman in Colombia or Morocco can, cheapen the goods she buys by negotiation with the vendor. She can only trudge from shop to shop looking for a better price, placing no value on her own time and energy. Even in her usual supermarket she will not be able to save time by going directly to the goods she wants, because the goods she buys regularly are periodically resited throughout the store so that she has to walk past tempting displays of goods outside her usual range. Manipulation of the unwitting shopper never ceases. Longer floor tiles in front of expensive items will make her feel more relaxed and expansive. Low-level displays will have her child shrieking for goods she had not intended to buy. Each shopping trip is a wild goose chase.

Nowadays the pedagogy of marketing is too sophisticated to gender the buyer as once it did. The consumer remains ostensibly unsexed, though the target of advertising has never been more obviously sexed. Considerations of political correctness require a current text-book of marketing theory to ask itself the question, 'Why do *people* shop?' and answer as follows, in carefully ungendered language:

- *Role playing*. Shopping is sometimes important to a person's role (e.g. a 'provider' feels that it is expected, important, and gratifying to shop for food for the household).
- *Diversion*. Shopping can offer a break from routine and is a form of recreation.
- *Self-gratification*. Shopping can offer us a sense of companionship when bored or can allow us to buy something nice for ourselves when we are depressed.

- *Learning*. Shopping allows us to learn about new products and new trends.
- *Exercise*. For some consumers, browsing is a regular form of physical exercise.
- *Sensory stimulation*. Shopping presents us with lights, colours, movements, scents, sounds, and so forth, much of which can be pleasant.
- *Communication*. Shopping provides opportunities to communicate . . .

And so on. Who can the sad individual be who needs shopping to act out a fantasy of being a provider (offering meals nobody really wants), to amuse her, to soothe herself by the acquisition of 'something nice', as a way of getting information and exercise in a jazzy environment and finding somebody to talk to? A man in search of most of these elements would go to a pub; women look for them in shopping because they are supposed to shop and not to hang about in pubs. Shopping is presented to women as recreation and they fall for the cheat. As *Tomorrow's Women* says of women in underpaid and dead-end jobs, who cannot find affordable childcare and whose husbands do not do their share, 'Outside work [they] enjoy spending and consuming for their own sakes . . . Consumption is a way of asserting individuality. It is a source of power as well as being fun. Work all too often reinforces powerlessness.' Recreational shopping implies the spending of money on frivolous things. Buying necessary things is unavoidable and has little novelty or entertainment value. Consuming for fun is part of female culture. From the time female children are old enough to identify the moving image, they will learn that there are pretty things they must have if they are to feel good. These begin with the girly accessories of dollies and dollies' accessories and proceed to clothes and fashion. On the one hand the girls' press educates them about girlness and what little girls should want and how they should look, but even more fundamentally and more pervasively it teaches little girls that they do not exist until they acquire. Theirs not to make but to buy.

In supermarkets men and women behave differently. Men on their own, especially if they are young, are usually buying beer and snacks. They want to get in, get the stuff and get out. So do the men who are with women, but the women want to involve them in the endless calculations about the best value, sell-by dates, ingredient lists and so forth. Will they get recycled toilet paper? If she wants. Most exchanges between men and women shopping together are more or less bad-tempered. The rule seems to be, if you love him don't take him shopping. Conversely, if he holds the purse-strings, taking him shopping just might bore him long enough and hard enough to force him to hand them over. The Birmingham City Plaza has now started a fashion by setting up a crèche where men may have drinks and sandwiches and watch TV while their wives are shopping.

Everybody knows I wear Gucci and Chanel and I feel a more valuable person if I have them.

Atsuko, Japanese schoolgirl prostitute

The science of fitting the correct level of consumption into the funds available used to be called home economy. It ought to be called home extravagance. Housekeeping expands to absorb the funds available in the same way that housework expands to occupy all the time available. If there is enough money to buy fresh-squeezed orange juice rather than the cheaper stuff prepared from concentrate, it will be bought. Anyone who really thinks that shopping is fun has only to study the body language and facial expressions of women in the supermarket, or the department store or the mall. What you will read there is not gratified desire but stress. Believe it.

oestrogen

Oestrogen makes women feel great and it shouldn't cost them a penny. Adult females make it themselves out of cholesterol converted by their gonads and their adrenal cortex first into progesterone, then into testosterone and then into oestrogen. The ovaries carry on producing oestrogen long after ovulation has ceased, more than twelve years in fact. The adrenal glands atop the kidneys produce oestrone to boost it; all steroid hormones are lipophilic, that is, soluble in fats and easily diffused through membranes. They bind with intracellular receptor proteins and the resultant complex binds to DNA. The scale of effects of this process is as yet hardly glimpsed. What we know and are prepared to say is that 'oestrogen lifts our moods and gives us a feeling of well-being'. It probably does that by influencing some of the neuropeptide transmitters in the brain that regulate how we feel and think, probably oxytocin and vasopressin, together with the enkephalins and dynorphins, opioids produced in the brain. Oxytocin is particularly interesting not only because it can be shown to have specific functions connected with arousal and orgasm in both males and females, but because neurons containing oxytocin receptors have been found in regions of the brain that suggest a role in bonding behaviour. Such data might give the impression that personality is a simple biochemical cocktail and can be changed just by upping some part of the mixture. In fact the cocktail has some 4,000 elements that are continually being shaken and stirred; the overall and ultimate effects of adding a jigger of something new are unknowable. It is too late to study the natural chemistry as we now have entire female populations in whom it has been disrupted by the administration of one kind of steroid medication or another.

The sex hormones oestrogen and progesterone are closely related to anabolic steroids and, like them, affect mood and behaviour. People suffering disruptions of their normal bio-chemical balance will report personality disturbances. The behavioural effects of added oestrogen are difficult to quantify; oestrogen will not increase libido, for example, as it exerts little action on the clitoris, but it does increase receptivity in that it controls the vaginal environment. We know enough to know that sex steroids are powerful and that they have complex inter-actions with other substances, which would seem to be good reason not to introduce similar substances that would replicate or exaggerate or annihilate any part of the wonderfully intricate sequence. In the case of recreational drugs reasonable people are only too ready to accept the idea that interference is fool-hardy; when it comes to exogenous oestrogen, which is a drug like any other, we are suddenly undisturbed by the prospect of lifelong dependency. Oestrogen is now being tried and found effective as a mood-altering substance; it has been used successfully as a symptomatic treatment for severe post-natal depression. Oestrogen seems to be as good for women as testosterone is bad for men.

Our culture, which sees happiness as something you put in your mouth or inject into your body, no sooner suspected that oestrogen, like serotonin, was a magic philtre that would restore and maintain equilibrium, health and well-being, than it began clamouring for more and more of it. Synthetic versions were swiftly patented, manufactured and sold. Yet exogenous oestrogen was no novelty; women had been using it for years in the form of contraception, without noticing any euphoric effect. The pharmacologists who developed 'hormone replacement therapy' saw at once that synthetic oestrogens did not produce the desired effects. They went back to natural oestrogen, a cumbersome and expensive product, harvested from the urine of pregnant mares. The mares are fitted with a collection cup attached to a hose and confined in a narrow stall for the entire eleven months of their pregnancy. As soon as possible after the birth of their foals, who are routinely slaughtered, the mares are reimpregnated and the urine-collection process begins again. Drug companies like Wyeth-Ayerst that currently markets its conjugated equine oestrogens as Premarin to eight million American women in return for a billion dollars a year are hardly likely to let the end-user glimpse the cruelty involved in the production of their elixirs. The whereabouts of the horse hormone farms and the numbers of animals involved are extraordinarily well-kept secrets. According to People for the Ethical Treatment of Animals, there are 80,000 mares on US urine farms.

If the pharmaceutical companies were to get women hooked the best time was at menopause when they were in oestrogen withdrawal and begging for a fix. At least that was what the researchers thought that hot flushes, joint pains, sleeplessness, etc., added up to. The new mixtures were the methadone rather than the heroin; like methadone they worked, kind of. For some reason the women did not stay hooked. The selling and the product design were relaunched time and again. Sub-dermal implants seemed to lose their effectiveness; women required bigger doses, the implants became ineffective more quickly, menopausal symptoms recurred at shortening intervals. The manufacturers of sex steroid preparations, like the manufacturers of cigarettes, had what they wanted, addiction, and they were just as unwilling to talk about it. An underground network of pushers was set up; women, all users themselves, held HRT parties, bring-and-buy sales and coffee mornings, to spread awareness so that women would ask their doctors to prescribe. Feminist rhetoric was used; male doctors who would not prescribe oestrogen were creeps who ignored women's needs and denied their rights. High on oestrogen, women thought they were doing it for themselves. They were actually doing it for Ciba-Geigy, Wyeth-Ayerst, Upjohn, Squibb-Novo and Novo-Nordisk Pharmaceuticals, Star Pharmaceuticals, ICN Pharmaceuticals, Roche, Solvay and Abbott, without even charging them for stamps and telephone calls.

Some impairment of insight is suggested by the kinds of rhapsodic publications that even physicians put their names to. Dr Lila Nachtigall assured readers of *Oestrogen: the new woman's dynamic / Oestrogen: how it can change your life* that:

Women who take oestrogen definitely tend to look younger than their years. Their skin remains smoother, moister, oilier and more flexible – in other words younger.

That doesn't mean you should take oestrogen for cosmetic purposes alone.

'Younger-looking skin' is just one of the magical consequences of HRT that researchers have been unable to substantiate; as far as laboratory investigations can establish, exogenous oestrogen has no effect on the epidermis or supporting structures. If you were to put fifty HRT users and fifty unmedicated women of the same age into a room, and tried to separate them out the result would no better than random. The difference between the two is subjectively felt rather than apparent, even though HRT users are more likely to dye their hair, wear bright colours and make-up than women who reject it. HRT cannot be advertised in any but the medical press but other products of the same pharmaceutical companies are the mainstay of women's magazine revenues. Ergo every women's magazine runs regular articles giving women the good news about replacement oestrogen; the women who read these publications have no idea that claims that replacement oestrogen prevents Alzheimer's and wrinkles cannot be substantiated. If they read the scientific literature they would not be much better off; claims that replacement oestrogen improves the voice, keeps eyes moist and prevents glaucoma are based on research financed by the drug companies. Research that concludes that HRT can cure the numbness and pins and needles in the hand caused by Carpal Tunnel Syndrome exists alongside research that HRT and the pill are contributing causes of Carpal Tunnel Syndrome. There is some work that suggests that women who use HRT for upwards of ten years can develop asthma, which in an elderly group should be a cause for concern.

Dr Nachtigall says that HRT 'may pave the way to a super sex life'. She does not say with whom. She mentions a patient who gave HRT up when her husband died but had to go back on it again. 'She is now sixty-eight and has four lovers!' What more could life have to offer? One of the things that researchers are very clear about is that while HRT keeps the vagina in penetrable condition it does not enhance libido. But when you're out of your skull on oestrogen little things like that aren't likely to upset you.

In an article in *Brainwork* J. Kinoshita speculated in the kind of way that inspires drug houses to finance the running of large-scale clinical trials, in this case of the effects of oestrogen given post-menopausally on the incidence of Alzheimer's disease:

Elderly women are more prone than men to Alzheimer's, but some physicians report anecdotally that those who receive estrogen do not develop the disease. Estrogen is said to enhance cognitive function.

What this actually means is that some GPs think that some of their older female patients might not have developed Alzheimer's because they were on replacement oestrogen. They have no idea which ones these might be or whether they would ever have developed Alzheimer's or whether some other factor such as non-exposure to environmental poisons might be involved. Once a large-scale trial has been set up it has its own momentum. A positive correlation of smoking with incidence of Alzheimer's has recently been observed. As for the effect oestrogen 'is said to' have on human 'cognitive function', the only evidence is from short-term administration of oestrogen to small mammals in the laboratory, animals not normally noted for intricacy of brain function.

Sex steroids can hardly be expected to be neutral in their effect on behaviour, mood, cognitive function and so forth, especially if we consider that the pharmacologic versions of sex steroids are administered at much higher levels than those occurring naturally. We are also beginning to realize that there are reciprocal interactions between steroids and behaviour. In other words, as hormones influence behaviour, so behaviour influences hormones. The more expert the endocrinologist, the more respect she/he has for the synergistic interactions of body chemicals; unfortunately most health practitioners have only an elementary understanding of endocrinology and are far too ready to believe in quick-fix remedies for perceived malfunction. Dr Ellen Grant, author of *The Bitter Pill*, describes the effect of HRT as 'like having a car stuck in a single gear'. Dr Grant is a founder member of the pressure group Doctors against Abuse from Steroidal Sex Hormones (DASH).

What is claimed for Alzheimer's is also claimed for cancers, except those of the endometrium and breast, which are considered oestrogen-dependent. The data are difficult to interpret. Women on replacement oestrogen are three times as likely to develop endometrial cancer as women who are not, but opposing the oestrogen with progestogens is thought to control the risk factor. British doctors believe that after stopping HRT women should continue to take progestogens for two years but American doctors have yet to be convinced of the usefulness of opposing oestrogen at all. Women on HRT have twice the rate of breast cancer after nine years, and women on combined regimes are four times as likely to have breast cancer after six years. HRT used to be denied to women who have had a brush with the disease, but now HRT users may also take tamoxifen if the risk of breast cancer is considered significant. The constant crying up of HRT has the effect of making women who are denied the therapy feel hard done by, when the truth is that most women who could use replacement oestrogen don't. The latest cross-national study of HRT users in Europe calculated current users as only one-third of women actually going through menopause and no more than 13 per cent of post-menopausal women. About a quarter of post-menopausal women reported use at some time. The figures for peri-menopausal use fluctuated wildly between countries, from 18 per cent in Spain to 55 per cent in France. In France the most popular method of administration is in the form of natural progesterone cream which is rubbed onto the thighs, which seems much more user-friendly than the combined oestrogen-progestogen regime favoured in Britain.

Still fortunes are to be made and professional clout to be accumulated by setting up large-scale cohort trials to track the incidence of the diseases of ageing in a post-menopausal population that faithfully persists in dosing itself with oestrogen. The difficulty will be to find that population, because if current trends persist women will use HRT during the period of menopausal discomfort as a symptomatic treatment and then abandon it. The drug houses, who anticipated easy pickings as women remained on their product for the term of their (un)natural lives, are perplexed. They want explanations of this poor compliance. They blame voices like my own crying in the wilderness, effortlessly overcoming the booming sound of their endless promotion of their product in the medical press, and the equally energetic distribution of free samples to GPs. The truth is that selling oestrogen as a panacea was a miscalculation. Nobody knows better than women that biology offers no free lunches. In women with wombs and ovaries oestrogen has got to be opposed by progestogens if uterine hyperplasia is not to result. This results in administration regimes that are onerous, especially when the adverse effects of exogenous progestogens, bloating, headaches, mood swings, etc., are taken into account. Then there is the question of monthly bleeding. Every year the drug houses present new methods of administration, tacitly admitting that they have not got the mixture right. There will be no definitive large-scale cohort trial of the prophylactic effects of post-menopausal oestrogen because there are insufficient examples of long-term use of any single method. In an article in *Science* in 1993 researchers recommended caution 'regarding the ever-changing practices of prescribing HRT'. In Britain DASH has begun a campaign to increase scepticism about the magical effects of exogenous oestrogen, especially in view of heightened susceptibility to thrombo-embolic disorders and the waning of oestrogen's effectiveness as a preventive of osteoporosis. Even the case for HRT as a protective against heart disease has been questioned.

Women have given HRT a fair trial and rejected it. No merchandiser could ask more, but whereas makers of detergents would simply introduce a new product, the pharmaceutical multi-nationals allege poor compliance as some kind of default in their client population. Women owe it to the public health authorities to eat up their pills and stay healthy. Not to take their HRT is almost as bad as smoking. Why, they will get heart disease like men do (though probably fewer thrombo-embolic disorders). They will die younger without HRT, goes the argument, which does not go so far as to point out that this represents a valuable service for the public health authorities. It is unthinkable that women would not be delighted to live out their lives dependent upon chemotherapy supplied at a price by the pharmaceutical biochemical superpowers.

Modern human females are much more highly oestrogenized than their recent ancestors. An Oxford zoologist calculated that over a mere 200 years the average number of menstrual cycles experienced by a European woman in her lifetime had increased from about thirty to 450. Her calculation is based upon the menarche's occurring earlier and upon the infrequent pregnancies that modern women can expect to carry to term together with shorter periods of lactation. If we add to this the artificially oestrogenized condition of modern woman post-menopause we end up with an astonishing 600 or so cycles. There is no precedent in the history of the human female for the raised and sharply fluctuating levels of circulating steroid hormones that we endure but, as we did not know what made the nineteenth-century female feel well or even if she felt well, we can hardly guess whether the modern women is better or worse off because of her vastly altered endocrinology. Only the rising cancer figures tell us that she is worse off. How you answer the question, whether individuals should be persuaded to live their whole lives in a state of chemical dependency, first upon contraceptive steroids and then on replacement therapy, depends upon your regard for the autonomy of the individual. If men would not live their lives this way, why should women? Even though all teenagers should by now be convinced that condoms should be their contraceptives of choice, British physicians have begun lobbying for the right to prescribe synthetic sex steroids to women under sixteen. The caponized woman is now the norm.

testosterone

Thirty years ago, when the world was in the grip of the Cold War, an emerging feminist could catch no glimpse of a future unless she tried to dispel the shadow cast by the nuclear threat. There was no doubting then that the military-industrial complex that would decide the fate of the world, whether in the Soviet Union or the United States, was constructed by men and run by men for men. It seemed equally obvious that feminism and pacifism had to overlap, if not to merge. Most of the members of the Women's League for Peace and Freedom were feminists. Though Margaret Thatcher was as least as bellicose as any male head of a western democracy, and thousands of women have fought under the aegis of the military-industrial complex, the feminist struggle against violence continues. In *The Female Eunuch* I argued that feminism would have to address the problem of male violence both spontaneous and institutionalized, but I could suggest no way of doing this beyond refusing to act as the warrior's reward. Even then radical women were demanding the right to aggression as a basic human right and women's groups were training in self-defence and martial arts. The assumption seemed to be that all human beings were violent unless they were deprived of the right to aggression by an oppressor. Freedom had to include the right to beat your enemies up. The outcome of a free-for-all seemed to me obvious: if violence is a right the strongest and the cruellest will always tyrannize over the gentle and the loving-kind. Only those women who were strong and cruel enough could join in the butchery. The rest would be butchered.

> I think women are just as aggressive as men but it's suppressed in us. With men it's totally out of proportion.
>
> Lesley of Silverfish

This was not an outcome that I could tolerate, so I argued feebly that women should devalue violence by refusing to be attracted by it or to reward the victors. In those days middle-aged ladies used to flock to the wrestling at the Deeside Leisure Centre on a Saturday afternoon and shriek like banshees as huge battered men mimed doing excruciating things to each other. The louder the grapplers roared in their histrionic agonies the more frenzied the bloodcurdling howls from the grapple-fans. Ladies who couldn't be there watched the live telecast. The heads of programming suddenly pulled the plug and TV wrestling was over. In the years that followed aggression was carefully studied, and we began to understand rather more about it. The role of women in fomenting male aggression is, I now believe, marginal, even irrelevant. Aggression is part of the currency exchanged in all masculine dealings. Male biochemistry and masculine enculturation interact to generate a threatening climate in which men, particularly young men, choose to live dangerously. Adrenaline is a drug which the violent man supplies of himself to himself. The flooding of fight-or-flight chemicals into the bloodsteam is pure pleasure; many of our entertainments consist in little other than the deliberate stimulation of terror. People who don't appreciate excitement, who can see no more point in going on the big dipper than in wilding or ram-raiding, who cannot watch films which are little more than realistic representations of people being tortured, blown up, mown down, cut in half or simply terrified, are pathetic. Our culture now depicts much more elaborate violence in more media more often than it did thirty years ago. Regardless of official ideologies our culture is therefore, by my judgement, less feminist than it was thirty years ago. Brutality, like other forms of pornography, damages everyone exposed to it. Violence disenfranchises all weaklings, including children, old people – and women.

Children, old people and women are all short of testosterone. Even ten years ago, testosterone was a word not often heard; nowadays the presence of testosterone in the environment is often remarked on. When the stands at the football ground are packed with vociferating fans it is described as a testosterone storm. When a driver kills another driver who cut him up at a corner, he does it in a 'blind testosterone rage'. Television programme-maker Paul Kozminsky described some people as thinking of child abuse 'as something bestial – out of too much testosterone'. By invoking testosterone a man can abdicate responsibility for his own behaviour.

The first time I took testosterone, I felt truly liberated. I'm delighted that my voice is deeper and I have a subtle difference in the way my muscles form. My sex drive has increased . . .

Janet 'Texas' Scanlon

Testosterone does seem to be powerful. Women who have been dosed with pharmaceutical testosterone as part of hormone replacement therapy report distinct and unnerving changes in personality, which are, as one might expect, increased tension and irritability, and clitoral sensitivity raised to the point of discomfort. When women began to complain of personality changes as well as irreversible changes in voice and distribution of body hair, HRT preparations containing testosterone were deleted. It would seem that testosterone is the hormone of dominance; a survey from Mount Sinai School of Medicine in New York found that, the higher up the career ladder women had risen, the higher their testosterone levels.

Researchers who study the influence of hormones on behaviour have the greatest difficulty in associating testosterone with any human behaviours whatsoever. They have injected all kinds of animals at all stages of development with synthetic testosterone to see how it affected their behaviour. They have juggled the naturally occurring oestrogens and androgens to see whether the role of receptors and sensitizers was more important than the action of the hormones themselves. Yet they still cannot define any specific influence of testosterone on the behaviour of the human male. Zoologists have less difficulty. The colony of Kenyan spotted hyenas that has the misfortune to be the subject of intensive study at the Berkeley campus of the University of California provided some fascinating data about the functions of testosterone. Adult non-pregnant female hyenas had plasma concentrations of androstenedione, the precursor of both testosterone and oestrogens, higher than those observed in adult males; testosterone levels in pregnant females increased until they were higher than those of males. Hyena pups, male and female, are born so aggressive that the mother hyena has to savage them to stop them savaging each other. Nevertheless, though zoologists might think being awash with testosterone sufficient to explain the astonishing ferocity of the hyena, the observer of human behaviour goes to enormous lengths not to incriminate it.

Research has long indicated that androgens, testosterone in particular, are linked not only with libido but with aggressiveness, particularly in the male. Animal research has been much more consistent in suggesting this hypothesis than human research has. However ... the fact that sexual awakening in the adolescent is associated with rises in testosterone level, does link it to libidinal urges and possibly to aggression.

Sexual awakening in the adolescent whom? we might ask. The writer, Ronald Langevin of the Clarke Institute of Psychiatry of the University of Toronto, chooses not to specify, but we know he does not mean girls. The testosterone levels of violent men have been measured time and again, and often, but not always, found to be higher than those in a control population. Violent sex offenders have been found, again not consistently, to have the highest testosterone levels of all. The effect of alcohol and drugs is variable; habitual use suppresses testosterone but occasional use can stimulate secretion, possibly as a feed-back effect of disinhibition. This raises a further possibility that violent men are not violent because they have more testosterone to cope with, but that they have more testosterone because they are more violent. Traditional patterns of male activity might have developed because they stimulate the secretion of testosterone. If a woman can have an oestrogen 'high', it seems likely that a man can have a testosterone 'high'. To assert baldly that the secretion of sex steroids responds to cultural and behavioural influences is to cause a good deal of unease, but the authority of John Money, who gave us the concepts of gender role and gender identity, could be cited in support: Money's argument is difficult but it is of radical importance.

The principle of multivariate sequential determinism is the ultimate and absolutely imperative foundation of any trustworthy theory of the development of human sexuality. Among

197

contemporary theorists, this principle is violated more often than it is obeyed. With ontogenic single-mindedness of purpose, people all too often follow a reductionist dogma. Theoretically they reduce the origins and development of human sexuality to a single and usually abstrusely defined determinant which typically belongs on one side or the other of the obsolete nature nurture fence. Foolishly, they juxtapose biology against the socioculturally acquired or learned, unmindful of the fact that there is a biology of learning and memory, mostly as yet undiscovered. Like the heredity environment protagonists, they wrongly equate the biological with the fixed and preordained, and the sociocultural with the unfixed and optional.

Money is arguing for a continual interaction between nature and nurture. The way we are conditioned affects the way we are biologically. In July 1997 Susie Orbach argued that there are ways in which 'we shape our individual biology so that psychological stress lays down neural pathways which, if repeated often enough, become like a personal template, inclining our emotions to choose one way rather than another'.

Male chest beating comes in the form of talking at length in meetings and then complaining when meetings overrun. Buttock-baring is now reduced to manly phrases such as 'going balls-out' on a project or its being 'cock-on-block' time.

Guy Browning, 'Office Politics'

Taking courage then from the notion of biology as alterable, we can entertain the possibility that ours is a culture in which elevated testosterone levels are sought, prized and rewarded, no matter how destructive the consequences. Consider the vogue of road rage. Young men are expected to drive aggressively; by driving aggressively and taking risks which involve another driver's having to brake to avoid a collision, they induce a completely avoidable state of tension in themselves which explodes into verbal and gestural violence on the slightest pretext. Though road rage is piously deplored in the media, many young men wearing the insignia of hardness, namely a shaven head, an earring and a thunderous scowl, make a point of displaying rage on every conceivable occasion, not least when they have been outdriven by a midde-aged woman in a more powerful car than their own. Testosterone converts fear into hostility; fear stimulates secretion of testosterone along with other body chemicals associated with aggression, and off float the pheromones into the surrounding air. Could it be that we enjoy being scared and angry more than we enjoy serenity?

As it is, young men, whether schoolboys, gang members or football fans, deliberately contrive war situations, in which they fervently hope to get beside themselves and accomplish historic exploits. Every week in Britain eleven men are badly wounded as a consequence of 'glassing'. Glassing is what happens when someone is hit with force in the face and head by another person wielding a broken glass or a bottle. The provocation for these attacks might be no more than jostling someone or accidentally spilling his drink. A jostler who does not apologize and immediately offer to buy the offended individual a replacement drink is in danger. The offended individual may signify a demand for appeasement by a 'hard stare' which may itself provoke a glassing from the offender. The results both immediate and long term can be spectacular, as the shards of glass slice through the blood vessels, nerves and tubes of the face and the delicate and vulnerable structures of the eyes. These incidents are so common that it would seem sensible to make pub and club drinking vessels out of plastic or toughened glass, but the threat of glassing seems to be essential to heterosexual masculine pub and club culture. The connection with drunkenness is obvious and prompts the question whether men prize alcohol partly because it weakens the inhibition that keeps reckless aggression bottled up. Indeed, the semantics of bottling up suggest that 'bottling', as glassing is also called, brings a pleasurable release of pleasurable tension. For there can be no

> *Frogger* for instance was hugely popular with girls. If you saw a cluster of teeny-boppers in a video arcade in the mid-eighties, odds are they were standing in front of a *Frogger* machine. Consider: it is impossible to be aggressive in *Frogger*. The object of this game is to dodge traffic and avoid falling off logs so you can reach your little frog nest safe and sound. It's a curiously non-confrontational game.
>
> J. C. Herz, *Joystick Nation*

doubt that some men get off on violence; there are men who enjoy fighting much more than sex. Women who do not realize that their own menfolk are of this species are at a permanent disadvantage in negotiating with them and therefore in constant jeopardy. The most chilling answer to the question 'Why did you hit me?' must be 'Because I enjoy hitting you', supposing any man were honest enough to say it. Gratuitous violence to women and children is usually disguised as some sort of righteous retribution.

As there has never been much investigation of women's attitudes to male violence it is impossible to judge whether women's attitudes have changed at all in the last thirty years. There is some, rather depressing, evidence that women are as thrilled by male hardness as ever they were. Marc Dutroux, in prison awaiting trial for implication in the Belgian paedophile murders, receives letters and presents from dozens of middle-aged women. Peter Sutcliffe, the Yorkshire Ripper, and Jeremy Bamber, convicted of the murder of five members of his family in 1985, regularly receive marriage proposals.

Harry Roberts, jailed for life in 1966 . . . for the murder of three unarmed policemen, also gets many letters from women explaining the erotic acrobatics they would like to perform for him.

German serial killer Thomas Holst was aided to escape by his psychotherapist, Tamar Segal, who was a lesbian before she fell in love with him. Explanations of this phenomenon are extraordinarily inadequate. Dr Glenn Wilson, reader at the London Institute of Psychiatry, is of the opinion that:

> Women see a man who is completely anti-social, living on the fringes of society, who has a high dose of testosterone. He is the kind of male not to be trifled with. They see that as having survival value for their offspring.

No-one actually knows whether killer males do have a high dose of testosterone or whether testosterone is of any value in protecting offspring. Human ethologists have pointed out that babies resemble their mothers because resembling their fathers could place them at risk from other men. A man who is violent is most often violent towards members of his own family. A woman who makes overtures to a jailed killer is not looking for a domestic partner; the fact that the man is caged is part of the attraction. Marriages between incarcerated felons and their pen-friends rarely survive the husband's release. A minority of women will be attracted to convicted killers because of their own history of sexual abuse. Such extreme cases are of less concern than the indications that many, perhaps most, heterosexual women fantasize about men who are mean and dangerous. As 'Sandra' told a reporter from *Cosmopolitan*, 'He treated me like a porcelain doll but I like sex a bit rougher. He'd try to sound tough and say something like, "On your knees, woman," but it didn't suit him. So I'd laugh.' If 'Sandra's' bloke had been of the testosterone-rich variety she might have lived to regret that laughter.

Sex is not well served by either testosterone or male hyper-fertility, men seem attached to both for reasons unconnected with women or reproduction. Historically young men have been trained, formally or informally, as a fighting force and their fierceness deliberately stimulated. As the soldier is expected to be unreflectingly aggressive and his traditional reward the opportunity to rape, we would not be surprised to find that much of his induction has manifested as effective because it has had the occult effect of raising his testosterone levels. If this is true, we might expect the testosterone count of the average Burmese Buddhist monk to be significantly lower than that of the average British squaddie.

Males bond in terms of either a pre-existent object of aggression, or a concocted one.

Elaine Morgan

Socio-biological explanations of the human male's competitiveness put it down to his vast fertility, which greatly increases his expendability at the same time as it greatly increases his reproductive opportunity. If this is true, we ought perhaps to rejoice that the human sperm count seems to be dropping precipitously. When we can see that we will need all the males we have got in order to survive as a species, perhaps male competition can be abandoned as entirely maladaptive. This argument only holds as long as we accept biology as a given: once we argue that gonadal activity is responsive to cultural and behavioural influences, we have to some extent undone the socio-biological hypothesis. By degrees over our long history, the human male may have, because of his capacity to learn and to teach, actually created his own hyperfertility along with his ability to ejaculate independently of any trigger stimulus connected with reproduction.

Aggressive men will not tolerate the least suggestion of aggression in women. Aggressive men will interpret a woman's speaking audibly, wearing trousers, buying her own drink as provocative. Some such astigmatism has led to the claim that in the last ten years women have become as aggressive and as violent as men. David Thomas, author of *Not Guilty: In Defence of the Modern Man*, argued that there was an epidemic of violence by women against men and that men were getting the worst of it. Warren Farrell has been defending the subjugated sex from the abuse of female power for thirty years. The first American battered men's support group was set up in 1993. Worldwide, women commit more than half the total number of child murders, especially of newborns, inflict the greater part of the physical abuse endured by children, about half the assaults involving brothers and sisters, half the assaults on the elderly and on spouses. In November 1997 the results of a British experiment in which injured infants in a hospital were monitored by hidden CCTV cameras were published; thirty-nine parents were seen on camera attacking their children, some no more than two months old. All but two of the parents were mothers. Nonetheless to equate female and male violence is misleading. Maternal violence is usually an extension of self-destructive behaviour. The kinds of attack perpetrated by women seldom use deadly force.

Though the violent woman is now a role model and girl gangs who vie with boys in their toughness and mindless brutality have been known for more than a hundred years, long before feminism urged women to express their rage in any way they could, the statistics have always shown that women's place is on the receiving end. In London in 1994 9,800 women were attacked by their male partners, compared to 887 men. What is more, most of the men were pushed, shoved and shouted at by the women; the women were punched, kicked and stabbed. In the British Crime Survey, which records the levels of crime experienced by a sample representing the whole population, 1.3

per cent of women admitted experiencing domestic violence as against 0.7 per cent of men; 81 per cent of the women who experienced domestic violence were beaten by current or former partners, only 45 per cent of men experiencing domestic violence were attacked by partners and 2 per cent by ex-partners. As Oliver James pointed out, the most significant predictor of being violent is simply being a man.

> The existence of the motor car lends strong support to the view that all men should be locked up from the ages of fifteen to thirty-five inclusive.
>
> Martin Amis, 1998

Men in cars are dangerous; 98 per cent of convicted dangerous drivers in 1995 were men and 89 per cent of speeding offenders were men. Men have more accidents, pay less heed to traffic lights, brake later and harder. According to DVLA figures there are more than 20 million male licence holders in Britain and 16 million women. The March 1997 issue of *Walk* magazine published by the Pedestrians' Association revealed that of 4,229 motoring fatalities in 1992, women had contributed fewer than a third. Home Office statistics show that men were responsible for 98 per cent of reckless driving convictions, 94 per cent of DUI convictions, 87 per cent of careless driving convictions. Of the drivers killed in single-vehicle accidents, 87 per cent were male. At weekends up to a thousand British lads will gather at a prearranged destination announced on the Internet for 'road raves' in which up to a hundred vehicles race on the public roads. All rural districts witness the phenomenon of 'boy racers' who take each other on in secluded country lanes. In April 1998 the British press reported the case of Jason Humble who, infuriated by the driving of a man in a small car ahead of him, shunted it three times at high speed until he succeeded in pushing it through the crash barrier into on-coming traffic. Both occupants of the small car were killed. Humble told the arresting officers, 'I think I am the best driver ever.'

Professor John Groeger, working on gender and road rage, explains the figures as consequences of the facts that men learn to drive earlier, are under greater peer pressure, and spend more time at the wheel: women, he says, will catch up with the aggression when they catch up with the stress and the responsibility. The International Astronautic Conference in Oslo heard that men, because they were aggressive, manipulative in relationships and did not always think before acting, made less good astronauts than women, who coped better with stress, got along well with others in the cramped space capsule, and thought before acting in difficult situations. Pluggers of the 'future is female' line like to tell us that women's management skills are different, because women are non-confrontational and more interested in compromise and settlement than in impos-ing their will. If aggression is fun and if the biochemistry of aggression can be stimulated by cultural demand, we cannot rule out the possibility that women will gradually become as dangerous to themselves and others as men are. If the non-violent woman is simply a subservient creature, too repressed to acknowledge her own murderous propensities, war will continue to be the human condition. War will not be rendered obsolete unless feminism and pacifism agree to persist in their historic cohabitation and build a culture of non-violence.

soldiers

There are half a million women soldiers in the world, all of them volunteers. Because of women's commitments to child-bearing and -rearing, they are never conscripted. Every woman soldier has chosen military life.

> The military is an equal-opportunity employer in terms of wages. Women's wages for comparable jobs in the civilian labour market are lower, and female unemployment is, in most countries, higher than male unemployment. A job in the armed forces, therefore, is a better opportunity for a woman than for a man.

The free choice of joining up would seem from this evidence to be to some extent a forced choice for women, much as it is for blacks. There are further benefits, in the form of free training and financial schemes and initiatives that favour service personnel that have come about solely because of the presence of women in the military. In 1991 the US Army Medical Research and Matériel Command set up a Breast

Cancer Research Programme which is directly funded by Congress to the tune of $135 million a year. From the beginning the approach has been innovative; since 1995 women who have been either successfully treated for breast cancer or are currently undergoing treatment sit on the committees that review grant applications and five of them serve along with the scientists among the twenty-two members of the Integration Panel which agrees overall priorities. When Congressmen attack the progamme as an example of 'the haemorrhaging of defense dollars for non-defense and highly questionable purposes', even pacifist feminists find themselves on the side of the feminists in the army and the National Breast Cancer Coalition who got this particular show on the road. If armies were formed to exterminate famine and pestilence women would have no objection to joining up, but modern warfare, like warfare through the ages, triggers, aids and abets the proliferation of both. Armies are very good at devastating the lives of civilian populations; they have made no headway whatsoever in conquering hunger or disease. The US Defense Department Breast Cancer Research Programme has yet to make any dent in the upward curve of the cancer death graph.

Suck my dick!

GI Jane

For even the most determinedly pacifist feminist, there can be no question of rescinding women's right to choose a career in warfare. If we are to have armies, women should have the right to be in them. Half of the women in the US armed forces serve in the nursing corps, which is neither shocking nor new; if women may work in one sector of the military, it stands to reason that they may work in others. In the British army at present 70 per cent of jobs are open to women who can pass the fitness tests.

If women are to be considered ineligible for weapons training and excluded from combat, they lose the special rewards and promotions offered to active members of combat units. Modern warfare makes fewer demands on physical prowess than it does on dexterity and promptness of response, and therefore restrictions on women's eligibility for combat units are unjustifiable. Where they remain in place women will progress through the lower ranks slowly, if at all, because the most direct avenues to promotion are closed to them. As long as a huge tranche of tax revenue collected from both sexes is invested in defence, the sexes should have equal access to the industry, and equal opportunity to acquire rank, wealth and power within it. Women who choose to find employment in military institutions want therefore to be allowed to bear arms and to fight. The feminist argument for women's participation in combat rests on three basic ideas, first, that men should not be represented as the sole protectors of women and children, second, that women should gain control of the deployment of force in their own interest, and third, that being prepared to defend one's country has been a prerequisite of first-class citizenship since ancient times. If the state has a monopoly of the legitimate use of force, women should have access to it and to the formation of policy, in the interests of their compatriots and or other women and their children.

Other feminists have had difficulty with this issue, because though military rhetoric always criminalizes the enemy (as for example someone who is going to rape your sister – or you), war cannot be compared to the defence or protection of the weak from assault by a criminal element. Besides, war nowadays is waged by virtually invulnerable professionals against extremely vulnerable civilian populations. In modern warfare women and children on the ground are in greater danger than the professionals who maim and kill them from a distance, without risk to themselves, and who will have the best of medical treatment if, by some mishap resulting from the unfortunate tendency of technocratic armies to unleash their killer technology against themselves and their allies, they should be injured. Forty thousand women, 7 per cent of the total contingent, served with the American armed forces in the Gulf War of 1990–1; eleven servicewomen died in the war, five in combat. Two were taken prisoner. We were never told the figures for deaths of civilian women and children in that war.

Nevertheless, repugnant as the thought may be that rich women are killing poor women for hire, equality demands that in a militaristic society women should be represented in the military. Kamlesh Bahl, chairwoman of the British Equal Opportunities Commission, was delighted when women were appointed to the command of two British Navy boats in the Gulf during the 1997 stand-off with Iraq: 'These appointments send a great message to all young people with aspirations of joining the armed forces, and hopefully signals a fresh, modern era in terms of the opportunities open to both sexes,' she said. Other women would have been loading and firing the big guns from the British Navy destroyers sent to make Madeleine Albright's war on Iraqi civilians.

In liberation struggles, in which the people are armed to resist oppression, women have always served.

> Instead of dying screaming, being raped by an aggressor army, it is a relief to face the army with your own weapon.
>
> Tamil Tiger

An unknown number of women fighters serve with the Tamil Tigers in Sri Lanka. Before they may bear arms they must spend a year learning the ideological justification for the armed struggle, and forming teams, either to develop liaison with the civilian populace, or to provide medical care, or to work in supply and logistics or to participate in combat. As the Sri Lankan army does not scruple to torture and execute civilians suspected of complicity in the Tamil insurrection, regardless of age or sex, Sinhalese women are already on the front line. The same was true of the Druze in Lebanon.

What happens to women in the military should convince us and them that equality is no substitute for liberation. Armies are crazy places, where masculinity contorts itself into conscientious inhumanity, whether there is an actual engagement in the offing or no. In the military the cult of stoicism goes so far as to seek to prove a man's right to his promotion by driving the pin of his new insignia into his breastbone. As masculinist networks, armies develop the usual patterns of consensual transgressive behaviour. Unofficially, senior officers have enjoyed the right to subject their male inferiors to ritual sexual abuse and humiliation. The recruits had the choice of enduring the traditional unofficial ordeals in silence or getting out. Armies need to be savage and they prove their savagery first by brutalizing or purging the vulnerable in their own ranks. Soldiers are not supposed to treat each other in atavistic and cruel ways, any more than they are supposed to rape enemy womenfolk, but they do.

Having sex with a woman and then killing her made one a double-veteran.

Vietnam veteran

The women who take the military option are aliens intruding on a masculine enclave. Bruce Fleming, who teaches English at the United States Naval Academy, describes graphically how deeply ingrained this masculinity is.

Military virtues invariably are expressed in 'male' language: the military prizes things such as hardness, toughness and strength – all metaphoric of male muscle or tumescence, or both. The very carriage required of people in the military is an exaggeration of male, rather than female, body language; its effect is to frighten aggressors: chest out, shoulders squared, body drawn to its full height. (Look at the gorillas in the zoo.)

Even military uniforms are made to flatter the male, rather than the female, figure, with their epaulets that broaden the shoulders, and the anonymous eyeshade of the male cover, or cap, which emphasizes the threatening body underneath ... Female midshipmen by contrast speak of their 'birth-control' shoes and look uncomfortable in the tight jackets of mess dress, which fit men as perfectly as breastplates ...

The male bond is created through exclusion, if not of women in particular, then of the female in the abstract. At the Naval Academy, we no longer exclude women, but (whether we admit it or not) we still exclude the female.

The men who used to have the military to themselves did not vote for the inclusion of women and by and large will not accept the presence of women, who are still not numerous enough to create their own ethos. The Sexual Discrimination Act was applied to the British armed forces in 1995; among the first cases brought was that of Lynn Goodall, an acting sergeant in the Royal Signals, who had been told when she attended a course for promotion, 'We don't want fucking women here.' She complained to a senior officer who said the trouble was that when she ran 'everything went the wrong way'. Until the institution of a concerted campaign to attract more women into the armed forces in April 1998, of 103,000 people in the army, fewer than 7,000 were women; 13,000 of the men were officers, fewer than 1,100 of the women. Women were fewer than 10 per cent of the RAF; of the officers more than 11,000 were men; women officers numbered less than 1,000. The position in the naval services is roughly analogous: 45,000 men, fewer than 4,000 women; 8,000 male officers, 457 female. Though men are not allowed by law to express their bitter resentment of women's invasion of their male precinct, no law can stop them feeling it. Unspoken resentments turn bitter and rancorous, and find tortuous underhand ways to break out. Sergeant Lynn Goodall got £47,500 damages; Alisa Cook, driven out of the 39th Field Regiment of the Royal Artillery after her promotion to lieutenant by a campaign of bullying, accepted an out-of-court payment together with a confidentiality agreement that prevents her from discussing details of what she endured at the hands of her fellow officers.

In the US armed forces 11 per cent of personnel is female; in most other armies the percentage is much lower, in the vicinity of 3 per cent. Being relatively isolated among men, and having no groups of their own to relax with, servicewomen find that they cannot hobnob with the men, who find their presence inhibiting. The process by which groups of rowdy men fall silent when a woman appears may be more instinctive than malicious, but it is functional ostracism, which inevitably undermines the servicewoman's confidence and, ultimately, competence. The servicewoman who capitulates by adopting masculine behaviours and pastimes, in an effort to become one of the boys, will find the inevitable rejection even more humiliating and disorienting. The traditional recreations of servicemen, their resort to pornography and prostitutes, and their use of alcohol, sort ill with a unisex army in which women are to be treated with respect. No thought was given to the presence of women among the US troops in Bahrain when the US Embassy hired three strippers to perform in Christmas shows for their entertainment. Though the Saudis had succeeded in getting the commanding officers to ban all drugs, alcohol and prostitution, British Air Force mechanics continued to paint pornographic female figures on their fighter bombers, though 1,000 British women had gone to the Gulf with them.

Civilians can only wonder what on earth was going on aboard the Royal Navy frigate HMS *Coventry* at Christmas-time in

1997. One raunchy Wren leapt astride a tubular sonar device and made moaning noises; another pulled down her leather pants to display a tattoo. Principal Warfare Officer David Bellingham was apparently chasing female ratings around the

> My friend in the team, we were in the field and the army was launching grenades at us. She jumped up to catch a grenade so that more Tigers didn't die. Her hands were blown to pieces, and her chest. She died and others' lives were saved.
>
> Tamil Tiger

ship in a Santa Claus hat and a pair of novelty underpants that played Jingle Bells. Claire Alcock, a twenty-two-year-old Wren, talked as tough as any of the lads; sex with a naval officer according to her was like a wisdom tooth extraction in that 'it hurts, there's a lot of mess and you end up with an infection'. The slap-and-tickle ended in tears. In January 1998 Bellingham was tried on eight charges of sexual harassment and sexual assault against four of the female ratings on his ship. He was cleared on seven of these, but the eighth was impossible to deny, Bellingham having chosen to have a sexually explicit conversation with Wren Alcock on the ship's intercom during an anti-submarine warfare exercise. He was found guilty of conduct prejudicial to good order and naval discipline, fined £2,000 and demoted from his recent promotion to Lieutenant Commander.

When women first joined the US Navy elite group of aviators, they tried to outdo the chest-thumping of their male colleagues. 'They talked tough and weren't prissy about sex, and one would occasionally show her spirit by grabbing a male colleague's crotch and shouting "Package check!"' At a post-Gulf War party in Las Vegas, drunken navy aviators from Tailhook forced twenty-six of their female colleagues, including fourteen officers, to run a gauntlet of men who abused them. Roxane Baxter who became a Navy flier twenty years ago recalled, 'One of the things I learned when I came into the Navy is that they didn't expect you to cry as a naval officer. The ideal naval officer was a man. You had to be like a man. And that was the message that a lot of women got.' Women had to join in rituals that humiliated them, as junior males had done before them, but the misogynist dimension made them peculiarly offensive. The Navy Inspector-General's investigation revealed unpleasantnesses such as the 'leg-shaving booth (where a male lieutenant would give women a high shave and "make them see God") and the belly shot ritual (in which alcohol was lapped from women's navels)'. As part of the entertainment at one 'wetting-down', as the promotion ritual is known in US Navy jargon, a pair of exotic dancers danced nude, and one of the women then performed fellatio on one of the men.

Pat Schroeder on the House Armed Services Committee argued that, in view of the male pecking order, as long as women were excluded from combat they would not be treated with respect. In the Gulf War the tender *Acadia*, which supplied and repaired destroyers but was not technically a combat vessel, was one of the first Navy ships to deploy women. When the ship left its home port of San Diego for the Middle East, 360 women constituted about a quarter of the crew; by the time it returned thirty-six of those women had been evacuated because of pregnancy. In the general population of the same age range and among military women in peacetime, one in eleven will be pregnant at any one time; nevertheless the Love Boat, as it became known, was frequently cited by Schroeder's opponents as an argument against a gender-integrated fleet.

Taking her chance Schroeder slipped a provision repealing the combat ban into a military-budget-authorization bill, and it passed easily. According to Peter Boyer, writing in the *New*

Yorker, there was then a push to train women aviators to accompany the aircraft carriers *Eisenhower* and *Abraham Lincoln* on their next deployments. That meant rushing women to the head of the training line, causing great resentment among the men who were pushed aside. When Kara Hultgreen was killed in an attempt to land her F-14 Tomcat on the *Lincoln*, many Navy people questioned whether she had adequate training or experience. The cause of the accident was given out as engine failure when it was actually pilot error, and Hultgreen was accorded the honour of burial at Arlington Military Cemetery as a pioneer aviator.

American women serving in the Gulf were in greater danger of being sexually assaulted by our own troops than by the enemy.
US senator Dennis DeConcini

As the US Navy struggled to rehabilitate its reputation after Tailhook, the spotlight turned to the US Army. In November 1996 investigators into allegations of sexual abuse at the Aberdeen Proving Ground's Ordnance Center in Maryland found that more than thirty female recruits claimed to be victims of rape, forced sodomy and constant sexual harassment. One officer was accused of rape, conduct unbecoming an officer, obstruction of justice, adultery and an improper relationship with a recruit. One staff sergeant was accused of multiple rapes, forcible sodomy and adultery and another of improper relations with female trainees.

On 7 November 1996 the US Army established a confidential toll-free sexual harassment hotline; by the end of the year 977 complaints had been listed as worthy of investigation; 145 of these are full-scale criminal investigations. At Fort Leonard Wood Missouri a drill sergeant has been convicted on sexual misconduct charges. In April 1997 the Aberdeen cases came to trial, with surprising results. Four rape charges and fifty-four lesser charges against one of the staff sergeants were dropped and he admitted sixteen counts of consensual sex with female recruits instead. Five of the twenty-two women involved claimed that they had been bullied into blaming only black officers. Racism being as embedded in the US Army as sexism, white women were used as they have been historically, to accuse and ostracize black men.

The situation in Britain is at least as confused. The Army Training Regiment at Pirbright in Surrey has been shaken by a series of scandals. A seventeen-year-old female private told an internal investigation that five corporals had taken turns to have sex with her after she had been rendered drunk and incapable at a passing-out parade party. A week later a lieutenant was fined £1,600 for taunting recruits in sexual terms. A week after that a sergeant was committed for trial at the Old Bailey for raping a recruit while she was at a stopover camp with other recruits carrying out training manoeuvres on Exmoor.

In March 1997 the US Army appointed Claudia Kennedy its first female three-star general; at the press conference she admitted that she had suffered repeated harassment from the time of her joining up, when there was no redress. She went on to protect her new peer group by saying that in the brave new unisex army any complaint was promptly dealt with. Notwithstanding, on 16 December 1997, a Pentagon panel recommended that men and women should be trained separately, live apart and serve in separate units. How often, when and where women-only units would see active service is anybody's guess.

sorrow

Mary the mother of Jesus is sometimes represented as Our Lady of Dolours, her heart pierced with seven swords, and a tear permanently suspended from her eye. Her grief is her glory. Twenty centuries since she watched her Son's long agony on the cross female sorrow has lost all dignity. Nowadays the word 'sad' is used contemptuously. To call someone 'sad' is to reject her as a dim-witted loser. Feeling sadness oneself is thought, by women as well as men, to be a symptom of an illness and in need of treatment. In fact sadness is the matrix from which wit and irony spring; sadness is uncomfortable and creative, which is why consumer society cannot tolerate it.

The silence that surrounds issues of anger, pain, guilt, shame and even love and joy can become an 'everyday silence' that inevitably leads to disempowerment, disillusionment and distress.

Sally Berry, Clinical Director, Women's Therapy Centre

Consumer culture sells antidotes to sadness, happiness in edible form, soul-numbing comfort. In the 1970s Valium was the most prescribed drug in the US pharmacopoeia. Nowadays Prozac is prescribed by the bushel, even though its biochemical pathways are still a mystery.

There is no medical condition called sadness. Doctors who treat it have to call it something else, usually depression. Since 1955 there has been a five-fold increase in depressive illness in the US; 6 per cent of the population are expected to have an episode of clinical depression by the time they are twenty-four. For reasons that are anything but clear women are more likely to suffer than men. This year 17 per cent of British women, slightly more than one in six, will try to kill themselves before their twenty-fifth birthday. One kind of depression, sometimes called reactive depression, is a response to life events such as bereavement, job loss, divorce, rejection. Another is the result of low self-esteem. Other kinds of depression are described as endogenous or biological, caused by genes or by fluctuating levels in certain body chemicals, serotonin or oestrogen. Women are twice as likely as men to suffer all of them, if the numbers who seek help are any guide. Dr Hugh Koch, a chartered clinical psychologist, quotes a Camberwell study that found that 25 per cent of housewives were clinically depressed. Other clinicians say that about 70 per cent of cases go undiagnosed. An assessment of episodes of illness as reported to British GPs in 1980–1 found that for every eight men treated for 'neurotic depression', there were twenty-five women. This is rather higher than has been observed in other studies, but the ratio is never lower than two women for every man reporting depression. Two-thirds of all prescriptions for psychotropic drugs are made out for female patients.

Women's tendency to depression was thought to be the result of disruption of their hormone balance by events such as childbirth and menopause but, whenever the matter has been scientifically investigated, no association between depression and hormone levels could be demonstrated. Assessments of levels of depression in women of childbearing age show no significant difference between women who have just given birth and women who have not. The startling suggestion has even

---

Now she can cope . . . thanks to Butisol (Sodium butabarbital) 'daytime sedative' for everyday situational stress.

---

been made that post-partum depression is more likely to be caused by exhaustion and lack of sleep than by hormonal turmoil. As for menopausal depression or involutional melancholia, post-menopausal women are the least likely of all to be depressed. Even the time of the month cannot be blamed for women's tendency to depression. In a study of 1,300 adults in the San Francisco area, Susan Nolen-Hoeksma of the University of Michigan found no difference whatever in the occurrence of depressive episodes between women who were premenstrual and women who were not.

New thinking on sadness suggests that it is the result of depressed serotonin levels. Once again we have to consider Money's 'multivariate sequential determinism' and ask ourselves whether depressed serotonin is the root cause of depression or whether response to depressing situations is biochemically expressed as depressed serotonin. Studies in animals that live in hierarchies have shown that secretion of serotonin responds to changes in status. Subordinate vervet monkeys have low serotonin levels; when the dominant monkeys were removed from the group, the winner of the subsequent battle for dominance had much higher levels of serotonin than before. Successful human students have high serotonin levels; people of low status tend to have low serotonin levels. Alcohol temporarily raises serotonin levels; Ecstasy causes a flooding of serotonin and ultimately damages the serotonin receptors. Prozac is one of a group of drugs known as Selective Serotonin Uptake Inhibitors. Whether it is ethical to tinker with the serotonin levels of rational people so that they have altered reactions to unchanged circumstances is a question no doctor is going to ask. A GP who suggested that a patient weep her cares away would be considered a sadist. Weeping is as much a disease entity as any purulent discharge.

These days it's the exception . . . for women to live 'happily married, humdrum lives' . . . I'm an ordinary fifty-year-old grandmother. My brother died at birth, my mother had a nervous breakdown, my first husband never paid bills, so we did moonlight flits around the country. He died at forty, leaving me with two children; my son got in trouble with the law. My second husband is an alcoholic. I've suffered with depression and have had affairs – mainly to stay sane. My son doesn't contact me . . .

Letter to *Woman* magazine, March 1998

If women's sadness can be considered biochemical and constitutional we can treat it with medication. We can put women on Prozac and they will think that they are happy, even though they are not. Disturbed animals in the zoo are given Prozac too, which rather suggests that misery is a response to unbearable circumstances rather than constitutional. The caged tiger is being treated not for the misfortune of being a tiger but for the misfortune of being in a zoo; female depression could as likely be a consequence not of being female but of an inhuman environment.

Things are different from when Sylvia Plath graduated with the highest honours from Smith College and her mother expected her to work as a typist before she got married, but in the last twenty years women have had a lot more pressure with careers and families, and men have not picked up the slack ... The next phase of feminism is how to have families that work. The 1950s nuclear family needed to be thrown out, but we haven't replaced it very well. There are still so many lonely children who need a community or some kind of family life. It should be everybody's issue, not a feminist issue – but it is, because women, as usual, have to figure it out.

Women's lives have become more, not less, difficult. They are better lives, but they are harder. If it could be shown that women have reason to be sad, they might be spared the stigma of being mad. A woman who accepts the label of mentally ill gives up her right to autonomy, loses her confidence in her own judgement and her prestige among her peers. Yet surely it is the person who feels cheery in unbearable circumstances who is irrational.

For years feminists have fought the good fight against the too frequent diagnosis of suffering women as mad or neurotic. Again and again they point out that women are disadvantaged in education, employment, opportunities, power and prestige, that the drudgery of cooking, cleaning and caring for children, the frail and the elderly is exhausting, that the solution lies not in medicating women or pathologizing distress but in changing the system. If the system is borne up by women nothing should be easier than for women to change it. We know that women are changing rapidly. Women no longer feel that they have to stay in unhappy relationships or that they have to bear children against their will. As more and more women work outside the home, as more and more women walk out of oppressive marriages, we might expect the quantum of female malaise to diminish. The evidence seems to be that it is getting worse. Thirty years ago we heard nothing about panic attacks, or anorexia or self-mutilation. Now the ikons of female suffering are all around us; the image of the battered woman is high fashion. The models reeling down the catwalks are stick thin, their faces cavernous and bruised, their hair matted. Scars and bruises are conspicuously worn. Hollow-eyed model girls seem to be saying, 'If I am to be I must hurt.' Lacking others prepared to injure them, it seems, they will hurt themselves.

Feminists have told and retold the story of misogyny, of male constructions of the female as unstable, irrational, malicious, subversive, revolting and so forth, as a way of explaining women's low self-image or lack of self-esteem. While there can be no doubt that over the centuries scholars and gentlemen have given free reign to their dislike of women, very few women would have been aware of what they were up to. Until the twentieth century women were excluded from the communities where such matters were discussed. The misogynist discourse usually, though by no means always, knew itself to be trans-gressive, because it originated in an attack upon the hallowed figure of the mother, the only female with whom celibate scholars had been intimate. Though women would have occasionally witnessed orgies of misogyny, witch-hunts and - trials for example, they were not in a position to extrapolate general principles from these, nor is it clear how they would have internalized anti-feminist generalizations to the detriment of their own self-image, as long as they were excluded from the culture of the male elite. The pre-literate woman lived within a self-validating female culture that was to be obliterated by the authority of the printed text. It is not until women learn to read that they internalize the masculine schema. When women become literate they are brought up sharply against the prevailing misogynies. They will only accept them if they are in the process of swallowing the masculinist cultural package of which they are a part.

When women, by one shift or another, wormed their way into institutions of higher learning, there were those who said that the experience would do them nothing but harm. The women, innocent perhaps of the real extent of woman hatred that festered within the groves of academe, stoutly asserted that their brains were strong enough to withstand the stresses and strains of study. In the very struggle to show that they were

What does the woman do when she realizes her father/husband/boss is a prime mover in her misery? Leave him? Change him? Most women have in reality little power in their lives and cannot simply leave the luxury of the consulting room and change their worlds.

Jane Ussher, 1991

equal to their self-imposed task, they imbibed the pernicious knowledge of men's fear and loathing. For the first time ladies, who had always been addressed with parodic courtesy, encountered the abuse that was the other side of the coin. The only way to progress in their chosen avocations was to learn with exemplary thoroughness what the senior males had unwillingly to teach them. Part of what they learnt was their own otherness. This process is far from complete.

Every woman who breaks into a previously male domain has to learn the same bitter lesson all over again. It would matter less that she discovers that men hate her if she did not love them and need to be loved by them. When she learns over many months that they will *never* admit her to true comradeship and that, whether she permits sexual familiarities or not, they will despise her, she is devastated. Men practise cruelty and discrimination in their relations with other men, as they jockey for positions in the pecking order and single out scapegoats to gang up on, but they cannot annihilate each other as easily as they can women. We can see in the psychiatric disorders that afflict the women who are driven out of the male enclaves of the police, the army, the navy, the fire brigade, what it is that makes women crazy-sad. It is not so much that men won't let us into the masculine race, it's that we want so much to join, and we take so much damage to our self-esteem before realizing that the situation is hopeless.

When we go in search of succour and consolation we find that people who do not know us know more about our lives than we do.

A woman who is unhappy, angry and withdrawn may be told by a psychiatrist that her hormones are in a flux, by a psychologist that her cognitions are faulty, by a sociologist that her environment is responsible, or by a psychoanalytic therapist that she is repressing her unconscious desires.

Or by a geneticist that it is in her genes. Or by a Freudian that she is maddened by penis envy. Any plan she might have of getting her life back under control is already scuttled.

To subvert the process we need to argue, not only that sadness is an appropriate reaction to afflicting circumstances, but that sadness is part of who women are and how they react to things. Women can bear pain better than men; that we can live with pain without indulging in orgies of self-pity and resentment is one of our strengths. In a poisoned world that becomes crueller and more unjust every day, sorrow may be dignified and rational. If the women of the tyrant nations do not grieve for the crimes of those nations, who will? We cannot enjoy the right to happiness until we have liberated sorrow; we cannot love the world until and unless we are conscious of losing it.

The strength of our feelings is one of the things about women that most unnerve men. They call our passionateness disparaging names, hysteria, lability, sentimentality, *sloppiness*. Now we are expected to apologize when we weep even if we are telling about the death of a child. When tears begin to flow you are said to have 'broken down', as if your personality was melting. Less than a hundred years ago when a woman wept other women would weep with her. Nowadays to be seen weeping is more embarrassing than being seen naked. You have to do it in a private place, in the toilet, in the car, in the dark, in

you say to me 'i make you happy'. you know you make me sad. you know that although my smile reaches from ear to ear, you make me sad. you know that although you make me fall on the floor i'm laughing so hard you make me sad. you know that because, no matter what my face is doing, what noise i am making, what i am saying, my eyes are sad. my eyes are filled with tears. that i may be smiling or laughing or talking, but at the same time i am crying. and you know you are the reason why.

Vique Martin, *Simba* 8

the cinema. Private as our vice of grieving is, it has its own tradition. Quentin Crisp has quaintly said that the most successful movies of the great age of cinema were made for a middle-aged woman with a broken heart. Millions of middle-aged women went to see them, over and over again, and very possibly all their hearts were broken. Why do women like weepies, why do they feel better after a good cry, if the heart is not overcharged? Women seek relief in tears where men seek relief in masturbation, which may be a distinction to be valued.

Women grow to be emotional athletes on a diet of rejection. As long as they take that rejection seriously, and continue to shriek their desolation, they are not diminished by it. Refusing to get over it is women's revenge. When Elizabeth Smart wrote her super-weepie *By Grand Central Station I Sat Down and Wept* she built herself into a far more significant person than the man who betrayed her. The heroic sorrower begins by saying, 'You do not love me as I love you', proceeds to saying, 'You did not love me as I loved you' and ends by saying, 'You could never love me as I loved you'. Male supremacy dictates an answer in the affirmative: 'You are quite right. It would be mad to love you as you love me. Keep taking the pills.'

> The unhappiness of many women would be eliminated if their men provided them with the same nurturance they offer them . . .
>
> Marilyn French, 1978

Women's reasons for sadness are not to be belittled or argued away, nor are they materially altered by piecemeal changes in economic and social circumstances. A woman's sadness derives from her powerlessness. Her powerlessness renders her vulnerable to a whole series of misfortunes that press on her without end. Her duty is, she learns daily from a thousand sources, to attract, that is, to be found attractive by others whose responses she cannot dictate. She hopes that it will be sufficient to be a nice person, a good girl, and she finds that this is not enough. She works hard, does well at school, gains a reputation for being clever and is liked only by her teachers. She is convinced that she is not beautiful, by the standards and stereotypes that can be seen on every side. Even if she is beautiful, she will not be so for long. If she has a measure of success in attracting, when age marks her she is doomed to lose her winnings and remain bereft. Nowadays women in their teens already feel that their maturing body is too matronly and expect rejection. The failure of the pair bond equals failure in everything. The woman who is never mated must grieve. If she is mated and left, she remains forlorn. The maintenance of the pair bond too often requires the gradual obliteration of her individual self. 'I want to make him happy,' she says, unaware that if he is not happy it has less to do with her than with any of the other factors in his life. If she tries to treat men as men treat women she toughens herself and tarnishes her self-image. If she bears no child, she is disappointed; if she bears a child she is sentenced to long periods of confinement at home with that child and sole responsibility for any problems that child may face. When it grows up she is not entitled to remain in close contact with it and must mourn its loss. If she terminates a pregnancy she must shoulder that grief too and struggle on. She may find satisfaction in her life's work, if she is so lucky as to have work worth doing, but she is likely to be left with nothing but that work. Poverty, drudgery and loneliness are valid reasons for sadness; beyond and beneath, far outreaching them all, is unrequited love. Love of the father, love of the partner, love of the child, all remain for the vast majority of women unrequited. A woman's beloveds are the centre of her life; she must agree to remain far from the centre of theirs. So desolate does she feel sometimes, that her own act of disinterested kindness to a stranger can move her to tears.

If we can agree that sadness is rational and that strong feelings are a kind of power in themselves, we should consider the possibility of deploying grief as a subversive force. If a woman bursts into a restaurant and stands over the table where her ex-lover is dining with his new flame and sobs and rails, we realize that her action is aggressive and powerfully disconcerting. The sobbing woman is out of order, embarrassing, unreasonable. We remember Princess Diana causing grim

> I want to be the girl with the most cake
> I love him so much it just turns to hate
> I fake it so real I am beyond fake
> Some day you will ache like I ache
>
> Courtney Love

foreboding at the Palace by avowing that she would not go quietly. When feminists protested against the Vietnam War they joined in the men's chants. 'Hey! Hey! LBJ! How many kids did ya kill today?' The words were inflammatory; the style was confrontational. The demonstrators invited retaliation and got it, with sticks and clubs and arrests. If women had mourned aloud, if they had wailed and beaten their breasts until tears drowned the wind, the police would have found it all but impossible to beat up on them. If the next time our governments propose to make war on a helpless civilian population we were to uncover our grief and guilt instead of our anger, how much difference might we make? If millions of people can weep uncontrollably for days on end about the death in his bed of an Asian dictator, we should be able to manage mourning aloud for a day or two about the violent deaths of thousands of women and children. Four out of five of the people whose grief for Princess Diana awed the world were women. Even the most hard-boiled of the lifestyle feminists realized that this thunderous explosion of grief was a female phenomenon and bickered in the media for weeks about whether the Princess had actually deserved it (as if any individual could actually have deserved it). The mourners said over and over, 'She was one of us. She identified with us'; it does not take a post-graduate degree in psychology to grasp that what they were saying was that they identified with her. Her suffering, as a wife disliked and scorned, as a lover betrayed and humiliated, was theirs. Her death gave mute women licence to keen and sob for their own pain. The British authorities are still reeling from the convulsion that contorted the whole country in August 1997 and has not spent its force yet. The Labour government is now moving to cloak its unchanged masculinist priorities beneath a gentler, more caring style of operation. For thirty years we have tried to run the feminist movement on women's rage but it was never present in sufficient quantities to drive us forward. If we can find ways of harvesting the energy in women's oceanic grief we shall move mountains.

sex

Sex at the end of the century is no longer a matter of intercourse. The sex of the millennium is pornography. Pornography is the sexuality of the information revolution, elaborated to achieve all the staggering impact of which the megamedia are capable, projecting the images of the best-known sex objects as far as distant planets in galaxies unknown. Tommy Lee videoed his conjugal relations with Pamela

> It's New Year's Eve, 1999. All the television networks have agreed to let me produce 'orgasms across America'. Every TV screen will be showing high-tech fine-art porn created by the best talent this country has to offer. At the stroke of midnight the entire population will be masturbating to orgasm for World Peace.
>
> Betty Dodson, *Sex for One: the joys of self-loving*

Anderson because he was more deeply in love with pornography than with her. He was signalling his fellowship with all the other men who spill their seed on the famously, preposterously erotic image of his abused wife. Women are not the point of pornography. Pornography is the flight from woman, men's denial of sex as a medium of communication, their denial of sex as the basis for a relationship, their rejection of fatherhood, their perpetual incontinent adolescence. The victims of pornography are men not women. Pornography makes men leaky vessels, and undoes the principal male virtue of continence. As men's real power dwindles, pornography is their refuge. Fear of commitment is inseparable from indulgence in pornography. Masturbation is easy; relationships are difficult. Relationships interfere with masturbation.

Cecil Lewis, who 'fought the Red Baron, wrote a bestseller, won an Oscar, saw the last Manchu emperor and still found time to seduce 500 women', died as old as the century in 1997. Perhaps we should be glad that we shall not see his like again, but the substitution of masturbation for seduction means even more loneliness for heterosexual women, loneliness that is keenest within the embrace of a lover.

Techniques of masturbation include 'the Slow Single Stroke, the Fast Single Stroke, the Slow Two-Hand Stroke, the Fast Two-Hand Stroke, the Cupped Hand, the Finger Stroke, the Wrist Pump, the Slap, the Beat, the Rub, the Squeeze Stroke, the Open-Hand Stroke, and the Vaginal Simulator Stroke'.

Susan Bakos, *Sexational Secrets*

Masturbation, which a man begins as soon as gonadal activity intensifies at adolescence, when it may take place several or more times a day, continues with gradually diminishing frequency all his life. At the beginning of the twentieth century masturbation was thought to debilitate an individual and frequent masturbation to be pathological. At the end of the century, though the word 'wanker' is still contemptuous and implies that an individual is feeble and worthless, masturbation carries no stigma. Among the effects of the poet Philip Larkin at his death was found a considerable collection of pornographic magazines which as the poet of solitary sex he had seen no need to destroy. At the end of the century masturbation is thought to be good for males and females alike, though there is no comparison between women's level of interest in masturbation and men's. According to Anne Hooper, 'Most women need to learn to masturbate.' No man does. An entire publishing industry has been built on men's insatiable appetite for aids to masturbation. The ten bestselling British porn magazines sell about two million copies a month, bringing in a yearly total of about £45 million. The American magazines *Playboy* and *Penthouse* sell about ten million copies worldwide each month.

The lads' magazine *loaded* for January 1997 sampled thirty-eight magazines, total cost £120.56, in search of 'page by page reliable porn'. The best were 'cheap, nasty and really filthy, great!'; the worst featured older women, women on the toilet, women with moustaches, 'girls who look like your best mate's bird's friend', or 'a bucketful of pigs'. The intrusion of another man into the imagery was enough to put them off: 'couldn't bang one out over this' was the verdict in such cases. Merchandising impersonal sexual stimuli is big business. The newspapers *Sport*, *Sunday Sport* and their associated titles are worth close to £500 million. Paul Raymond of the Soho sex revues, proprietor of the porn monthlies *Escort*, *Mayfair*, *Men Only*, *Club*, *Razzle* and *Mensworld*, is supposed to be worth something like £350 million. To the soft-porn magazines *Penthouse*, *Knave*, *Fiesta*, *Club* and *Hustler* that sell about half a million copies a month must be added niche magazines like *Big and Fat and Forty Plus* that sell about 10,000 per month. Models for these magazines are paid about £300 a session, photographers between £1,000 to £2,000.

As part of its endless crusade to bring men and women to

simultaneous orgasm, *Cosmopolitan* magazine for January 1997 invited men to explain their sexuality. Sean Thomas boasted that 'Male lust is like a great river crashing down to the sea – put an obstacle in its path and it will merely find another route.'

> The whole idea of sexy Chinese girls wearing tight superhero costumes, fighting, then having sex is possibly the finest development a cinema man could hope for.
>
> Jonathan Ross, 1997

It is one of the commonplaces of pornography grossly to exaggerate the volume of ejaculation. Male sexuality is actually more like a sluggish trickle meandering across a delta, dissipating its force in trillions of channels; twentieth-century men are like De Sade's jaded aristocrats, so sated with sexual imagery that they must behold ever more bizarre and extravagant displays before they can achieve potency. Mark explained to *Cosmopolitan*, 'When I see a perfect babe on the street, I am overwhelmed. I know I'll never be able to have her so I get depressed and then usually go and masturbate to get rid of the sadness. I'm not sure women really understand this – why men like to masturbate so much.' There is a little bird that says that Mark does not know why he masturbates so much either; if masturbation was more effective in driving away grief than intensifying loneliness funerals would be orgies of jerking off.

The acceptance and promotion of men's auto-erotic activity means that men are more likely to dispense with the services of actual women who are more demanding than their fantasy partners and interfere with their pleasure. Men whose fantasies are replete with exaggerated imagery of synthetic womanhood are likely to respond badly to the realities of actual female bodies. Every heterosexual woman shares her partner with the fantasy females of commercial pornography out of which her partner's sexual imagery has been assembled. If she cannot drive out her partner's fantasy fucks she might as well impersonate them. The success of the Anne Summers Party Plan, which merchandises split-crotch panties, cupless basques, PVC

A boy who claims not to masturbate is lying. All boys do it and there's no reason why they shouldn't. Most teenage boys masturbate anything between about one to five times a day. Fact!

Bliss magazine, February 1997

---

thongs, peephole bras, whips, shackles, gags, slave leashes and collars, French maid, schoolgirl and nurses' outfits to chaste suburban wives in their own homes, represents women's final capitulation to their partners' reliance on commercial pornography. The Anne Summers Party Plan was dreamed up by Jacqueline Gold, after Gold International took over the Anne Summers sex shops when the original proprietors had gone into voluntary liquidation. Gold International was built up on the proceeds of pornographic magazine publishing and telephone sex lines; the company holds a 50 per cent stake in the newspapers *Sport* and the *Sunday Sport*.

People who come to know their pleasure by masturbation will replicate the most successful combinations of mental images and physical action at the very time when they are supposed to be most intimate with another person. The great appeal of blow-jobs is that the real and present woman is least able to interpose her personhood on the interaction when her face is impaled on the penis. In some British circles women are now expected to perform fellatio on demand. British men are not expected to return the favour and seldom do. As far as sex is concerned both equality and liberation are further off than ever. Masturbation is as easy for women as it is for men but they are simply less interested in it; most women still need or think they need actual contact with real men in order to feel any significant amount of pleasurable tension and subsequent release. As long as women need relationships with real men more than men need relationships with real women, women are at a disadvantage in sexual negotiations.

After thirty years of feminist struggle there is vastly more pornography disseminated more widely than ever before. To mountains of print have been added pinnacles of video; in the United States in 1997 rentals from porn videos were worth $4.2 billion. Exponentially reproducing pornographic images are populating cyberspace. At the end of 1997 the newsagency chain W. H. Smith announced that it was withdrawing from sale some of the oldest established soft porn mags because of falling sales. A good deal of what used to be available only in dedicated magazines is now to be seen in general circulation magazines while, for the man with more specific needs, television channels like the Playboy Channel, the Adult Channel and Television X supply pornography twenty-four hours a day; much more is available on satellite cable channels. According to the *US News and World Report*:

> In 1996 Americans spent more than $8 billion on hard-core videos, peep shows, live sex acts, adult cable programming, sexual vices, computer porn and sex magazines – an amount much larger than Hollywood's domestic box office receipts and larger than all the revenues generated by rock and country music recordings. Americans now spend more money at strip clubs than at Broadway, off-Broadway, regional and non-profit theaters, at the opera, the ballet, and jazz and classical music performances – combined.

For 'Americans' read 'American men aged between seventeen and forty-five'. In the early Seventies the market was worth at most $8 million or so. In 1997 8,000 hard-core videos were released in the US; 25,000 stores rent and sell hard-core videos.

The real action however is on the Internet where the commonest key-words are 'sex' and 'pornography'. An ever-increasing number of websites cater for all tastes, including tastes for sex with children and animals. *Guardian* columnist Mark Lawson reported that by the time he logged off on 14 February 1997, one sex-based website had been visited 608,059 times. The bi-monthly Xnet – 'Everything men want – direct from the Net' – carries addresses for more than 500 porno-graphic websites, as well as CD-roms offering hundreds more links to sites.

Maybe the tango is better than sex.

Sally Potter

The digital videocamera no sooner appeared on the market than men were using it to send live footage of themselves masturbating into cyberspace to impress the children whom they were already importuning by e-mail. Among the earliest e-mail messages were many of the kind that Alan Paul Barlow used to send to teenage girls: 'I'm feeling really horny – I think Oscar is making a statement. We both want you very much. I'm thinking about you, & he's thinking about Love Bunny and tingling like mad.' An English priest amassed so many paedophile fantasies that he built a series of computers to store them in; by the time he was arrested he had accumulated a data-base fifteen times the size of the *Encyclopaedia Britannica*.

The conventional notion is that because men are continually manufacturing sperm they constantly accumulate sexual tension which generates an endless succession of intrusive erotic fantasies which become more insistent until some action is performed to dispel them. This pseudo–physiological explanation of masculine genital obsession is simply an excuse for men's deliberate entertainment of fantasies which they endlessly elaborate in search of more effective stimuli. Men work on their fantasies, growing them on a sumptuous diet of pornography in every available medium. They wilfully construct the elaborate fantasy edifice that towers in their minds and enjoy exploring it. The lengths to which they will go in search of genital stimulus vary from the pathetic to the bizarre to the criminal. The nadir of Seventies nerd-sex was a flotilla of cases of men reporting at casualty departments of British hospitals with badly lacerated penises: curiously all of these men had been vacuum-cleaning in the nude and their penises had been inadvertently sucked into the Hoover Dustette. Most bizarre are the cases of auto-strangulation in which men intending to half-hang themselves in search of brain-sucking orgasms hang themselves in earnest. His family must still blush for the memory of British MP Stephen Milligan found dead on his kitchen table, dressed only in stockings and suspender belt, an orange in his mouth and a polythene bag over his head. Of the thirty known paraphilias, or 'perversions' as they used to be known, none is the speciality of women though, under pressure from the competition, they are learning to fake them.

The man who uses the Internet to prey on children believes that the children are knowing, willing participants in his fantasy, as does the man who expects his adult partner to play out the roles he casts her in in his fantasy, as schoolgirl, nun, whore, whatever. A partner who asks a woman to dress up is well within his rights. A woman who considers herself sexually sophisticated has to be prepared to be all things to one man. There is no suggestion that the man is simply masturbating, using a woman much as Colin Laskey, Roland Jaggard and Anthony Brown used 'hot wax, sandpaper, fish hooks and needles . . . spiked belts, stinging nettles and a cat o'nine tails'. Nor is it suggested that women owe it to themselves not to let themselves be used as sex aids. Marriage counsellors have been known to encourage couples having sexual difficulties to look at pornographic magazines and videos together, though it is not the woman who will be turned on by such visual stimuli.

'Sexuality,' according to Courtney Love, 'is the most subversive thing.' She proved it by pulling a breast out of her stage

> A woman is like a sponge. You pour pleasure in the top and she keeps sucking it up until it drips out the bottom, but she still absorbs more. They can never get enough. I'm very jealous of women's ability to do that.
>
> Joel Ryan, Heaven on Earth Escorts

costume and shouting, 'See, I've got my tit out!' at a time when exposed tits could be seen by the hour on even the softest of the TV porn channels. Jaundiced observers might suspect that Love is, or was, more interested in creating a sensation by any means possible than she is in subverting the system that has made her rich. P. J. Harvey too believes that hanging her breasts out is a radical act, whether on her first album or on the cover of *New Musical Express*. The sexual display of Harvey and Love is considered to be different from Page 3 stuff because it is not enforced capitulation to the male gaze but their own raunchy exhibitionism, of a piece with talking loud and dirty, with the aim of intimidating men rather than turning them on. This would be more believable if the overwhelming impression projected by Love clones were not one of undemanding availability, bodies barely hidden by torn slips, bed-tousled bleached hair with dark roots, scars, cuts, tattoos and a welter of smeared cosmetics, as if they had just been gang-raped by the men they are pretending to intimidate. If women bought their records one would feel less dubiousness about their feminist credentials. As it is boys vastly outnumber girls as buyers of indie rock, grunge rock, rock/blues, etc., the girl bands included.

Sexuality might be the most subversive thing, but female sexual display, even the most grotesque, is pure conformism.

Love and Harvey might both be surprised to learn that a quarter of a century ago, when genital display was not an everyday phenomenon, one of the old feminists they deplore tried the same tactic. Believing, as Courtney Love does, that there is

> When I was fourteen, it was considered the hallmark of feminine success and popularity to be able to perform the perfect blow job.
>
> Naomi Wolf, 1997

nothing more subversive than sexuality, she decided to defy the male gaze not by uncovering her breasts, which is the female display that males find least intimidating, but by displaying her vagina and her anus. There were historical precedents for this kind of female protest. When Maheude wanted to show her utter contempt for the oppressors of the poor in Zola's *Germinal*, she turned her back, parted her legs, stooped and threw her skirts over her head, displaying her split buttocks, as if to say, 'You can kiss my big, fat, smelly arse!' However wild the disorderly scenes engineered by girl rock bands in the late twentieth century, they pale into insignificance in comparison with the riotous bare-ass displays of the midinettes of Paris who danced the original can-can.

The intention of the twentieth-century feminist was at one stroke to demystify the entire female body, which at that stage was being revealed piecemeal in the public prints. The display was less hostile than the girl riots of today are meant to be. For shock value it was probably on a par with Donita Sparks's pulling a tampon out of her vagina and flinging it into the audience when L7 was on stage at the Reading Festival of 1992.

What the 'early feminist' learnt from the pointless surrender of her own privacy is that female genital display is a weapon that can only inflict injury on the displayer. Though male genital exposure frightens women, female genital exposure, whether intended to be hostile or alluring, reinforces men's sense of their own superiority. As long as men think of women's bodies as commodities offered for their consumption, there is no liberation to be had either in taking clothes off or in keeping bodies covered. There has been an attempt to encourage women to take the same attitude, by including images of partly clad pop stars and footballers in girls' and women's magazines, but there is no comparison whatever between these and the plethora of images of mostly anonymous women juggling huge breasts and pouting wetly at the camera in men's masturbation mags.

In the 1970s a veritable mythology of female orgasm developed, from the wondrous G-spots, which had only to be touched to set off deep and shuddering orgasms, to the belief that the true, the deep, the genuine female orgasm was the most sensational and uplifting experience any human is capable of, enough in itself to explain why so few women bother climbing Mount Everest. If you could get the biggest thrill of all with your vibrator without even stirring from your warm bed, who would bother toiling up a freezing mountain for weeks on end? The mythology of the female orgasm could be considered the last ideological push of the heterosexual establishment. If only women could have been endowed with a sexual response that exactly mirrored the male experience of ejaculation and

---

Woman has sex organs just about everywhere. She experiences pleasure almost everywhere.

Luce Irigaray, 1986

---

orgasm, the continuing cohabitation of the sexes might have kept its position as the dominant lifestyle. Nothing, however, could disguise the fact that, where male response tended to the mechanical, female response continued to manifest as unpredictable. Only radical lesbians were able to handle the idea that female sexuality might not be symmetrical with male sexuality and that reconstructing it to fit might result in a net loss of delight.

Some laconic remarks by heterosexual Lucretia Stewart in *Punch* of all places suggest that this penny might be about to drop:

> Personally, I've always thought it was possible to exaggerate the importance of orgasm, believing that in many cases it's better to travel hopefully than to arrive. As any fool knows, the best stage of a love affair is the early stages, when you are in a state of constant, frenzied, unsatisfied desire. Once a man knows how to satisfy you there is no mystery, and within lie the seeds of boredom.

A man who knows which buttons to press to get his partner to come and dutifully presses them in every sexual encounter is seeking to produce in his partner stereotyped orgasms rather like his own. Clearly these are not what women want, or the sway of the vibrator would be far greater than it is.

Nobody nowadays would question the notion that sex is good for you. Sex is not just good for you, it is absolutely essential to good health. Here is a 'specialist' advising menopausal women: 'Staying sexually active is a must. Regular sex or masturbation stimulates the blood flow into the vaginal area, reducing dryness. The muscle contractions during orgasm promote the health of the vagina.' Ergo, if you haven't got a partner or your partner isn't interested, you have to have sex with yourself. Going without could lead to a sick vagina. A great many menopausal women have no partner on hand; some have never had a partner at all. If they have not masturbated regularly their vaginas are presumably all sick as parrots. Lack of interest in masturbation is an illness in itself, to be treated by investing in

commercial pornography. If you fall asleep during masturbation, which tends to become a rather lengthier business as you
get older, you are clearly in a truly pitiable condition. Those of
us who experienced the waning of desire as a liberation are
beyond redemption. 'Lack of sex drive' is now a symptom as
telling as sleeplessness. Even old people will be considered in
poor health if they have no sex drive and if, having sex drive,
they are unable to put it into action. People in old people's
homes are now encouraged to get it on.

In 1997 *American Demographics* published the results of an
analysis of sexual behaviour based on the General Household
Survey of 10,000 adults. About one in five of them had not had
sex at all in the previous year and only one person in twenty had
sex at least three times a week. About 15 per cent of them
accounted for 50 per cent of the sexual activity. One of the
authors of the report, Geoffrey Godber of Penn State
University, remarked thoughtfully, 'It appears to everyone that
we are a hypersexual society. In reality, people stay home a lot
by themselves.' If he had been a typical product of graduate
school he would not himself have been having sex more than
once a week, according to his own research.

> This is my favourite vibrator, the Pocket Rocket. Use it when
> you're in a traffic jam.
>
> Ava Cadell, sexologist

If we are prepared to accept that women's relationship with
babies might be erotic without being genital, we have also to
countenance the idea that men and women are actually sexually
incompatible. This may not always have been the case; men,
like women, start life as babies with a generalized whole body
response to caresses. Both baby boys and baby girls make love
to their mothers, with eye contact, lip contact and whole body

response and baby boys don't get erections while they are doing it. Marcuse's arguments about the making of the one-dimensional man are now out of fashion, but there can be little doubt that men's bodies are, as it were, de-eroticized during

> I have come to believe ... that female biology – the diffuse intense sensuality radiating out from the clitoris, breasts, uterus, vagina; the lunar cycles of menstruation; the gestation and friction of life which can take place in the female body – has far more radical implications than we have yet come to appreciate.
>
> Adrienne Rich, 1977

the process of masculinization, so that the penis is the only sanctioned erogenous zone. That this process fails fairly often is obvious; many men retain erotic interest in being penetrated rather than or as well as penetrating, and find themselves responding in unexpected ways to stimulation of parts of the body far from the penis. Absence of erection is not necessarily absence of arousal but in our society it is always interpreted as such, because in sex, as in everything else, we have superimposed a performance ethic. Even in this we may be rescued by our children, who have developed their own sexual culture. Among Los Angeles high school students 10 per cent of those who describe themselves as 'still virgins' have engaged in oral sex, with girls as likely as boys to be getting the pleasure. Today Los Angeles, tomorrow the world? Will sex scenes in blockbuster movies start showing cunnilingus instead of the missionary position? That really would be radical.

love

mothers

It may be that persecution of mothers is a permanent feature of patriarchal societies, but at the end of the millennium contempt for the mother seems to have assumed a new dimension. At Wigstock, New York's annual gay extravaganza, in Tompkins Square Park in 1993, a huge Australian man took the stage.

Accompanied by a blaring cover of the Beatles' 'All You Need Is Love', he strode forth in a knee-length skirt, a bulging floral print jacket, and a menacing nylon mask that zipped up the back and had openings for his eyes and mouth. Makeup had been applied directly to the mask; his lips were rendered huge, clown-like. White cotton tights and dark sensible shoes with a small heel completed the look . . .

After a minute or two, half singing, half shrieking into a microphone, he clambered up on to a table set up in front of the enormous Wigstock scrim of candy-coloured images of girls – or rather boys as girls. Facing the audience he lay back on the table, screaming and moaning, as if he were going into labor. He then parted his legs and a human figure began to emerge from between them – a nude woman, slathered in 'blood', sausage links and slime . . . the sight of her crawling from between Bowery's legs was heart-stopping.

Mothers bear children in pain, feed them from their bodies, cherish and nourish and prepare to lose them. The old way of depriving the mother was to remove her boys to the masculine establishment, the men's house, the boarding-school, the mine, the army, the bank, the factory, and her girls to the families of the men they married. Variations of this pattern are virtually universal in human societies where mother-right struggles against father-right for power over children. When sons empower a mother, and bring daughters-in-law to her household, she may expect rewards for her long service and wield a measure of influence. Where the only family is the nuclear family mothers have few prospects. Instead of growing, their households will shrink; if their children prosper, the mothers will have no claim on that prosperity. 'Mother' is not a career option; the woman who gave her all to mothering has to get in shape, find a job, and keep young and beautiful if she wants to be loved. 'Motherly' is a word for people who are frumpish and suffocating, people who wear cotton hose and shoes with a small heel.

What or who is the greatest love of your life?
My son, Gabe.

Interview with Joan Baez, 1998

Among Pirandello's *Six Characters in Search of an Author*, written in 1921, is a mother, wearing a fixed mask of *dolore*, that is, pain *and* sorrow, with waxen tears fixed in the hollows of her eye-sockets and along her cheeks. Her emotional intensity is experienced by the other characters as a tyranny from which they must escape if they are to survive. Mothers are a soft target; Pirandello was much praised for his insight into the stifling dynamic of the traditional family. At the same time the accepted ideal of feminine beauty became boyishly slim and hipless, the broad hips and full bosom of maternity as monstrous as motherhood itself. Femininity has remained slim and virginal ever since. Women are suffered still to bear children, but they are not permitted to show any sign of their maternal function. After bearing a child they have to 'regain their figures' at all costs as soon as possible. The mothers in TV commercials advertising 'disposable' nappies are all as lean as whippets and heft bonny boy babies who weigh half as much as they do.

English literature had never interested itself in mothers or motherhood; vilification of mothers is a recurrent theme whether the writer is Jane Austen, George Eliot or Charles Dickens. The only good mother was a mother who died young, leaving a shining after-image against which all other mothering figures could be measured and found wanting. Although male writers did not shrink from describing the throes of childbirth and even childless D. H. Lawrence considered himself qualified to describe maternal feelings in proliferating detail, until recently women have written little or nothing about the emotional cataclysm of becoming a mother. The experience of falling desperately in love with one's baby is by no means universal but it is an occupational hazard for any woman giving birth. Most of the women who find themselves engulfed in the emotional tumult of motherhood are astonished by the intensity of the bliss that suddenly invades them and the keenness of the anguish they feel when their child is in pain or trouble. Labour is the hardest work any human being is ever called upon to do, but it comes to an end and is sooner or later forgotten. The condition of motherhood is never over, never forgotten. Once a woman has a child her capacity for suffering widens and deepens beyond anything she could ever have imagined.

Whether her relations with her children are good or bad, whether the children turn out well or ill, they will cause her pain, because she is so much less important to them than they are to her. There are some societies where this is understood and women are treated with special respect because of it, but not one of them is Anglo-Saxon. English people sneer at the Italians for being ruled by their mothers; having to go to *la mamma*'s house for dinner every other Sunday, capitulating to her need to see her children, to be consulted, to be respected, to be loved, is seen as pitiably backward.

> But my lost woman evermore snaps
> From somewhere else: 'You did not love me.
> I sacrificed too much perhaps,
> I showed you the way to rise above me
> And you took it. You are the ghost
> With the bat-voice, my dear. I am not lost.'
>
> Patricia Beer, 'The Lost Woman'

Every night the television news brings us images of the suffering mother which we hardly register for what they are. Whether she is the African refugee with her collapsed infant in her arms or the white-haired Chechen woman searching the streets for a body or the Palestinian whose son has fallen foul of the Israeli army or the Iraqi sitting by her dying child's hospital bed, she is a mother and her suffering has the extra dimension of a mother's pain. Many of the women who will die of hypothermia in Britain in a harsh winter are mothers but that entitles them to nothing.

Motherhood is regarded now as a sort of personal indulgence. Cracker-barrel psychologists tell us that mothers become mothers out of carelessness or selfishness or narcissism or because they want something to love. Historically societies have nurtured and promoted the mother–child bond. In village

India and Pakistan the new mother is still kept away from strangers, in a calm and lazy place, in close contact with her baby's body, secure in the certainty that the arrival of the new baby brought joy to everyone around her. To mark her new status and prestige she is dressed in new clothing, given new jewellery, called by a new name, feasted and fêted. In such societies girls learn mothering from their earliest years, usually by mothering their brothers and sisters. Universal induction of females into motherhood no longer prevailed in western society when *The Female Eunuch* was written. In the years that followed, population panic reduced still further societal demand for children, who were seen no longer as assets and delights in themselves but as a drain on resources and a clog on life's pleasures. Mothers and babies are not welcome in adult society, in cinemas, theatres, restaurants, shops or buses. The quality of a working woman's life takes a nose-dive when she has a baby; examples on all sides show her more plainly than words that the foreseeable future is composed of equal parts of worry, guilt and exhaustion. Such dissuasives are as nothing before the implacable desire of some women to enter the passionate world of motherhood.

Like a passionate affair that ends and gets redefined as a fluke, a mother also learns to forget the erotic bond she once had with her baby – a perfect intimacy that may never be recaptured.

Marni Jackson, *The Mother Zone*

Everyone knows that birthing is a dangerous time for a woman but most of the professional attention around her is concentrated upon the child being born. Everything necessary will be done for the child no matter how premature, how small or how sick but, if the mother becomes one of the 3,000 women each year who will suffer severe post-natal illness, chances are

there will be no specialist treatment available for her. Tracy
Forshaw suffered severe depression after the birth of all of her
children. Seven days after bringing her third child into the
world she unlocked her husband's gun cupboard, took his
shotgun and used it fatally on herself. Though bodies as
eminent as the Royal College of Psychiatrists have regularly
deplored the inadequacies in the management of post-natal
psychiatric disorders, there are still no more than 500 specialist
beds. In a sane society no woman would be left to struggle on
her own with the huge transformation that is motherhood,
when a single individual finds herself joined by an invisible
umbilical cord to another person from whom she will never be
separated, even by death. If she gives up her child for adoption
she will feel unbearable pain at the site where her child is attached
to her and she will mourn for that child all her life, forever
searching the faces of strangers for a sight of her child's eyes.

The last irreducible function of a mother is to take the
blame. Everything that afflicts her child in later life will be a
mother's fault if only because there is no-one else to blame,
other relationships having withered away. A major purpose of
psychoanalysis is to put the patient 'in touch with her hostility
to her mother'. Eating disorders are often described as resulting from unresolved conflicts with the mother. Now marriage
breakdown too is mother's fault. Doreen Goodman, representing the pressure group What about the Children?, wrote
to the *Guardian* in February 1997:

Marriage breakdown is yet another sign of attachment disorder,
which the World Health Organization has recently included in
the International List of Recognized Diseases (100th edition).
Those affected have never had a mother's selfless commitment
modelled for them when they were children, nor experienced
their birthright of an unbroken one-to-one attachment that
gives them the confidence in themselves, trust in others and
ability to communicate, on which a true marriage is based.

Mothers who do display 'unbroken one-to-one attachment' have been blamed for dominating their children. Attachment disorder, if such a thing exists, is as likely to stem from the smallness of nuclear family units as from any other cause. The father, be he absentee or abusive, gets off scot-free. It's not 'your mum and dad' who really 'fuck you up', just your mum.

> My children cause me the most exquisite suffering of which I have any experience. It is the suffering of ambivalence: the murderous alternation between bitter resentment and raw-edged nerves and blissful gratification and tenderness.
>
> Adrienne Rich, *Of Woman Born*

Blaming the mother begins before the child is born. In 1998 a Finnish study found that having been born unwanted by the mother was the crucial factor in subsequent development of schizophrenia. Academic papers are published every year showing that foetal undernutrition in middle or late pregnancy leads to disruption of the development of the baby because some organs have too few cells. Mothers with flat bony pelves bear children with small heads and a heightened chance of stroke. The thinnest mothers bear children with the highest risk of heart disease. Low birth weight has been linked to high blood pressure and diabetes. Every day new information incriminates the uterine environment; mothers who did not take folic acid in early pregnancy, who drank a glass of wine as the cells of the blastocyst were dividing, who smoked, who habitually drank coffee, tea or cola in pregnancy are to blame for their children's ill-health. In Greenville, South Carolina, Cornelia Whitner is doing eight years for bearing a child addicted to cocaine; other women elsewhere are being charged with felonies for the same reason. In Racine, Wisconsin, Deborah Zimmerman has been charged with drinking her baby to death.

The mother is no longer referred to as a person but as a place, the 'uterine environment'. Optimum uterine environment is now, we are told, the clue to a child's intelligence. If

> Traumatic experiences in the womb lie at the root of all sorts of psychological disorders.
>
> John Turner, psychotherapist

under such pressure you start worrying about whether you are doing the right thing by your baby you might end up doing the worst thing of all, experiencing stress, which will muck up the blood supply to the foetus. It is only a matter of time before a superior maternal environment is designed and built. If Dolly the sheep can develop in an artificial uterus, so can Dolly the person.

Perhaps the belief that the parent with responsibility is the least able person to bring up a child is simply an aspect of the mind-set of an ageing society. A nation of grandparents is the most likely to disapprove of parents and find fault with their performance. However it has come to pass, it is clear that mothers are harried rather than helped. Nearly half the mothers of British children under five already work outside the home, most of them to service the family debt. A controversial British study found that the children of mothers who work full-time were twice as likely to fail their GCSEs as the children of women who worked part time. Stay-at-home mothers had nothing to congratulate themselves for – their children had the worst pass rate of all. Even those who have good jobs and make enough money to pay a nanny find that the employers' demands are not compatible with the demands of children. As a company director and mother Sally Bevan found herself cramming an eighteen-hour day into eight hours.

The worst thing was never being able to relax at home. I went: rush hour, work madly, rush hour, walk in, nanny goes straight off duty, and it's 'Mummy, mummy, mummy'. I couldn't bear the clutching hands, and it was so unfair on the girls, at such an important time for them. I never had any time to myself. Sometimes, driving home, I would just drive round in circles listening to the radio, just to be alone with no demands being made. I was really angry about it. It left me exhausted and depressed though I didn't realize till later. After eighteen months I resigned, then I spent two years at home on Prozac, and now I've set up on my own.

The strangest thing about this account is the invisibility of the girls' father, Sally's husband, when Sally was working primarily to help pay the mortgage they had taken out together. The mother's role is necessarily deeply involved with the child, administering nutriment and comfort, socializing and teaching everything from speech and table manners to road sense and human relationships.

Look around today and you'll see lots of women without children, who wouldn't dream of having them – they're having far too nice a time. They look at those who do have children, who have a terrible time, and who don't have enough disposable income, and feel sorry for them.

Fay Weldon, 1997

In view of the delegation of all the most important aspects of a child's socialization and development to the mother it is remarkable that when it comes to securing the co-operation of professionals her judgement is so seldom respected. Jane Gregory knew that her daughter was having severe problems but a health visitor had to notice that the child had poor head control before the brain scan that her mother had been begging for could be arranged.

'We were told it was normal and that Chrissy was a delayed developer. I tried to ask questions but was dismissed as being neurotic.' She sneaked a look at the paediatrician's notes and read: 'Mrs Gregory came to see me, worried as usual. Asked <u>again</u> if her daughter was handicapped.' Mrs Gregory was right; her daughter is severely handicapped. Even if she had been wrong, if she had been irrationally over-anxious, she should have been helped. Her questions should have been heard and answered, not simply dismissed. Such casual contempt does not prevent health professionals from delegating all the hard work of day-to-day caring for difficult cases to the mother, who is the only one of the battery of carers who is not in receipt of pay. A mother desperate to alleviate her child's pain and frustration will acquire all the skills necessary for medical research of a high order. As befits a champion shopper she will comb the world for specialists and specialized treatments to give her child the very best chance of a normal life. She will raise funds to take the family to Florida or Hungary or New Zealand in search of the best care. Conversely

---

Because she has borne five children
And her belly is criss-crossed
With little tongues of fire . . .

Give her honour
Give her honour, you fools,
Give her honour

Grace Nichols, 'Because she has come'

---

a mother may decide that her child has been tortured enough and should be allowed to die with dignity. And once more her judgement is likely to be questioned, reviled, and ultimately rejected.

Who should be a mother? Now that we no longer require all women to produce as many babies as possible and indeed seem to feel that women should be producing as few babies as possible, women cannot avoid making a choice whether to realize their reproductive potential or not. Fewer and fewer seem to be choosing the motherhood option and we are constantly told that those who do are the wrong ones. Teenaged girls from poor backgrounds are far too ready to have children, so they say, and women of high achievement are unwilling. In 1971 one in twelve British families was headed by a single parent, in 1986 one in seven, and by 1992 one in five. Mothers are 91 per cent of lone parents, most of them separated, divorced or widowed; 35 per cent have never been married, 10 per cent are under twenty. One in three births in England and Wales is now outside marriage. In the early Nineties the fear arose that hordes of very young women were 'getting themselves pregnant' (the term was actually used) just so that they could get a council flat and live off the state. Right-wing tabloids vied to produce the most shocking stories of entire housing estates peopled by none but feckless girls and their bastards, at the expense of the properly married folks and their legitimate issue who were passed over in the housing queue. In September 1993 Wandsworth Borough Council led the way in removing single mothers from their positions of priority on the housing list. Within days of being elected new Labour announced plans to get single mothers back to work, as if they did not already have full-time jobs.

According to Evelyn Shaw and Joan Darling, women have actually stolen mothering away from men.

Women themselves, by culturally controlling the access of men to births, to infants, and to young children, have excluded them from the contact that apparently fosters 'maternalistic' feelings seen in other mammals. By doing so, women have reinforced the myth that biology is destiny and that the female of our species is the only one who should care for the children.

Shaw and Darling can imagine a time when men struggled to be admitted to the birthplace while women held the door against them, ignoring their pleas to be allowed to spend more

---

I feel more relaxed now. Working full-time, it was a struggle. I never seemed to have much time or money. The one thing I do miss, though, is adult company. Work did provide some kind of social life, and I can now go days on end without having a decent conversation.

Deborah Benady, freelance writer and single mum

---

time with infants. Now we know why men found so many things to do outside the house, why they invented football and pub culture and all their other expensive and time-consuming leisure pursuits. It was because women cruelly kicked them out of the nursery, bruising and crushing their maternalistic feelings. Not that one would wish to deny that men's maternalistic feelings could be switched on; men knew better than to allow that to happen, maternalistic feelings being so inimical to freedom and self-interest. When 70 per cent of human societies still deny males access to the birthplace, it seems more common-sensical to conclude that the ruling class, i.e. males, who generally get to do whatever they choose, has never made any concerted effort to invade it.

Being female helps with mothering, but it is not enough. The biological family of mother and child is vulnerable; it needs protection and support. Mothers need sustenance, physical, mental and spiritual. In western society the person who is expected to provide that sustenance is the mother's husband or partner, but only if he chooses. A woman without a partner and with children is usually a woman in trouble. The very fact that she has children will militate against her ability to provide for them; employers feel that despite her need to put food on the table every day, she will be unreliable because she will absent herself from her place of employment if her children are sick.

In Britain, despite growing national prosperity, one in four children is growing up in poverty. Whether a mother is bringing up her children on social security or on the proceeds of her waged work, she is under as much scrutiny as if she were a paid state employee. All kinds of officials have the right to inspect her, her house and her children, and assess her performance, but none of them seems to have a duty to help her. Her neighbours are encouraged to keep an eye on her, though not to help her. As a mother who cannot cope will have her children taken into care, mothers are terrified to admit that they are having difficulties. In the summer of 1996 Julie Lane wandered away from her four-year-old boy who was found in a seaside park; days later she was found a hundred miles away by a railway line in a distressed state and committed to a mental hospital. Samantha Perkins ran away, leaving two sons, eight and nine years old, alone in the house. She got as far as a seaside guest-house before ringing the police and confessing what she had done. No charges of neglect or desertion were brought, because the little boys were obviously well cared for until the day their mother tried to run away from her own grief at the deaths of both her parents and the breakdown of her marriage, tried and failed.

> Everything from the shameful wages of day-care workers to the isolation of the at-home mother is evidence of how, despite lip-service and pedagogical theories, our culture remains inimical to children and the people raising them.
>
> Marni Jackson, *The Mother Zone*

You and I need all the mothers we can get. Governments rely for the funds that run our societies on tax on current earnings;

the people now in work pay for the care and support of the people who are not in work. As the workforce shrinks and life-expectancy increases it becomes harder and harder to pay the social security bill. We all need the children being born now and we need them to grow up as well-educated, useful people, not circling aimlessly round the poverty trap. In *The Female Eunuch* I argued that motherhood should not be treated as a substitute career; now I would argue that motherhood should be regarded as a genuine career option, that is to say, as paid work and as such an alternative to other paid work. What this would mean is that every woman who decides to have a child would be paid enough money to raise that child in decent circumstances. The choice, whether to continue in her employment outside the home and use the money to pay for professional help in raising her child, or stay at home and devote her time to doing it herself, should be hers. By investing in motherhood we would inject more money into childcare which is the only way to improve a system that at present relies on the contribution of disenfranchised, low-paid, unresourced and unqualified women. The sooner we decide that mothers are entitled to state support to use as they wish, the less it will cost us in the long run. We will be told on all sides that we can't afford it. If we weren't paying to send aircraft-carriers to the Gulf and any other place Bill Clinton thinks a sabre should be rattled, we could afford it. It is a question of priorities. Dignified mother-hood is a feminist priority. A permanent seat on the UN Security Council is not.

fathers

What kind of a parent is a father? A father is the provider of the sperm that fertilizes an ovum to produce a pregnancy that, all being well, will end in a live birth. He may not even know that he has done it. He may not care whether he has done it or not. Contraception is still women's business. Socio-biologists are convinced that men seek every opportunity to pass on their genes and sociologists have told us that patriarchal systems of control over women were set up so that men could be certain that they were indeed fathers, but it appears to a naive observer that men are more concerned to evade paternity than to claim it. If men did care whether a child carried their genes or not they would have used DNA testing to identify which of their offspring warmed themselves at other men's fires. In fact they have used it for the opposite purpose, to deny responsibility for the children of women they know they have had sex with. In July 1998 a DNA paternity kit costing £300 came on the market in Britain; the client was to take a swab from his own cheek and a swab from the child's and send them to the DNA Testing Agency at Keston in Kent for analysis, with results five weeks later. The agency's advertisement in the *Sunday Sport* ran, 'Whose child is it? Are you really the father? The curious, suspicious or disbelieving who just want peace of mind can now conduct paternity checks in the comfort of their own home.' Only days before, the Labour government had announced that henceforth unwed fathers *who signed the birth certificate* were to have the same rights in law over their offspring as fathers married to the children's mothers. Once again men get the whip hand; they can exercise paternal rights or evade parental responsibilities – as they choose. The genetic father cannot be forced to sign but the genetic mother may well be forced to allow him to, regardless of her wishes. It seems unlikely that there will be many men picketing registrar's offices yelling for the right to put their names on a child's registration, but very likely that the few who do will be motivated principally by hostility to the mother who is denying them access to her children. In 1998 fewer women entered a father's name at registration of their children's birth than ever before in history; the trend seems set to intensify.

Jobless Andy Burn has NINE children by NINE women – but pays only £5 a week to support them.

Sun, 27 March 1998

Men are equally uninterested in and unwilling to take responsibility for their spermatozoa. A father may choose to be totally unknown to both mother and child by supplying his semen to a sperm bank. Such a man would have to be utterly incurious about any conception that might ensue and uncaring that children carrying half his genes have been born. In the late twentieth century thousands of children are being born who will never be allowed to know who their genetic father is. Any society that allows this to happen clearly does not consider that siring presupposes any kind of relationship at all, regardless of pious resolutions about the unwed father's rights. In Britain the Human Fertilization and Embryology Authority supplies a 'donor information' form which purports to provide one-line information under the heading 'interests' and 'occupation', leaves optional a physical description, and makes no mention of academic record. In January 1998 Ruth Deech, chairman of the HFEA, used the authority's Internet site to warn women away from applying for donor sperm by mail order because 'No questions are asked and browsers are invited to pick from an array of potential biological fathers', neatly encapsulating the very reasons why a woman might prefer to use an Internet supplier. Neither the HFEA nor the Internet suppliers think it appropriate to supply the sperm donor's name. If they did they would have no product.

For all the palaver about men playing full parenting roles, fathers desire, seek, contrive and protect their anonymity. When Aurore Drossart claimed Yves Montand as her father in 1989 and a French judge ordered that he provide material for DNA testing, Montand stalled. He was claimed by death before the order could be enforced. In 1994 another court found on the basis of testimony and a strong family resemblance that Aurore Drossart was indeed Montand's daughter. Because Montand's adopted daughter refused to accept the verdict an

---

Each year in Britain around 50,000 men over the age of forty become fathers ... Most older fathers have had one family already while young. How many children should people have on this overcrowded island?

Minerva, *BMJ*, 18 January 1997

---

order for exhumation of Montand's body was issued. There was an immediate outcry. Prior consent is a condition of genetic testing. The right to anonymity of even a dead father had to be respected. To everyone's amazement the exhumation carried out on 11 March 1998 disproved Drossart's claim. Exhumations of other great men are pending; the reluctant fathers include Giacomo Puccini, Sir Harold Acton and Juan Peron. Even when children distinguish themselves fathers continue to lie doggo, as the fathers of Paula Yates and Eric Clapton chose to do.

The law is rather less concerned to assign paternity than to allow men to escape from it. In the US a man who donates sperm for the insemination of a woman known to him at her request is held legally liable for child support for at least twenty-one years, but a man who donates his sperm anonymously to a medical authority that will use it as it sees fit, without consulting him, has no liabilities whatever to any child born with half his genes. A man having unprotected intercourse with a woman may claim that he had no intention of being a father, believed that the woman was practising contraception so that the child was, as it were, stolen from him by deceit; if he was to be held responsible notwithstanding and made to support his child, other men might begin to see urgent reasons for controlling their own fertility. As it is men retain the freedom to acknowledge their children or not, as they will, and this is a freedom they look like being able to retain. Any man subject to a challenge from any woman who claims that he is the

---

21 April 1998, St Charles, Missouri
Hospital worker Brian Stewart is arrested for injecting his eleven-month-old son with HIV-infected blood in an effort to evade child maintenance payments.

---

father of her child can invoke a basic human right in refusing to supply any of his bodily substance for DNA testing, and so beat the rap. In the case of a married woman inseminated by sperm from a donor not her husband, her husband is considered in law the father of the child, rather than the inseminator; the old law that children born in wedlock are assumed to be offspring of the man the mother is married to still prevails. Strangely that same society continues to trumpet about the role of a father in family life, principally in order to discriminate against women who find themselves raising children without the co-operation of a father.

In 1993 as part of a campaign to revitalize family values, the British government set up the Child Support Agency. Its job was to track down the absent parents of unsupported children and force them to contribute to their maintenance. In 1994, only 4,900 of the absent parents were mothers. In 1998 out of a total of 742,000 cases, 37,300 were mothers. The absent parents would be assessed according to their ability to pay and the money taken from their pay packets at source by the agency. The idea seemed simple enough. The government wanted to get back what it had contributed to the upkeep of unemployed lone parents and children from the absconding parents. The result was uproar. The uproar came first from the fathers who were already paying maintenance directly to mothers and found themselves having to pay twice. It came also from men who had settled at divorce for a single lump sum pay-off, or had given the family home to their wives in lieu of maintenance, and found themselves having to pay up anyway. It came also from second wives complaining that the agency discriminated against second families. It came from men who had been wrongly identified as fathers of children by women other than their wives. It came from men who threatened suicide for any of a variety of reasons. It came from single mothers who were already dependent upon Income Support and objected to being denied their right and thrown into dependence upon men whom they no longer wanted in their lives. Anti-CSA fathers got together in a campaign that they actually called 'Colluding to Defraud the State'; they persuaded their ex-wives to declare that they had good cause to fear violence from their estranged husbands so that the CSA cases would be dropped. The proportion of women claiming to be afraid of estranged husbands rose from 15 per cent to more than 70 per cent in 1997. By March 1998 there were 572,000 claims unprocessed, most of them older than a year. One solution floated by New Labour was to make absent parents pay 9p in the pound for a single child and 12p for two, to be collected along with income tax and paid to a new agency which would pay the money directly to the carer. Within weeks the scheme had been jettisoned. In July 1998 the number of British children growing up without any support whatsoever from absent parents was estimated at 1,700,000 – one in six of all children.

> Can't pay, damned if they will pay, fathers seethe with passions the state delves into at its peril.
>
> Polly Toynbee, April 1998

Fathers are as adroit in evading their responsibilities in the US where only 20 per cent of maintenance orders are paid; in the District of Columbia, Illinois and Tennessee the percentage is half that. So inefficient is the service, which is run by the individual states, that there has been talk of having it taken over by the federal Internal Revenue Service. The US federal government has set up a $2 billion computer system to help states track absentee fathers, but most are unable to make use of it, as they have neither the personnel nor the money nor the political will to follow up on the information and collect what is owing.

As fathers men exhibit the same variability that they do in other spheres of human activity. The worst parents are men; the best parents (so we hear) are also men. To 1.8 million

American fathers who have been awarded custody of their children must be added an estimated 2 million stay-at-home dads. Congress has voted the states $2 billion to be spent over the next six years on 'fathering promotion activities'. As men discover how little child-rearers are valued, perhaps they will begin to agitate for recognition and decent rates of pay. The isolation of home-makers is combated by stay-at-home dads by using the Internet where they can spend as much time on chatty websites as stay-at-home mums were reputed to spend on the telephone. The National Fatherhood Initiative has already had $100 million's worth of donated time to air its radio and TV commercials. Stay-at-home mums were taking the easy option and doing what came naturally; stay-at-home dads are heroes.

From a child's point of view a male parent can define his own role. He can function as the mother's lover or the enemy of the mother, or position himself at any point between the two. He can be authoritarian, or permissive, or inconsistent. A father can choose his fathering style as well, on a spectrum from cuddly and extremely accessible to controlling, critical and distant. Results of a survey commissioned by the British charity Care for the Family, carried out by MORI and published in June 1995, revealed that 15 per cent of fathers

> Women have done an excellent job of selling mothering as the task from hell, destroying both confidence and career prospects. So what man in his right mind would want to take it on?
>
> Adrienne Burgess

spent no time whatsoever with their children on weekdays and most fathers gave their children less than five minutes a day; daughters received even less attention than sons. An NSPCC survey of a thousand kids between the ages of eight and fifteen found that 20 per cent of them could not recall doing anything with their fathers during the previous week. Only 37 per cent had done something with him in the house or garden. An older study by the Joseph Rowntree Foundation came to the conclusion that middle-class men who claimed to be doing more work around the marital home were actually doing less than previously.

For many girls, their father is the object of an unrequited love, in that he is less interested in them, less mindful of them, than they passionately want him to be. They learn from his indifference that they are unattractive, that they will sooner or later be rejected by the people whom they love most. As they fail time and again to command and hold their father's full attention, their self-confidence wavers. This early disappointment can have life-long consequences. In March 1998 Judi James, author of *Bodytalk*, told a *Guardian* journalist, 'I believe women are still capable of holding themselves back in the workplace. They make gestures of defence, or even submission, when they need to be making gestures of confidence and control. The big salary and title don't mean that much if your gestures are saying "Like me! Like me! I'm just a little girl and I won't get in your way, really."' Even James herself may not have realized that she was seeing the employee–employer relationship as the perpetuation of the daughter–father negotiation. In view of the endless examples of harassment of women by their employers and superiors we must ask ourselves if these negotiations too will lead either to failure, that is, rejection by the father because he does not like you, or to abuse, in that he comes to see you as an object of sexual interest. It seems that the acceptance of women as citizens and co-workers requires the redemption of the father–daughter relationship, but we need to ask ourselves whether no father is not after all better than a bad father. At present no father is much easier to come by, and much more frequently encountered than a good father.

A good father, according to Joan Minninger, is one who 'validates' his daughter.

The women who come into therapy unsure of their worth and numbed to their own desires are women who have not had their worth and their desires validated. A father validates his daughter's desires by cheering her on as she learns to sit, crawl, stand, walk, talk, swim, ride a bicycle and make her first wish list for Santa Claus. He continues the process later by helping her with her homework and showing up for her recitals, sports events and class plays. Still later he wants to get involved in her college plans and support the career she wants. But it all begins with being there for her first, great, fundamental achievements as an infant human being.

Easy, isn't it? All a father has to do is turn into a mother.

I saw an advertisement recently in an American magazine. It was for plastic breasts which dispensed real milk. They are designed to be worn by men so that fathers, too, can share the joy and pleasure of breast-feeding.

I thought it was a joke. It wasn't.

Ross Benson, *Express*, 1997

On 7 January 1998 the London *Daily Mail* ran a front-page picture of a woman with a black eye. She had been hit by her husband, an actor in a television series who was having an affair with another woman. She was quoted as saying, 'I honestly feel it's my fault. I must have got the marriage wrong . . . When I look at myself and look where he's hit me, I feel like I've deserved it.' Gee gosh, the papers roared, what has feminism accomplished if a faithless husband can punch his innocent wife and she will take the blame for it? Feminists can tell a woman a thousand times that men's cruelty towards her is not her fault, but, if she knows herself to be unloveable and is only waiting for each relationship to go the same way as the relationship with her father, their words will have little impact. We know where she is coming from but that does not mean that we can get her to jump the tracks laid when she was a tiny girl by the failure of her first love affair, her love affair with her father. She learned then that she was unworthy, that she did not have what it takes to have and hold a man. Little girls are supposed to be rejected for their mothers; in a divorcing society they get to be rejected altogether. As successful coupledom has little understanding of non-genital tenderness and innocent body contact, it is a rare (non-abusing) father who can permit himself any degree of physical intimacy with a daughter. He either sees her as a 'little cracker' and keeps his distance in case she should go off, or does not see her as interesting at all. She tries to find ways of getting close to him which only increase the tension in the situation. The more abject she is the more he is repelled.

As a psychotherapist, I had worked with hundreds of clients of both sexes. I had seen how, for women, their sense of worth-as-a-woman and worth-as-a-person was rooted in their experience of their fathers. I had observed them re-enact their struggles with their fathers, over and over, with other men. I had seen that even absent fathers have influence – that their absence is their influence.

Joan Minninger, *The Father–Daughter Dance*

It is a truism of the study of gifted children that the motivation depends upon the attitude of the opposite-sex parent. Mothers offer boys unqualified stimulation and encouragement; not a boy but is sincerely convinced that he is unique and wonderful and entitled to the best of everything, including academic honours, if he wants them. Girls, relying on the critical, conditional endorsement of a male parent who is rather less interested in their achievements, are much less secure. Instead of seeing tests and examinations as opportunities to show off, they dread being found out. While boys are taking plenty of time off to relax, let off steam and unload the tension, the girls wind themselves up tighter and tighter, until they are doing more and more work for less and less result, proving what they have always known, that they are stupid and silly after all. Boys approach examinations with strategies for providing what will serve; girls are both over-prepared and under-prepared. They tend to know too much about the subject and not enough about the examination. They will have to struggle to get their teeming knowledge compressed into anything like coherent form, and have taken no steps to see that it can be done in the time available. The typical career of a high-achieving girl keeps her ahead of the boys until sixteen plus, when she begins to falter and the boys streak past her. This check operates at precisely the point where she is being encouraged to become more inner-directed, to identify her own goals and pursue them, rather than carry out tasks under direction for praise from an authority figure. She is probably working harder than

> I always say to my children 'You should have suffered a little more because it's good for you' . . . It may sound awful but I was pleased when my son Elan's first movie wasn't a success. I was worried that it would hit big and that he'd never learn.
>
> Vidal Sassoon

ever but the return is diminishing, not because of the occult operations of puberty or PMT, but because of her lack of what gifted boys have in abundance, confidence in their own abilities.

The difference is nowhere more strikingly illustrated than in the televised quiz show *University Challenge*. All-male teams are common and are over-represented in the high scores; most teams field a single woman who provides very few of the answers to the questions, not necessarily because she does not know them, but because she is less aggressive and shy of shouting out an answer that might be wrong. The lowest score ever achieved on *University Challenge* was scored by an all-woman team from New Hall, Cambridge. The same inhibiting factors that operate against women in televised quizzes also bring them down in examinations. Once the pattern of anxiety-driven over-work is set, the young woman has installed her own glass ceiling. She will never be able to give of her best or even to know her best for what it is. She will watch as people who are trying half as hard as she bound up the ladder past her and say to herself, just as the battered wife does, 'It's because I'm not good enough.' She may not even be able to see how effectively other (mostly male) people are deploying the hard work that she has done for their own advancement rather than hers.

A mother does not have to be female, but it helps. Yet, at the end of the millennium the very word 'mother' is disappearing into the de-sexed word 'parent'. The vicissitudes of the Child Support Agency and the sufferings of unsupported mothers are evidence that mothers need support not from an erstwhile sexual partner but from the communities in which they live. Their children are everybody's children. Everybody should play the father's role by contributing to our children's maintenance through income tax. And the amount of revenue devoted to parenting activities should be enough to develop the pre-school sector along professional lines, with proper systems of licensing, assessment and review. To keep sane every adult needs contact with children; it is time we all played the validating father. Whether men opt in or out of parenting will remain their choice, as it always has been.

daughters

As the fabric of patriarchal society has cracked under the strain of women's insurrection every kind of putrid matter has burst out of it, none of it more bewildering and appalling than the facts about sexual abuse of children. In 1971 Louise Armstrong and other American feminists defined the role of father–daughter incest in conditioning women for a life-long role of submission to male sexuality and male definitions of female sexuality. According to their analysis incest was not an exotic rarity but sanctioned behaviour that came with the territory, a fiefdom of the mother's lover. To many this position seemed extreme, as extreme as its companion tenet, 'All men are rapists.' That was before the testimonies began to come, and keep on coming until it seemed there would be no end to them. Celebrity after celebrity described how men *in loco parentis*, genetic fathers and stepfathers had forced their attentions on girls too small, too bamboozled, too afraid to seek help or protection.

The feminist account of incest was usually countered by the bald assertion that, as mothers too sexually abused their daughters, and fathers and mothers both abused sons as often as daughters, father–daughter incest could not perform the specific functions alleged for it in the conditioning of the silenced, annihilated female. As Liz Kelly of the Child and Women Abuse Studies Unit at North London University points out, it was feminists who reminded us of the uncomfortable fact that, while women do sexually abuse children, 'it is overwhelmingly men who sexually abuse. Neglect is a woman's crime. Physical abuse appears to be equal, but not if you take into account how much more time women spend with children.' At the level of the child's experience abuse is secret, though the imagery of child abuse is to be seen on every billboard and television set. Abuse is the secret thing the girl child and daddy do together, their private game, so it is difficult now to guess just how common genital contact between fathers and daughters actually is. The child and the abuser both repress the experience; when it resurfaces there is no objective reinforcing evidence. It is the easiest thing in the world to accuse grown women alleging abuse at the hands of their fathers of imagining things; what a Freudian would say is that pre-adolescent girls fantasize taking the mother's place, much as the Wolf Man fantasized the primal scene, and in adulthood the fantasy cannot be distinguished from a true memory. Even when the fathers admit that some hanky-panky had taken place, they deny that the experience was traumatic. Because penises give men pleasure, they think that the people on the receiving end must be having pleasure too.

In a family where nakedness is usual the small girl may see her father's genitals as enormous, threatening, literally in her face. She may be intensely interested in her father's penis; if she climbs into daddy's bed of a morning she may be moved to play with his erect penis. What should he do? If he is separated from his wife and his daughter is on an access visit, he should run for his life. One word from his daughter to her mother and he is in deep trouble. Only the child has the option of

innocence; the adult cannot allow the contact to continue. Even
if the little girl seems heartbroken she may not climb into
daddy's bed any more. The prevalence of father–daughter sex

> Girl and boy babies are like kittens and puppies. Boys are noisy
> and messy and get wet and shake their fur at you. And it's true
> that a dad can be more affectionate with a daughter; with a boy,
> even when they're six months old, you're on the brink of hav-
> ing that conversation that begins, 'This is all very well, but you
> have to stand on your own two feet.'
>
> Martin Amis, 1997

abuse is as unknowable as the prevalence of rape. Just as only
women truly know whether a sexual contact was consensual or
not, only children know if contact with an adult was experienced by them as abuse. Abusive contact need not necessarily
involve penetration.

It is probably fruitless to try to pin a date on a gradual and
imperceptible escalation from healthy and comfortable affection
to kisses on the lips, to being Daddy's 'special' girl, to goodnight snuggles in bed that went on too long and were too
intimate, to early-morning unwanted snuggles when the rest of
the household slept, to fondling, to open-crotch photographs of
a miserable and passive little girl with her nightie pulled up
above her waist. At what point in the sequence did behaviour
slip from normal to abnormal, from loving to abusive? In his
memory, clearly, it never did.

A third of the 3,964 calls taken by the London Rape Crisis
Centre in 1995 came from women who had been sexually
abused as children. The Women's Support Project in
Strathclyde receives 250 calls a month from women seeking

counselling because they or their children have been abused. Usually abuse begins with being 'daddy's girl', with daddy playing the role of admiring suitor, taking too many kisses, too many of them when no-one else is around. The distance between accepted courtliness to flirtatious little girls and inappropriate utterance is minute, non-existent perhaps. Among the first behaviours a little girl learns is how to get the best out of daddy; she may begin the ogling and the pouting; she may climb all over daddy, triumphing in his weakness for her. Daddy may respond by bouncing her on his leg. It did not need Freud to point out the similarity between this activity and sexual intercourse. Fathers can capitulate or they can distance themselves, censoring all body contact, refusing all kisses, terrified of their own peremptory sexuality and the tyranny of their incessant sexual fantasy.

Girls practise on their dads. What are we supposed to do with girls? Slap them on the face if they give us that look?

Jeremy Irons

Feminists called for an end to the sanctioned abuse of daughters by fathers and stepfathers but, if a father is a mother's lover, it is difficult to see how he could avoid the rejecting behaviour that constitutes emotional abuse; if a father is sexually interested in children he will not reject their innocent advances, but take advantage of them. Either way the kid gets it. It seems, however, mistaken to assume that the distant father and the sexualizing father must be contrasting types. In his much admired memoir, *As If*, the poet and critic Blake Morrison chooses to present himself as the father of three children, two sons and a daughter who is the middle child. She is mentioned as 'just born and hardly breathing in her caul, as if she were clay, the colour of earth, waiting to be shaped', unlike her livelier elder brother. The book contains reported conversations with both the elder and the younger boy but from this daughter not a word; though the narrator mentions taking her and her friends to school in the car in the morning we are not told how old she is. Chapter 10, 'Sex marks', begins:

> It's early evening in the bedroom, a sweet breeze through the sash, the heat of a honeysuckled July. Skirtless, jumperless, she lies on the floor (I lie her on the floor), her hair settling about her like a silky parachute. She turns away and laughs, stretching her left arm to a book just behind her . . . I unbuckle her shoes and pluck them in turn from each heel, tickling it seems, for she turns her head away from the book and giggles. The tights next . . . Practised, instinctive, not stirring from her page, she lifts her bum to let the seat of the tights pass under, and then I roll them down her moly thighs and gleaming calves.

Who can this female be? How old can she be? The use of the present tense to confer sensuous immediacy delays the reader's realization that this abandoned siren is in fact the narrator's daughter, whose (presumably) baby body is being minutely detailed in appetizing terms. The narrator describes himself running his finger along the underside of the child's foot, noticing sweat beads in the arch and the caterpillar softness under her toes. He unbuttons her blouse

> down to the last button, which as it comes away brings with it the right side of her blouse, exposing her right nipple, hollow navel and rosepink butterfly hovering on the waistband of her white pants.

The striptease continues.

> Between finger and thumb I take hold of the waistband by her little hip-juts and pull the knickers off . . . Finally naked now

she pedals her feet and skirls with laughter, though whether at her book or at her nudity it's hard to say. Here am I, kneeling at her feet. And there she lies, a fizz of cream on the floor.

She won't get up from the floor

which leaves me impatient but marvelling at her body – tilty nose, avalanche of hair, pale nipples, soft stomach, candid slit – and pondering my part in it.

From the chapter's opening the 'fizz of cream' aka the 'dairy squiggle' on the floor has never been identified as the narrator's daughter, unless we count the unfortunate reference to 'his part in it' in which, if the rules of syntax applied, 'it' should refer to the child's body, or her 'candid slit', metonymically (possibly) her genetic inheritance. The reader must register the child on the floor as a sex object before she is permitted to get her head around the relationship in which this female stands to the narrator, in forced complicity with the depersonalizing male gaze. She has no option but to follow the itemization of the parts of the child's body as if it were a suggestive menu. What is knowingly and deliberately demonstrated in this whole passage is how fathers, including the most responsible and virtuous, can regard their daughters, working on a titillating memory of them as scrumptious, sensual and irrational while denying their present reality. Female readers will also be aware that the female child is presented as fanciable, delectable even but not likeable. I am grateful to the artfulness of Morrison's writing for the insight into how the distant father and the sexualizing father can be one and the same.

The association of inappropriate ideas leads the narrator further.

A child in my lap, being read to, and I find myself erect.

Not so long ago finding oneself erect would have meant

springing involuntarily to one's feet. The narrator identifies his penis with his self, as is common enough in our time. The corollaries of such identification are distasteful. Love me, love my penis (as I do). The narrator goes on to express his horror at the very idea of a child's knowing of his erection or touching it, because it goes without saying that in reality he is a good clean-living guy, but the damage has already been done. The violating text in which his daughter is laid on the floor naked and splayed for all the world to savour in fantasy will outlive her. Failing to stop her investigating an erection (supposing she should take it into her head to do such a thing of her own accord) would be no violation at all, for erections are themselves innocent, not horrifying or even, often, a manifestation of desire.

The received opinion used to be that the men who directed their sexual feelings towards children were a special group of inadequate individuals; nowadays such inadequacy appears very much commoner than we like to believe, indeed so common that it can hardly be distinguished from normality. It is understood that heterosexual men fancy young things, that youth itself is a turn-on, but no-one is quite sure how young is too young. Why after all are sexy young women called 'babes'? The word 'babe' is current slang in the rave culture; a super-

---

Basically, what we hope is that their fathers are going to look at them and think, 'Gosh, what a little cracker.'

Spokeswoman for Vivienne Westwood,
explaining the choice of thirteen-year-old
models for her 'Red Label' show, February 1997

---

cuddlesome young woman is a 'real babe'. Why do Japanese schoolgirl prostitutes call their clients 'papa-san'? Do most men want to fuck their infant daughters, real and metaphoric?

The fact that governments have to pass laws establishing the age of consent shows that such laws are necessary. Two of the three heroines of the successful film *The First Wives' Club* sneered that the women who replaced them were twelve years old and skinny, without remarking that these proclivities in their husbands were verging on the criminal. If we teased out the tendency until we can see it in all its ugliness, we might find ourselves having to admit that men are attracted to the infantile female in the same measure that they are repelled and revolted by the adult child-bearing female. As long as the infantile female is only pretending to be a child she may survive her fatherly lover relatively unscathed; if she is starving herself to prevent the anatomical evidence of adult womanhood from becoming visible, she is already in deep trouble. If the condition for retaining a man's love is to refrain from growing up, she is doomed to lose that love sooner or later.

The many men and few women who get sexual gratification from the children who are dependent on them want to say that their behaviour is normal. Children have sexuality; sexual interaction is normal as long as no-one is hurt. The feminists are outraged; there is no match between the child's sexuality and adult sexuality. What might begin as mutually gratifying play becomes pathological sooner rather than later. Children involved in sexual congress with adults develop pathological behaviours, using sex as barter in non-sexual encounters, grooming smaller children in order to have sex with them. They might also be sleepless and more anxious, suspicious, timid or aggressive than childen should be. The feminist argument is that incest is both so common as almost to be considered normal *and* devastating. Abuse in childhood prepares the growing woman for a lifetime of abuse. She learns as a child to capitulate to male sexuality regardless of her own inclination or pleasure, just as she learns that her body has a special significance that she can neither comprehend nor control. Her own desire or lack of it seems irrelevant; the sexual agenda has been set elsewhere, in another time. Is it possible that little girls have no choice but to love daddy and daddy no way of responding that is not guilty?

Enter the academics whose job is to take the heat out of the situation and render the question academic. Because there is so much incestuous behaviour, they argue, prohibition is impos-sible, so what we look for is explanation and under-standing. They use the spurious language of children's rights: children have the right to express themselves sexually and with whom better than with members of their own families? The feminists are in a jam; do they deny child sexuality and neuter young females at a stroke or do they hold fast to their condemnation of incest as oppression? The experts wanted to say that incestuous behaviour was driven by love; the feminists knew different. The experts rather scuttled their own case by producing a new stereotype of the 'incest mother' who tacitly offered her children to her lover to make up for what she could not give him, youth, freshness and innocence. Now they speak of divorced men getting back at the mother by sexually abusing the children they have access to, a strategy that can hardly be called loving.

Ever since Othello killed his wife because he loved 'too well', women have been murdered by love, with love and through love. Where once love was a many-splendoured thing, begin-ning with love of God, love of one's neighbour, love of one's brethren and love of one's parents and kin, long before it found expression with a sexual partner, now the word is steeped in sex. Families have decayed and fissioned, mothers have lost their right to the lifelong love of their children, which should be the paradigm of non-invasive love, and the couple rules, OK. Orgasms are the sign of the love of the couple. Orgasms have very little to do with love; sphincters have no souls. The man who terrorizes a woman, who telephones her all through the night, who parks his car outside her house for weeks on end, who sends her terrifying packages and follows her wherever she goes, thinks that 'love' gives him the right to do so. You might as well say that foxes 'love' rabbits, which they surely do. Jack loves Jill not as Jill loves Jack but as Jill loves chocolate. 'Love' is the name given to sexual appetite which can be experienced by the object as the rabbit experiences the fox.

Phoebe (not her name) was only eight when she fell in love with her thirty-year-old uncle. That's what she says, not what the experts say. She says that she seduced him. For four years they had a sexual relationship and then she went away to school. She missed him so terribly that she told one of her schoolfriends, who saw where her duty lay and immediately informed their house mistress that Phoebe had been a victim of abuse. Experts were called and action was taken. At first Phoebe simply denied the whole tale, but she was not believed. She was medically examined and tricked into confessing. In vain she struggled to convince them that she loved her uncle and had felt no fear in his company, that nothing had been done that she resented. They told her that she was still in the grip of her abuser and that nothing could be done for her unless she got in touch with her terror and rage. Eventually she produced enough terror and rage to satisfy them and her uncle was prosecuted and imprisoned. Phoebe has never forgiven herself for betraying the love of her life, which has been a mess ever since.

Most people, feminists included, would think that Phoebe's uncle got what was coming to him. Whether Phoebe seduced him or not, he should have put himself out of danger of succumbing because he was the adult. He was in control of where he went and what he did in a way that she was not; he could have avoided her. As a feminist I have to put Phoebe first and consider the devastation wrought on Phoebe by this whole business. If Phoebe's juvenile sexuality had been recognized, if enough attention had been paid to the way she interacted with her uncle, if she had had a closer relationship with her parents, this story would have been different. Little girls fall in love with inappropriate objects all the time; if they are lucky they never get near enough to them to become drawn in as Phoebe was. Some may see Phoebe as a lonely little girl, in whom no-one was particularly interested, until she latched on to her uncle who was only too easily interested. She was probably interested in him rather than his penis; the chances that he was interested in her undeveloped mind rather than her immature body are slim. Which is simply the point that the feminist analysis of abuse has been trying to make. Women are taught by hard lessons like these even from early childhood that the only way to power and value is manipulation of male sexuality.

The experts are right; these behaviours are less aberrant than normal. They may be outlandish and extreme, but they are manifestations of the governing principle that runs the every-day. Women are expected to relate to men who are older than they are; husbands are meant to take over the role of fathers and assume authority over their wives; the juvenile status of the wife is a continuation of the daughter role. This pattern is more apparent in Britain than America where men marry younger and the age difference between spouses is less. As women become more adult, male anxiety becomes more acute. Men turn away from the potentially threatening to the vulnerability of the girlie. We know that little girls flirt with their fathers and that little girls can be exhibitionistic. We also know that current fashions stress the infantile characteristics of the young female body. Fashion-conscious young women show their flat navels and narrow midriffs under skinny tops and over skimpy skirts and hipster pants, in a not-quite-grown-up version of the titillating outfits devised for smaller girlies:

> In the shop window are models of little girls in short dresses and white socks – each model contriving to hold her skirt up to reveal her child's knickers underneath. Within the store are rack upon rack of girls' underwear, swimwear and sleepwear – lacy, feminine and emphasizing the promise of immature or

non-existent breasts beneath the ruffles and satin. How are fathers – and men in general – supposed to respond?

The dismissive answer is to say that men are not supposed to respond at all – it is not men who shop. How are women supposed to respond if not to register and highlight the seductiveness of little girls? Is it not the 'incest mother' who attires her little daughter in peek-a-boo styles and sends her in to coax daddy away from sport on television and get him to take her upstairs and put her to bed? It is certainly true that the little girl has sexuality; how can we be sure that she is not being taught every day and every way to deploy that sexuality as a child relating to an adult? Why do men give their girlfriends cuddly toys? Why do lovers talk baby-talk? Every Valentine's Day British newspapers run over with infantile babble – daddy and daddy's girl are at it again.

sisters

There was a time when feminists signed off their letters 'Yours in sisterhood'. The sororal ideals were dear to us then, perhaps because of the increasing rarity of the experience of having actual sisters as distinct from political ones. By sorority we meant something not quite like brotherhood, and quite unlike the absurdities of elitist sororities on American university campuses. We meant a relationship linking equals in a loose but strong network that acknowledged no leaders, imposed no sanctions and indulged in no peculiar or secret rituals. The sisterhood was to be as different from the groups formed by men as could be, having no hierarchies, no passwords, no secret signs. Sisterhood was in your face.

In the non-human world sisterhood is more evident than brotherhood. There are no all-male species, but all-female species are relatively often found. Gall-making wasps, saw-flies, at least nineteen species of lizards, are all female. There is an all-female variety of fish in the Gulf of Mexico. Amazon mollies pirate sperm from other species to fertilize their eggs but produce only females. Beehives and ant communities are full of sisters, working side by side. In all kinds of mammal species sisters live together, ovulate simultaneously, bear their young at the same time and suckle them together. Motherhood is shared among whales, dolphins, elephants, species that are paragons of intelligent social organization. The females of various species of raccoon, pig, goat, mongoose and rodent, co-operate in sisterly fashion by breast-feeding each other's young. Lionesses hunt in a group, wait on the single adult male in the pride, and raise their young together. Domestic cats, if they bear their kittens at the same time, will often spell each other, one taking on all the kittens while the other rests and then taking her chance for a rest when the co-mother returns.

Some primate females establish old-girl networks and smoothly carry on their daily endeavours through a dominant-subordinate relationship that would make the human female reel.

In many primate groups, baboons, macaques, chimpanzees and lemurs, for example, older sisters nurse little sisters. Tendencies among women living together to ovulate simultaneously probably represent some kind of mammalian residue. Kathleen Stern and Martha McLintock, psychologists from Chicago, devised an experiment to test this phenomenon. Volunteers provided samples of their underarm moisture on cotton pads which were then wiped on the upper lips of other women; more than two-thirds of the receivers of the swabs altered their menstrual cycles to coincide with those of the donors. Cycles were both lengthened and shortened, which indicated to the researchers that two different pheromones were involved.

Ann Oakley in *Sex, Gender and Society* noted that there are human societies, such as the Samoans, the Alor, the Bororo and the Arrenta, where sisters work together to raise children and share breast-feeding. Matt Ridley pointed out in *The Origins of Virtue*, 'female elephants aggregate in groups, but the groups

are not hostile, territorially competitive or fixed in membership
. . . It is an intriguing fantasy to imagine ourselves like that.
Indeed female human beings are like that already.' But are they?

> For there is no friend like a sister
> In calm or stormy weather;
> To cheer one on the tedious way,
> To fetch one if one goes astray,
> To lift one if one totters down,
> To strengthen whilst one stands.
>
> Christina Rossetti, *Goblin Market*

Female human beings do not often live together, nor do they
choose to rear their young co-operatively. What socio-biological
accounts like Ridley's suggest is that perhaps they could. If we
can perhaps we should, but there are strong societal pressures
forcing women away from each other.

In white Anglo-Saxon Protestant society there is no tradition
of sisterhood. Historically women born of the same parents
marry out of those families, taking as their primary relationship
that of a spouse and subsequently a mother. Our sisters, if we
have any, have to take a back seat, as aunts to our children, with
no greater claim on us than our husbands' sisters. Sisterhood is
a relationship conducted, if at all, by telephone. All too often
sisterhood degenerates into sibling rivalry. If we comb the
history of women for famous sisters we find very few, and fewer
still whom we could take as models. More work needs to be
done on the dynamic of the relationship between even the
best-known sisters, Cassandra and Jane Austen, the Brontës,
Christina and Maria Rossetti, Virginia Woolf and Vanessa Bell,
and the Mitfords.

The notion that all women were 'sisters', bound together across ethnic, class, generational and regional lines by their common experiences as an oppressed group, was the most powerful, utopian, and, therefore, threatening concept feminists advanced in the 1970s.

This statement, made by Susan J. Douglas in *Where the Girls Are*, bears closer examination. In patrilocal systems, where women live in their husbands' houses, biological sisters have a tough time hanging together, unless they remain virgins. Non-biological sisterhood too was thought appropriate for virgins only. Non-biological sisters have never at any time in history or in any significant human society been bound together except in convents and the hospitals that grew out of the old religious institutions. Nurses are called sister by analogy with the nuns who had cared for the sick before Florence Nightingale. The word sisterhood still suggests some kind of conventual cultus, tainted with self-flagellation and self-starvation in the throes of religious mania. The media were quick to seize on this way of characterizing feminists as an order of fanatics led by one false prophetess or another. Feminists tried to beat them to it by taking names like WITCH (Women's International Terrorist Conspiracy from Hell) but the jokes they made themselves were usually turned against them. Deliberately loony feminist nonsense was always quoted as if its inventors had been unaware of its looniness.

Clearly there is no sisterhood. There might be in the bigger sense but that's spearheaded by very strong women.

Phyllis Nagy

Political sisterhood was always going to be difficult. As Florynce Kennedy told me in 1971, 'You watch out for those

sisters, honey. They'll suck the marrow out your bones.'
Sisterhood also loosed off some unpleasant vibrations in those
men whose elder sisters beat them up and pulled their hair
when they were small. For whatever reason sisterhood was a
tough word and a difficult idea.

As soon as sisterhood gained any ground as the primary
relationship between women, it was bitched by the brotherhood
as other oppressed groups began loudly to complain that
feminism would undermine their struggle. The International
Socialists, the Workers' Revolutionary Party, any and all black
power groups, levelled bitter accusations at middle-class
feminists, that they were elevating their petty bourgeois
concerns over the life-and-death struggle of the genuinely
oppressed. More to the point, as the women of Students for a
Democratic Society or Red Mole or Black Dwarf or whatever
recognized their oppression and went off to join feminist
demonstrations and consciousness-raising groups, there was
no-one to do the typing or make the coffee.

To climb out of the beds of the student revolutionaries was
not to step into a fully formed sisterhood. Sisterhood had to
find a local habitation and a name; somehow it had to become
visible and to become visible it needed an organization. Once
there was an organization, there were leadership contests. Once
there was one organization, there were others competing to
recruit amongst the same population. Before feminism had had
time to develop even a fledgling analysis of women's oppression
and its causes, would-be feminist ideologues of widely varying
levels of sincerity and insight began attacking other feminists.
Radical groups sailed into revisionist groups, NOW sneered at
Red Stockings. The media identified 'newsworthy' candidates
for leadership and massaged their images briefly before setting
up cat-fights between them. I was dubbed 'High Priestess of
Women's Liberation', though I had done nothing but write a
book; Gloria Steinem was 'the New Woman'; Betty Friedan
was 'the Mother Superior'. There was never any shortage of

feminists ready to do each other down; the most contemptuous reviews a feminist writer could expect to get were those from the pens of her sisters which, of course, were the only ones she cared about. Newspaper after newspaper set women to interview women, with a clear instruction to get knocking copy which was duly supplied, usually by neophytes who had no idea that they were infinitely replaceable and would be replaced whether they bucked the trend and were true to themselves or not. The treatment of Catherine McKinnon when she visited Britain in 1995 was typical. She was almost invariably questioned by very young women with only the haziest idea of what she was about, who reacted very badly and turned in reams of lampooning copy if she showed the slightest sign of annoyance at their wasting of her time. No newspaper in the world would bother to set up a demonstration of sisterhood, when female mud-wrestling can be had on demand.

Thirty years ago feminist texts were attacked by all kinds of people, so that feminists had to invest a great deal of energy in defending feminism against the forces of darkness. The forces of darkness having been by and large routed, feminist texts are now reviewed by feminists who are then forced into adversarial positions. They could refrain from reviewing each other's books and thus retain each other's friendship, but the issues are issues they care about, the subject is their subject, and they need the money so in they wade. This very book was 'reviewed' by Maureen Freely for the tabloid press a year before it was published and denounced as 'pap', though she had not seen a word of it, neatly illustrating the way exploited female hacks pluck down the feminist intellectual establishment with their own hands. University libraries burst at the seams with the hundreds and hundreds of women's studies titles that are published every year and hundreds of thousands of students incessantly investigate and expound feminist issues, but media feminists remain untroubled in their ignorance. Ros Coward actually went so far as to declare in the *Guardian* that 'The media is now the only place where discussions take place.'

However stormy or disloyal your relationship with your sister, you do not have sex with her. Of all forms of intra-familial incest, sister-fucking is the rarest. As our relationship with the oppressor was transacted through sex, it seemed clear that sisterhood should be different, with as much as feels comfortable of whole body contact, snuggling and cuddling even, but no genital involvement. Enter those lesbians who made genital involvement with women a condition of sister-hood. This was a contradiction that many feminists could not handle, specially when it came in the form of harassment of a rather familiar kind. After having been told for years that our radical credentials would be placed in doubt if we did not put out for this or that male activist, we were now being told that if we didn't let another woman climb aboard we were not feminists. As far as I was concerned having the hard word put on me by Jill Johnson was no different from getting it from Abbie Hoffmann, except that being incurably heterosexual I found Hoffmann marginally less unattractive. Throughout the

> when we met, I tell you
> it was a birthday party, a funeral
> it was a holy communion
> between women, a Visitation
>
> it was two old she-goats butting
> and nuzzling each other in the smelly fold
>
> Michele Roberts, 'Magnificat'

Seventies I toured America giving lectures on 'Feminism and Fertility' and, in every other lecture-hall, a small group of lesbians would sit itself under my nose and wait until I was fifteen minutes into the lecture before shouting that I was an anti-feminist because I was only addressing heterosexual women. The objection was easily dealt with but the snarling hostility that accompanied it infuriated the majority who had been enjoying themselves until this phony war broke out. Florynce Kennedy had told me that oppressed people special-ize in 'horizontal hostility'; as they cannot confront 'the Man' or anyone else in a position of power, they can only attack people as vulnerable as themselves. Sometimes the campus newspaper would represent the event as a brawl, though the disturbance lasted no more than a minute or two, in the same way that the mass media orchestrates an endless series of knock-down drag-out bouts between women as a distraction from the main event.

It was in the nature of the lesbians' struggle that they should mount guerilla activities of a spectacular kind and become far more visible in media terms than the women who were strug-gling for a better deal from the men they loved too much to get really tough with. Sisterhood demanded that a feminist identify herself with all feminist manifestations, that she defend the right of women who cannot bear the thought of a penis anywhere near them to conceive and bear children, male and female, that she explain Gloria Steinem's critique of marriage as prostitution, that she defend the right of women to become priests or rabbis or Marines or to sit on the boards of munitions companies if they want to, trying to create a consensus where none existed.

Even more questionable than the suggestion that sisterhood unites women across class and ethnic lines is the claim that sisterhood binds women of different generations. Sisters, by definition, belong to an age set. Sisters are close because they learned their language at the same time, they grew up with the same youth culture or lack of it, they went through their life-changes more or less simultaneously, bearing their children in the same epoch and burying their parents together. This community of experience is the *sine qua non* of actual sisterhood; to expect that political sisterhood include women of both our grandmothers' generation and our granddaughters' generation is too much by more than half. As more and more women realize that our society is even more rotten with ageism than sexism, sisterhood cannot come to their aid. Feminism is as youthist as any other radical movement. 'Old feminists' exist to be sneered at by young feminists, and when the young feminists, who are usually not as young as they think they are, bait them they can expect to be chastised. Big sisters have been known to wallop pestilential little sisters from time to time. The little sisters make a tremendous fuss of course, screaming and yelling for months on end, but they usually recover well enough to do it all over again.

Part of the pejorative connotation of the word 'sisterhood' is the imputation of an unthinking consensus, when sisterhood could be thought with equal justification to confer licence to disagree without rancour. There never was a time when feminists all sang from the same hymnbook, nor should there have been, because the nature and dynamic of sex oppression needed to be uncovered and argued over. From the outset it was clear that paradox was an inherent characteristic of the female dilemma; the contradictory expectations that drove the super-feminine menial to the medicine cabinet extended beyond actual circumstances to the very definition of the female condition. Every day and in every way women are required to assert and to deny their womanhood simultaneously, and this contradiction, rather than the feelings appropriate to one's reproductive or sexual or social circumstances, is what sisters should be prepared both to understand and to interrogate. At the very first feminist meetings, the question of whether men should be admitted was debated with great fervour, called 'ferocity' by the press. Non-separatist feminists were dubbed, with a blithe disregard of etymology, humanists; separatist feminists who thought that women could not discover their

own point of view within male-dominated groups were called
man-haters. Anyone who argued for doing it both ways was
simply inconsistent. Conventional analysis will not tolerate
paradox; theoretical feminists were asked to decide whether
'woman' was a social construction or an essence. If they had
been allowed to take a book as conscientiously unacademic as
The Female Eunuch seriously, they might have had their cake
and eaten it too, for the argument there is that female is essence
and feminine social construct. Deciding which behaviours
mirror female and which the castrated form of feminine is not
easy, until menopause burns off the impurities. What remains
in the crucible after that proof is the whole woman.

The trouble is not that *Sisterhood is Powerful*, as the title of
Robin Morgan's book has it, but that it isn't. Sisterhood does
not rule and will never rule, OK? The principle of sisterhood is
power-sharing, which is another name for powerlessness. In a
society constructed of self-perpetuating elites a grass roots
movement exists to be walked on. Elites tumble down but the
grass survives to spring again through the thickest pavement.
All studies of gender difference agree on one thing, that
females are less variable than males. If men and women were
poppies, both the tallest and shortest poppies would be men.
The women would cluster around the median, the norm. If we
look at intelligence or mathematical ability we can see the same
phenomenon. Men are, as it were, built for competition, already
separated out into winners and losers, while women are built
to understand each other, to co-operate, to pull shoulder to
shoulder. Indeed, we could see the historic pattern of binding a
woman to a man and forcibly separating her from her female
peers as a precaution against the development of a female
tendency to agglomerate. Men are afraid of women in groups.

One of the advances in the last thirty years has been that
women's friendship is now a serious topic, and an entrenched
value in women's lives. Girls' magazines treat the vicissitudes
of friendship with more seriousness than the endless flummery

about boys. Women's 'being there for each other' features in soap operas. Women students consider themselves bound to accept each other's word without question, flying in the face of the prejudice that women are incapable of loyalty or trust. Only when sisterhood is real can sisterhood become powerful. We are on the way.

the love of women

Women love all kinds of things, places, animals and people. They can love a place with so gut-wrenching a passion that they dream of it every night. They can love animals with such tenderness that they would die for them, whether in a burning house clasping an old cat in their arms or under the wheels of a lorry loaded with live calves for export. They can love a child or an adult person with a devotion that never flags through long years of toil and struggle. They love undaunted by ill-treatment, abandonment or death, returning good for evil. They do not kill the things they love but cherish them, feed them, nurture them, remaining more interested in them than they are in themselves. They do not come to love the objects of their love by fucking them. With many of the creatures they love the longest and the most deeply they have no genital contact at all. Each man kills the thing he loves, or so a man once wrote. God forbid that I, a woman, should suggest that the love of men is essentially proprietory or predatory, or cruel or consuming, or destructive or degrading, but it is strange that when all love is expressed in masculinist culture by fucking, no word should have more destructiveness packed into its meaning than 'fuck'. 'Fuck' and 'destroy' are not cognate in women's language; women do not teach children the verbal assaults that use the verb 'fuck'. In the last thirty years women have acquired the right to use the word 'fuck' in the same senses and contexts as men do, and they have used it, as unthinkingly as they have accepted the notion that nothing is more despicable than to behave like a cunt. In verbal sparring women want to give as good as they get; it would not be the first time that, in using men's weapons against men, women have hurt themselves.

The heterosexualization of desire requires and institutes the production of discrete and asymmetrical oppositions between 'feminine' and 'masculine', where these are understood as expressive attributes of 'male' and 'female'.

Judith Butler, *Gender Trouble*

The expression of women's non-sexual love grows every year more difficult. The love of sexually active women for their sex partners may be projected on screens all around us, but the vast well of non-sexual love remains hidden. More than 80 per cent of RSPCA volunteers are women. Millions of women sit knitting garments that nobody wants because the hours of fiddling work give them an opportunity gradually to release the intolerable pressure of their unspoken love. Millions of women spend hours shopping for presents because those hours are a blessed time when they can think continually about the people they will give the presents to. And they will be told, 'Oh Mum/Gran'ma/Auntie/Sis, you shouldn't have.' For the secret lover the time and money have been well spent, indulging her obsession and easing her overloaded heart. Even if her extravagance means she must go without, she knows she is not being generous, for every time she feels the pinch, her gnawing love will be assuaged.

Whom a woman loves rather depends upon where she is in the series of transformations that compose a woman's life. When she is a baby she loves a composite creature, herself-and-her-mother, then she loves her daddy, then as she approaches the menarche she goes through a tumultuous phase of manic boy-craziness which may also coincide with intimacy with another pubescent girl. The males who are the object of pre-teens' obsessions are beardless, cute, 'gorge', 'babetastic', 'love-gods', 'stud-muffins' and 'lush-buckets'. They are more childlike than masculine, and sometimes convey an explicitly transsexual message, like Boy George whose outrageously camp image was plastered all over girls' bedroom walls in the Eighties. By constantly refashioning himself as an androgyne Michael Jackson has retained and expanded a vast audience of pre-teens. It is more important to pubescent female fans that boy bands and boy stars appear to be uncommitted to any sexual partner than that they be heterosexual. Leonardo di Caprio's manager, who is also his mother, is well aware that the girl fans who crowded the pavements to see him when he attended the London première of *The Man in the Iron Mask* in March 1998 would have been as chagrined to see him with a woman on his arm as they were delighted to learn that he brought his grandmother with him so that she could meet the Queen. The suggestion of adult heterosexual activity would be hardly less damaging to his image than the suggestion of adult homosexual activity. The girls wanted him to be a child, literally a babe for them to cuddle in fantasy. He obliged by acting shy and mildly embarrassed by their eldritch shrieks of 'Le-oh! Le-oh!' Though the consistency in teeny-bopper preference for ephebous boys rather than men suggests that their sexual preferences are not yet fully heterosexual, girls' magazines always assume that their readers wish for success as boy-magnets and harbour no lustful feelings towards their own kind. Lesbianism is never mentioned; though they celebrate mateship between girls ('Boy friends come and go but friends are friends forever') the magazines do not discuss the possibility of sexual intimacy with girl mates.

Later in life too a woman's erotic interest appears to move away from conventionally masculine types to effeminate males. The adoring audiences of Liberace were, as the adoring audiences of Barry Manilow are, middle-aged women. While Liberace could exaggerate his effeminacy and they would only drool the more, he had to conceal the extent of his actual sexual activity, if he was to retain their adoration. So he pretended to be a virgin queen for as long as he could, until a rejected partner exposed him as a demanding and aggressive lover. The painted fops and carpet-knights of the seventeenth century were both effeminate and successful with women; the lounge lizards of the twentieth century were also suspected of being in league with lustful females to betray the honest love of true-hearted working men. If a lady's man is by definition effeminate, what does that tell us about the lady's sexual preferences? Men rather than women seek rough trade. The logical extension of such questioning could lead us to ask whether there is anything natural about heterosexuality, and even to suspect that if heterosexuality is not in future to be buttressed by law and religion and family pressure it will collapse.

The girls who write to teen mags often refer to 'hormones going haywire' as a cause of injudicious behaviour. They have been taught that their juvenile feelings are not to be acted upon and become used to denying themselves the satisfaction of acting out their desires. Heterosexual preference would appear to establish itself fairly late in the pubescent girl, and it would seem that homosexual preference does not emerge until even later. Most lesbians, 58 per cent according to one study and 84 per cent according to another, have had heterosexual experience. Between a quarter and a third of lesbians have been married at some time in their lives. Sappho herself was a wife and mother. This suggests that female homosexuals are not mirror images of male homosexuals; at the age of twenty 27 per cent of men have established homosexual or bisexual patterns of behaviour as against 11 per cent of women, but by age thirty-five the proportion is 13 per cent for both sexes. In 1953 Kinsey reported that 28 per cent of women had had sexual experience involving another woman. A heterosexual woman who enjoys sex with a woman has only a 50 per cent chance of developing a lesbian identity. How women move from hetero-sexuality to homosexuality has been little studied; the possibility that such women might be rejecting heterosexuality as unsatisfying and have consciously or unconsciously gone in search of a different kind of love has been little explored, in contrast with the never-ending attempts to find some biological component in sexual preference.

Though most male homosexuals recognize their orientation in the course of promiscuous sexual contacts, many women have to fall in love with another woman in order to identify themselves as lesbian. Adrienne Rich famously fell in love with a woman at the age of forty-seven, after having lived as a wife and the mother of three children.

I have an indestructible memory of walking along a particular block in New York City, the hour after I had acknowledged to myself that I loved a woman, feeling invincible. For the first time in my life I experienced sexuality as clarifying my mind, instead of hazing it over; that passion, once named, flung a long, imperative beam of light into my future. I knew my life was decisively and forever different.

At forty-seven Rich was on the cusp of the peri-menopause; her bodily chemistry was changing, yet she was not encouraged to think of herself as changing but to believe that the real she had been until that time silenced and denied. If her marriage were to be considered a fraud and her motherhood a mistake, the conclusion would have to be that more than half her life was wasted or lived wrong, though Rich never devalued her experience of motherhood. It seems more profitable to consider the possibility that there was a change, that new feelings and attitudes had developed out of changing conditions and consciousness. Certainly emerging lesbians often do explain that they had no lesbian sexual orientation before falling in love with a woman, that they lived the usual female life and liked the usual female things, suggesting that becoming lesbian was a developmental phase rather than the uncovering of underlying pathology or genetic inheritance or any other kind of immutable essence. The essentialist would argue that the lesbian was her real self that had at last emerged, devaluing all her other relationships. It is at least as likely that the woman has changed, that she has developed from being the subordinate partner in a heterosexual relationship which is predicated upon her relationship with her father and moved to a new kind of relationship between equals. According to Julie Burchill who had two husbands and one child before opting for same-sex love with Charlotte Raven:

The sex-rev failed because, Freudian or not, it failed to ask what women want. In presuming that wham, bam, thankyou Sam was going to look wildly attractive from where we were sitting, the sixties sex evangelists revealed themselves as the appallingly inept lovers they must have been. No wonder all those sixties free love chicks became lesbians in the seventies.

Burchill for one seems to believe that there is no such thing as sexual identity, or rather, that sexual behaviour is as much a response to prevailing realities as an expression of immutable self. If men were more like women, it might be possible for women to retain their sexual interest in them. Burchill pointed out in the same article that men 'come off like a rocket' and, whether homosexual or heterosexual, seek sexual opportunity avidly and insatiably, while women require much more in terms of commitment, time, communication and caress.

> In the Seventies, lesbianism was perceived as a feminist, political act by the burgeoning women's rights movement, and there were many rules to the sapphic sex act. To avoid the patriarchal power structure developing, lesbians weren't meant to maintain eye-contact, fetishise breasts or even permit one partner to get on top of the other. You have to admire these women for their principles and political commitment – even if it did mean that no one came for an entire decade.
>
> Alice Fisher, *Esquire*

When sex was medicalized in the late nineteenth century, unorthodox sexual orientation became pathology, a kind of congenital disability for which the heterosexual and healthy should feel pity. Lesbians like Radclyffe Hall presented themselves as intersexuals, marked out by God to be lovers of women or live in wretched celibacy. Amazingly ingenious experiments to prove homosexuality inborn continue to this day; most recently Dennis McFadden and Edward G. Pasanen of the University of Texas measured the echoes that certain sounds produce in the inner ears of 237 men and women and found that the inner ears of fifty-seven heterosexual women produced louder echoes than did those of sixty-one homosexual and bisexual women, whose range was closer to that of men, leading the researchers to the opinion that homosexual and bisexual women may have been exposed in the womb to higher levels of androgens and to some extent masculinized as a result.

Results of research into traits supposed innate in homosexual individuals are published every year. We have learnt that gay men are more likely to have gay brothers than straight men and that lesbians are more likely to have lesbian sisters. It has been proposed that the degree of exposure to androgens in the uterine environment is the precipitating factor but in view of the fact AIS males, who did not develop masculine characteristics because they were insensitive to the androgens in their mother's amniotic fluid, are not necessarily attracted to men rather than women, this explanation of homoerotic sexual orientation seems unlikely. Though females with Congenital Adrenal Hyperplasia are bathed in their own androgens *in utero* and may be born with what appear to be external genitalia, they do not often acknowledge homosexual feelings. In 1991 Simon Le Vay examined the brains of nineteen gay men, sixteen heterosexual men and six women, to see whether there were significant differences in a region of the hypothalamus that was important in regulating sex-differential behaviour in animals. There was more variation within the three classes than there was difference between them, but Le Vay interpreted his data as suggesting that gay men and heterosexual women have a feature of brain anatomy in common that they do not share with straight men. Laura Allen and Roger Gorski then found another feature of brain anatomy, the anterior commissure of the corpus callosum, that tended to be bigger in women and homosexual men than it was in straight men. Such research, based as it is on minute samples, seems footling at best but it could be used by those who would impose heterosexuality as the only acceptable expression of human eroticism to justify the treatment of deviance as a defect in need of correction. Contrariwise it could be used to show that as God created all kinds of sexual orientations He must approve of all of them. Neither position would be comfortable for the woman seeking to protect her right to change.

Straight people often think that lesbians are masculinized women and male homosexuals are feminized men. The assumption that people who are attracted to the same sex must share characteristics of the opposite sex is part of a larger assumption, that heterosexuality is the only sexuality and all sexual activity is a more or less distorted version of it. All that is possible as far as the straight person is concerned is role

> Pleasure is something which passes from one individual to another; it is not something secreted by identity. Pleasure has no passport, no identity.
>
> Michel Foucault

reversal, one lesbian woman in each couple playing the part of a man; one homosexual man in each couple playing the part of a woman. If this were the case, homosexual people could neither abolish nor transform the basic dynamic of human sex relations but only imitate it. Actually, as homosexuals deny the validity of the prescription of a single kind of relationship as orthodox, healthy and normal, they can claim the full spectrum of deviance. Homosexual forms of sexual expression are extra-ordinarily various. Some homosexual lovers are so obsessed by the imagery of penetration that they use arms, fists and instruments to penetrate more effectively, others experience no urge to breach the body outline at all. Gay men are more interested in dildoes than either straight women or lesbians are, and so on, through every conceivable permutation that fantasy can suggest.

Homosexual relationships vary in levels of sexual activity, varieties of sexual activity, and degrees of monogamy. Male and female patterns of homosexual behaviour are also different. If a male homosexual gets off the tube train at Lancaster Gate in the hope that some like-minded male is loitering to give or take a blow-job in the five minutes between trains, both are men in pursuit of casual sex and behaving malely, regardless of who sucks what. Lesbians may not share the male appetite for lavatorial sex but they do not choose to imitate heterosexual penetration behaviour either. The subversive truth seems to be that same-sex love-making is not a substitute for or an imitation of other-sex love-making but an out-and-out rejection of it.

Though some homosexual people may clamour for the right to marry in imitation of the heterosexual establishment, they are far outnumbered by others whose sexual ambitions are less orderly, even anarchic. The process by which the authorities will seize the opportunity to tame homosexual relationships by bringing them within the purview of the law has already begun. A law permitting same-sex marriage was passed in Holland on 1 January 1998. The first lesbian marriage in Holland was celebrated at the stroke of midnight on 14–15 January 1998 when Irma van Praag married Anna Kreuger. As a female comedian remarked bitterly, if the law has its way, after five years of married life homosexuals, like heterosexuals, will be celibate.

---

i never thought it would happen to me either . . .
until one day
for some reason
these things i'd subconsciously been hiding
started to rise to the surface when i kissed her –
and a long overdue series of changes began to occur
   i tossed in my marriage
   i began to find my voice
   i began to be happy
   i threw away my pills

   and i fell in love for the first time

cherie aitken

In 1908 Gertude Stein and Alice B. Toklas went through a secret marriage ceremony and lived together thereafter until

Stein's death in 1946. Neither woman ever so much as flirted with anyone else. This kind of utter commitment is as common among lesbian couples as it is rare among homosexual couples. Though some lesbians are exhibitionistic they are a minority. The spectacular festivals organized by the homosexual community, from the British Miss World Competition to New York's Wigstock to the Sydney Mardi Gras, showcase stupendously flamboyant men rather than women. It is too soon to say whether the Miss Lesbian Beauty competition, first staged at the London Café de Paris in 1997, will develop into an annual tourist attraction. Lesbianism remains for the most part discreet and modest. When Angela Eagle, junior environment minister in the British Labour cabinet, came out as lesbian in September 1997 she promised that she would not aim to become a spokesperson for lesbians and that she would not attend functions with her partner whose name was never given. None of the gay males in the Labour parliamentary party has a regular partner with whom not to be seen and those who are out came out in order to be spokesmen for gay rights. Male pop stars who are out as gay flaunt their sexuality, while a lesbian rock musician remarked ruefully that the glare of public attention had cramped her style: 'From being an old slag prior to success, I've become a withdrawn shell of a person.'

Socio-biologists never tire of telling us that men are promiscuous by nature because they are actively accumulating reproductive opportunity. They do not explain why homosexual men, who deposit their seed in sites where no reproductive opportunity can be said to exist, are even more promiscuous. Promiscuity may be one male characteristic that lesbians will soon acquire; lesbians may one day hang out in toilets, parks and clubs looking for a quick tumble, but so far they do not. One intriguing piece of evidence suggests that female monogamousness is not innate. The Israeli singer Dana International, Eurovision winner in 1998, was until recently a man called Yoran. As a man, she said, 'I used to have sex up to ten times a day. Now I'm a woman I play by their rules. It isn't nice to have sex with lots of men. Ordinary women don't do it, so neither do I.' (A feminist reading such stuff doesn't know whether to split her sides or tear her hair.)

Women's sexual orientation could well be as volatile as other aspects of a sensibility that can respond in tumultuous puberty to the erotic appeal of the pubescent boy or girl and in maternity to that of the child. The essentialism of so much of our thinking about sexual orientation functions as an oppression in itself. On all sides women are being challenged to make up their minds, to behave predictably, to accept a label and get themselves under control so that others can control them. This pressure comes from all sides; for the woman who becomes sexually involved with another woman it is as likely to come from the lesbian community as anywhere else. Many lesbians, not all of them feminist, challenge the reality of 'bisexuality', understood as the capacity to feel intense erotic interest in people of both sexes. The bisexual female is a frequent performer in heterosexual male fantasy; when such a large proportion of pornographic imagery displays women pleasuring each other in order to arouse a single on-looker male, it is perhaps understandable that a lesbian would reject the stereotype. It is also understandable that she would reject the notion of herself or her lover as making do with lesbian sex until James Bond should happen by and sort her out. Even so, women may still want to claim the right to be erotically interested in people of either sex or uninterested in genital contact with either. Both options are nowadays likely to be construed as denial of an underlying reality.

Lesbianism was known before the second feminist wave, even well known and celebrated, but as an interesting rarity rather than a common phenomenon. The Amazones of Paris insisted on their extraordinariness; they were gifted women, artists, and therefore freaks. The lesbianism of the last thirty years is rather different, down-home, democratic and unpretentious.

Lesbians now insist on the sexual element in women's love. Once upon a time a married woman with the usual relationship with her husband could put her girlfriends ahead of him both in her estimation and in the time she chose to spend with them, without being suspected of genital contact with them. Women could choose to live together for the duration of their lives, sharing everything, and not be suspected of sexual involvement. These companionable states of affairs are now impossible. At the end of the millennium the only love is sexual love, and close women friends must appear to be in regular genital contact, whether they are or not. Some would rejoice at the recognition of women's right to sexual intimacy with other women but others might feel pressured by the duty to act out feelings they do not have, especially if constantly told that they are either in denial or frigid. In the 1980s, when various studies reported a low frequency of genital interaction in lesbian relationships, especially in those of long duration, it was interpreted as evidence of ignorance and inhibition. At the same time that the institutionalized elderly were being incited to sexual activity, lesbians were being urged to spice up their lives. The late-twentieth-century ideal of sex as a process leading to orgasm rather than intimacy, focused on thrill rather than serenity and security, is itself masculine. In California, where the pressure to eroticize lesbian relationships was strongest, some of the most radical lesbian women take testosterone so that they can feel towards women as rapists do.

Women who identify themselves as lesbians do not view lesbianism as a sexual phenomenon first and foremost.

Lilian Faderman

When it is said that it is a woman's privilege to change her mind, what is meant is that it is not her right. Yet change is inbuilt in womanhood; at all phases of her life a woman changes. Even the most essential of her aspects, her body, will change, in its outward shape and in its inner chemistry. It would be strange then if her sexuality did not change too. When people speak of women 'coming out' as lesbian they imply that there is a true self who is a lover of her same sex who has been hidden behind a facade of heterosexuality. For men coming out usually means the ending of a lie; they have been passing as heterosexually active and interested in women when they were actually having sex and lots of it with men. Lesbians are different; between three-fifths and four-fifths of gay women have had heterosexual experience and functioned apparently adequately in a heterosexual role. They were not active as homosexuals while pretending to be 'normal', as men might be, but actually living the lives of heterosexual consorts, wives and mothers. If neither homosexuality nor heterosexuality is innate, if both are socially constructed, none of us needs lose hope that she may yet meet the woman of her dreams and love as she has never loved before.

single

According to zeitgeist expert Charlotte Raven, feminism 'succeeded in making the single state respectable'. As long as it was synonymous with grim virginity, spinsterhood was supremely respectable. The most famous and influential women of the post-suffragette era were the unmarried lady professionals who gave their lives to running schools, hospitals and orphanages and inspecting factories and prisons. Having placed public duty before marriage they were awesome figures. Men could have both a marriage and a profession, but not women, because being a wife, unlike being a husband, was a full-time job. The single women themselves did not realize that having a wife was a necessity if one was to have a successful and rewarding professional career. It did not occur to them that a professional woman might need a wife just as much as the professional man did, but they saw very clearly that they could not combine the duties of a wife with the demands of a profession. The necessity of a professional woman's remaining unmarried chimed in nicely with the demographic fact that, as a result of squandering men's lives in foreign wars, there were not enough men to go around. Allowing women entry to the professions went some way to solving the problem of the maiden aunt, who was rescued from ignominious dependency upon her married relatives by being allowed to earn her own living. Most working women duplicated outside the home the functions carried out by women in the home. In the office the secretary took care of her male employer, kept him supplied with tea or coffee, typed his letters, kept her counsel, earned his confidence, protected him from troublesome clients or bailiffs, and brightened up the workplace with those little feminine touches. In millennial Britain male bosses still expect their female secretaries to carry out a range of wifely duties not mentioned in the official job description. For centuries nursing, whether of babies, the sick or the dying, was done by women at home; when it moved into hospitals a gang of women was recruited to accompany it. Both these professions were dead-end; there was no climbing upwards into the boss's seat; the rift between doctors and nurses was only bridgeable by marriage. Nuns cannot become priests, but they may serve on the altar.

LIVELY ATTRACT F
39, likes cinema, dining out & sport. WLTM M for l'term r/ship. Ldn.

The situation of single women has changed most radically in that unmarriedness now has nothing whatever to do with virginity. Many people who are not married are not single either, because they have what is now called a 'partner', meaning a person they have sex with. Modern etiquette requires that no distinction is made between common-law wives and legally wedded wives or between same-sex partners and other-sex partners or live-in partners or drop-in partners.

The role played by feminism in bringing about this radical social shift is debatable. It could be argued that women's increasing economic independence removed part of the rationale for marriage. If a husband is one who supports a wife and children he is fast becoming obsolete – not because of feminism but because it takes two pay packets to run a home with 'all modern conveniences'. The voluntarily stay-at-home wife is now the prerogative of rich men only; about half the mothers of children under five work outside the home and many more would do if there was adequate, affordable daycare. Feminism was reborn in the late Sixties because it coincided with this sea-change. The stay-at-home wife was coming to the realization that confinement in the home was exclusion from everything that mattered, from mental stimulation to adult company.

Among the consequences of the loosening of sexual mores is that the single state is now less respectable than it has ever been. When people can cohabit informally by mutual agreement, singleness signifies, not a lack of opportunity to pair up, but failure to pair up. There was always a sickly cast of rejectedness about spinsterhood, which was seen not so much as a woman's own choice as the result of not having been chosen. The stereotype of the spinster was that she was a starchy, forbidding creature that men could not warm to. The less she had of male

---

February 14, 1998

Marisa Tomei, Glenn Close, Gloria Steinem, Winona Ryder, and Whoopi Goldberg, all dressed in red velvet, perform Eve Ensler's *Vagina Monologues*.

---

attention the more angular and repellent she became. She began life as a wallflower, the girl nobody danced with, and she continued as unbought merchandise 'on the shelf'. Though the free expression of contempt for 'old maids' is now anathema, fundamental contempt for the unattached female is still in place. Nowadays her miserable condition is explained as a result, not of her lack of appeal, but of her inability to commit herself through narcissism or frigidity or disrupted pair-bonding in childhood. Any explanation of her singleness as the willed consequence of the utter resistibility of the offers she has received simply will not do.

The absurdity of the notion that there is someone 'out there' for everybody is obvious to anyone who has thought about it for more than five seconds. Women's lives would be a lot easier if they started from the opposite premiss, that there is nobody 'out there' and they might as well get on with life and work. Many women are doing exactly that, working towards holidays or career plans or sporting excellence without bothering whether they have a date or not. How many others are fretting about 'getting and keeping a man' can be guessed from the continued success of *Cosmopolitan*, but there is no way of telling how many women there are who are simply not bothered. Even Sharon Stone, of unbelievably perfect beauty, plus wit, plus charm, plus talent, had been known to ask half-seriously, 'So how come I can't get a date?' The men her name has been coupled with (including the man she married) have been markedly deficient in all the qualities that distinguish her. Men don't like knowing that their partner is worth two of them from any point of view let alone from all points of view. They want to feel needed, we are told. Which is where feminism does come in. One thing feminism indubitably did do was to paint on walls all over the world the heartening message that 'a woman needs a man like a fish needs a bicycle'. Unfortunately feminist graffiti were not spectacular enough to blot out women's need to be needed. Like Nancy reeling round the stage in *Oliver!* bawling 'As long as he needs me' – as if Bill Sykes needed her more than any other soft and silly woman he could prostitute and beat up – women continue to build up their fantasy picture of the men who couldn't do without them.

That foolish self-delusion cost Nancy her life, but torch singers go on belting out her fatal song as if it made some kind of heroic sense, as if it was something other than a prelude to murder.

It would take more than feminist graffiti to counter the message being blasted out by all media that real women long for commitment and real men are terrified of it. Bridget Jones will soon be the world's best-known thirty-something female without a boyfriend. *Bridget Jones's Diary*, begun as a news-paper column by Helen Fielding, tirelessly and tiresomely enumerates the heroine's drinking, eating and sex problems and rang so many bells that the book, an updated version of the old Mills & Boon scenario where girl eats heart out over (not-so-rich) Mr Wrong until (extremely-rich) Mr Right makes his play on the second last page, became a bestseller. Bridget, whose head has room for little other than beauty routines, sexual fantasies, envious thoughts and narcissistic panic about her looks, is thin enough to get her man. She will soon be baring her empty little soul in cinemas and on video. *Bridget Jones's Diary* has already spawned a gaggle of imitations in print and on screen, all featuring sassy career women who are insecure, needy, anxious about their body-image and disappointed in love.

Though the once-incessant clamour to marry-and-have-babies has weakened to the mere ticking of a biological clock, women begin to panic about their failure to find a sexual part-ner at an astonishingly early age. They begin to date in their pre-teens and in Britain they tend to do so in couples. *Just Seventeen*, which is read by girls several years younger, devotes eight pages to 'how to land your ideal lad', readers' most embarrassing 'pash palavers' and the 'foxiest first-date outfits around' in its number for 15 January 1998. 'Lush lad' Robbie, born in 1980, expressed his view of the dating game in exactly the same way as his grandfather might have done:

I love the thrill of the chase and all the excitement that comes with it, but once it becomes permanent the spark always goes.

In the short term I'm pretty romantic. I'll take a girl out to dinner and show her a good time. But once girls start feeling settled, they often change. They need commitment and want to speak on the phone every night.

Jakov, sixteen, also found that 'relationships always end up getting heavy', for all the world as if women were still as monogamous and men as polygamous as ever they were, despite the best attempts of feminism, proto-feminism, pseudo-feminism and Guerilla Girls. In March 1998 'Guilt-ridden, 15' of Hampshire wrote to Alex of *Bliss* magazine: 'I've been seeing my boy-friend for five months, but recently we started drifting apart. Now I've made a mess of things by two-timing him with another lad. I know I should make that break, but I just can't bring myself to do it.' Alex replied, 'Some people drag out relationships because they're afraid of being single' – at fifteen years of age. A boy, 'Fed-up, 12', wrote to Andrea the therapist because of a girl who was constantly calling him and wanting to hang out with him. 'I wouldn't mind seeing her occasionally but I don't want to be her best mate,' he explained, afraid of commitment already, at twelve years old. As mothers of teenage boys can testify, girls do keep calling and wanting to hang out, and boys keep going fishing and forgetting to return calls.

Inexplicably the repellent practice of dating or 'going out with people', as Bridget Jones calls it, appears to have survived. Seventeen-year-old Robbie clearly thought that it was his responsibility to buy a girl food and pay for her entertainment. *Marie Claire*, the magazine 'for women of the world', in amongst the endless promotions for fashion, slimming foods and anti-wrinkle creams, runs articles on men who give women wonderful presents. Though the women claimed to give presents in return, it was the spectacular generosity of the males that was on display in the form of jewellery, clothes and holidays, which were listed with the price tags appended. If *Marie Claire* had run an article on women giving lavish presents to men, the men would have seemed belittled and the women desperate. Serious gift-giving like paying the restaurant bill appears to be a gendered activity – which is odd considering that men's toiletries are marketed to women. Women shop for men on a daily basis, but this giving is like women's cooking, a lesser activity with none of the resources and the creativity that go into men's gift-giving. And to think it is more than sixty years since Carole Lombard gave Clark Gable a roomful of doves.

> Men still think they have to pay for our dinner (fools). So we get to spend more money in Joseph.
>
> '100 reasons why it's good to be a
> girl', *Minx* magazine, April 1998

As recently as August 1995 Imogen Edwards-Jones agonized in *The Times* over the fact that a woman still cannot ask a man out for a date.

Our generation chose to underwire their bras, not burn them. We're the sexy minxes who chop the masculinity off executive toys. We're the girls who ditched the dungarees and popped on lipstick. We're post-feminists and yet we're still too wet to invite boys out for a drink.

What cannot be done in person can be done through the small ads. All newspapers, even the tiniest local rags, now carry dating services called 'Meeting Point' or 'Soul Mates' or 'Introductions'. Most carry a chilling caveat:

Be safe & be sure.

Have great fun using this service but make sure you follow these simple rules when arranging your first meeting.

1 Always meet in a busy place.
2 Always make the meeting in daylight hours.
3 Always tell a close friend or immediate family where you are going and at what time you are expected back.
4 Always try to arrange the first meeting without giving away personal details such as address or phone number.
5 Control the situation from the outset.
6 Always be firm and calm if the meeting is not working out as you had hoped.

In the *Cambridge Evening News* 'Meeting Point' for Friday 27 December 1996 forty-nine advertisements appeared, of which twenty were inserted by women. The women, four of whom were single mums, sought 'fun and friendship'; two were lesbians, of whom one wanted 'a soul mate for intellectual discussions' and another 'feminine female for friendship and hopefully loving relationship'. Most of the men specified an age group or demanded a younger woman; six wanted her also to be 'slim'; one bucked the trend by asking for 'buxom'; many demanded GSOH, that is to say, a woman prepared to laugh at their jokes, as well as 'genuine, warm, loving, attractive, sincere, loyal, fit, tall, active'. Men and women tend to use newspaper dating services in roughly equal numbers and about half of both sexes will be in their thirties.

The first British dating agency, Dateline, was founded in 1966 and now claims 35,000 members who pay £150 a year for the privilege of being on the register. Introduction agencies now claim to carry at least 120,000 clients, 15 per cent of whom have been on their books for more than two years. Upmarket agencies charge as much as £700 per year's membership. At the other end of the spectrum are the agencies offering hot dates, casual contacts, and 'instant contacts with wild women worldwide'. People who cannot meet other people in this crowded world can woo each other telephonically on chat lines, which seem to be no more than yet another aid to masturbation masquerading as a cure for loneliness. Singles bars still do good business. Unattached people may invest in singles holidays where they will be thrown into propinquity with other unattached people in skimpy clothing, amid quantities of cheap liquor and hot weather, all propitious for what is euphemistically called love. Supermarkets now run singles nights, with special checkouts where singles can get talking to each other while musicians provide the food of love. Such desperate signalling on the part of women must invite the kind of cynical abuse hinted at in the safety instructions provided for users of newspaper dating services, but as long as there is money to be made from this kind of procuring, the market continues to grow.

Nexus opens the door to life as a secure and fulfilled single person in, what seems like, a world of couples.

We are not a marriage bureau or a dating service and yet, between members, we have an average of 2 marriages, or setting up house together, each week, that happens naturally and is nothing to do with us.

The cult of coupledom would be less destructive to women's peace of mind if so many women were not half of a couple and had no realistic hope of ever being so. Women head the overwhelming majority of single-parent families and they are far less likely to remarry than the men they divorced. By the year 2020 a third of all British households will be occupied by a single individual, and the majority of these individuals will be female. Out of 3.8 million British women in their thirties almost a million are single or divorced. The Office for National Statistics forecasts that a quarter of all women will be single by the year 2020. Even in Kuwait, where marriage was universal a generation ago, matchmakers estimate that there are 40,000 spinsters. A twenty-six-year-old graduate working in a Kuwaiti government ministry said to Kathy Evans of the *Guardian*, 'I want a Western-style marriage, like you see on television, where responsibilities are shared.' The higher the expectation of egalitarian marriage the shorter the duration of actual marriage.

> Whatever happens it is hell for the woman. Getting out of a relationship is very hard but the alternative is living with it for the rest of her life.
> PC Debbie Roberts, Domestic Violence Unit, Norwich Police

Not only are many women not at present half of a couple and not likely to become so, they are also sexually inactive, which is a dereliction of their duty to themselves and the body politic. There is very little they can do about this, bar spending a fortune on body, clothes, face and hair, because, though they can signal availability in a dozen ways, they cannot actually 'make themselves attractive'. The power to make an object attractive lies with the beholder of the object not the object itself. As a woman grows older her chances of mating on any but humiliating terms grow less and less. The constant pressure to be sexually active, which has replaced the old pressure to reproduce, actually places unmated women in jeopardy, and fills them with anxiety and the sense of failure. It is the greater pity then that so many feminists accept and perpetuate the notion that people who are not sexually active are of no account. So let this feminist say it again, 'No sex is better than bad sex.' Bad sex is bad for you. Looking for sex can be humiliating, disappointing and dangerous. Making yourself available can mean putting yourself in jeopardy. No sex does you no harm at all. As many a sole woman out there knows, being single and free is bliss compared to the misery inflicted by an unfair partner, good though the sex may have been. Besides, the things you want don't tend to turn up until you have given over looking for them.

wives

The prestige of the mother having withered away to nothing, the wife is supreme among women. The ascendancy of the female consort above mothers, daughters, sisters, colleagues is illustrated every day by the prominence we give to the so-called First Ladies. The first First Lady, created by the press whether she liked it or not, was Martha Washington; wherever American influence has spread, the cult of the First Lady has gone with it. The likes of Indira Gandhi and Benazir Bhutto, who became world figures because they were daughters, are far eclipsed by the women who become visible in every newspaper on earth because they are wives. Hillary Rodham Clinton was invited to address the UN Women's Year Conference in Beijing not because she is a career woman but because she sleeps in the same bed as a head of state. The unedifying precedent was set twenty years before when Imelda Marcos addressed the UN Conference in Mexico City at the inauguration of the first UN Decade of Women. Mrs Clinton's advisers recommended a baby-pink suit for the occasion, to powder over any suspicion that she might be something of a feminist.

A First Lady must not only be seen at her husband's side on all formal occasions, she must also be seen to adore him, and never to appear less than dazzled by everything he may say or do. Her eyes should be fixed on him but he should do his best never to be caught looking at her. The relationship must be clearly seen to be unequal. A male head of state with an adoring wife can afford to utter pro-feminist sentiments of the most resonant; their impact will be effortlessly neutralized by the spectacular subservience of his wife. That this smiling silent supermenial had a career of her own adds insult to the injury. The power of Hillary Clinton's well-trained brain is principally demonstrated to the American public in her spirited public defences of her husband against charges that he has cuckolded and humiliated her.

Ambitious male politicians must be seen to be happily married, whether they have any stomach for womanflesh or not. However liberal views on homosexuality might have become, no party would put up for the top job a politician without a presentable consort. In the 1960s Edward Heath could head the British Conservative Party as a bachelor; in the 1990s William Hague could not. The politician's wife is expected to display all the wifely virtues, that is, she must look good, but not too good, dress well but not too expensively, speak when she is spoken to, come when she is called and laugh at her husband's jokes. She must never be caught sneering or frowning or yawning or slouching or looking anything but perfectly groomed. No matter how interesting she is in her own right, no matter how effective she is in her own field of operations, the media will be interested in her only as the sexual partner of a great or potentially great man. British journalists charting the rise and rise of Tony Blair were less interested in his wife's legal career than in the kind of knickers she wore. Though as Cherie Booth QC she is a leading barrister, she is expected to drop everything and accompany her husband on all foreign trips. When she went with her husband to the four-day meeting of world leaders in

Denver in June 1997 a hairdresser went with her so that she could have her hair done twice a day. By the time she accompanied her husband to the Middle East in April 1998 she was being recoiffed at least three times a day.

Newly-weds represent 2% of the US population, and 13% of all retail and service sales. In the six months surrounding a wedding, spouses will complete 58% of all cutlery sales, 41% of all stereo sales and 25% of all bedroom furniture sales.

Given the conspicuous success of the best-known wives it is hardly surprising that women are still keen on getting married. In England in 1997 about 300,000 women got married and 160,000 women got divorced. For all the changes that are supposed to have taken place in the last thirty years the ghastly figure of the Bride still walks abroad. She has invaded all regions of the world; women whose mothers were married in kimonos and sarongs now get themselves up in dozens of yards of white satin, tulle and lace. In millennial Britain newspapers still carry pages of photographs of Saturday's brides; glossy magazines run page spreads on the most lavish weddings. *Hello!* magazine exists on a diet of actual weddings, *Bride* magazine on notional weddings. Every children's pantomime ends with the wedding of the Principal Girl and the Principal Boy: the most glittering costumes of gold and silver sequins, diamante, lurex and lamé process onto the stage; the nuptial tableau blazes with firework brilliance and seconds later the curtain falls. The pantomime is over. Mannequin parades also end with a bridal finale as the apotheosis of the designer's vision. The average cost of the short-lived orgy of conspicuous consumption that is a white wedding in *fin-de-siècle* Britain has risen to £10,151: the wedding dress costs in the region of £750; 98 per cent of couples host a reception for an average 111 people; 81 per cent treat themselves to a dream two-week honeymoon for an average of £2,275.

> Do not put such power into the hands of husbands. Remember all Men would be tyrants if they could.
>
> Abigail Adams

To revivify an ailing soap opera all you need is a wedding. The white wedding with tulle, orange-blossom, bridesmaids, flower-girls, page-boys, bridal showers, honeymoons, trousseaux and a list at the smartest shop in town is a ritual insisted on by women, by the bride and the mother of the bride. The cost used to be borne by the father of the bride but these days more and more brides finance their own extravaganza. The groom still celebrates the end of his bachelorhood by spending the eve of the wedding drinking with his male friends and may be so hung over in the church that he hardly registers what is going on. His mates may have decided to inspire him to resist the process of domestication by hiring a prostitute or two to dance naked or jump out of a cake. The assumption is that the bride-groom is an unwilling participant at his own wedding which is the courted female's last hurrah before she settles down to the drudgery of wifehood.

These days when the bride and groom have usually cohabited before the wedding, the bridal whiteness must be interpreted as the sign not of virginity but of chastity, in that the bride will henceforth have sex with her husband only, forsaking all other. Children of the couple may even be present at the ceremony; children that the bride or groom have had by other people may also be present at the ceremony. Wedding as pantomime has largely replaced wedding as sacrament. People who have lived together and found it good simply decide to have a party. Unfortunately some of the briefest marriages are those that follow a long period of cohabitation. Nobody quite knows why this is so. The theory is that unforced cohabitation is less oppressive than sanctioned cohabitation. Marriage does make a difference; even when the marriage service does not contain the bride's pledge to 'love, honour and obey', it acts in the interest of a husband rather than a wife. In the most secular and perfunctory weddings, in the bleakest registry offices, the registrar asks the bride to sign her 'maiden name' for the last time when she signs her marriage lines, as if she were kissing herself goodbye. Though the bride herself may not feel that she has left the family of her father and been taken into the family of her husband, the ancient dynamic still prevails. His friends will now be her friends but her friends are unlikely to become his; even if her parents are not entirely displaced by his, his will take precedence. The dynamic of mutual accommodation that propelled a couple's informal cohabitation is unnecessary once marriage has confined them. As both are bound, the power will come to be concentrated in the person best prepared to take advantage of the situation, and that person is the male partner. Having been so lucky as to acquire a wife, he begins to take the liberties that husbands have traditionally taken, comes and goes as he pleases, spends more time outside the connubial home, spends more money on himself, leaves off the share of the housework that he may have

> We look for communion
> and are turned away, beloved,
> each and each
> Denise Levertov, 'The Ache of Marriage'

formerly done. She sees her job as making him happy; he feels that in marrying her he has done all that is necessary to make her happy. The less she expected it, the more generous he feels for having done it. To her anxious question, 'Do you love me?' he has an easy answer. 'Of course. I married you, didn't I?'

The interesting thing about this particular con is that men need marriage more than women do. A man without a wife is fragile; prisons are full of men who never married. Unmarried men are more likely to die violently. Married men score the highest on psychological well-being, followed by single women, then by married women and last by single men. This is partly because unmarried men are a self-selecting group who have been unable to find wives for some of the same reasons that they find themselves in trouble. A wife, whose first duty is to stand by her man, reassure him, build up his confidence and attend to his creature comforts, is an asset to any man; performing such a role is not necessarily advantageous to the performer. Yet marriage is represented to women rather than men as a sign of success so effectively that failure in a woman's pair-bonding will neutralize success in any other field. Success which might put pressure on her pair-bond is success too dearly bought. Magazine after magazine offers young women advice on how to get their man to commit himself; there is nothing comparable in men's literature. Men buy literature about men's toys and pastimes; women buy magazines about men and relationships. Though young men are more likely than young women to commit suicide because they cannot lose their virginity, and have searing anxieties of their own about

---

61% of men find sport more exciting than their girlfriends or wives.

Total Sport, April 1998

---

relationships, relationships are not represented to them as the only things of value in their lives. This fundamental asymmetry distorts all youthful male–female interaction: the girls put too much into their sexual relationships and set too much store by them, making demands that immature males cannot afford to recognize.

The sacrament of Holy Matrimony is supposed to turn a woman and her husband into one flesh that no man can ever sunder. Most people nowadays have no notion of sacramental union or of a sacramental sign; Holy Orders may be undone and priests abandon their sacred vocation and take a wife, and marriage may be as easily erased. Thinking of marriage as a sacrament serves only to obscure the entirely unsatisfactory nature of marriage as a contract. Occasionally one hears of agitation for a 'new' marriage contract, as if there had been an old one. Contracts require terms and conditions that are negotiated and agreed. When a woman agrees to unite herself to a man in holy wedlock, does she agree to clean his house? To bear his children? Does he agree to keep her and her children? Can either be penalized for failure to supply the services agreed? A husband may expect his wife to clean his house and wash his clothes, but she need not be aware of this. The matter will not necessarily have been discussed. He may expect her and her children to live on what he earns but he has not actually undertaken to provide her with sufficient funds and he cannot be made to supply her with sufficient funds – unless she leaves him, and there is a divorce settlement. Strange that we should have settlements for divorces but not for marriages. A man and a woman who have got to know each other principally by 'going out' together or 'dating' may have quite different ideas about such crucial matters as housekeeping, diet, religion, money, children. Ideally these will have been discussed but, in the rather febrile atmosphere of courtship, it is not easy to give due weight to disproportion and asymmetry in expectations. Rather, it is assumed that spouses will grow together as they experiment with lifestyles and find one that suits them both.

In post-industrial societies it is individuals who marry; the nuptial agreement is seen as involving two people only. Even the children they may have together are not parties to the agreement between spouses. That agreement has been reliant from the first on the intensity and durability of the sexual

> So for your face I have exchanged all faces,
> For your few properties bargained the brisk
> Baggage, the mask-and-magic-man's regalia.
> Now you become my boredom and my failure,
> Another way of suffering, a risk,
> A heavier-than-air hypostasis.
>
> Philip Larkin, 'To My Wife'

attraction between them. If the sexual attraction should lose its potency, if another attraction should eclipse it, the marriage is deemed dead. Such a system is bound to fail; no person can guarantee to be sexually attracted to another for as long as they both shall live. Sex is too anarchic a force and far too responsive to fantasy to serve as the mortar holding together the essential building blocks of society. In defiance of the obvious, modern morality holds that to marry for any reason other than sexual love is to commit a great crime and to court disaster. From accepting that sexual attraction is the essential condition of the initial coupling and establishment of the pair-bond we have moved on to supposing it to be an essential condition of its continuance. Modern marriage is fragile because the demands made upon it exceed the tensile strength of the initial sexual bond.

Studies of the frequency of sexual intercourse between spouses are neither numerous nor reliable, but they all demonstrate the same pattern. The frequency of marital sexual intercourse declines precipitously after the first year before levelling out to a steady shallow decline. Wives are not sexy. Male sexuality demands the added stimulus of novelty. A wife has both a duty to keep her male mate interested and no realistic chance of keeping him interested. She is not even allowed to try keeping him on starvation rations so that she begins to exhibit some of the charms of rarity if not novelty. She has instead to enter into his fantasies and agree to impersonate the various female figures that turn him on. She is not allowed to object that an honourable wife should not be required to come on like a prostitute. If her husband is revolted by her in pregnancy, or when she is breast-feeding, she has to make it up to him or be prepared to lose him. She has no authority as the mother of his child to insist that he shapes up and gets his head together to be a husband and father rather than a boyfriend. Marriage therapists suggest strategies for reviving a husband's flagging interest: dressing up, talking dirty, hiring porn videos to watch together; agony aunts all advise that to let the sex go out of your marriage is fatal. Wives in their fifties are advised to take replacement hormones so that their husbands can still have sex with them.

> A few men fantasize about slow gentle sex with a woman they love. Mostly though, the sex they see in porn movies is the sex men really want, but daren't ask for. Hot, adventurous and jumbo filthy dirty.
>
> Grub Smith, *Minx* magazine, April 1998

The married couple owes it to each other to remain sexually active and sexually interested in each other, though even this mutual obligation is nowhere spelt out. The partner who loses sexual interest is therefore already in default and may put up with a good deal of default on the other side in an attempt to compensate. The wife who does not fancy her husband may excuse her husband's infidelities and neglect, thinking that because she has not 'been any good' to him, she has brought the situation upon herself. This after all seems to be the iron mechanism that actually underlies the mystery of marriage, that a wife thinks herself continually at fault, a husband never. Even where his affections are engaged, a man will chastise a woman who does not perform as he wishes by withdrawal of intimacy; this tactic is not available to most women because their partners would have no difficulty in ignoring it, whereas a woman treated by her partner with coldness and distance is stricken with panic and capitulates at once.

In December 1997 a conference called 'The Chaos of Love' organized by the charity One plus One was told that only 25 per cent of couples were satisfied with their marriage after seven years. Only 56 per cent of women said that they would choose the same man if they had their time over; 71 per cent of men said that they were satisfied with their wives. In 1970 only 66,700 British women had initiated divorce proceedings themselves; by 1989 that figure had risen to 134,400. Three-quarters of all divorces in Britain and Wales are now sought by women, though their standard of living after divorce is bound to plummet. The most commonly alleged grounds for divorce are husbands' adultery and/or unreasonable behaviour; the husband who bothers to defend the action is a very rare exception to the rule. In Britain now one in every 2.3 marriages ends in divorce, more than anywhere else in Europe. The reasons are clearly a reduced tolerance on the part of women of the miseries of marriage. What is remarkable about individual cases is how hard wives struggle to rescue a marriage, taking back unfaithful husbands, apologizing for violent husbands, working to keep idle husbands, drug addicts, drunks and wastrels. On 19 November 1993 the *Independent* reported on four cases: a sixty-one-year-old woman who endured twenty-seven years of marriage with a man who despised her, beat her and kept her in ignorance about his own movements; a forty-nine-year-old married for twenty-three years, whose husband left her for another woman, returned and then began another affair; a thirty-four-year-old whose husband used his knowledge of the abuse she had suffered at the hands of her father to get his own kicks, gave up his job and let her keep him and the four children she had by him; a thirty-year-old whose husband attacked her, squandered his severance pay, cashed in their endowment policy, cancelled their pensions payments and allowed debts to build up without telling her. All of these women had children and all struggled to remain in their unbearable marriages for the children's sake.

More and more women now refuse to put up with being lied to, beaten and betrayed by the fathers of their children. The truth behind the so-called decline in family values is that the illusion of stable family life was built on the silence of suffering women, who lived on whatever their husbands thought fit to give them, did menial work for a pittance to buy the necessities that their husbands would not pay for, put up with their husbands' drinking and their bit on the side, blamed themselves for their husbands' violence towards them, and endured abuse silently because of the children. The honour of the family was served if the appearance of unity was maintained; all marriages were happy marriages. The most vocal abuse of the feminists of the Sixties and Seventies came from women insisting that they were happily married. Feminists were often asked why more of the women who phoned in to radio and TV programmes would not admit the justice of the feminist critique of marriage. The answer was as obvious as it was painful. The wife who admits to outsiders that she is unhappy is throwing in the towel; a woman who has worked hard at being a wife for year on year has made an investment in her marriage that will be irrevocably lost the moment she admits defeat.

For women divorce carried and still carries high penalties. Very few husbands agree to support their wives at all generously, supposing that they can afford to. Strangely the same men who have been divorced for adultery and unreasonable behaviour have less difficulty in finding new spouses than their innocent ex-wives do. It seems there is never any shortage of women who will commit adultery with married men and that even women who call themselves feminist are perfectly willing to marry a man who has already rendered a wife or two acutely miserable. One of the women who told the story of her divorce to the *Independent* added a rider: 'One thing that riles me is how our men-friends colluded in keeping his secret. They knew all about his vices, yet nobody said a word.' Against a woman men defend and protect each other, right or wrong; women are all too ready still to accept a man's view of his relations with women, and to understand men whose wives, with much longer and closer experience, don't understand them. When women are ready to believe that a man's saying 'My wife doesn't understand me' means 'I behave unreasonably towards my wife', feminism will have got to first base. One wife is all any man deserves.

power

emasculation

It has long been believed that women, whether they are loving mothers, willing consorts or non-compliant bitches, will drain men's virility if they get the chance. Everyone who has ever discussed male potency has been driven by worry that men weren't what they used to be. It is nearly four hundred years since Alexander Niccholes lamented that women were obliged to dress suggestively, their breasts 'embared', as if the world had grown 'barren through increase of Generations' and men had lost their potency. There has never been any shortage of nerdy, gormless wimps for moralists of Niccholes's kidney to produce in evidence. Renaissance moralists thought that

> All men are feminists now. It's the only way to pull chicks.
> Rik Mayall

teaching men the arts of dalliance, so that ladies would persuade them to waste their manly substance in the pursuit of pleasure, slackened both their muscles and their resolution. All kinds of whores, from the lowest serving-wench to the most resplendent concubines, were blamed for the existence of simpering, vacillating, lily-livered men, carpet knights, or lounge lizards, as my father's generation called them. Tribesmen in New Guinea still remove their sons from the women's longhouses so that they can be turned into warriors; spending time with a woman in her garden will weaken even an adult man, who must stalk and rape her in the forest instead. Since the beginnings of recorded history, a woman's man has been considered less manly than a man's man.

The breaking of the second wave of feminism in the late twentieth century brought a new kind of accusation, that the stridency and aggression of feminists had screwed phallic anxiety to such a pitch that men were finding themselves unable to perform the sex act. German sex therapists are now blaming men's limpness on women's having better jobs than men. Sexologists produce paper after paper at conference after conference charting the rise in the numbers of men seeking treatments for impotence. The evidence is mostly worthless, for no account can be taken of the immense number of variables involved, let alone the fact that sex therapy is a brand-new variety of quackery and has therefore not much in the way of historical data with which to compare the new figures. Smoking, alcohol consumption and medication all have a demonstrable effect on erectile function; feminism has none.

The breaking of the second feminist wave coincided with a vast increase in the practice of effective contraception. For the first time in human history the human vagina was always and everywhere accessible. This was only true in the developed or rich world; reports of impotence were, needless to say, emanating from that same world. Men who had been kept on relatively short rations of sex and therefore in a constant state of genital tension were easily convinced that if increased opportunity should arise they would be equal to it. When sexual opportunities proliferated, their bluff was called. Tumescence became harder to achieve. Men began to feel pressure to perform, complicated by embarrassment amounting to anguish at any failure to perform. Things have reached so pretty a pass that the merchandisers of Viagra®, an erection-capacitating pill to be taken an hour before sex, tell us that 40 per cent of men will have experienced difficulty in achieving or sustaining erection by the time they are forty. When Viagra was launched in April 1998 36,000 prescriptions were dispensed in the first week. The number of American men suffering from 'impotence' is estimated at 30 million. Such huge figures suggest that what is being regarded as a dysfunction is merely a naturally occurring variation of normal function.

> In 1996 male cosmetic surgery was a $9.5 billion industry nationwide.
>
> American Academy of Cosmetic Surgery

In the *New Yorker* for 30 October 1995 appeared a remarkable article by Susan Faludi that traced the agonies of the male performers in pornographic movies as they and the whole film crew and studio team 'waited for wood', that is, for an erection good enough to film. Virtually all of the male porn stars had, in Faludi's words, 'bailed out of sinking occupational worlds that used to confer upon working men a measure of dignity and a masculine mantle but now offer only uncertainty'. Faludi finds the cause of male insecurity in the collapse of the prestige and power of the working man, caused not by the assault by women upon job opportunities but by structural change in the job market. 'Suddenly, in the eighties and nineties, ornamental occupations became the job oases.' Said a senior porn star to Faludi: 'We're the last bastion of masculinity. The one thing a woman cannot do is ejaculate in the face of her partner. We have that power.' The crux of the article was the account of the suicide of Cal Jammer. Jammer, like many male porn stars, had begun having serious and costly 'problems with wood' and was rapidly becoming unemployable. His explanation was that he was having problems with his wife. When he shot himself on the doorstep of her house he had gone there intending to shoot her.

If Cal Jammer had read the *New Yorker* for January 1997, his problems with wood might have been over. Amid the usual advertisements for books and international real estate, he would have found a full-page advertisement of a kind not often seen in the up-market press, for a penis-stiffening injection.

> This causes the erection to occur like it would naturally by relaxing the smooth muscle and allowing blood to become trapped in the penis. The erection usually takes only 5 to 10 minutes to develop. This allows for the natural progression that typically comes with foreplay, so you and your partner can enjoy a complete sexual experience . . . Priapism, a condition in which an erection lasts longer than six hours, was reported in less than ½ of 1 per cent of all patients. The most common side effect . . . is mild to moderate pain after injection. In clinical studies this was reported by about one-third of patients; although only 3 per cent discontinued use for this reason.

Now you know why Viagra is expected to make a billion dollars for manufacturers Pfizer by the year 2000.

Free erectile dysfunction clinics are now appearing in public hospitals. Sister Biggins at Doncaster Royal Infirmary sees 2,000 men a year and can help 98 per cent of them with either a vacuum pump, or an injection, or inserting a pellet into the penis and rubbing for ten minutes. Sister Biggins, who is brim-full of snappy euphemisms for the standing male member, told *Woman's Own* that hers was the 'most rewarding job in the world'. As an example of the power of her ministrations she told of 'one old boy of 86 [who] hadn't had an erection in years.

He had an injection and found himself standing to attention as he was cycling home. He was so excited he fell off his bike.' Well done, Sister Biggins. Cycling may have contributed to the old man's problems in the first place. God forbid that any woman should belittle the importance of male impotence, but female sexual dysfunction, a vastly more pervasive problem, has never enjoyed the services of a single Sister Biggins. Both male and female dysfunction could be caused by the same mistaken emphasis on penetrative sex as the only real sex. It is not women who have set the penetration agenda. It is men who assess sexual performance as if it were a variety of pile-driving. Faludi looked on as T. T. Boy, described as a 'life support system for a penis', turned in another sterling performance for Caballero Home Video: 'He ground away on the actress . . . with the regularity of a jack-hammer . . . After a while the grinding turned to pounding, the bed and the façade of the bedroom walls rattling in time. I was beginning to feel like an observer on the set of *Earthquake*.' Doctors are already concerned that men will over-use Viagra; if they watch T. T. Boy too often they well may. Phallic anxiety is generated in men by themselves and other men. Women have nothing to do with it.

In 1996 an organization calling itself Concern for Family and Womanhood embarked on a Campaign for the Feminine Woman. Its proponents want to emphasize the importance of natural sex roles, 'the submissive feminine woman, the natural feminine role of wife and mother in the home and the responsible, protective, dominant man'. The break-up of the family, sexual deviance and rising crime were all in their view due to 'the emergence of those unnatural beings, the assertive aggressive man-aping woman and the weak equality-indoctrinated man'. Feminism they said is 'a dangerous cancer and perversion in human society which must be eradicated'. Emasculation used to be the fault of women who melted their men with tenderness and caresses; now it is the fault of women who clash with men. Concern for Family and Womanhood seems to think that if women speak out and assert themselves, men will not clash with them and grow strong in conflict with them, as they would in conflict with other men, but mysteriously cave in and go floppy. The hero seeks out a strong, high-mettled horse; why should he not also seek out a strong, high-mettled woman? There seems no obvious reason why a strong man should be able to husband his strength only in partnership with a weak woman – unless of course male strength is a delusion that can only be maintained as long as it is not challenged by genuine strength, which is, I am sure, not what Concern for Family and Womanhood actually meant.

If masculine dominance and feminine submission were natural, we might expect the hammer–anvil pattern to survive undisturbed by the activities of a small and much reviled bunch of people called feminists. If in the past masculine dominance was only assured by keeping all the economic and legal power in the hands of men, there can be nothing natural about it at all. We would expect that when women became economically more independent they would refuse to bow to male authority or put up with betrayal or bullying, which seems to be what they are doing. Our mothers usually accepted their husband's infidelities in the same spirit that they made do with whatever share of their husbands' earnings their husbands felt like giving them. Nowadays women who would never dream of calling themselves feminists refuse to endure humiliation within marriage. Even agony aunts in the mainstream women's press do not hesitate before suggesting separation from her partner as the obvious remedy for a woman's unhappiness. A social system that depends upon the misery of half of the people is not worth perpetuating. We are only now beginning to wise up to the harsh realities that underlay the unquestioned sway of the breadwinner, who believed himself invulnerable in his own house even when he had physically and sexually grossly abused the people whom he should have been protecting. The greatest irony about husband-as-protector is that he was too often the most dangerous person his wife or his children would ever have to face.

Are there any reasons for believing that men are becoming weaker? Certainly workers are weaker than at any time since the mid-nineteenth century. Workers are now expendable, as they never were before. This powerlessness has not been visited upon them by women but by other men, the bosses who saw to it that the machines which could have liberated their employees from drudgery and repetitive tasks replaced them instead. A man who cannot earn his living is unmanned, long before he sees some woman taking a job he could have done. When he sees women in work and men like himself out of work it is practically inevitable that he will decide that the woman has taken his job and brought him to his present humiliating dependency. Unemployed men are fragile; fragile men are dangerous, especially to women and children.

Concern for Family and Womanhood connect the assertive, aggressive man-aping woman with sexual deviance, as if women's abandonment of a submissive posture has caused some kind of upsurge or outbreak of sexually deviant behaviour. Conventional moralists, unnerved by the sheer numbers of men apparently driven into the arms and beds of their own sex, often seek to blame the phenomenon on repellent women of one kind or another, usually a dominating mother who has overriden her son's autonomy and prevented his developing adult, heterosexual preferences. Such observers assume that men who have sex with men in preference to women are less masculine than other men. Male homosexuals are often thoughtlessly described as effete or effeminate, 'poofs' or 'nancy boys', as if it took less effort to penetrate an anus than it does a vagina, though the opposite is clearly the case. Heterosexuals might suppose that homosexual men come in two distinct varieties, those who penetrate and those who are penetrated, butch and bitch as they are sometimes known, but few gay men have not played both roles. The male penetration agenda applies with added force to gay male sex; a man who never plays the role of penetrator will be called a doormat and slide to the bottom of the pecking order. A man who is too often forced to submit will complain that he is 'always on his knees'. Likewise, in prisons, the most influential inmates are those who exert control over their environment and their fellow convicts, while the most despised and vulnerable are those who are sexually used by them or others.

Same-sex buggery is a sub-section of the culture of masculinity. Though the masculinity culture is not itself a constant and varies at least as much and as rapidly as any cultural phenomenon, certain motifs and characteristics are usually present in some form or another. The process of masculinization is often described as hardening or toughening, words that have their own phallic colouring. Mother's milk must be driven out of the young boy, so that he is no longer a milksop. Indeed, the whole process can be described as a flight from the female, the driving out of the woman. A man is continent; he contains himself, and neither speaks nor moves unnecessarily (the strong, silent type). Tears are typical of the female, who is a leaky vessel, so masculine men have no use for them. In military castes buggery of juniors by their superiors is a version of ordeal. Having endured the pain the juniors arrive at the privileged position of inflicting it on their subordinates as they gain in status. Straight men howl in outrage when told that gay men are a by-product of the same process that shaped them. They will point to the day-to-day collaboration between gay men and older women as evidence that gay men are frozen in momma's-boy mode.

As far as sexual culture is concerned men are no more or less masculine than they have ever been. From a biological point of view men are becoming, though not necessarily less potent, very much less fertile. A healthy young man should manufacture about a thousand sperm every second, day and night, while a woman takes twenty-eight days to bring one follicle to popping condition. This vast disproportion is immensely important in the ordering of human affairs; men could be neither promiscuous nor competitive if their fertility was anywhere near as low as women's. They would have to be careful what they did with their seminal material rather than squandering it in masturbation or chance encounters or buggery. A steep decline in male fertility would completely change the complexion of relations between the sexes – if the human race did not die out first. The human male has always produced a high proportion of defective spermatozoa, 40 per cent misshapen and 20 per cent immobile, but nowadays the overall number of sperm in the ejaculate appears to be dropping steeply. Though there are fertility experts who stoutly deny this and reject the evidence, research into the problem continues at a frenetic pace. The alarm was first raised in 1974; researchers at the University of Iowa assessed the sperm counts of men about to undergo vasectomies and found them to be less than half those of the previous generation. Other reports from

Philadelphia and Houston followed; in 1979 a senior biologist published data that seemed to prove that somehow these researchers had erred and no such decline in sperm numbers could be observed elsewhere in the research community. In

---

Did you know?

If you use a tourniquet (such as a rubber band) around a man's penis to prolong his erection and prevent ejaculation, never leave it on for more than half an hour – the blood could clot and cause gangrene in the penis.

Cosmopolitan, February 1997

1992 Danish researchers compared all the data on sperm counts going back as far as 1938 and found an undeniable decline from about 86 million sperm per millilitre in 1944 to 59 million in 1990. As the volume of sperm in the average ejaculation had also declined the drop in overall fertility was greater than the drop in concentration. The most methodical study, from the Hôpital Cochin in Paris, revealed that the sperm production of 1,351 men had declined by more than 2 per cent per year between 1973 and 1992. Appalled by his results, the director of the laboratory made a special study of an age cohort who had been abstinent for three or four days before their sample was taken; in this group the decline in fertility was even more marked, 3.7 per cent per year. A Parisian man born in 1945 had a sperm concentration of 102 million per millilitre, a man born in 1962 half that number.

Nobody knows what is going on. Some deny that anything is going on. The researchers' first instinct was to look for something that was feminizing men and the obvious candidate was synthetic oestrogen, the residue perhaps of oral contraceptive pills remaining in recycled water after treatment. This proved to be no more than a biological version of the blame-it-on-women theme, for no oral contraceptive residue could actually be found in drinking water. Antibiotic use, lifestyle toxins such as nicotine and tetra-hydracannabinol, mumps, chickenpox, low-level venereal infections such as trichomonas and chlamydia, pesticides, radiation, stress, tight underpants, automobile exhausts, growth-promoting hormones in beef production, caponizing hormones in chicken farming, all were considered and all found to have effects upon male fertility at some stage and at some level. The blame-it-on-women theme re-emerged with the growing awareness that the exposure of males to the damaging compounds must have been intra-uterine, during gestation, because the dates of birth were the critical correlate in establishing the steepness of the decline.

There is one sure way of lowering a heathy man's sperm count, which is to dose him with testosterone. Women's fertility was deliberately disrupted by supra-physiological doses of oestrogen, which worried nobody one bit. As nobody knew how much testosterone men had to start with, nobody knows whether unmedicated men may not now be over-testosteronized. If men were hooked on their own testosterone and deliberately stimulating testosterone secretion by their own behaviours, their sperm production would fall. We could try counting the sperms of football hooligans and joy-riders before, during and for weeks after their climactic experiences, but we still would have little insight into the elaborate synergies involved in healthy spermatogenesis. We have always supposed that in men masculinity and virility and fertility were different names for the same thing. The sooner we cotton on to the fact that the three are not only different but possibly antagonistic, the sooner men will be released from their own thraldom to tyrannical gender roles. Millions of Viagra pills are swallowed worldwide because men are hooked on their hyper-masculine gender roles, to the point of being desperate to act more masculine than they are. For more erections they are prepared to risk their lives and health by playing ducks and drakes with their blood pressure. They might say that they are spending the money (£5 per pill) and taking the risk for women, and they might believe it, but they are wrong. It is not women who need men's erections, but men. Any man has easier and surer and safer ways of bringing a woman to orgasm than by slamming a Viagra-driven organ into her, ways that are unacceptable to him because a female lover might use them as effectively as a man. In making love the way he does he defines himself as a man. The success of Viagra tells us two things, that the penetration agenda oppresses men as well as women, and that they have not taken even the first step towards their own liberation.

fear

Women are afraid of men. Women can be routinely insulted and humiliated for years on end, repeatedly raped and sexually abused and yet keep silence, made to endure a life of kicks and blows from a husband, because they are afraid. They endure unending agonies because they have been made to believe that if they run away, they will be followed and much worse will be done to them and to their children. The beaten woman does not call the police because she knows that sooner or later, once the police have finished with the man who is oppressing her, he will return and do something unimaginably worse than any of the abominable things he has already done. The woman paralysed by terror exists in her own mind as well as that of her abuser to be abused. She can see no way out, no possible rescue, because fear has blinded her.

> A life lived in fear is a life half lived.
>
> *Strictly Ballroom*

Margaret Atwood once asked a group of men why they found women threatening. 'We're afraid that women will laugh at us,' they said. And she asked a group of women why they felt threatened by men. 'We're afraid of being killed,' they said. Perhaps women are more frightened now than they have ever been, because now women do not have extended families to defend them; there are no brothers to administer rough justice to men who have threatened or assaulted them; there are no sisters to lend solidarity; the mother is a figure of no importance. Perhaps the streets are more dangerous than ever because so many women walk alone. Perhaps.

All the evidence seems to show that, frightened as women undoubtedly are, they are frightened of the wrong thing. The worst is already happening to women and it is being inflicted not by strangers on the dangerous streets but by their nearest and dearest at home. Crime surveys show that most crimes against women remain unreported. In the US 38 per cent of women experience sexual molestation in youth, 24 per cent endure rape in marriage, and nearly half are victims of rape or attempted rape at least once in a lifetime, some repeatedly, some at the hands of groups of men, nearly all at the hands of men they know. The British Crime Surveys reach much the same conclusions. There are many reasons why women do not report sexual assaults; chief among them is fear. There is one thing worse than being sexually abused and that is being killed. In the developed world 4.4 per cent of females die of injuries, of one sort or another, compared with 10.3 per cent of males. In Latin America and the Caribbean life is significantly more dangerous for males, 13.9 per cent dying of injuries, while the figure for females rises only to 4.8 per cent. The most dangerous country for females is understood to be China, with 10.7 per cent of females dying of injuries compared with 12.2 per cent of men. The safest area for men might appear to be India, where only 7.3 per cent of males will die as a result of injury, whereas 5.7 per cent of women will meet that fate.

Even from the cloudy vastnesses of these figures one thing emerges with clarity, that males are always and everywhere more likely to die a violent death than females. In the culture of violence the rule is 'kill or be killed' which translates to 'kill and be killed'; of the 606 culpable homicides recorded in Britain for 1993, 375 of the victims were male and 231 female. These figures compare with FBI statistics of 60 per cent of homicides as male on male, compared with 24 per cent as male on female. Of the 70,000 or so people maliciously wounded in Britain each year about two-thirds will be young males. The most likely perpetrators are young males. Our sons are always and everywhere in more danger than our daughters, both of committing crimes of violence and being the victims of crimes of violence, but it is our daughters we are afraid for and whom we teach to be afraid for themselves.

When questioned about the fear of crime young men confess to feeling least; the indices of women's fear of crime are three times those of men. That fear has been taught to women by those who want to protect them. We tell our daughters not to speak to strange men, not to dawdle when they are running errands, to come straight home from school. In 1990 during an umpteenth rape scare police visited university campuses to warn young women and to advise them to attend self-defence classes. As a university teacher, I cannot but be aware of women students' perennial concerns about security; every year we were asked to install even more security lights, to eliminate shadows, to cut down shrubberies, to organize cross-campus buses, so that our students might feel less vulnerable. The result of all our efforts was that they feel even less safe. Occasional attacks on women students still occur but the real risk is far less than women's perception of it.

Homicide figures for England and Wales tell us that 40 per cent of the women who suffered a violent death at the hands of a man were killed by their spouse or lover, 22 per cent by a family member and 19 per cent by someone who was known to them. Only 12 per cent were known to have been killed by a stranger, and yet it is strangers that women are taught to be afraid of. On 4 January 1996 the *Independent* newspaper reported a survey conducted by a motor leasing and retailing

---

Women are 80 per cent of agoraphobes.

---

group that had found that nearly three in five women feared being attacked in their cars. One in four said they were not prepared to drive alone at night on motorways or country roads; 60 per cent of them felt even more vulnerable on public transport. A 1998 Middlesex University study found that two-thirds of women in Finsbury Park would not go out after dark; one woman in eight avoids public transport. Such fear is not rational. If anyone should be afraid of strangers it is men, for the largest proportion of men killed, 38 per cent, were killed by strangers, only 35 per cent by people known to them, 12 per cent by family members and 6 per cent by a spouse or lover. Yet we do not tell men to avoid places of promiscuous resort or of known danger. Victimology studies tell us that there are such things as dangerous places and that the people who resort to them are taking a risk. As far as young men are concerned dangerous places are 'where the action is'.

Feminists have argued that the emphasis upon women as targets for attack functions as an instrument of social control. The object is not protection but the engenderment and maintenance of fearfulness. No sooner had the news reached Britain that the drug Rohypnol was being used to spike women's drinks so that they could be sexually assaulted with impunity and retain no memory of the event, than Graham Rhodes set up a charity which he called, after the street name of the drug, the Roofie Foundation. The object was to 'raise awareness' and fund a helpline. The publicity read: 'If you are a woman living anywhere in Britain you should be afraid . . . very afraid.' Such rhetoric has the same effect on women as the breather on the telephone, the obscene caller, the man who follows a woman in the street or chases her car on the motorway, the man who displays his penis. All such men are sniffing for the scent of female fear. Submissive behaviour on the part of the female is their reward.

Some feminists have tried to counter this kind of victimization by teaching women self-defence as a cure for fear. Self-defence is fine as long as you are not physically weaker or less agile than your assailant. Most of the men who are killed by other men have been involved in a violent interchange in which defence and aggression have become confused. To be ready to defend oneself is less abject than cringing beneath any and every kind of assault, but should a woman carry a cosh on her key-chain or keep mace in the glove box of her car? Should she attempt to mimic the alien culture of violence? The men who live within the culture of violence are there because they enjoy it; they become hooked on the adrenaline rush of living dangerously. Is a woman who trains seriously in order to feel less vulnerable likely to get the same fierce pleasure out of displaying her power over weaker or more cowardly people?

A man is following me . . .
I hear him close behind stepping faster
we criss-cross the street together . . .
all my life I have moved with his shadow
pacing the street in this slow mad dance

Jennifer Rankin, 'A man is following me . . .'

The woman who prepares for combat is capitulating to an ever-present vision of herself as the object of attack. The only sure inference we can make about the woman who carries a cosh on her key-chain is that she is frightened.

Perhaps men, like dogs, unconsciously scent fear, find it gratifying and exciting and ultimately interpret it as a cue for attack. Men who are afraid of other men can replenish their manhood at the expense of women who are afraid of them. One aspect of victimization that has been very little investigated is the extent to which seeing oneself as a victim prompts victim-type behaviour and whether victim-type behaviour inspires the offence against the person. A person who begs 'Please don't hurt me' may be introducing the idea of attack into a so far uncommitted interchange. We are told that screaming is a good idea, but is it? What is a wimp after all, but a frightened person? In the animal kingdom fear and flight inspire pursuit; the scent of fear is a stimulus to all carnivores including man. If we are encouraging women and children to behave as quarry are we not pandering to the male's fantasy of himself as predator? By inculcating fear and encouraging fearfulness we may make women and children more vulnerable, but there seems no other option.

The alternative, to encourage bravado, might be to reap the whirlwind that catches up most of the men who die at the hands of other men. Men's experience of violence seems to show that refusing to feel fear is more dangerous than showing it. The infants who are murdered every year are incapable of feeling fear; they do not understand that keeping on crying will place them in extreme jeopardy and so they die. Time and again we read of little girls who were beaten to death because they would not shed tears or beg for mercy, 'naughty', 'sulky', 'rebellious', that is to say, proud and brave little girls.

Female fearfulness may be, like the timorousness of rabbits or deer, adaptive. To suppose this is to suppose that males actually are predators and females their prey, a situation which, if it exists, needs to be neutralized by civilization, rather than enshrined in statute and in custom. Men do not hunt and eat women. The truth is rather that female fearfulness is a cultural construct, instituted and maintained by both men and women in the interests of the dominant, male group. The myth of female victimhood is emphasized in order to keep women under control, so that they plan their activities, remain in view, tell where they are going, how they are getting there, when they will be home. The father who, if his teenage daughter is out at night, insists on collecting her and bringing her home in his car is unconsciously instilling fear into her at the same time that he consciously exercises control over her. His teenage son is at greater risk, but the gendered nature of fearfulness means that his father would not dream of offering to gather him up in the midst of his mates and drive him home. The myth of female victimhood keeps women 'off the streets' and at home, in the place of most danger.

The atmosphere of threat that women feel surrounded by is mostly fraudulent. The sight of a man exposing his genitals causes fear; the man who exposes 'himself' is almost always rewarded by the sight of submissive behaviour as women passing by avert their eyes and hasten their steps. Submissive behaviour may be what such a man can exact by no other means. In the case of flashing, the proper response would seem to be hilarity and ridicule, to deny the flasher his kick. A middle-aged woman used to enjoy trotting around Cambridgeshire villages naked under an army great-coat. 'What do you think of that then?' she would say to surprised shoppers, as she held the coat open. 'Very nice, dear,' they would say. In law women are deemed incapable of indecent exposure. A woman's body signifies nothing; a man's body, or rather the attachment to a man's body, signifies power over life and death.

To complain to police is to reinforce the flasher's belief in his penis's magical power to amaze and appal. In truth the man standing with his pants down is extremely vulnerable, not least through the thin-skinned genitalia themselves. In a society where women had not been successfully victimized a man who displayed his genitalia to passing women and girls would inspire ridicule rather than dismay. He could expect to be stripped of his trousers and driven through the town, maybe stood naked from the waist down in the pillory for a day or two, and pelted with kitchen refuse. What women feel in the late twentieth century has been investigated by Sandra McNeill, who lists three stages of reaction: first, fear, shock and disgust, then anger or outrage, then guilt, shame or humiliation. When she asked the women what they were afraid of, she expected them to say 'of rape'. What they said was that they were afraid of death. Why should a woman who sees a man with his pants open and turkey-neck and gizzard hanging out feel mortal fear?

Indecent exposure began its existence as an offence under the criminal law in 1824 as a section of the Vagrancy Act; and applied to any man caught 'wilfully openly lewdly and obscenely exposing his person with intent to insult any female'. The wording had to be specific because penises were relatively often seen when men urinated; presumably ladies who had penises waggled at them in the 1820s were annoyed rather than frightened and complained of an impertinence rather than a threat. Then they connected the visible penis with excretion rather than with rape or death. In the 170 years intervening the symbolic importance of the phallus has grown as its visibility has waned. At the close of the twentieth century the penis is the one part of the human body that has not been explored in all its variety and detail; instead it is hinted at in the advertising imagery of chocolate bars that explode in the mouth, in the silhouettes of weapons of mass destruction and the shapes of vehicles that cleave the universe. With the disappearance of the actual penis from common view and its replacement by the fantasy phallus has come the thoroughly modern anxiety about penis size, just as a cultural anthropologist would expect.

One of the women in McNeill's sample interpreted the act of unveiling the penis in this way: 'He was saying "I might be an old slob but I've still got more power than you have. I've still got this. I can keep you under control."' In fact the old slob had no power over the woman that the woman herself did not grant him; if she threw a stone hard at his crotch, he would soon discover the real vulnerability of his genitalia. Reporting indecent exposure to the police is mostly useless because the offence must be witnessed by the arresting officer at the time of the arrest. More important, in my feminist scheme of things, is the consideration that to complain to the police, rather than throwing a pail of slops over the reprobate, is to be obliged to exaggerate the power of the limp dick. The complainant is obliged to lose her time and trouble and tangle up a lot of public money in attempting to discipline a nuisance.

In 1993 Jalna Hanmer and Sheila Saunders said of a series of sexual offences against women – the touching up by a seventy-year-old man of an eighteen-year-old woman as she got onto a bus, flashing, an old man masturbating in front of a visitor – 'These crimes may legally be minor, while the impact on women may be major.' It is my opinion, considered and reconsidered over forty years, that the only way forward is to work to reduce the impact of such misdemeanours on women, rather than to expect the courts to track down all offenders and invoke the law in all its severity. It is up to women to render the exposure of the male organ as trivial and meaningless as the intentionally grotesque exposure of women's bodies already is. The penis is not, and should not be treated as, an awesome thing. By protesting against the exposure of male genitalia as a crime against the body politic we exaggerate the disruptive power of the phallus.

Donna B. Schramm describes the horror of rape in these terms:

Rape can be the most terrifying event in a woman's life. The sexual act or acts performed are often intended to humiliate and degrade her: bottles, gun barrels or sticks may be thrust into her vagina or anus; she may be compelled to swallow urine or perform fellatio with such force that she thinks she may strangle or suffocate; her breasts may be bitten or burned with cigarettes.

Most of these acts could be performed by someone without a penis. By choosing to describe the horror of rape in terms of generalized sexual assault Schramm raises the possibility that the least terrifying kind of sexual assault is the actual rape. Moreover the fact that a sex act may be meant to humiliate and degrade should not necessarily mean that it does humiliate or degrade. We do not have to accept the rapist's script. If women are to reject the role of natural-born victim, they will have to reject the ludicrous elevation of the humble penis to the status of devastating weapon. The extent to which women have followed the phallocratic script was memorably illustrated when Lorena Bobbitt cut off her husband's penis instead of his head. It is illustrated every time women against rape suggest that castration would be an appropriate punishment. The most pressing need must be to demystify the penis; to perpetuate the mystique of the penis as a sacred object the mere sight of which is death is to act in our own worst interest. Of all the parts of a man that can hurt, a penis is the least.

loathing

No statement in *The Female Eunuch* caused more derision and amazement than the sentence, almost always misquoted, 'Women have very little idea of how much men hate them.' That sentence meant what it said: women don't know how much men hate them, when men hate them, or why. Enid Golightly was sleeping peacefully in her bed one night in August 1996 when her husband bashed her on the head with a club hammer with such force that fragments of bone were pushed more than an inch into her brain. Her husband was a

---

In my country one woman dies every ten days because of serious abuse by a man in her immediate family or a close acquaintance.

Marianne Eriksson, Swedish MEP

---

fifty-four-year-old vicar with a record of exemplary service to others; his bishop declared that he considered Golightly a good

Christian and a friend, and that was after he had been convicted at Newcastle Crown Court on 17 January 1998 of causing Enid grievous bodily harm with intent, and sentenced to five years. Golightly claimed to have found his wife lying naked in a pool of blood at the foot of the stairs. According to the police the pool of blood was in the conjugal bed. When her husband was sentenced Enid screamed in anguish, 'Five years! What am I going to do?' She had given evidence for the defence. 'I know he would not do anything like this to me,' she had said. The police, the judge and the jury disagreed. Even so, for most of the sixteen months that it took for the case to come to trial, Golightly had been free on bail to live at home with his wife who now has some impairment of brain function. Every day of the trial husband and wife had come into court hand in hand. The Bishop said, 'The Church deeply regrets one of its clergy being in this situation.' Not a word about Enid.

When Jacqueline Newton left her husband she had absolutely no idea that he would mix hydrochloric acid with a paint-stripper that he knew contained a carcinogen, put on his helmet, drive his motorbike to the off-licence where she worked and spray the corrosive inflammable mixture all over her face and body, then pursue her as she fled screaming and pour more of the stuff over her as she lay curled up in a terrified, agonized ball on the floor of a storeroom. It never occurred to her that the man who visited her in hospital every day was the man who had done his best to disfigure and maim her. When she made a televised appeal for her attacker to come forward she let him sit beside her. The police knew at once what she was so slow to grasp, that the man who was solicitous for her was the man who hated her most in the world.

A few men hate all women all of the time, some men hate some women all of the time, and all men hate some women some of the time. We do not know whether one kind of woman-hater predominates or whether all three kinds exist in roughly equal proportions. When Susan McDonald began an affair with Milton Brown in May 1996 she had no suspicion of the depths of vicious loathing that lurked beneath his cool exterior. When he started knocking her about she told herself that it was

> The Wu Tang have a lovely little song in their
> repertoire about defecating on girls after sex.
>
> Julie Burchill

because he thought she was unfaithful, i.e. because he loved her. Despite the beatings she kept on seeing him. At last, after an especially savage beating, he refused to let her leave his flat, except for the evenings when he walked her to the local soup kitchen to get something to eat. He stabbed her in the left arm with a rusty horse pick and refused to allow her to seek medical treatment. He beat her up again so badly that he broke the injured arm and several ribs. That night on the trip to the soup kitchen she finally ran away.

Milton Brown seems to be one of the men who hate all women all of the time. By the time he began systematically abusing Susan McDonald he had been charged four times with rape. One of the victims was a twelve-year-old girl who was too terrified to face him in court. Though he must have been guilty of statutory rape at least, forty-four-year-old Brown was allowed to plea-bargain; for pleading guilty to two charges of unlawful sexual intercourse with the child he was, unbelievably, put on probation for two years. Susan McDonald had only been able to get away from him on the way to the soup kitchen because his attention was distracted by the sight of a woman passer-by who was obviously drunk. He followed her, indecently assaulted her, and marched her back to his flat where he subjected her to a ten-hour ordeal. When the case came to trial Brown, who was defending himself, kept this woman in the witness box for two days while he took her through her statement again and again. Another woman who met Brown outside a Soho jazz club accepted his offer of somewhere to live and went home with him. Brown raped her at knife-point three times in fifteen hours. He kept her in the witness box for three days. Milton Brown managed to transform his legal right to defend himself into a licence to torture two women for days on end before an audience who could not intervene.

> Men do not beat women because of low self-esteem. They are not a fringe group of society with emotional problems that need to be pitied. There is no cycle. A man beats a woman for any reason. Not because she becomes 'more assertive'. But because she is there, as a target, with anything used as an excuse.
>
> Vique Martin, *Simba* 9

This pleasure has proved difficult for other woman-haters to resist. The precedent was set by Ralston Edwards who had so fantasized about the unparallelled opportunity for torture that his trial for raping Julia Mason offered him that he had kept the clothes in which he raped her unwashed for the occasion. The woman judge was obliged by precedent to allow Edwards all the time he needed to conduct his defence; if she had not he would have had grounds for appeal. She had also to be careful not to appear to be persecuting him in case she should arouse the sympathy of the jury. As a result Edwards had the pleasure of keeping his victim in the witness box and cross-questioning her for six days. Robert Roscoe, chairman of the Law Society's criminal law committee, declared that it was 'a very unfortunate incident, but . . . just one case which is unlikely to be repeated'.

Roscoe was wrong. As he spoke a Japanese student who had been raped by five young men was enduring thirty-one hours of cross-examination by their barristers, in an ordeal played out over a record twelve days. The judge told the defendants, 'For over thirty hours this girl had to relive the ordeal in a public court and in front of total strangers. Outrageous suggestions were put to her on your instructions. You, not your counsel,

> Inconvenient as it may be, the reality is that one can have great sex with someone one neither loves nor likes; indeed under the right circumstances hatred is an effective aphrodisiac.
>
> Dennis Altman

added insult to injury and heaped further humiliation upon her.' The fortitude displayed by the anonymous 'girl' student, who appeared in court unsupported by any member of her family because she had spared them the knowledge of her humiliation, was not enough to make a woman of her in the male judge's eyes. No sooner had the woman-haters twigged that there was a possibility of using the courtroom as a torture chamber than they were all doing it. Floyd Bailey followed the precedent set by Ralston Edwards and made the woman who was the subject of a rape case against him describe his genitals in graphic detail.

The Labour Home Secretary is now searching for a way to protect the victims of rape from such ordeals but, if he cannot do so without compromising the rights of defendants, there will be no remedy. Feminists have argued for twenty years that the legal system enshrines contempt for women and operates against them, and have been denounced as shrill and unreasonable for doing it. In 1981 Lynne Griffiths went into a newsagency next door to the bank where she worked and was served by a man called David Daniels who began to pursue her with letters and telephone calls. In 1983 he was jailed for life, after admitting one rape and three attempted rapes. He had stabbed one of his victims and threatened to cut another's breast off. He continued to persecute Lynne Griffiths from his prison cell; in 1992 she wrote a letter telling the South Wales police that she had never had a relationship with Daniels and that she was afraid that if he was released on parole she would be his next victim. Parole was denied. Daniels issued a writ for defamation but the case was dismissed as frivolous and an abuse of process. Daniels appealed. Cherie Booth QC argued at the Court of Appeal that Lynne Griffiths's letter was indeed libellous and Daniels should have the right to sue. The three judges agreed. The immediate result was that Lynne Griffiths had to pay the costs of the earlier court action, estimated at £50,000, and will have to be prepared to pay the costs of a High Court libel action as well.

The deeper the morass of misogyny through which we all have to wade the more vociferous the condemnation of anyone who dares to mention it. It is as easy to vilify women as man-haters, which they most emphatically are not, as it is difficult to challenge men on the grounds of their woman-hatred, which is real, pervasive and obvious. Any woman who points out the obvious fact that men hate women will herself be branded a man-hater who has brought men's hatred upon herself.

> Let's say I committed this crime . . . Even if I did do this, it would have to be because I loved her very much, right?
>
> O. J. Simpson

There is no point in trying to establish reasons for men's hatred of women because hatred is irrational. A woman trying to understand men's cruelty to women is confronted again by a simple antipathy, which is what sexism means. Sexism is an antipathy to persons of the opposite sex, whether felt by men or women, but in fact felt by men. Though all kinds of women are reviled as man-haters no woman has ever tortured a powerless man in the way that some men torture powerless women.

Women do not have the vast vocabulary of insults for men that all men apply to women every day. Nothing that any Englishman can call anybody is worse than the word 'cunt'. A prick though contemptible is a lovesome chap by comparison. Men whether straight or gay revile cunt.

James Smith is now fifty years old and in jail. In 1980–2 he had a relationship with Tina Martin, whom he used as a punch-bag even when she was pregnant with his child. In 1982 Smith began a relationship with a fifteen-year-old whom he tried to drown. Then he met Kelly Ann Bates. She was fourteen. Three years later, as he held her prisoner for a month, he amused himself by gouging out her eyes, stabbing her in the eye-sockets, and cutting her on the ears, nose, eyebrows, mouth, lips, scalp and genitals. He scalded her on the buttocks and left foot and burned her thigh with an iron. He broke her arm and crushed her hands. Ultimately he drowned her in the bath. In England and Wales two women every week die at the hands of the man they live with. When any woman is killed the most likely suspect is the man she lives with. The death is usually the denouement of a long history of hatred, hatred that the brutalized woman interpreted as love gone awry.

WHOA – Women Halting On-line Abuse – has opened a site at whoa.femail.com

---

Men's cruelty to women cannot be explained as simple aggression or even blind rage. The British Medical Association issued a report in July 1998 estimating that more than one in four British women experienced domestic violence, ranging from being punched, choked or bitten to being forced to have sex against their will, and recommended that all women patients be asked about their experience of domestic violence as is already done in the US. The same report noted that attacks on women were more likely when they were pregnant. Domestic violence is not simply a saga of broken bones and black eyes, of mayhem and fisticuffs. Violent partners also persecute their womenfolk with threats and insults, justify their savageries as provoked by the women themselves, and keep them in a state of terrified contrition. It is in vain to wonder whether men would beat up on women less if women were more submissive or whether standing up for yourself would be a better strategy. Men bash women because they enjoy it; they torture women as they might torture an animal or pull the wings off flies or kick the supporter of an opposing team as he lies helpless on the ground, because they get off on it. Better educated men get the same thrill from torturing their partners verbally, undermining their confidence, sneering at them, jerking them about emotionally. Once a woman finds herself in this sadistic cycle there is only one thing she can do. She cannot hope to wean her partner off his savage satisfactions, or blunt his sense of grievance, or get him to love her as she deserves. She can only leave him. And he will follow her, threaten her, shine the lights of his car into her house at midnight, get his friends to join in terrorizing her. An abusive partner is the most faithful partner of all; addicted as he is to the pleasure of battering and abusing his woman he cannot let her go. And that goes as much for the pin-striped city gent who spends his leisure time humiliating his wife as for the stabber and gouger.

> Sometimes boys say really NASTY things about the way you look, talk or act. But believe it or not it could just be their way of telling you that they like you!
>
> *Shout* magazine

We have realized at last that rape has nothing to do with lust and everything to do with loathing; sexual harassment too is based in hatred and resentment of the female interloper. What we have to understand now is that loathing has its own pleasures and they are addictive. A brutal man can feed his habit for many years undetected. Even now when awareness of rape, sexual harassment and domestic violence is much higher than it was thirty years ago, it is an unlucky man who meets with any kind of punishment. In London in 1997 of 512 reported incidents of domestic violence, only 103 resulted in arrests; only thirty-one men were subsequently charged, and nine of the women subsequently withdrew the charges. Only nineteen of the cases came to court, and only thirteen men were convicted. Only two went to prison; the rest paid fines, or did community service and two were conditionally discharged. Domestic assaults are regarded as lesser crimes than non-domestic assaults; the perpetrators face the lesser charges of common assault rather than actual or grievous bodily harm, and the charges are more likely to be downgraded. In British law a man who has brutally murdered his wife can defend himself by producing evidence that he was provoked, that his wife goaded him so incessantly that he finally 'snapped'; if the defence succeeds the offence will be commuted to man-slaughter and the killer may even walk free from the court with no heavier sentence than a year or two's probation. Provocation as defined by law may consist in no more than words, the dreaded 'nagging'. Nagging is simply complaining that no-one is listening to, grievance relay that gets nowhere. It is never appropriate to answer a word with a blow; any legal system that enshrines a man's right to silence someone who is speaking offensively by beating her to death is barbaric. The annual successes of the provocation defence in cases of wife murder are all the evidence we need of the continuing inequality of women before the law.

The battered woman can hope for little in the way of redress as long as she persists in hoping against hope that she can keep her family together by forgiving her abuser or by taking the blame upon herself. Her blind faith that her batterer loves her when in fact he loathes her may cost her her life. The most effective schemes to counter domestic violence are those that insist upon the cessation of the abusive relationship. In Britain the Norwich police arrest abusers and take them out of the home; once an abuser is excluded from the home his partner is entitled to a panic button on her telephone and on a pendant she can wear around her neck. Pressed, the button sends a signal to the emergency operator who alerts police and records everything that is going on. The police are clear that there is no cure possible within the relationship; the women themselves find this conclusion much harder to reach, because they simply cannot believe how much their men hate them.

The powerlessness of women to find either protection against abuse or redress for abuse is as evident in cases of sexual harassment and rape as in domestic violence. Most rape and sexual harassment occur beyond the reach of the law; both are embedded in the texture of everyday dealings between men and women. A date turns to a rape when the lovelessness of the man's interest can no longer be disguised. Marital sex turns to rape in exactly the same way. In both cases the woman is slow to sense the implacable hostility that looks at her out of her man's eyes. Women are raped, abused and harassed not by rampaging strangers but by men they see every day, men they thought they knew or men they thought they could ignore. Dig it. The man is not born who will not hate some woman on occasion. Odds on it will be the woman with the greatest claim on his love. The law and the police can do nothing to protect her as long as she persists in the fond delusion that what looks and feels like hatred is really love.

masculinity

Masculinity is to maleness as femininity is to femaleness. That is to say that maleness is the natural condition, the sex if you like, and masculinity is the cultural construct, the gender. Where once feminists talked of sex discrimination, they now usually refer to gender roles, because the cultural construct is what can and should be changed; sex, as a biological given, is less susceptible. The distinction is rather like the one to be found between the genotype, which is what is written in the DNA, and the phenotype, which is how that immense text is quoted in actuality. The potential of the genotype is enormous;

> A man feels himself more of a man when he is imposing himself and making others the instruments of his will.
>
> Bertrand de Jouvenel, *Power*

the phenotype is the finite creature that is all that can be made of almost limitless possibility in a single lifespan in a single set of circumstances.

In June 1997 a report in *Nature* argued that masculinity (as distinct from maleness) was genetic: David Skuse of the Institute of Child Health and workers at the Wessex Regional Genetics Laboratory had been studying Turner's Syndrome, which is a consequence of being born with only the X of the final pair of chromosomes. Though they have no uteri or ovaries these single-X individuals are classified as female. They usually grow up to be short in stature and infertile. The researchers found that the single-X 'girls' displayed 'masculine' characteristics in that they were insensitive, demanding and obtuse. The researchers explained this as a lack of the feminine traits of intuition and sociability, on which girls usually score higher than boys, the inference being that these were carried in the second X. The single-X individuals who inherited their X from their mother had more problems of social adjustment than the ones who inherited their X from their father. Peter McGuffin and Jane Scourfield of the University of Wales Medical College welcomed the information.

> There has been a tendency to play down the possible role of biology in accounting for psychological differences between men and women. For the first time we have evidence about the location of a gene that plays a part, challenging the prevailing belief that gender differences are largely culturally determined.

If we look more closely at what the new information actually amounted to, this interpretation seems rather too definite. The Skuse team had graded eighty-eight Turner's Syndrome individuals on an unsociability questionnaire; those whose X chromosome came from their fathers scored five out of a possible twenty-four, those whose X came from their mothers scored nine, but this compares with scores for a control population of four for the boys and two for the girls. The Turner's Syndrome children would appear to have rather more serious socialization problems than normal XY boys who scored closer to XX girls.

An 'unsociability' test that establishes a high of twenty-four when the norm is between two and four would seem to contain a number of significant variables; did the whole group of single-X 'girls' display the same or contrasting kinds of unsociability? How much of the single-X truculence could have been explained by differential treatment from carers and parents? And so on.

> He [President Clinton] embodies a masculine virility that has been under attack in the States for so long.
>
> Katie Roiphe

For all the hoo-ha Skude and his team had not proved that masculine men are born. They had certainly not done anywhere near enough to counter the vast amount of research on how they are made. That process begins when the carer who thinks a child a boy readily offers it food when it cries; the same carer, thinking a child a girl, will allow it to cry longer and will soothe rather than feed it. This sounds preposterous but it has been proved in a famous series of experiments, in which subjects were given wrapped-up infants, and randomly told that the infants were male or female. When told that female babies were male, the subjects treated them as male, responding quickly to their vociferations and interpreting them as demands for food. When told that male babies were female, they let them cry longer and were comparatively reluctant to offer them food. Observers of breast-feeding have likewise observed that male babies are fed more often and for longer at a time than female babies. Mothers perceive boy babies as hungrier and as better feeders than girls; what this means is probably that they enjoy feeding their boy babies more than they enjoy feeding their girls, for whatever reason. We know less about these mechanisms than we should because as little work has been done on the psychology of breast-feeding as on every other aspect of the well woman's function. The boy baby learns that he can have what he wants and quickly, the girl baby that she has to learn patience. Boy babies are cooed to on a different note. They are potty-trained later. The sociability and intuitiveness that Skuse valued in XX girls is simply biddability by another name, and there is a distinct possibility that it has its roots in the insecurity that the little girl feels in her relationship with both her parents.

> Do you think that men are any good for anything? It seems to me that men are ruining the world.
>
> Nina Simone, 1997

Then there is the vexed question of father-love versus mother-love. Daughters will develop more self-confidence if their fathers are encouraging and appreciative of their efforts, but fathers seldom give such matters much attention and, if they do, usually demand objective verification of a daughter's merit before giving encouragement. The self-confidence of boys, on the other hand, is reinforced by mothers' attention which is abundant and rarely conditional. Whether it be because a girl's first love affair (with her father) is inevitably a failure compared to a boy's effortless conquest of his mother, or the outcome of interaction of more complex and mysterious causes, boys grow up convinced that they are lovable regardless of their appearance or their behaviour. The saddest, smelliest, most shambling male individual still imagines that women will find him attractive and is prepared to act on the assumption. And he considers himself entitled to criticize any and all aspects of a woman's appearance as harshly as any other male.

Until comparatively recently both boys and girls were dressed alike and looked alike until a boy was breeched and his hair cut into a manly style. As long as his mother's milk was in him a boy was expected to be girlish, a milksop; his tears were no shame to him. The age at which induction into masculinity was to commence was indeterminate and unstable, especially as mothers wept and railed at the mere thought of giving their babies up to the brutality of schoolmasters, who were expected to teach them to bear pain without flinching as a condition of teaching them anything else. Elizabeth Barrett Browning is thought to have exaggerated a tad in keeping her son's blond curls trailing over his shoulders until he was almost in his teens, by which time it was thought too late to make a man of him. Though we might hope that schoolmaster brutality is a thing of the past, comparatively young men have experienced extreme brutalization at the hands of schoolmasters. An article in *loaded* magazine described teachers who punched boys in the stomach and hit them with sticks. This is one of them:

> A brick shithouse with a ruddy face and unusually thick eyebrows, he was an ex-army man with the morals of a housefly and a temper meaner than the Moscow winter. A man who might have been put on earth for the singular purpose of terrorizing each and every adolescent male under his charge.

The persistence of the expression 'to make a man of [someone]' is the best possible evidence of the deliberateness of the streamlining of the male person into the masculine man. Repeatedly the boy is told that he is about to be made a man of, especially when he joins some paramilitary organization, the scout movement, the cadets, the school officer training corps. At a slightly less belligerent level, he is encouraged to take part in team sports, to get used to rough and tumble and learn to take his punishment 'like a man'. If at all possible he will usually take as his model his father, present or absent, alive or dead. The primary virtue of masculinity for the young man is courage, manifested as stoicism in everyday vicissitudes and as belligerence when threatened. A man is supposed to be unflinching, hard in every sense. So he is taught to control his gestures, to keep his hands and arms still and his face expressionless. His body outline is to be contained and imper-

> My uncles would take me out just to learn how to fight and the lesson was, don't lose the fight or else your uncles are going to give you a hiding.
>
> Jonah Lomu

meable. Real men do not fuss or scurry. It is not women who have foisted this requirement upon men but other men, who prove their own hardness by constantly challenging other men to repeated trials of physical and mental strength. Women often connive at the process; some mothers will taunt their sons if they think them cowardly; some wives and sweethearts will incite their men to attack other men in their defence. Generally, however, though women make boys out of babies it is men who make men out of boys. Though in these enlightened times schoolteachers may encourage boys to express softer feelings, even to weep, in the schoolyard, on the playing field and in the street, compensation for this erosion of masculinity is exacted with interest. Young males form groups behind dominant individuals and prove themselves by conflict with rival groups; at the same time they jockey for power and seniority within the group. The group may be nothing more macho than a cricket team but, even when the game is played in the correct sportsmanlike fashion, individuals are caught up in the drama of acquiring and losing prestige.

Men do not only give orders; they also take orders. A masculine man's attention is focused upon his role in the various groups to which he belongs and from which he gains verification of self-worth. If he spends time with women it is partly or even mostly because he wants to demonstrate his prowess to his mates; he owes no loyalty to the women whatsoever. If it might improve his status he will surrender a woman with whom he has been intimate to another man and feel no qualm of jealousy. Young women are slow to grasp their irrelevance to the emotional centre of a masculine man's life, mainly because young men are the emotional centre of young women's lives. To be successful young men have to achieve a measure of respect from other men; this is the spring of all their behaviours, in the workplace and at play. They have to acquire a vast amount of lore, principally about sport, but also about cars and other boys' toys, subjects upon which girls are uninformed and stupid, and they have to keep it up to date, which requires attention. For a man who is not imposing physically there is the resort of humour; if he is amusing enough he will be caressed by the hard men he cannot emulate.

Despite advances towards sexual equality, many men still feel embarrassed when they have to buy nappies. They fear people will think them henpecked husbands ordered by their wives to buy the nappies. Proudly placing a six-pack [of beer] alongside the nappies sends out the message that the man is really a he-man.

Nick Green, Tesco Clubcard manager

Wherever men are gathered together, in the pool hall, at a restaurant, you can see the wannabes waiting on the dominant males, studying their reactions, gauging when to defer and when to challenge. There will always be one man who can silence the others with a look; most will defer, one may challenge or mock challenge, giving the leader a chance to strut his stuff, and there will be the junior males, who seek to ingratiate themselves by stepping and fetching, and grooming the silverback. The presence of women in such groups distracts the men from the work in hand – if they acknowledge women's presence, which they usually don't. The conversation is between males; when women make a contribution the men ignore it and respond to the last utterance by a male. Often the only woman present is the silent, smiling consort of the dominant male, who is gratified if his subordinates pay her an appropriate measure of attention. The kind of consort who is exhibited in this way is usually particularly decorative; the top honcho is pleased to see his henchmen afraid to catch her eye or speak to her, even as they dream of such executive totty for themselves.

Masculinity requires the creation of dangerous situations, actual or symbolic. The myth that feeds masculinity is that every boy should become a strong and resolute warrior capable of defending his women and children from attack by other males. In stature he should be bigger than a woman, and more heavily muscled. As a US Navy officer wrote in the *Navy Times* in July 1989:

> Warriors kill. If someone cannot kill, regardless of the reason, that individual is not a warrior. Men make the best warriors in comparison to women because men are better at killing in war.
>
> Women cannot compete in a battlefield as they cannot compete in professional sports against men. Women do not hold even one Olympic record for strength or speed. Women are weaker and slower on average as well. Strength, not weakness, wins battles and wars.

As a typical masculinist statement this deserves analysis. 'Killing in war' is here represented as a gendered activity, with the unstated inference that any man who is not good at 'killing in war' is less of a man. The role of modern technology which, being inanimate, must be gender-free, is transferred to a mythical supermale who is good at killing not because he is equipped with devastatingly effective weaponry but because he is some kind of an athlete. Only a minute proportion of males will ever come within reach of an Olympic record, but the achievements of male record-holders empower all men. The implication that the weakest man must be stronger and faster than any woman whatsoever is obviously absurd. The ultimate effect of the myth of masculinity is to generate anxiety in the vast majority of men who cannot live up to it. The cult of masculinity drives many a man who knows himself to be unaggressive and timid to opt out of conventional manhood altogether. Masculinity run riot creates the situation it most dreads, the wholesale effeminization of men who cannot play its game.

Masculinity is a system. It is the complex of learned behaviours and subtly coded interactions that forms the connective tissue of corporate society. Women who are inducted into masculinist hierarchies are exported tissue, in constant danger of provoking an inflammatory response and summary rejection. The brokers of Wall Street are typical of a self-selecting masculinist elite in that they bond by sharing intensely transgressive experiences. Juniors will recommend themselves to the alpha males by persecuting underlings, and in particular, women. The men of one Wall Street brokerage firm used to hold drinking parties in the 'boom-boom' room from which women were excluded. Any woman who dared to make a complaint about the incessant verbal abuse and physical harassment she was subjected to would be dealt with after hours in the boom-boom room, where a lavatory bowl hung from the ceiling. Fifty-year-old stockbroker Pamela Martens described Wall Street as 'an old boy network where that barbaric aggressive behaviour has to be cloned if you want to advance'. The British Stock Exchange is no more civilized: a successful trader used to be known as a 'big swinging dick' and women as either 'babes', 'mums' or, if they were thought to be at all feminist, 'lesbians'.

Female interlopers are often quite unaware of the intensity of the inter-male negotiation and consolidation going on around them. When push comes to shove the guys repair to the men's room and plot their strategy. The woman who thinks her male

> The time has come for all guys to come out of the locker room. Don't be ashamed of that fetid jockstrap and those toxic sweat socks. Leave that toilet seat up proudly! The time has come not only to live openly guy but to embrace the whole guy lifestyle.
>
> 'Guy Pride', *Maxim* Manifesto, March 1997

colleagues are dealing with the case on its merits rather than as a pawn in a long-term power play will only remain in her position of eminence as long as she serves their purposes. It is no accident that women inducted into male hierarchies so seldom identify with other women or advance the interests of other women. They wouldn't have risen so far in the organization if they did. The most obvious case of this mechanism at work was Margaret Thatcher, imported into the Tory hierarchy as an irritant, only to prove strangely successful and so extend the men's tolerance to an unprecedented degree, and ultimately to be unceremoniously, ageistly, sexistly dumped.

According to Ken Auletta, writing in the *New Yorker*, women executives in the American entertainment business believe that 'women are better managers – more nurturing, more collegial, more communicative, more instinctual – and that these strengths mesh better with the corporate culture of teamwork and partnering which is emblematic of the information age. And as women gain authority, most of them believe, our movies, our music, our television, our software, and our other communications will improve.' The accompanying photograph showed twenty-four utterly conformist apparently pre-menopausal females; none wore glasses; almost all were smiling, decorously rather than broadly; all wore lipstick, suits and heels; all were carefully coifed; more than half were blonde.

If we have them to thank for the current state of entertainment, rotten as it is with the crudest misogyny, drunk as it is on extravagant and trivialized violence, they must be a very curious bunch of women. The old rule probably still holds good; if women are running the front office, power must have taken refuge somewhere else. Insisting on women's management style as fundamentally softer and more accommodating is a very good way of ensuring that power stays where it is, in the men's room.

equality

Unpopular feminists 'fight' for liberation; popular feminists work for equality. In *Who Stole Feminism?* Christina Hoff Sommers argues that the bad feminists, i.e. the gender feminist activists, stole the movement from the good, i.e. the mainstream equity feminists who adopt a moderate, unpretentious posture. 'They embrace no special feminist doctrines; they merely want for women what they want for everyone – a "fair field and no favors".' These are the feminists everyone can like. The least liberal people will agree that women should get equal pay for equal work – provided they actually do equal work. Women should have equal opportunities, provided they do not demand special considerations and are prepared to do as a man would do, that is, to put the job first. Equality means taking the rough with the smooth, sharing men's oppression as well as their privileges. The champions of equality smile grimly as women force their way onto the building site, to carry hods with the men, and go out on patrol with the police, and fight fires with the fire brigade, work the graveyard shift alongside the men, run the gauntlet with men. If US Navy pilots get pinned when they get their wings, then we'll drive pins into the chests of women fliers too, ho ho. Now we all can see whether women are equal to equality. No more victim politics; women have to show that they are tough enough to hold their own in this [man's] world. A woman is not a wimp.

Sweet dreams, Nina, always one of the lads.
On a wreath at the funeral of PC Nina MacKay, killed in the line of duty

---

There seems to be no shortage of women prepared to train hard and qualify for the toughest of men's sports. Steeplechase jockeys are amongst the toughest men on earth; time and again their bodies are crushed and broken in racing accidents and time and again the mended jockeys climb back into the saddle and run the same risks all over again. Astonishingly women have qualified to ride as professionals; in 1977 Charlotte Brew got the ride on Barony Fort in the Grand National steeplechase, one of the most dangerous horse-races in the world. Those who had never been happy to see women riding alongside men spoke out. Women's skulls are thinner than men's, they said; in their own interest, women should have been prevented from riding professionally. The argument is persuasive until we ask

---

25 February 1998
Britain's 'strongest woman', tri-athlete Jo Amies-Winter, died in her bed at the age of 23. Traces of cocaine, alcohol and Prozac were found in her blood. At a competition in 1997 she threw a 25-kilo tyre further than any of the men.

---

ourselves whether amateur riding is any safer. Perhaps women should be prevented from riding altogether, if their skulls are so fragile. What the women jockeys would say is that they want to be allowed to take their chances. If the prospect of death or injury does not deter them it should not influence others to deny their right to participate. Other questions arise when we consider who jockeys are and what kind of control most of them have over their own lives. Few jockeys die rich. Owners, who risk neither life nor limb, are the ones who are rich.

In May 1995, in Copenhagen, with 3,000 live spectators and another 3.5 million people watching on Danish TV, Jane Couch, the 'Fleetwood Assassin', won the women's world welterweight boxing title. In the tenth and final round, in the words of *Guardian* sportswriter Nick Varley:

> Couch is about to be crowned champion but her once-white crop-top is a blood-stained deep pink, her eye is black and swollen, and her cheekbone looks broken, which indeed it is. But the source of the blood is Sandra Gieger, who had her nose broken in the second round. She was undefeated in her previous 25 fights but by the end of her 26th she had fractures of the hand, fractured ribs, and had also lost her crown.

In November 1996 the Amateur Boxing Association of England announced that women and girls over ten years of age will be allowed to fight as amateurs and to fight competitively from October 1997. The first schoolgirl bouts were fought in March 1998. Even the supporters of boxing as a fit occupation for young men were horrified. Dr Adrian Whiteson, medical adviser to the British Boxing Board of Control, was quoted as saying,

> I'm terribly concerned about this. I don't think enough is known about the potential risks to women for such a decision to be made. Blows around the breast or chest can induce bruising and the nodule which results is difficult to distinguish from cancer. No one is saying it increases the chances of cancer but

no surgeon is going to say 'Carry on'; he's going to remove the lump. Even if women wear breast protectors, they would have to be made of steel to stop bruises occurring. We also need to know much more about what is happening during the period, when the woman is shedding blood, making her more anaemic. She could be boxing without realizing she is pregnant.

In February 1997 Jane Couch appeared before an industrial tribunal to protest against the refusal of the British Boxing Board of Control to grant her a licence and Dr Whiteson was forced to trot out his unconvincing arguments all over again. Ultimately it seemed that Couch would be denied her licence not because she might box when pregnant or bruise her breasts and get nodules, but simply because the BBBC rules do not allow professional boxers to wear any covering above the waist.

I recently gave my best mate Iva a black eye when aiming for her arm. Fisticuffs are a normal part of our drunken bonding sessions.

Emily Sheffield

Boxing is dangerous regardless of gender and professional boxing is less rather than more dangerous than amateur boxing. Only the day before the decision of the British Boxing Board of Control was published, doctors had turned off life support for twenty-five-year-old Fabrizio de Chiara, brain-dead as a result of a killer punch. What remained when the shouting about women boxers had died down was the question why anyone, regardless of gender, would fight for a living. Historically boxing has been a way that poor boys with no better opportunities have tried to fight their way out of squalor and hopelessness. There are always more losers than winners; ultimately the only winners are the fight promoters who buy and sell the fighters like prize performing animals. A boy who decides to sell himself as a boxer is rather like the peasant who sells a kidney for cash he can earn no other way. Women boxers now appear on the under-card at Mike Tyson fights; pin-up girl Christy Martin earned $75,000 as the under-card of the Holyfield–Tyson fight.

The notion of equality takes the male status quo as the condition to which women aspire. Men live and work in a frighteningly unfree and tyrannical society, constructed upon the oppression of junior males by senior ones, on grooming of favoured males for succession at the expense of others, on confederacies and conspiracies, on initiation and blooding rituals, on shared antisocial behaviour, on ostracisms and punishments, practical jokes, clannishness and discrimination. As soon as a woman enters a male preserve, be it the police, the military, the building site, the law, the clergy, she finds herself in an alien and repellent world which changes her fundamentally even as she is struggling to exert the smallest influence on it. As these masculine realms have been constructed to withstand outsiders and have grown stronger and more effective in doing so over many generations, they are virtually incapable of transformation. Aspirants to rank in such groups have to learn the ropes and then bounce their rivals onto them. The woman who becomes the leader of a conventional political party can only do so because she has become tougher than the men in it. It was often said of Margaret Thatcher that, despite her frothy bows and four-inch heels, she was the only man in her cabinet.

'We fight for our rights, and not for privileges. Business has no gender,' said Ann Diamantopoulou, Secretary of State in the Greek Ministry of Development, to the assembled company at the OECD conference on Women in Small and Medium Enterprises held in Paris in April 1997. Betsy Myers, director of the White House office of women's initiatives and outreach, declared that 'Women's equality is defined by empowerment, and the ultimate empowerment is entrepreneurship.' The right to credit is not a human right, nor is equality 'defined' by empowerment, nor is entrepreneurship the only kind of power, though it has a great deal to do with oppression and exploitation. The business establishment is as intensely and instinctively hierarchical as all masculine structures are and competition is its modality. Women have tended to start their businesses using their own credit or the credit of their families, many by simply borrowing on their credit cards, because banks would not deal with them and they had no entrée to the old boys' network. They are routinely charged higher rates of interest and given less time to pay, because they are considered worse risks than men, which is clean contrary to the facts of the case. Whatever Diamantopoulou thinks of the gender of business, business thinks it is male, and not only male, but lean, hungry, predatory and hostile. Diamantopoulou said more than she knew when she said, 'What for men is a natural success is a conquest for women.' Dogs eat dogs naturally, it would seem, but bitches may be different. Certainly, women bosses are regularly described in the lifestyle pages as tougher and meaner than men, which can be largely interpreted as a perception on the part of employees that decisiveness and straightforwardness become stridency when manifested by a female. We also learn that women's businesses expand more slowly than men's, the implication being that this is not because they do not have access to venture capital but because women are naturally less competitive. Women in business like women everywhere are pushed and pulled in opposing directions, which they emblematize by the way they present themselves – business suit but plenty of leg in sheer stockings and high heels, lots of lipstick, nails and scent. They mustn't remind anyone of the last hated female in authority, the schoolmarm. The high-heeled shoe itself is a marvellously contradictory item; it brings a woman to a man's height but makes sure that she cannot keep up with him. All pornography features the high-heeled shoe.

American sex manuals advise that women wear them even to bed.

The Wilson government of 1975 that brought in the Sex Discrimination Act along with the Equal Opportunities Commission was made up of businessmen and lawyers. The Sex Discrimination Act was designed to give more progressive people the illusion that women's oppression had been recognized and that something was being done about it and at the same time to reassure conservatives on both sides of the House of Commons that no great changes were likely to ensue and business could go on exactly as usual. There was never the remotest chance that employers would find themselves facing expensive adjustments to wages policy even though the act would create thousands of hours of lucrative work for lawyers. The first cases taken up by the Equal Opportunities Commission created to enable enforcement of the act seemed chosen for their iffiness. Case after case was argued interminably only to be lost. The obfuscation worked perfectly until the hearing of the cases of the women in the Armed Forces who were wrongfully dismissed for being pregnant. Those cases were unique in that the grounds of dismissal were so clearly stated as to be undeniable. The attitude of the legal establishment itself to equality is best illustrated by the composition of the panel of 116 barristers from whom pleaders for the government in the civil courts are chosen; there are no women on the main panels for common law and Chancery work, or among the standing counsel who handle specialist cases; thirteen of the seventy-one members of the panel of junior counsel are women. As the plum jobs in the Attorney General's department are not advertised but awarded according to 'secret soundings' within the old boy network, the Sex Discrimination Act is deemed not to apply.

The Sex Discrimination Act is so effective a tool for striking down any attempt at reverse discrimination, because such attempts have to state their purpose clearly. If you want one level of a carpark to be for women only, you have to say so clearly and obviously, and crash down comes the act. This is anything but an unintended consequence. It is obvious from the wording, that all parts of the act applying to sex discrimination against women 'are to be read as applying equally to the treatment of men', that the act was designed to be a protection against any pressure for reverse discrimination. Well-meaning people were outraged when the Equal Opportunities Commission helped to fund the scuppering of the Labour Party's plan for all-women shortlists by invoking the Sex Discrimination Act but the parliamentary Labour Party heaved a vast and heartfelt sigh of relief. Only six of the nine regions had been able actually to draw up all-female lists; in the northwest only one woman had been selected. Every poll revealed that the all-women shortlists policy was a vote-loser and massively unpopular. The Sex Discrimination Act got New Labour off the hook with its spurious pro-feminist credentials intact. The SDA has been used to prevent the Royal Automobile Club from giving priority to calls from lone female drivers, to prevent the setting up of a firm of all-female taxi-drivers, and to outlaw women-only swimming sessions at leisure centres.

The beauty of the Sex Discrimination Act is the beauty of the English legal system generally, that is, that a person who wishes to put legislation into effect has to bring an action on her or his own behalf and must devote to it vast amounts of time, money and energy before a result of any kind can be expected. Large corporations have lawyers on retainer; individuals fighting cases have either to fund themselves or to avail themselves of legal aid, in which case their costs will come out of any eventual settlement. Both sides can appeal, in which case no action is to be taken on the appealed decision as the cases trail from court to court for anything up to seven or eight years. The law's delays mean little to corporations; for working people they are crushing.

Sue Edwards worked for nine years as one of twenty-one women among the 2,033 drivers employed by London Underground; when her son was born in 1988 she was working a five-day week and swapping shifts to fit in with arrangements for childcare. In November 1991 London Underground changed the shift system to something they called a Company Plan, which involved a flexible roster spread over a seven-day week, with a 'Single Parent Link' to enable parents to adjust to the new timetabling. In the event the Single Parent Link never materialized and Edwards was forced to take voluntary severance. After three months the Company Plan was abandoned but London Underground did not reinstate Edwards. By July 1996 two tribunals and subsequent appeals had found in her favour, but London Underground continued to appeal and she had still received no compensation. Edwards did not give up; in June 1998 she won her case for the third time. London Underground applied to the House of Lords for leave to appeal again. At the time of writing Edwards had yet to receive a penny in compensation and her huge legal bills remained unpaid. It is to be hoped when it arrives that her compensation is adequate and that her costs do not absorb too much of it, for, if her career follows that of other women who have successfully prosecuted discrimination cases, she may never work again.

For the young women who now outnumber young men graduating in law, life in chambers can be a nightmare of discrimination amounting to outright persecution and harassment. A report by legal recruitment consultants Reynell published in January 1997 found that a quarter of women solicitors have suffered sexual harassment and almost half have been disadvantaged because of discrimination on grounds of sex. Yet women lawyers seldom bring cases under the Sex Discrimination Act. As lawyers they know better. In their struggle to build a career, even if the women lawyers won their cases, they would lose their prospects. A woman involved in a sex discrimination case, whether she wins or loses, is thenceforward known as an expensive troublemaker, despite the reassurances in the act that the fact of bringing a case should not be held against an employee and that recriminatory behaviour would be treated as discrimination. One of the peculiarities of the act is that since 1988, as a consequence of verdicts in individual cases, a case brought under the act is the only way to seek for redress of grievance caused by sexual harassment and as such peculiarly ineffective. For one thing, it seems that there is no way even to bring a case unless harassment has been a cause of resignation or dismissal. Law, with its long hours and compulsory hobnobbing, is just one of the professions that are poorly adapted to the needs and priorities of women. Indeed, most high-earning professions cannot be successfully practised without the support of a stay-at-home wife.

Women have been full members of British police forces since 1915 when they were recruited specifically to deal with prostitutes. Later women police constables were used as an ancillary force to deal with women and children and remained uninvolved in general police work. In 1975 it was decided that women should be involved at all levels of police work, including the use of firearms. In September 1996, Pauline Clare, Chief Constable of Lancashire, was quoted as saying:

> I have never labelled myself a feminist, though I have always respected the feminist movement and its aims. I think many of those have now been achieved: you need only look at the way we have improved equal opportunity in the workplace to realize the significant impact feminism has had on our way of life.

Only a few months earlier, in May 1996, an industrial tribunal heard the case of PC Karen Wade of the West Yorkshire Police who claimed harassment by three male colleagues. One of the officers giving evidence was Sergeant Jane McGill who said that, in her twenty-six years in the police force, she had been indecently assaulted four times and had been addressed using inappropriate sexual language countless times. As she spoke, she was embarrassed to find her eyes full of tears. She was asked when the last instance had occurred. 'Last week,' she said, struggling to regain her composure. Having to admit in a public forum that one has endured belittlement and abuse for so long compounds the injury; women treated routinely in such ways gradually come to see themselves as worthless. Sergeant McGill's experience is not unusual; the attempted integration of women in the police force was met by more or less covert insult, harassment and humiliation. Now, out of a total of 125,000 or so police, 18,000 are female, by no means enough to neutralize the masculinist culture that they have inherited.

An anonymous policewoman explained to journalists:

> ... the sexism started on my second day. When I made a complaint I was sent to Coventry by the whole lot of them. It ranged from trying to shove things up my backside to writing really crude things about me on notepaper. I became a firearms person, that didn't matter. I was a top student, that didn't matter, and, in the end, because of all the hassle involved in complaining, I blew my attempts to get into another department. Either you try to be one of the boys, or you're on your own and you become a target.

In September 1996 it was decided that, in order to avoid the kind of bad publicity surrounding the Wade case, neighbouring North Yorkshire Police would settle the cases of Libby Ashurst, formerly a detective constable at Harrogate, and Amanda Rose, a constable seconded to the CID at Harrogate, out of court. In order to raise the necessary £110,000 North Yorkshire Police took twenty-five patrol cars off the road. The public was outraged, the more because Ashurst's payment was more than ten times the maximum she could have got from an

industrial tribunal. Because of the accompanying confidentiality agreements, all the press could find to publish were
bizarre glimpses of life at Harrogate: the women had been told
to wear short skirts, stockings and suspenders when they were
in the buildings; an officer had appeared naked in an office with
a lost property ticket dangling from his penis; male recruits had
run down corridors with bulldog clips attached to their nipples;
an officer who refused to wear a loud tie was locked in a dog
kennel for three hours. The Chief Inspector who apparently
ordered these peculiar rituals was later convicted of five out of
eight charges of gross misconduct. In such cases we need to ask
ourselves, not whether the police force is a fit environment for
women, but whether it is fit for human beings.

A built-in tension exists between this concept of equality,
which presupposes sameness, and this concept of sex which
presupposes difference. Sex equality becomes a contradiction
in terms, something of an oxymoron.

Catherine McKinnon

Few of the many women who have suffered as members of a
British police force have been as fortunate as Ashurst and Rose.
In August 1995 Inspector Cydena Fleming of the Lincolnshire
Constabulary complained that since she had been so foolhardy
as to reject the advances of one officer and to give another a
poor report, her life had been made very difficult indeed. Her
complaint was ignored, but anonymous telephone calls were
made to her superiors accusing her of sexual misconduct and
the social services were told that she had been neglecting her
two children. In an attempt to collect evidence that she was
being victimized Fleming hid a voice-activated tape-recorder in
her locker. When it was found she was suspended for 'oppressive
behaviour'. During the run-up to a hearing at an industrial

tribunal she found that the constabulary was nobbling her witnesses by warning off anyone who intended to support her and promoting only the ones who kept their lips buttoned. The hearing, which took sixty-one days and cost £600,000, found in February 1998 that she had indeed been the victim of a set-up, though she was unsuccessful in a charge of sexual discrimination. After two years' suspension her warrant card was at last returned to her, all disciplinary charges were dropped, and she took a transfer to Humberside.

Every week brings new evidence of the struggles of women in male-dominated professions. A woman in a masculine institution is always an outsider; as long as women remain small minorities in such institutions they can be subjected to extreme pressure, as the men close ranks. What is beyond doubt in these cases is the hostility felt by the men who are intent on making the women feel threatened and unwanted. These are not cases of chivalry misinterpreted or sexual high-jinks but of deliberate victimization using sexual aggression. It is safe to say that self-defining male elites always gang up on outsiders, especially if they feel that the outsiders have been forced upon them. In the military and the police, Jews, Sikhs, Hindus, West Indians, Pakistanis and gays have all experienced victimization based on race or sexual orientation rather than gender. Aggravated sexual abuse of gay men is routine in certain hypermasculine environments, on some oil rigs, for example. As sexual violation, actual or mimed, is the commonest form of domination behaviour among vertebrates, it is to be expected in all-male institutions, such as prisons, where the establishment of a hierarchy is crucial. Civilization is incompatible with such mammalian residues; if the participation of women in male elite corps means that bullying and victimization die out then immediately cannot be soon enough but at this stage the cost to the women themselves seems rather too high.

The solution, say the proponents of equality, is to bring the numbers of women to parity, in which case the institutions in question will be unrecognizable. The cult of equality means that this cannot be done, because women will not be recruited in large numbers unless some policy of reverse discrimination is adopted and reverse discrimination is illegal under the law of equality in both Britain and Europe. In 1995 more men than women made complaints of discrimination to the Equal Opportunities Commission. If it is illegal to discriminate on grounds of sex it is illegal for all purposes, even for the sake of equality itself.

Grotesque oppression of working women is not limited to the traditional male professions and redress is no less difficult to secure. The only female director of IT consultancy Optika was put through an extraordinary ordeal in February 1995 when her birthday surprise came in the form of a twenty-three-year-old man posing as a job applicant, who handcuffed her, stripped to a G-string with a toy elephant's trunk, then removed his G-string and threw her over his shoulder. At the time she seemed to take this grotesque jape in good part but she made no secret of her anger with the managing director and was dismissed for gross misconduct two weeks later. She brought a case for sex discrimination and lost. To the lawyers' glee, she will appeal. A consultant with General Accident Life Assurance claimed to have been 'driven to a nervous break-down' by her senior manager, whom she accused at an industrial tribunal of bullying and 'old-fashioned chauvinism towards women in the Leicester office'. Eventually she resigned, sued for sex discrimination and lost. She too will appeal. Of the 3,850 female secretaries who responded to a survey conducted by the *Guardian* in 1998 15 per cent said that their male bosses had asked them to have sex or to perform a sexual act. Their bosses also expected them to perform menial tasks, to make coffee, buy lunch, buy presents for wives and mistresses and children; 31 per cent said that it was their job to remind their bosses of anniversaries and birthdays. One employer demanded details of his secretary's menstrual cycle so that he could know when to expect PMT. According to the definition in the Sex Discrimination Act you discriminate against a woman when you treat her 'less favourably' than you would treat a man or impose upon her a condition or requirement which you would also impose upon a man but which a woman would find harder than a man to carry out, or which is itself unjustifiable and 'is to her detriment because she cannot comply with it'. The significant words in this formulation are all minefields.

> In a civilized society, no one should have to choose between a job and a life.
>
> Maureen Freely

If employers were not allowed to discriminate there would be no point whatever in the job interview. The difficulty in getting the SDA to work in favour of an individual who has suffered from sex discrimination is to prove that a particular individual or corporation is discriminating solely or principally on the grounds of sex or marital status. All the discriminator has to do to refute the imputation of an infringement of the SDA is to adduce a different ground for discrimination; it is not that a woman is a woman but that she is 'difficult', 'unreliable', 'slovenly', 'indiscreet'; the publicity given to sex discrimination cases means that this bad reference is anything but confidential. The law is a costly and cumbersome instrument that the powerful manipulate in their own interest. The men who complained to the Equal Opportunities Commission were more successful than women had ever been. The difference is partly one of solidarity; allegations of discrimination need supporting evidence and women are still more likely than men to be disloyal to their same-sex colleagues. Female journalists are more ready than men to sneer at women seeking redress for systematic humiliation, perhaps because they themselves have had to endure it without complaining. Witness Carol Sarler, journalist, who characterized women's complaints of harassment as 'Poor little me, the boss made a rude joke, the other sailors teased me, help, I can't cope.'

> I couldn't get pregnant at the *Observer*.
>
> Polly Ghazi

Men's culture is hierarchical; junior males are systematically humiliated by the silverbacks, most obviously among military castes, the police, the fire brigade and any groups that pride themselves on toughness. The vulnerable in such groups will be hardened or forced out. Women who resist both processes will bring about a fundamental change in such institutions, but the process is of vegetable slowness. Until it is completed we will not have the right to call ourselves civilized. Litigation English-style is irrelevant; what we need is a system of assessment of the performance of employers, corporations and authorities that will facilitate official enforcement of fair employment policies by imposing rewards and penalties. If we had such a thing the Houses of Parliament would have swingeingly to fine themselves for persisting in men's club procedures that are clearly to the detriment of women and family life.

It is virtually impossible to separate the idea of equality from the idea of similarity. If we accept that men are not free, and that masculinity is as partial an account of maleness as femininity is of femaleness, then equality must be seen to be a poor substitute for liberation. Arguing in terms of equality or difference permits two kinds of neutralizing of pro-feminist pressure: one cites the concept of equality to women's disadvantage, as in the notion that women are entitled to equal pay for work 'of equal value' – a meaningless concept that serves to enshrine women's work as permanently subordinate – the other institutionalizes the contrast between men and women, treating widows differently from widowers, mothers from fathers, wives from husbands. What we find is that when it is in men's interest to plead equality, they do; when it is in their interest to plead difference, they do. A male soldier who wants the right to wear his hair long pleads equality; a male tennis player who wants to go on being paid twice as much as his mixed doubles partner will plead difference. A man who wants paternity leave will plead equality, a member of the MCC who wants to exclude women will plead difference. Quite the most cynical application of equality rhetoric was made in April 1997 by one of the California clinicians responsible for implanting a fertilized ovum in the treated womb of a woman who as a result gave birth to a baby at the age of sixty-three. 'Men can become fathers in their fifties, sixties and even beyond,' he said. 'So why not women?' There is in truth no comparison between the way men become fathers at any time of life and the way women become mothers. The passing on of their genes involves men in no risk whatever to their health; pregnancy for a post-menopausal woman involves a complex work-up in which the womb is prepared for its foreign host; the older woman runs an elevated risk of circulatory disorders, stroke, heart attack and the diabetes of pregnancy. The denial of real difference can be as cruel as forcing different-sized feet into a single-size shoe.

> Sexism killed [Janis Joplin]. People kept saying she was just 'one of the guys' . . . that's a real sexist bullshit trip . . . She was one of the women. She was a strong groovy woman. Smart, you know? But she got fucked around.
>
> Country Joe McDonald

In September 1996 the British press carried stories of a rise in the number of complaints of misconduct made against nurses. In 1985–6 there had been 339 complaints; by 1994–5 the number had risen to 883, of which 115 were referred for hearing by the professional conduct committee of the UK Central Council for Nursing, Midwifery and Health Visiting. As a consequence forty-five nurses were struck off for a variety of offences, including theft of drugs, abuse of elderly patients, theft of patients' money, sexual harassment and sexual relationships with patients. Nothing was made of the fact that 50 per cent of the accused nurses were men, although they are only 9 per cent of nurses overall. To tease out the differences between male and female nurses might have led to sex discrimination which would never have done. When it comes to promotion and office-holding, male nurses are as over-represented as they are in the crime figures.

The equality argument has probably gone as far as it can go; the terminus has been reached by Patricia Pearson whose life work is fighting for equality for women on death row. Pearson argues that women have got away with murder for far too long because of the sexism of investigators who are so reluctant to believe that women are capable of killing that they ignore the obvious, and have allowed child-smotherers and husband-poisoners to go on killing people when they could have been stopped. Pearson points out that the women who are caught are treated too leniently; though one in eight of the Americans arrested for murder is a woman, women account for only one out of seventy people on death row. Only two of the 432 people executed since 1976 were women. This according to Pearson is not because they were considered less of a risk to the public than male killers, but because they were not allowed to take responsibility for their own actions. In 1996 when the death sentence of Guinevere Garcia was commuted against her will to life imprisonment, Pearson argued in the *New York Times* that the decision demonstrated gender bias. Equality demanded that Garcia, who had been systematically abused by men all her life, should be put to death without further ado.

In exhorting men who have the right to be cruel to other men to abandon their sexist chivalry and extend their cruelty as unsparingly to women, Pearson shows that equality is an utterly conservative aim. Equality is cruel to women because it requires them to duplicate behaviours that they find profoundly alien and disturbing. Men like the masculine world that they have built for themselves; if enough men had not enjoyed what they euphemistically call the 'cut and thrust' – the sanctioned brutalities of corporate life – such behaviour would never have been institutionalized and women would not now be struggling with it. In constructing its male elite, masculinist society contrives to be cruel to most men, all women and all children. If women can see no future beyond joining the masculinist elite on its own terms, our civilization will become more destructive than ever. There has to be a better way.

girlpower

The longest revolution has many phases, false starts and blind alleys, all of which must be explored before a way through can be found. One of these is the brief and catastrophic career of 'girls', 'girls behaving badly', 'girls on top'. Though the career of the individual bad girl is likely to be a brief succession of episodes of chaotic drinking, casual sex, venereal infection and unwanted pregnancy, with consequences she will have to struggle with all her life, the cultural phenomenon is depressingly durable and the average age of acting out kinderwhores grows ever younger.

> Don't be scared of being a GRRRL – there is a difference between girl and GRRRL. A girl has fallen for the lies and bullshit put in front of her via TV/magazines/religion/ parents, all corporately/government sponsored. GRRRLS KNOW BETTER.
>
> Jasmine in *Sawtooth* No. 1 (1993)

Girls themselves claim descent from the ur-Girl, Madonna, who has been said to have launched the new stereotype in *The Girlie Show*. It is probably truer to say that they are descended from Buffalo Girl, Vivienne Westwood, who with Chrissie Hynde used to stick her buttocks in the faces of beholders at The Sex Shop in the King's Road in the 1970s. In Westwood's collection for spring 1990 Sara Stockbridge wore tights decorated with the commonest kind of lavatory-wall drawing of a penis, with the title 'Half-Dressed City Gent'. Madonna's display of conscientious harlotry was healthy by comparison. The next heroine of girl culture was Courtney Love, whose bleached hair straggled over a raddled face scarred with lipstick, who used drugs, got drunk, occasionally assaulted people and let herself be photographed snogging girls, with unfocused eyes and lipstick smeared to her hairline. Courtney's best buddy was Drew Barrymore, who added flipping her breasts out on talk shows to the gallimaufry of bad behaviour. Enter Björk Gudmundsdottir who, though a mother, proved that she was still a girl by grabbing a woman journalist by the hair, shaking her head violently, throwing her on the ground, jumping on her and banging her head on the floor five times.

Madonna's mouthiness was at least as important as her muscles in placing her as the figurehead for succeeding generations of aggressively randy, hard-drinking young females, who have got younger with every passing year, until they are now emerging in their pre-teens. They are served, that is to say indoctrinated, by a new group of commercial magazines, whose contents are consumed over and over in the unfillable gaps between soap operas and phone conversations. *Bliss*, *Minx*, *Mizz* and *More* – 'Smart Girls get *More* every fortnight' – exist to sell young women cosmetics, clothes, underwear and entertainment; the sales catalogue of trashy clothes, gooey lipstick, gaudy hairdye, pimple creams and cold-sore lotions is moored to self-discovery quizzes, true confessions, tips for getting laid and endless prattle about 'totty', whether it be boy bands, football players or teachers at school.

Sugar, price £1.50, dubs itself 'Britain's number 1 girls' mag'. A regular feature, 'How embarrassing!', compiled out of readers' contributions, tells of dancing in a leotard stuck up one's 'bum crack', offering cat food instead of munchies to a boy, tampax instead of cigarettes ditto, farting, and trying to chat up a boy with a piece of popcorn up one's nose. 'Pesky poo' told of how Sue of Edinburgh panicked that one of her turds would not flush away, wrapped it in loo paper and stuffed it in her handbag, where her date found it. Information about David Duchovny included the fascinating detail that 'he farts human farts. Yep! During an interview on the set of his new film, *Playing God*, due to hit the UK some time next summer, Mr Duchovny shocked – and gassed – all his fellow actors with a stonkingly honkingly, earthling power-guff! *Pheweee.*' Farts are something of a leitmotif in *Sugar*. Jarvis Cocker is a hero because he raised the skirt of his jacket and waved his farts at Michael Jackson, and 'boys' were reported as saying under the rubric 'you girls are weird': 'Your farts smell funny. You eat the same stuff we do, yet your farts always smell of rose-water not rotten eggs. How do you do that?'

My mother's generation were very much about screaming and shouting about being locked in a cage. Then the cage was eventually opened. My generation is more about ignoring it, stop moaning and get things done.

Björk

The issue of *Sugar* for February 1997 advertised itself as 'packed with hot crumpet', in this case, 'cute boy-types', 'fresh out of the *Sugar* totty oven'. If equality meant role-reversal,

Sugar was anxious to claim it, by treating men, or rather boys, as sex objects. There is nothing new in this, since Ganymede was carried off by Jupiter; the difference is simply that *Sugar* sells to sub-teens who are boy-mad. The possibility that they are already sexually active is squarely confronted in articles that ask 'Are you ready for sex?' and proceed to list 'the scary facts' about chlamydia, genital warts, cervical cancer and pregnancy. It is strange to see child-abuse help lines and pregnancy-counselling services listed on the same page for the same readers. It is assumed that all young readers are aware of green issues and passionate about animal rights.

The manufacturers keen to get into this market were Nike, perfumiers, cable TV, record companies, Boots the Chemists, makers of sanitary protection, mail-order suppliers of jewellery and clothing, cold-sore creams, Wella hair-colouring products (an eight-page promotion), T-zone skin care range, World Vision, Clearasil and the national Drugs Helpline. The editorial trod a precarious path between endorsing the anti-social aspects of youth culture and protecting its readers who are all much younger than the fourteen- and fifteen-year-old finalists in their model competition.

In England in 1999 the girl is the counterpart of the lad but her preoccupations are very different. She experiments with make-up, colours her hair, spends a good deal of time in her room watching soaps and listening to boy bands, and goes shopping whether she has money or not. Nothing in *Sugar* magazine suggests that a girl can have a life apart from lads, that she has any interests of her own beyond make-up, clothes and relationships, that she will ever get a job or travel, that she plays any sport, that she has ever read a book. *Minx* magazine advertises itself as for 'girls with plenty of balls', but what this means is simply that girls who read it will be encouraged to take liberties rather than fight for them.

Men write in the girls' magazines, principally advising the girls on the way boys think about them. In *Looks* magazine, aimed at 'real girls', Michael Hogan warned about overdoing the tomboy act.

> You know the kind of girls I'm talking about . . . the ones who flounce into your local in a micro-mini and PVC vest, making pensioners choke on their peanuts. Who drink like fish, smoke like troopers and laugh like a drain at anything remotely crude. Who have half the blokes drooling and the other half hiding in the loo.

Lairy-girls, also known as 'warrior-babes', are sexually aggressive, so much so that Hogan was moved to observe: 'grabbing his arse and sticking your Wonderbra in his face will make him think Benny Hill's been reincarnated in female form'. Hogan's squeamishness is echoed by the children's charity Kidscape which reported a 55 per cent increase in calls from girls complaining of being bullied by other girls in the 18 months up to March 1998 and put the phenomenon down to the pernicious influence of the Spice Girls. Said the director of Kidscape sternly: 'Picking up the attitude of a popular group and turning it into the aggression more traditionally shown by boys needs to be stopped.' Message: boys have the right to aggression, girls don't. Girls must be stopped, though boys clearly haven't been. Bullies would have actually learnt their craft more effectively by watching the war waged by the rock media against the Spice Girls, whose imminent humiliation and failure was prophesied and prematurely gloated over in every issue. Feminist responses to the Spice Girls depended upon whether their activities were perceived as self-regulating or whether they had been manipulated into acting out a marketing concept. In millennial society, alas, you can't have one without the other.

The cynicism of the merchandisers of bad-girl culture is perfectly reflected in the brutal lay-out of girls' magazines, some of which are as expensive as the glossies sold to older women. From them the emerging girl learns that the only life worth living is a life totally out of control, disrupted by debt, disordered eating, drunkenness, drugs and casual sex. Their

> The question for babe-haters among us is are these girls turning themselves into temporary sex objects because they've let their identity be consumed by the male-gaze or are they doing it for themselves? I can't help thinking this issue is still with us, because the boys, in comparison, don't dress or act like sex objects.
>
> Tom Marcus, *Mixmag*

editors would say that they are telling it how it is, in which case nobody else is. The little girl who pores over this sinister muck has no way of knowing whether the life described is real or not. All pre-teens go through a boy-crazy period which they used to survive because they were not sexually active, the boys of their own age being in no way able to take advantage of the situation. In *fin-de-siècle* teen sexual culture boys are represented as infinitely desirable and at the same time worthless, treacherous and crap in bed. The preceptors of girldom would say that they are empowering heterosexual girls to express their own sexuality and telling them the truth about male perfidy, so that they will not suffer the pernicious erosion of self-esteem that used to accompany the awareness of having been dumped several times in succession. In fact they are telling them that any sexual interaction is better than none; that a cool girl gives hand-jobs and head, fakes orgasm and has less flesh on her limbs than a sparrow. The models in the propaganda of girldom are 'victim-babes', the thinnest in the business.

Originally feminists expressed dislike of the word 'girl' for much the same reasons that black men refuse to answer to 'boy'. An adult woman is called a 'girl' in order to emphasize her inferior status. In England, where a male driver who is tentative at traffic lights or signals the wrong way is still quite likely to be called a 'girl' with as much venom as a woman is called a 'cow', the word carries an extra loading of contempt. English men have not quite shed their repellent habit of referring to the women who work for them as 'girls', as if insisting upon their junior, inferior status, no matter what their age. In Australia men used to refer to their secretaries as 'their girls' as in 'Ring my girl, she'll take care of it.'

Feminists soon saw the potential in the word 'girl' aggressively used, as by the great Guerilla Girls, 'conscience of the art world' in New York in the mid-eighties. At the same time a series of posters and badges announcing 'girlpower', that 'girls can do anything' and that 'it's really good being a girl' addressed themselves specifically to school-age women, in the hope of influencing their career choices and building their confidence. Similarly, *Geekgirl* tried to attract girls into information technology: 'Girls need modems'. Lesbians initiated their own cable TV 'Girlie Network'. Feminist guerilla desk-top publishing of the early 1990s produced *Riot Grrrl*, which developed a pro-girl feminist philosophy out of punk and Indie rock, to be followed by *Girl Power!*, *Alternative Sex*, *Feminaxe*, *Shocking Pink*, *Bad Attitude*, *Subversive Sister*, *Raging Dyke Newsletter*, *Jane*, *Gutter Girl*, *Garbles*, *Crumpet Frenzy*, *Scars and Bruises*, *Cooties*, *From Far Off*. These small-circulation magazines dealt with the whole spectrum of young women's protest, including self-mutilation; many proclaimed their same-sex orientation. As *Riot Grrrl* explained:

> Under the guise of helping us spread the word, corporate media has co-opted and trivialized a movement of angry girls that could be truly threatening and revolutionary, and even besides that it has distorted our views of each other & created hostility, tension and jealousy in a movement supposedly about girl support & girl love.

Among the fossilized remains of the feminist fanzines that can be seen in the commercial girls' magazines are frequent articles on 'best mates' and how to relate to them. It took little to convince publishers that there was huge marketing potential in women's magazines that would admit that women much younger than the readers of *Cosmopolitan* were interested in having fun, that is to say, sex. Out of the gang-rape of feminist guerilla performance and publication by the mass-circulation print industry was born the hybrid boy-mad girls' press.

In the USA at this time there were several magazines designed for the teenage market.

> *'Teen* was the worst one of all. The teenage girl was dumb, the magazine implied. She cared only about clothes, make-up and boys, but (the editors foolishly and dangerously reasoned) she did not have sex, drink or experiment with drugs.

But American advertisers would not buy space in a magazine that addressed the tougher issues facing teenage girls. British advertisers, though equally powerful, are less squeamish. As long as twelve-year-olds spend their pocket money on *Bliss*, *Sugar*, *Minx* and *More*, and badger their parents for the money to buy the lipsticks and hairdye and padded bras they see on every page, advertisers will gladly pay over the odds for space. What do they care if our daughters refuse healthy food, slobber their bright faces with make-up and hang around bus-stops in the hope that they will get to share an alco-pop and cop off with a boy?

The publishers of the commercial girls' magazines in America and in England agreed on one thing, that lesbianism would not sell. From the first the commercial girls' press was overwhelmingly heterosexual; all that has changed in the endless preoccupation with snogging boys is the specificity of the contact. At the end of the century the only thing a cool girl can allow herself to expect from a lad is his penis, which is also called 'great sex'. In *Looks*, which pretends to address young women in their teens but never refers to its readers as anything but girls, a feature called 'The Ultimate Shag' argued that a man's sexual performance was signalled by his hair: 'Which hairstyle spells "big package" to you? ... And which style implies "lacking in the tackle dept"?' A 'girl' called Vivienne was quoted as stating, 'My motto is: "If it's limp on his head, it'll be the same in bed."'

The language of independence conceals utter dependence upon male attention, represented as difficult for a girl to get and all but impossible for her to keep. Any boy who dipped into this literature would get an immediate and vivid impression that girls are abject in their need for the most casual and uncommitted male attention, and think of very little else. He is more likely to read boys' rock magazines where he will learn that women are 'gagging for a shagging' and that the cool attitude is one of contemptuous indifference. The lead singer of Reef will tell him, 'I mean, after a gig, if a girl comes up to you, you can take her in the bogs, or outside, and shag her, if you want.' In *Kerrang!* magazine for 18 January 1997 'Shag Monster' Paul Stanley of Kiss boasted, 'When women asked if I'd respect them in the morning, I'd say, "I don't even respect you now!"' What red-blooded male would settle for being a nice boy when he could as easily become a love rat or shag monster?

> Girls are taking on boys at their own game – and they won't rest until they've drunk them under the table, snogged their faces off and puked up in their laps.
>
> Jo Hawkins, *Bliss* magazine

It is hard to reconcile the emptiness of the girls' press with what we know about pre-teen and teenage girls at school. They do play sport and music, they are into theatre and dance, and they get the best academic results. What the girls' press tells them is that none of this counts because it will not get you into bed with a lovebucket.

The same preoccupations were reflected in *The Girlie Show*, which was 'created' by David Stevenson, Channel 4 controller of entertainment and youth programmes, as 'a celebration of women in the 1990s'. *The Girlie Show* celebrated women by naming the wanker of the week and sitting on a sofa in the shape of bright red blow-up lips. According to Angela Neustatter, the show traded on 'the fashionable, and non-sensical construct of sugar and spice turned to galvanized steel, a generation of sexually confident, dangerous gals who can match men for balls and bravado'. Did it celebrate women or titillate sad, middle-aged men? There were girls who said, 'Yeah, I fake orgasms.' And girls who modelled their boyfriend's penis out of Play-doh. And discussions of well-filled underpants. And attempts to fill underpants with shriek-making stuff such as jellied eels. Even so *The Girlie Show* got three million viewers. When an interview with a convicted shoplifter provided handy hints for beginners the Independent Television Commission had to intervene.

American supermodel Rachel Williams presented the show, resplendent in spiky hair and pierced lip, and known to have left her male lover for a woman. Williams likes to display her breasts in the street as well as on the catwalk as she did in Vivienne Westwood's Fall show of 1996. Williams was joined by northerner Sara Cox: 'I really look up to my dad, Len. I'm such a daddy's girl. He's chuffed to bits that I'm on the telly, but he's not too happy about me saying things like w[anke]r on TV.' Ms Cox 'can't bear women's grown-up shoes' but lives in trainers. The first series was co-presented by Clare Gorham, half-Swiss, half-Nigerian and adopted. Gorham was feminist enough to hope that the show would discuss issues of concern to young women in a frank and forthright way. Instead she found herself having to wax a man's bottom and judge a Sexy

Fireman contest. 'We had to be ball-breakers, proving we could match men in any lewd, crude behaviour . . . I do think we have to redress the balance there has been, where men have objectified women and made fun of them for years, but not by going to extremes,' she said, and was dropped from the show as a result.

In 1996 the Spice Girls' hit 'Wannabe', which sold two million copies, won three awards in The *Smash Hits* poll. Charlotte Raven wrote rancorously of these 'ever-so-zeit-geisty chicks': 'The boys want to fuck them, the girls want to be them and feminists want to hail them as the feisty new exponents of that post-oppression jive.' Raven fulminated that 'having a giggle has come to be seen as a protopolitical act' and denounced the young women as 'a bunch of charmless never-weres'. Vivienne Westwood also slagged them off quite unnecessarily. The five, who were known to most of their public only as Posh Spice, Baby Spice, Ginger Spice, Sporty Spice and Scary Spice, and were given little chance of displaying individual personalities to go with their mix-and-match image, were quite anodyne. They danced energetically if not well and they had a reasonable ratio of flesh on their bones – and they had achieved an educational level not aimed at by the dead-eyed emaciated models who are featured in *More*.

The only feminist actually to hail the Spice Girls' line about 'being who you wanna' and 'not taking any shit' as revolutionary was American Kathy Acker. Acker felt that after her sojourn in England in the Eighties feminism had entered a dark age until the constellation Spice Girls arose in the Heavens to show by their radiance that feminism can be fun. The Spice Girls did make a difference because their most passionate fans were eight-year-old girls. In April 1998 a conference on children's oral culture learned that whereas half the space in school playgrounds used to be taken up by a self-selecting group of boys playing football, girls' clapping and dancing games were taking over. Items in the repertoire included an adaptation of the Teletubbies' opening song in which Dipsy was stabbed through the heart and shot in the head. Attagirls!

The propaganda machine that is now aimed at our daughters is more powerful than any form of indoctrination that has ever

---

Feminism isn't over, it didn't fail, but something new must happen – Riot Grrrl. Feminism taught us to think more carefully and see the oppression but is now constantly put on the defensive and made reactive. Riot Grrrl is offensive and active – it feels no guilt, gives no justification. Constraint and sexist attitudes can just fuck off. Next time a bloke feels your arse, patronizes you, slags off your body – generally treats you like shit – forget the moral high ground, forget he's been instilled with patriarchy and is a victim too, forget rationale and debate. Just deck the bastard.

Girl Power

---

existed before. Pop is followed by print is followed by video and film, and nothing that a parent generation can do will have any effect other than to increase the desirability of the girlpower way of life. Nobody observing the incitement of little girls to initiate sexual contact with boys can remain unconcerned. Regardless of the dutiful pushing of condoms in the girls' press, the exposure of baby vaginas and cervixes to the penis is more likely to result in pregnancy and infection than orgasm. We know that some of today's young women regard oral sex as little more than a courtesy routinely offered by cool girls to demanding boys, the girls themselves having no expectation that any man would ever do as much for them. The girls' press does not question this inequity; rather it reinforces the idea that boys are nabobs who can get any kind of sex anywhere and mostly cannot be bothered. To deny a women's sexuality is certainly to oppress her but to portray her as nothing but a sexual being is equally to oppress her. No-one doubts that teenage boys have peremptory sexual urges, but they are never depicted as prepared to accept any humiliation, endure any indignity, just to get close to some, any, girl. Nor are they pushed to spend money on their appearance or to dress revealingly or to drink too much in order to attract the attention of the opposite sex. In every colour spread the British girls' press trumpets the triumph of misogyny and the hopelessness of the cause of female pride.

liberation

Now that women are acquiring a measure of confidence and beginning to kick free, men are retreating deeper into their own virtual world. As the extended family has crumbled under the pressure of urbanization, increasing landlessness and economic change, men, no longer constrained by their elders to live as husbands and fathers, have backed away from women and children. A quarter of all the families in the world is headed by a lone female. In North America, Europe and North Africa the proportion is about a fifth, and rising steeply; in the Caribbean, Latin America and sub-Saharan Africa it is about a third, and rising. As Debbie Taylor explains in *My Children My Gold*, the phenomenon is not one of 'increase in single motherhood, but the decline in responsible fatherhood around the world'. Wherever they are, fatherless families represent the poorest section of society. In the United States, the richest nation in the world, the income of the single-parent family is one-third that of the couple family. The lives of single mothers consist of love and work which are their own rewards. For this loyal, unsparing labour there is no recognition, no promotion, no security, no help. Whatever we may think about the ideologies of different feminisms we must see that a feminism that does not address this situation is ostrich feminism. Women's liberation must be mothers' liberation or it is nothing. Whatever other aspects of women's oppression we foreground in our individual circumstances we have to be aware that the kind of feminism that sees getting membership of the MCC or the Garrick Club as a triumph is lifestyle feminism that gives tacit support to a system that oppresses women worldwide. A 'new feminism' that celebrates the right (i.e. duty) to be pretty in an array of floaty dresses and little suits put together for starvation wages by adolescent girls in Asian sweat-shops is no feminism at all.

> I'm a Guerilla Girl and I'm not angry.
> Anger is not a part of our vocabulary.
> Guerilla Girls

Though women need reliable ways of regulating their fertility, we must not simply assume that what mothers in poverty want to be freed from is motherhood itself. Population control, even if it did not deliver women into the power of the pharmaceutical multi-nationals, is not the right answer to the need for child support all over the world. We will be told that technology no longer requires a vast labour force, that these children are a product that is not marketable, and that money spent on them simply perpetuates the problem of too many mouths to feed, in other words, that the children of poor women should not have been born. 'Tough-love' is the cry. Women know too much about tough-love to want to inflict an institutionalized version of it on other women. Feminism has to believe that a technology that cannot feed its people is worse than useless. We do not exist to serve technology; technology exists to serve us. As soon as such an idea is formulated we glimpse the abyss that yawns between the aims of technocratic society and human need. With modern technology nobody needs to die of the diseases of malnutrition any more; every year untold millions of people do just that. We could distribute food rationally from places of plenty to places of scarcity; we don't. We could provide everyone on earth with clean water; we don't. We could use our standing armies and billions of pounds' worth of *matériel* to protect people against the consequences of natural disasters; we don't. There is an unmet need for family planning around the world, but if we acknowledge no responsibility for feeding and educating children we need not trouble whether they were wanted or not. Such skinny brown children will make small demands upon the ecosphere and they will soon die off. To read of Nicaraguan women walking up to fifteen miles to camps where they will be sterilized by tubal cautery without anaesthetic and given a couple of Ibuprofen before they walk home again, is to feel with sickening certainty that lifestyle feminism has been a sideshow. The main event, the worldwide feminization of poverty, is a tragedy that is moving inexorably and unseen to an unimaginably terrible dénouement.

Being a woman has only served me well. Like I say, I look like a woman but I think like a man, and that has served me well on the business end. I knew what I had to sell, and I knew if I could sell somebody on the idea I could make us all a bunch of money.

Dolly Parton

We do not need to travel south or east to see the feminization of poverty in process. We can see it at work in our own countries, and we know what it produces, exhausted, anguished women and children who are desperate and angry, who will express their reckless rage in a thousand ways each more ingenious and destructive than the last, children who despise us. In our own rich societies poor children present serious problems; the modish term for it is 'social exclusion'. The socially excluded are people with no stake in society. It ought to be obvious that people will only invest in society if society has invested in them. In a rich society every child born is entitled to a decent living. The primary carer who socializes and nurtures her/him is entitled to our support, gratitude and respect. The teachers who continue the process are entitled to prestige and significant reward. We will be told that we cannot afford to pay mothers and teachers, but of course we can. All we have to do is to shift priorities. At the same time that we insist on women's being able to eschew motherhood for themselves without suffering a diminution of their femaleness as a consequence, we will have to promote motherhood as an institution. If fathers abscond, motherhood will have to be financed by all of us, because we are all ultimately beneficiaries. Childcare should be seen as a career option, whether it is done by mothers caring for their own children, or by professional carers who look after the children of others. We cannot afford to continue in the daft belief that child-raising can be left to the informal sector or the black economy or unpaid familial labour. Some will say that treating mothers decently will bring about a chain-reaction population explosion but they are wrong. A rise in women's education is the most reliable predictor of falling birth rates. Even if motherhood is reclaimed, the numbers of women opting for it will continue to decline, because the experience of motherhood is perceived to be unrewarding, no fun, all pain no gain, even where poverty is not a factor. Especially where poverty is not a factor. The immense rewardingness of children is the best-kept secret in the western world. As the emerging elites of the developing world model their lives on ours, bearing children will be seen more and more as a passport to marginalization. Which is all the more reason to treat the women who still choose the motherhood option with respect and appreciation.

The most powerful entities on earth are not governments but the multi-national corporations that see women as their territory, indoctrinating them with their versions of beauty, health and hygiene, medicating them and cultivating their dependency in order to medicate them some more. As these same corporations control research and the dissemination of information, women are helpless before their advance into every area of human existence. Women's crafts have been cheapened, commercialized and mass-marketed back to them in stereotyped forms. Women have lost their control over food and the rituals of food-giving have withered away. The female sector is disappearing as women are inducted into a neutered workforce. Though these processes were well advanced when *The Female Eunuch* was written, it was a year or two later that I found myself arguing for the recovery of women's culture, of open-ended un-monumental art forms that were continuous with living, the creativity that makes everyday life balanced and elegant.

> The unique consciousness or sensibility of women, the particular attributes that set feminist art apart, and a compelling line of research now being pursued by feminist anthropologists all point to the idea that female biology is the basis of women's powers. Biology is hence the source and not the enemy of the feminist revolution.
>
> Alice Echols on cultural feminism

Equality feminists know very little about the heroic struggles of women artists who have insisted on difference, returning again and again to the female body, whether they be seventy-two-year-old Nancy Spero with her ebullient installations of bacchantes serving themselves orally and vaginally with elegantly curved dildoes or Mona Hatoum with her videos of pulsing, glistening female entrails. Such dense and complex enactments of difference can make little headway against the world-conquering, hard-bodied, missile-breasted stereotype of masculinist fantasy, unless women pay them attention, and make them famous by following them in droves as little girls flocked to the Spice Girls. Some of the most powerful art is produced by women like Orlan who carve the insignia of the stereotype into their own flesh. Women's poetry too turns back again and again to the immediacy of the body and women's transformational experience.

Some say that women shall not be free until they are liberated from womanhood itself. Judith Lorber looked forward to an age when we might no longer ask at birth what sex a child is, because it will be of no consequence.

> When we no longer ask 'boy or girl?' in order to start gendering an infant, when the information is as irrelevant as the color of the child's eyes (but not yet the color of skin), then and only then will women and men be socially interchangeable and really equal. And when that happens there will no longer be any need for gender at all.

There is a considerable body of evidence that no matter how gender-free their upbringing, children will invent gender for themselves. One of my god-children amazed me one day by refusing a sweet on the grounds that sweets were for 'greedy boys'. All she had ever been told was that in our all-female family we did not eat sweets. She had gendered the activity of sweet-eating all by herself. Though she always wore pants and wore her hair short and had no dolls and didn't cry when she fell down because she was brave, she knew she was a girl and as unlike a boy as might be. The animal world will remain sexed, if not gendered, and the child would be dead from the neck up who did not wonder whether she was the kind of animal who could have puppies or not. Lorber was delighted with Donna Haraway's vision of women of the future as cyborgs:

> The cyborg is a creature in a post-gender world; it has no truck with bi-sexuality, pre-Oedipal symbiosis, unalienated labor, or other seductions to organic wholeness through a final appropriation of all the powers of the parts into a higher unity . . . the cyborg is resolutely committed to partiality, irony, intimacy and perversity. It is oppositional, utopian and completely without innocence . . . I would rather be a cyborg than a goddess.

'So would I,' says Lorber. If freedom is an out-of-body experience this feminist wants none of it. This female eunuch wants to be at ease in her body, unembarrassed about her body, proud and protective of her body, the body she has now. She wants to be freed from forever criticizing it, chastising it and forcing it to submit. It is more wonderful in every way than any production of our technology; no computer can perform a millionth of what her brain can, no man-made tool is a hundredth as efficient and versatile as her hand. Women may well find that the liberation struggle becomes a struggle to defend the female body, the source of all bodies, against the cyber-surgeons who will inherit the hubris of those present-day surgeons who think they make better breasts than God. The breasts surgeons make do not lactate, have no blood supply, are cold to the touch; they may look like breasts but in truth they are nothing but huge raised scars. The female body is not our enemy but our strength; it is not our sex that confines us but the hatred and disgust of others for our sex. If we begin to share their contempt we are finished.

Some radical feminists have looked forward to a future when children would no longer be born of women, seeing the functions of gestation and parturition as intolerable burdens. That future may be almost upon us, but it will not bring liberation unless it has been desired and designed by women themselves. Refusing to be defined, discriminated against and disadvantaged because of our female biology should not be confused with a demand to be deprived of it. Women (like Vietnamese villages) cannot be liberated by being destroyed.

There are a few set-piece numbers, though none of them is very elaborate, and the first, with the catchy title of Plough my Vulva, doesn't get things off to the best of starts.

Andrew Clements describes an avant-garde opera

In *The Female Eunuch*, long before Pre-Menstrual Syndrome had been invented, I suggested that, though there was nothing repulsive in menstruation itself, perhaps women would rather not menstruate. I had not thought so far as to suggest eliminating women's cyclical pattern altogether, nor had I considered the transformational nature of women's life experience. Men become very early set in their ways as lifelong Arsenal fans, lager drinkers, burglars, bankers, whatever, and usually continue in their chosen tramtracks for the rest of their lives. Women change, and change radically, as they pass through their climacterics. Each change seems to bring its own enlargement of awareness or sensibility and, though I consider that women in our time almost certainly menstruate too often, I have come to find women's changeability a value in itself, and a necessary corrective to masculine rigidity. Adaptability is the insignia of the female; survival rather than victory is her success. In a disaster-prone world this is a characteristic too valuable to jettison.

In the early days feminists learnt a great deal from Black Power; they learnt what it was to be a colonized people and they understood themselves to have been colonized. They saw the black people celebrating difference but, in place of singing and dancing that womanhood was beautiful, they studied. They studied women and they studied gender. They set up thousands of women's studies courses in universities, and millions of students enrolled in them and the universities pocketed their money and used it to buy prestige by developing traditional

> I think women are stronger than men. I make them stronger in my books. The sort of men I like are life's losers. They struggle gallantly, but they really ought to be left in peace. Life is just a bit too much for them.
>
> Penelope Fitzgerald, 1998

disciplines and hiring high-fliers (male). Though the women's studies courses brought in lots of students and lots of money, the women who ran them were infinitely replaceable and regularly refused tenure. Academic feminists expected recognition from the institutions that bred them; they worked and waited in hope and that hope was denied. Again and again, they found themselves passed over, except for a conspicuous few.

The black people knew that there was no point in pretending to be white and no point in imitating the white man's achievements or espousing his value system. They talked of doing their own thing, though they were only too well aware that their thing would appear so transgressive that it would be called crime. The white women were not sure what their own thing might be. How much of their traditional culture was slave culture; how much of their sensibility was what Florynce Kennedy would call nigger nobility? Should they learn to be as competitive, aggressive, lecherous and cruel as men? It is probably too soon to say that women *cannot* succeed in being as competitive, aggressive, lecherous and cruel as men, though I suspect that to be the case. What we can say is that to be as competitive, aggressive, lecherous and cruel as men is to be as fragile and miserable as men. Professor Keefe of Ohio University has found out what we all knew already, that women bear pain better than men, though he could not explain why. Much of the unbearableness of pain is caused by resentment of pain. Ability to endure is women's strength; rage would fritter away the kinetic energy contained in that strength, which is women's advantage. Because we bend, we do not break.

Women are versatile, tough, and contain within their variability all that falls within the range of normal; men are freaks of nature, fragile, fantastic, bizarre. To be male is to be a kind of idiot savant, full of queer obsessions about fetishistic activities and fantasy goals, single-minded in pursuit of arbitrary objectives, doomed to competition and injustice not merely towards females, but towards children, animals and other men. What the cliché that men know what they want and women don't know what they want really means is that women are conscious of all kinds of conditions that affect the desirability of any particular option at a particular time and in particular circumstances, while men formulate goals and pursue them in a single-minded manner. Single-mindedness is generally assumed to be better than multiple-mindedness because single-mindedness leads on to success in a highly competitive world. In a competitive world that imposes higher and higher standards of achievement, failures infinitely outnumber successes as more and more is sacrificed for less and less. Single-mindedness, which blinds an individual to the costs and risks associated with any course of action, is mostly maladaptive. Single-mindedness produces hideously anti-social behaviours, from paedophile rings to waging war. If the male is doomed to competitiveness by his Y-chromosome, his hyperfertility makes him expendable; his enemies are not the females, whose co-operation he needs to encompass his aims, but other males, all other males. The phenomenon of men's aggregating themselves into hierarchies which both acknowledge and threaten the rule of the alpha male is explicable in these terms. Perhaps it is appropriate to see females as programmed to seek a way to live together rather than fight, not by enforced subservience but by the low fertility that ensures their survival.

There has always been a confederacy between women and rebels against masculinist conditioning, be they homosexual, transvestite or transsexual, and these are relationships that feminists should continue to foster but not at the cost of denying their own perception of female reality. We can recognize the anti-male and the she-male without having to accept them both as female. To do so would be to confirm the negative view of women as simply non-males, penis-less people. When it comes to impersonating the feminine stereotype the trans-vestites and transsexuals are better at it than we are and we may as well let them get on with it. Feminists must work, as so many women artists are working, to give an imaginative shape to female potency so that it can be recognized for the awesome thing it is. If that means that we have to warn men off from messing with us, so be it.

> With their heads and their bodies finally liberated, with their eyes wide open, women will no longer be like those blinded horses who turn in circles round the wheel to which they are attached; they will no longer turn blindly, lovingly around you, Sir . . . They will no longer bury themselves in you.
>
> Françoise Parturier, 1986

No animal society exists in which non-competitive females could wrest control from competitive males who would then submit to their sway. Such a system would be a contradiction in terms. Usually the non-competitive females choose to live as a society of females and children with or without a single male leader, segregated from the unmated males. Advanced human societies regard such segregation as backward, assuming that it has been forced upon females by male tyranny, which has at the same time imposed seclusion. We are less aware of the cultural segregation in which we live; we do not see that masculine men flee domesticity and pursue a galaxy of concerns that hold no appeal for women, in which women do not participate except as a way of being close to men. The women who penetrate masculinist enclaves are usually unwelcome, kept on the periphery and treated as a sexual commodity if they are noticed at all. Women cannot force a change in such male behaviour because, as the men don't care if they are there or not, they have no bargaining power. The dignified alternative is for women to segregate themselves as men do; heterosexual women fear that men would find such segregation very much less irksome than they would themselves. So teenage girls continue to ring up boys who would rather go fishing. More than three million British males go fishing as often as they can. Women of any age are not welcome on the river bank. The only way to correct such asymmetry is for women to make a conscious decision not to want men's company more than men want women's. If that means segregation, so be it. If the alternative is humiliation, there is no alternative.

If we proceed on the assumption that the rise in lone-female-headed families reflects what men want, it is but a short step to deciding that they should pay for it through their taxes. More and more we are finding that matrilocal families including grandmother-figures and aunt-figures have established themselves from the fall-out of the nuclear family. Such segregated communities may hold great advantages for women and children, especially if they can find ways of incorporating older women who are now the majority of the elderly living alone on benefit. Governments could encourage a more rational use of housing stock and more caring in society by taxing households containing more than one occupant less than households with a single occupant, in diametric opposition to the British poll or council tax system. Whereas tax allowances to heterosexual couples clearly advantage one way of life over another, a household tax allowance would privilege all co-habitation systems, straight and gay, including the several-women-with-children unit. This would make sense in fiscal terms because people living in groups can take care of each other and should require less intervention than sole occupants with no-one at home to help if they meet with illness or accident. It might also mitigate the grim architectural consequences of a predominance of single-occupancy housing units. The family is dead, long live the family. The word 'family' actually means not kin-group but household. Maybe, instead of dating services, we should set up household-formation services to help like-minded individuals to set up house together.

The price list for [Angela Marshall's] show at the Decima Studios in Bermondsey, south-east London, was £25 and oral sex for a small picture, £50 and full sex for a medium-sized picture, while the purchase of a large painting at £75 would be enough for 'anything kinky'.

Guardian, 18 April 1998

The personal is still political. The millennial feminist has to be aware that oppression exerts itself in and through her most intimate relationships, beginning with the most intimate, her relationship with her body. More and more of her waking hours are to be spent in disciplining the recalcitrant body, fending off the diseases that it is heir to and making up for its inadequacies in shape, size, weight, colouring, hair distribution, muscle tone and orgastic efficiency, and its incorrigible propensity for ageing. More of her life is wasted cleaning things that are already clean, trying to feed people who aren't hungry, and labouring to, in, from and for chain-stores. Too much of her energy is sapped by being made to be afraid of everything but her real enemy, fear itself. She spends too much time waiting for things that will not happen, hoping for support and reinforcement that are withheld, apologizing for matters beyond her control, longing for closeness to the ones she loves and being reconciled to distance.

> No one can be perfectly free until all are free; no one can be perfectly moral until all are moral; no one can be perfectly happy till all are happy.
>
> Herbert Spencer

The second wave of feminism, rather than having crashed onto the shore, is still far out to sea, slowly and inexorably gathering momentum. None of us who are alive today will witness more than the first rumbles of the coming social upheaval. Middle-class western women have the privilege of serving the longest revolution, not of directing it. The ideological battles that feminist theorists are engaged in are necessary but they are preliminary to the emergence of female power, which will not flow decorously out from the universities or from the consumerist women's press. Female power will rush upon us in the persons of women who have nothing to lose, having lost everything already. It could surge up in China where so many women divorced for bearing girl children are living and working together, or in Thailand where prostitution and AIDS are destroying a generation, in Iran or anywhere else where women are on a collision course with Islamic fundamentalism, or anywhere the famished labourer sees luxury foods for the western market grown on the land which used to provide for her and her children. And the women of the rich world had better hope that when female energy ignites they do not find themselves on the wrong side.

notes

recantation
3   Julie Burchill, *Guardian Weekend*, 1 August 1998.

warm-up
8   Julia Gaynor, 'You sucker!', *Company* magazine, March, 1997, p. 61.

10   Angela Phillips, *Guardian*, 29 January 1998.

the superpower that grinds the life out of the world's women: see, e.g. Geoff Simons, *The Scourging of Iraq: sanctions, law and natural justice*, second edition (New York, St Martin's Press, 1998) and *Cuba – the impact of the US embargo on health and nutrition in Cuba* (Washington DC, US Committee of the World Health Organization and the Pan American Health Organization, 1997).

12   Naomi Wolf, *Fire with Fire: the new female power and how it will change the twenty-first century* (London, Chatto & Windus, 1993), p. xiv.

14   feminists in academe: D. C. Stanton and A. J. Stewart, eds, *Feminisms in the academy* (Ann Arbor, University of Michigan Press, 1995).

15   Susan J. Douglas, *Where the Girls Are: growing up female with the mass media in America* (London, Penguin Books, 1995), p. 236.

Larry Elliott, *Guardian*, 18 January 1997.

16   Iris Marion Young, *Throwing like a Girl and Other Essays in Feminist Philosophy and Social Theory* (Bloomington IN, Indiana University Press, 1990).

18   Alison Jaggar, Introduction, *Living with Contradictions: controversies in feminist social ethics*, ed. Alison M. Jaggar (Boulder CO, San Francisco and London, Westview Press, 1994), p. 11.

body
beauty

24   BDD: *Guardian*, 11 July 1996. BDD is a recognized psychiatric disorder; see, e.g. K. A. Phillips, M. M. Denight and S. L. McElroy, 'Efficacy and safety of fluvoxamine in body dysmorphic disorder', *Journal of Clinical Psychiatry* 59:4 (April 1998) and D. B. Sawyer, T. A. Wadden, M. T. Pertschuk and I. A. Whitaker, 'Body image dissatisfaction and body dysmorphic disorder in 100 cosmetic surgery patients', *Plastic Reconstructive Surgery* 101:6 (May 1998), pp. 164–9.

25   RuPaul from D. A. Keeps, 'How RuPaul ups the ante for drag', *New York Times*, 11 July 1993 H23.

26   Diet Breakers, Church Cottage, Barford St Michael, Oxfordshire, England, OX15 OUA; up-to-date information on organizations promoting healthy eating can be found on the Internet under http://www.healthyweightnetwork.com.

27   Demi Moore's fitness regime: *New Woman*, February 1997, p. 31.

28   today's granny: Virginia Ironside, *Woman and Home*, February 1996. Cher: *Newsweek*, November 1987.

29   botulin toxin: J. Guerissi and P. Sarkissian, 'Local injection into mimetic muscles of botulinum toxin A for the treatment of facial lines', *Annals of Plastic Surgery*, 39:5 (November 1997), pp. 447–53. Injections of Botox (Clostridium botulinum toxin) to eliminate frown lines, 'crow's feet' and suchlike 'dynamic wrinkles' are advertised on the Internet by the University of Michigan Center for Facial Cosmetic Surgery (http://www.med.umich.edu/cfs/botox.html), Advanced Dermatology Associates Ltd (http://www.adaltd.com/botox.html) and the Seattle Laser Treatment Center (http://www.seattlaser.com/botox.html) among others.

30   Barbie, Ann Treneman, *Guardian*, 27 November 1996; Richard Kelly Heft, *Guardian*, 24 December 1997. See also M. G. Lord, *Forever Barbie: the unauthorized biography of a real doll* (New York, Morrow, 1994); Sybil De Grein and Joan Ashabraner, *The Collectors' Encyclopedia of Barbie Dolls and the New Theatre of Fashion* (Paducah KY, Collector, 1992); Erica Rand, *Barbie's Queer Accessories* (Durham NC and London, Duke University Press, 1995) and the periodicals *Barbie Bazaar* and *Barbie Fashion*.

31   Miss World: *Guardian*, 23 November 1996. See also the Miss World website, http://www.qlcomm.com/missworld

manmade women

35   Dr Takowsky: as seen in the first part of the four-part TV series *Hollywood Lovers* (September Films) aired on ITV channels in the UK on 8 January 1997, quoted by Nancy Banks Smith in her review 'Squishing the fat gives new definition to leotards and televised sleaze', *Guardian*, 9 January 1998.

       Christine Williamson: press, 25 October 1997.

36   Lowri Turner, *Guardian*, 27 May 1993, quoted in 'Fashion Plates, Empty Plates' by Judy Sadgrove.

       ban on Silastic prostheses: press, 18 February 1998.

37   report of independent review body: press, 20 February 1998.

37–8   B. E. Cohen, T. M. Biggs, E. D. Cronin, D. R. Collins Jr, 'Assessment and longevity of silicone gel breast implants', *Plastic Reconstructive Surgery* 99:6 (1997), pp. 1597–1601.

       breast-feeding and implants: *Journal of Rheumatology*, May 1997 24(5).

       Silicon Support UK: up-to-date information on local and international support groups can be found on the Internet at the website of the Coalition of Silicone Survivors, http://www2.private.com/~coss/coss/sshead2.html#supportgroups

38   Karen Watson: letter to *Now* magazine, 3 July 1997.

40   'She's 75 . . .': Dr Novack, quoted in *Cosmopolitan*, August 1996.

41   Jan Breslauer, *Playboy*, July 1997.

       Laura Horbury, letter to *Now* magazine, 3 July 1997, p. 10.

42   The bikini-clad violinist is the Finn Linda Lampenius who has posed for *Playboy*. She now calls herself also Linda Brava; for a taste of her act, try http://home.vpress.se/andreas/linda.html. Her official website is http://www.ul.com/ubl/cards/015/6/32.html.

womb

44   Courtney Love: Poppy Z. Brite, *Courtney Love: the real story* (London, Orion, 1997), p. 101; Susan Wilson, *Hole: Look through this* (London, UFO Music, 1995).

45   Josepha Grieve: 'Screen Bodies: the body and computer technology in contemporary Australian art'. *Women's Art Magazine* 63, March–April 1995.

46   Linda Grant: *Guardian*, 19 August 1997.

47   Orlan, 'I do not want to look like . . .' *Women's Art Magazine* No 64, May–June 1995. See also Orlan et al. *This is my body . . . This is my software* (book and CD Rom, London, Black Dog Publishing, *c.* 1996).

48   Hippocrates: 'De Mulieribus', *Hippocratic Writings*, ed. int. G. E. R. Lloyd, trans. J. Chadwick et al. (London, Penguin, 1978).

49   D. H. Lawrence, *Lady Chatterley's Lover* (London, etc., Penguin Books, 1994) p. 247.

50–1   Fiona Shaw, *Out of Me: the story of a post-natal breakdown* (London, Viking, 1997) pp. 13, 13–14, 17, 22, 31–2, 97–8, 174.

51   Premenstrual symptoms are now classified in different ways depending on whether the symptoms are physical or mental; the psychiatric version of extreme distress is called 'Premenstrual Dysphoric Disorder' (PDD); P. Y. Choi and S. McKeown, 'Premenstrual dysphoric disorder: what are undergraduate women's qualitative experiences of the menstrual cycle?' *Journal of Psychosomatic Obstetrics and Gynaecology*, 18:4 (December 1997), pp. 259–65 suggest that the important influences on women's perception may well be cultural. For updated information on current attitudes to PMS see the Understanding PMS website on the Internet (http://tor-pw1.netcom.ca/~visprint/smal/html).
        Edward Shorter, *A History of Women's Bodies* (London, Allen, Lane and Unwin, 1983), pp. 286–7.

52   Dinora Pines, *A Woman's Unconscious Use of her Body: a psychoanalytical perspective* (London, Virago, 1993), pp. 48, 85, 91.

53   HFEA statements on surrogacy: HFEA leaflets *Egg Donation* and *Donors and the Law*.

breasts

56   Laura, Cardiff: letter to *Now* magazine, 3 July 1997, p. 10.

57   Dr Cathy Read (author of *Preventing Breast Cancer: the politics of an epidemic*, London, Pandora, 1995) in *Everywoman*, May 1995.

58   Leland Bardwell, 'Husbands', in Linda France, ed., *Women Poets* (Newcastle upon Tyne, Bloodaxe Books, 1993), p. 41.

60   Elisabet Helsing and F. Savage King, in *Breast Feeding in Practice* (Oxford, Oxford University Press, 1982) p. 31.
        Elizabeth Garrett, 'Mother, Baby, Lover', France, op. cit., pp. 141–2.

60–1   woman who gave up breast-feeding: Pam Carter, *Feminism, Breasts and Breast Feeding* (Basingstoke, Macmillan, 1995), pp. 141–2. See also Linda M. Blum, 'Mothers, babies and breast-feeding in late capitalist America: the shifting contexts of feminist theory', *Feminist Studies*, 19:2 (Summer 1993), pp. 291–311.

63   Tanya Hatherall, *Sugar*, 28 February 1997.
        breast awareness: it is worth noting that 'Breast Awareness Week'

was instituted in 1984 by ICI (Imperial Chemical Industries) whose wholly owned subsidiary Zeneca manufactures tamoxifen.

64   link between abortion and breast cancer: *Guardian* , 12 October 1996; the Danish study was reported in the *New England Journal of Medicine* 336 (1997), pp. 81–5.

breast pain: D. N. Ader, C. D. Shriver, 'Cyclical mastalgia: prevalence and impact', *Journal of the American College of Surgeons*, 185:5 (November 1997), pp. 466–70.

breast polycystic disease and diet: *Surgery*, 1979, J. P. Minton et al. See also S. Franks and F. Neumann, eds., *Polycystic Ovarian Syndrome: a new approach to treatment* (Chester, Adis International, 1993).

evening primrose oil: Judy Graham, *Evening Primrose Oil*, third edition (London, Thorson's, 1993).

65   J. C. Elmore, M. B. Barton, V. M. Moceri, S. Polk, P. J. Arena, S. W. Fletcher, 'Ten year risk of false positive screening mammograms and clinical breast examinations', *New England Journal of Medicine*, 38:6 (16 April 1998), pp. 1145–6, pointed out that over a ten-year period one-third of the women whose breasts were examined as regularly as recommended will have had a false-positive result which necessitated further work-up.

65–6   Professor Michael Baum originally suggested scrapping of mass mammography in a letter to the *Lancet* which was picked up by the *Sunday Times* for 3 September 1995, setting off a media controversy that ran for some time. Professor Baum's considered position is set out in Chapter 13 'Screening and Breast Awareness', of Michael Baum, Christine Saunders and Sheena Meredith, *Breast Cancer: a guide for every woman* (Oxford, Oxford University Press, 1994), pp. 147–158.

67   Swedish study: N. B. Jurstam, L. Bjorneld, S. W. Duffy, T. C. Smith, E. Cahlin, O. Eriksson, L. O. Hafstrom, H. Lingaas, J. Mattsson, S. Persson, C. M. Rudenstam, J. Save-Soderbergh, 'The Gothenburg breast screening trial: first results on mortality, incidence and mode of detection for women aged 39–49 years at randomization', *Cancer*, 80:11 (December 1997).

For a recent discussion of the situation see S. Moritz, T. Bates, S. M. Henderson, S. Humphreys and M. J. Michell, 'Variation in management of small invasive breast cancers detected on screening in the former South-east Thames region: observational study', *British Medical Journal*, 315:7118 (15 November 1997), pp. 1266–72.

alternatives to radiation mammography: S. H. Heywang-Kobrunner,

P. Viehweg, A. Heinig, and C. Kuchler, 'Contrast enhanced MRI of the breast: accuracy, value, controversies, solutions', *European Journal of Radiology* 24:2 (February 1997), pp. 94–108 and S. G. Orel, 'High resolution MRI imaging of the breast', *Seminars in Ultrasound CT and MRI* 17:5 (October 1996), pp. 476–93 and M. Funke, V. Fischer, and E. Grabbe, 'MR–mammography: current status and perspectives', *Aktuelle–Radiologie* 6:3 (May 1996), pp. 130–5.

68   Johanna Johenson: press, 25–27 June 1996.

class action for over-radiation: press, 10 January 1998.

69   breast cancer epidemic: see P. M. Lanmtaz and K. M. Booth, 'The social construction of the breast cancer epidemic', *Social Science and Medicine* 46:7 (April 1998), pp. 98ff.

The change in priorities and approach is heralded by articles such as P. Hopwood, 'Psychological issues in cancer genetics: current research and future priorities', *Patient Education and Counselling*, 32:1–2 (September–October 1997), pp. 19–31.

research funding: in Britain the current state of affairs can be monitored on the Internet at http://www.easynet.co.uk/aware/contacts. The US National Breast Cancer Coalition runs a bigger site at http://www.natlbcc. org/

See also Sharon Batt, *Patient no more; the politics of breast cancer* (Charlotte Town, Gynergy Books, 1995).

food

72   Connie Bensley, 'Cookery' in Linda France, ed., *Women Poets* (Newcastle upon Tyne, Bloodaxe Books, 1993), p. 56.

74   Jean Earle, 'Jugged Hare', France, p. 123.

75   Marya Hornbacher, *Wasted: a memoir of anorexia and bulimia* (London, Flamingo, 1998), p. 286.

76   youth culture: see, for example, 'Group Anorexia: the deadly way women bond', *Cosmopolitan*, February 1997, pp. 33–5.

78   self-starvation: see Suzie Orbach, *Hunger Strike* (London, Penguin Books, 1997).

Debra Gimlim, 'The Anorexic as over-conformist: towards a re-interpretation of eating disorders', in Karen A. Callaghan, ed., *Ideals of Feminine Beauty; philosophical, social and cultural dimensions* (Westport CT and London, Greenwood Press, 1994).

79   Elaine Feinstein, 'Rose', France, p. 137.

pantomime dames

80   gender dysphoria: D. Denny, *Gender Dysphoria: a guide to research* (New York, Garland Publishing Inc., 1994).

81   Dwight D. Billings and Robert Urban, 'The sociomedical construction of transsexualism: an interpretation and critique', *Social Problems*, 29 (1982), pp. 266–82.

82   current trends in neovulvavaginoplasty: R. B. Karim, J. J. Hage, J. W. Mulder, 'Neo-vaginoplasty in male-to-female transsexuals: review of surgical techniques and recommendations regarding eligibility', *Annals of Plastic Surgery*, 7:6 (3 December 1996) pp. 669–75.

      the importance of rhinoplasty: J. J. Hage, M. Vossen, A. G. Becking, 'Rhinoplasty as part of gender-confirming surgery in male transsexuals: basic considerations and clinical experience', *Annals of Plastic Surgery*, 39:3 (September 1997), pp. 266–71.

      voice improvement: H. F. Mahieu, T. Norbart and F. Snel, 'Laryngeal framework surgery for voice improvement', *Review of Laryngology, Otology and Rhinology*, 117:3 (1996), pp. 189–97.

83   follow-up-studies, e.g. P. J. van Kesteren, H. Asscheman, J. A. Megens, L. J. Gooren, 'Mortality and morbidity in transsexual subjects treated with cross-sex hormones', *Clinical Endocrinology*, 47: 3 (September 1997), pp. 337–42, and K. Midence and I. Hargreaves, 'Psychosocial adjustment in male-to-female transsexuals: an overview of the evidence', *Journal of Psychology*, 131:6 (November 1997), pp. 602–14.

      Judith Lorber, *Paradoxes of Gender* (New Haven and London, Yale University Press, 1994), pp. 20–1.

84   Lawrence Cohen, 'The pleasures of castration: the post-operative status of hijras, jankhas and academics', in *Sexual Nature, Sexual Culture*, eds. Paul R. Abrahamson and Stephen D. Pinkerton (Chicago, University of Chicago Press, 1995); see also Serena Nanda, 'The hijras of India', *Journal of Homosexuality*, 11:3–4 (1986), p. 38.

85   Janice Raymond, from *The Transsexual Empire: the making of the she-male* (Boston, Beacon Press, 1979), p. 114.

86   AIS males: *Guardian*, 25 February 1997.

87   sexing of newborns: Mahin Hassibi, 'Designing sex, playing God: have doctors gone too far?', *On the Issues: The Progressive Woman's Quarterly*, summer 1998, p. 15. See also R. M. Viner, Y. Teoh, D. M. Williams, M. N. Paterson, I. A. Hughes, 'Androgen insensitivity syndrome: a survey of diagnostic procedures and management in the UK', *Archives of the Disabilities of Childhood*, 77:4 (October 1997), pp. 305–9.

Tracie O'Keefe: *Guardian*, 25 February 1997.

89   Simon Reynolds and Joy Press, *The Sex Revolts: gender, rebellion and rock 'n'roll* (London, Serpent's Tail, 1995), p. 64.

90   The case of 'W': *Guardian*, 2 August 1996.

adolescent transsexuals: see P. T. Cohen Kettenis, S. H. van Goozen, 'Sex reassignment of adolescent transsexuals: a follow-up study', *Journal of the American Academy of Child and Adolescent Psychiatry*, 36:2 (February 1997), pp. 263–71.

91   Louisa Young: *Guardian*, 29 July 1996 (tabloid, pp. 6–7).

transsexuals in the sex industry: S. Greenberg, 'The new wave', *Advocate*, 633 (13 July 1993).

female-to-male transsexuals: H. A. Bosinski, M. Peter, G. Bonatz, M. Heidenreich, W. G. Sippell and R. Wille, 'A higher rate of hyperandrogenic disorders in female to male transsexuals', *Psychoneuroendocrinology*, 5 (22 July 1997), pp. 361–80.

91–2   Mark Rees, 'Becoming a man: the personal account of a female to male transsexual', *Blending genders: social aspects of cross-dressing and sex-changing*, ed. R. Ekins and D. King (London, Routledge, 1996).

manmade mothers

96   Robert, Lord Winston, *Infertility: A sympathetic approach to understanding the causes and options for treatment* (London, Vermilion, 1996), p. 3. See also his interview in the *Sunday Times*, 27 April 1998, and *Making Babies: a personal view of IVF* (London, BBC Books, 1996).

98   born of a pig or an incubator: see, for example, G. Corea, *The Mother Machine: reproductive technologies from artificial insemination to artificial wombs* (New York, Harper and Row, 1986) and Sarah Franklin, *Embodied Progress: a cultural account of assisted conception* (London, Routledge, 1998).

99   ovarian hyperstimulation: Carl Wood and Alan Trounson, *Clinical In Vitro Fertilization* (Berlin, Springer-Verlag, 1989) p. 15.

100   egg donation: *Guardian*, 12 August 1997. See also A. Simon, A. Revel, A. Hurwitz and N. Langer, 'The pathogenesis of OHSS [Ovarian Hyperstimulation Syndrome]: a continuing enigma', *Journal of Assisted Reproduction and Genetics*, 15:4 (April 1998), pp. 202–9.

101   Mara Lane, egg donor: *Woman's Own*, 13 May 1998.

For discussion of the role played by the media in changing attitudes to IVF see Jose Van Dyck, *Manufacturing Babies and Public Consent: debating the new reproductive technologies* (London, Macmillan, 1995).

101–2   adverse outcomes: see G. Corea, R. D. Klein et al., *Man-made Women: how new reproductive technologies affect women* (London, Hutchinson, 1985) and current numbers of *Issues in reproduction and genetic engineering: a journal of international feminist analysis* (New York, Pergamon Press).

103   Professor Craft: *Guardian*, 23 July 1996.

105–6   Shulamith Firestone, *The Dialectic of Sex: the case for feminist revolution* (London, Jonathan Cape, 1971), pp. 233–4.

abortion

107   the history of abortion law reform: Cynthia Gorney, *Articles of Faith: the abortion wars, a frontline history* (New York NY, Simon & Schuster, 1998). See also Norma McCorvey with Andy Meisler, *I am Roe: my life, Roe vs Wade and Freedom of Choice* (New York, HarperCollins, 1994), pp. 89–90, 95, 99, 126–8, 133.

107–8   deep moral conflicts: Janet Hadley, *Abortion: between freedom and necessity* (London, Virago, 1996) and Rosalind P. Petchesky, *Abortion, a Woman's Choice: the state, sexuality and reproductive freedom*, revised edition (Boston, Northeastern University Press, 1990).

108   abortion and organized crime: in 1978 the Chicago *Sun-Times* conducted an investigation resulting in a week-long series of major articles which were later issued separately as *The Abortion Profiteers*.

109   Cardinal Winning: *The Times*, 10 March 1997.

110   Pamela Pickton, 'Letter to two babies who never were', *Everywoman*, September 1995.

        German abortion laws: *Guardian*, 1 August 1996.

111   letter to the *Lancet*: Jayshree Pillaye, *Lancet* 348 (17 August 1996), p. 9025.

        MPs on abortion: *Guardian*, 4 December 1996.

        MORI poll results: press, February 1997.

114   Joan Earle, 'Menopause' in Linda France, ed., *Women Poets* (Newcastle upon Tyne, Bloodaxe Books, 1993), p. 125.

115   non-surgical abortion: see *Medical Methods of Termination of Pregnancy: report of a WHO scientific group* (WHO Technical Reprint Series, 1997) and D. J. Majahan and S. N. London, 'Mifepristone (RU486): a review', *Fertility-Sterility*, 68:6 (December 1997), pp. 967–76 and J. R. Goldberg, M. G. Plescia and G. D. Anastasio, 'Mifepristone (RU486): current knowledge and future prospects', *Archives of Family Medicine*, 7:3 (May–June 1998), pp. 219–22.

mutilation

119   Bondo society: press, January 1997.

clitoridectomy in the US: Martha Coventry, 'The tyranny of the esthetic: surgery's most intimate violation', *On the Issues: The Progressive Woman's Quarterly*, summer 1998, pp. 16ff.

120   intersexual newborns: see above, p. 85 and n.

letter to the doctor of *Woman* magazine: 13 April 1998, cf. *Cosmopolitan*, December 1996, 'Plastic surgery for sexual pleasure'.

criminalization of FGM: E. T. Ortiz, 'Female genital mutilation and public health: lessons from the British experience', *Health Care for Women International*, 19:2 (March–April 1998), pp. 119–29 and F. L. Key, 'Female circumcision/female genital mutilation in the United States: legislation and its implications for health providers', *Journal of the American Medical Women's Association*, 52:4 (Fall 1997), pp. 179–80, 187. *Proceedings of the Oxford Symposium on Sexual Mutilations*, August 1998.

121   attack on cultural identity: See Adela Apena, 'Female circumcision in Africa and the problem of cross-cultural perspectives', *Africa Update* 3:2 (1996).

anti-male-circumcision movement: NoCIRC and NORM UK (National Organisation for Restoring Men). See also R. S. Immerman and W. C. Mackey, 'A bio-cultural analysis of circumcision', *Sociobiology*, 44:3–4 (Fall–Winter 1997) pp. 265–75. See also R. S. van Howe, 'Variability in penile appearance and penile findings: a prospective study', *British Journal of Urology*, 80:5 (November 1997), pp. 776–82. Stephanie Welsh, 'Like Mother, Like Daughter', *On the Issues: The Progressive Woman's Quarterly* 5:4 (Fall 1996), pp. 28–31.

122   'beliefs and practices': *The State of World Population 1997* (New York, UNFPA, 1997), p. 25.

124   Claire Keighley-Bray: 'My sister's death almost killed me', *Bliss* magazine, April 1998, p. 40.

See also K. C. Perkins, 'Adolescent trends in the late twentieth century: fad or societal alienation?', *West Virginia Medical Journal*, 93:6 (November–December 1997), pp. 313–6.

125–6   Jane Shag Stamp, *Shag Stamp* No. 6, 1996.

126   A. R. Favazza, 'The Coming Age of Self-Mutilation', *Journal of Nervous and Mental Disorders*, 186:5 (May 1998), pp. 259–68.

128   episiotomy: Gemma Mitchell, 'Stitched up', *Everywoman*, July 1996.

130   John A. Walsh in Elizabeth Davis *Heart & Hands: a midwife's guide to pregnancy and birth*, third edition (Berkeley CA, Celestial Arts, 1997), p. 149.

131   Marina Abramovic: interview with Guy Hilton, 'Fifty is just the
       beginning', *Make*, 73 (December 1996–January 1997), pp. 3–5. A
       Film and Video Umbrella programme of selected video and perfor-
       mance pieces by Abramovic can be found on the Internet at:
       http://www.beyond2000.co.uk/umbrella/html/abramovic.html
       Wendy Cox: *Guardian*, 15 October 1996.

132   non-surgical treatment for heavy uterine bleeding: I. S. Fraser, C.
       Pearse, R. C. Shearman, P. M. Elliot, J. McIlveen, and R. Markham,
       'Efficacy of mefenamic acid in patients with a complaint of menor-
       rhagia', *Obstetrics and Gynaecology* 58 (1981), pp. 543–51.

132–3 epidemiology of hysterectomy: K. M. Brett, J. V. Marsh, J. H.
       Madans, 'Epidemiology of Hysterectomy in the United States: demo-
       graphic and reproductive factors in a nationally representative
       sample', *Journal of Women's Health* 6:3 (June 1997), pp. 309–16.

our bodies, our selves

136   Helene Cixous: 'The Laugh of the Medusa' from *New French
       Feminisms: an anthology*, ed. Elaine Marks and Isabelle de Courtivron
       (Brighton, Harvester Press, 1991), p. 251.
       For a fuller discussion of the monitored pregnancy see Barabara Katz
       Rothman, *The Tentative Pregnancy* (New York, Norton, 1993).

139   human papilloma virus: M. J. Arends, C. H. Buckley, M. Wells,
       'Aetiology, pathogenesis and pathology of cervical neoplasia', *Journal
       of Clinical Pathology*, 51:2 (February 1998), pp. 96–103, and J. Hall
       and L. Walton, 'Dysplasia of the Cervix', *American Journal of
       Obstetrics and Gynaecology*, 100 (1968), pp. 662–7.
       unreliability of Pap test: W. C. Fetherston, 'False-negative cytology
       in invasive cancer of the cervix', *Clinics in Obstetrics and Gynaecology*,
       26 (1983), p. 929; N. D. Morrell, J. R. Taylor, R. N. Snyder, *et al.*,
       'False-negative cytology rates in patients in whom invasive cervical
       cancer subsequently developed', *Obstetrics and Gynaecology*, 60
       (1982), p. 41.

140–1 assessments of cervical screening: A. M. Foltz, J. L. Kelsey, 'Annual
       Pap Test: A dubious policy success', *Millbank Memorial Fund
       Quarterly*, 56 (1979), 426, cf. L. W. Coppelson and B. Brown,
       'Estimation of the screening error rate from observed detection rates
       in repeated cervical cytology', *American Journal of Obstetrics and
       Gynaecology*, 119 (1974), p. 953. See also the editorial in the *British
       Medical Journal* 314:533 (22 February 1997), 'Screening could seri-
       ously damage your health'.

142   B. Sevin, J. H. Ford, R. D. Girtanner, W. J. Hoskins, A. B. P. Ng,
       S. R. B. Nordqvist and H. E. Averette, 'Invasive cancer of the cervix

after cryosurgery; Pitfalls of conservative management', *Obstetrics and Gynaecology*, 53 (1979), p. 465.

144   Dundee study: C. A. Mackenzie and I. D. Duncan, 'The value of cervical screening in women over 50 years of age: time for a multi-centre audit', *Scottish Medical Journal*, 43:1 (February 1998), pp. 19–20.

Strathclyde cervical smear: *Guardian*, 29 April 1993.

145   Dr Angela Raffle: *Guardian*, 3 February 1998.

mind
work

152   Joseph Pleck: from Helen Z. Lopata and Joseph H. Pleck, *Research into the interweave of jobs and families*, 3 (Greenwich CT, JAI Press, 1983), p. 39.

All Work and No Play: the sociology of women and leisure (Milton Keynes, Open University Press, 1986); E. Green, S. Hebron and D. Woodward, *Women's Leisure, What Leisure?* (London, Macmillan, 1990).

155   lazy gorilla: Irene Elia, *The Female Animal* (Oxford, Oxford University Press, 1985), p. 210, quoting Kelly Stewart, 'The birth of a wild mountain gorilla'.

160   'Women are doing better than ever in the workplace': Charlotte Raven, 'Me, myself, I', *Guardian*, 9 September 1996.

160–1   Cambridge University study: press, 6 December 1996.

housework

166–7   George Soros: *Guardian*, 18 January 1998.

170   Sharon Maxwell Magnus: *Guardian*, 23 July 1997.

171   'The loneliness of a long-distance wife', *Woman and Home*, February 1997, p. 61.

shopping

175   Wendy Cope, 'My Lover', in Linda France, ed., *Women Poets* (Newcastle upon Tyne, Bloodaxe Books, 1993), p. 89.

Helen Wilkinson and Melanie Howard, with Sarah Gregory, Helen Hayes and Rowena Young, *Tomorrow's Women* (London, Demos, 1997), pp. 22, 61, 62.

176   Loreto Keech: letter to *Woman* magazine, 13 May 1998.

183   men's crèches: press, 29 March 1997.

Japanese schoolgirl prostitute: 'Bliss Global Report: Japanese schoolgirls live for designer clothes and some are going to any lengths to buy them', *Bliss* magazine, March 1997, p. 24.

oestrogen

184   J. B. Becker, S. M. Breedlove and D. Crews, *Behavioural Endocrinology* (Cambridge MA and London, MIT Press, 1992), pp. 32–3, 380–81.

185   oestrogen as a psychotropic: B. Sherwin, 'Hormones, mood and cognitive functioning in post-menopausal women', *Obstetrics and Gynaecology* 87:20 (1996); A. J. P. Gregoire, R. Kumar, B. Everitt, A. F. Henderson, J. W. W. Studd, 'Transdermal oestrogen for treatment of severe post-natal depression', *Lancet*, 347 (1996), 930–3.

186   urine farms: Leora Tannenbaum, 'The bitter pill: bombarded by propaganda on Premarin, we can't trust our doctors and we can't trust ourselves', *On the Issues: The Progressive Woman's Quarterly*, Winter 1998.

      People for the Ethical treatment of Animals is a worldwide organization. Their official Internet website is http//:www.peta-online.org

187   the waning efficacy of HRT: B. Ellinger, O. Grady, 'The waning effect of post-menopausal oestrogen therapy on osteoporosis', *New England Journal of Medicine*, 329 (1993), pp. 1192–3.

      Lila Nachtigall and Joan Rattner Heilman, *Oestrogen: the new woman's dynamic / how it can change your life* (London, Arlington, 1987), p. 20.

188   HRT and Carpal Tunnel Syndrome: M. S. Sabour, H. E. Fadel, 'Carpal Tunnel Syndrome – a new complication ascribed to the pill', *American Journal of Obstetrics and Gynaecology* 107 (1972), 1265–7; G. S. Dieck, L. J. Kelsey, 'An epidemiologic study of carpal tunnel syndrome in an adult female population', *Preventative Medicine* 124:9 (1985), pp. 63–9; L. J. Cannon, J. Bernacki, S. D. Walter, 'Personal and occupational factors associated with Carpal Tunnel Syndrome', *Journal of Occupational Medicine* 231 (1981), pp. 255–8; R. Confino-Cohen, M. Listner, H. Savin, R. Lang, M. Ravid, 'Response of Carpal Tunnel Syndrome to hormone replacement therapy', *British Medical Journal* 303 (1991), p. 1514.

      a super sex life: Nachtigall and Heilman, pp. 77, 82.

      J. Kinoshita, *Brainwork* (2, 1992).

189   Dr Ellen Grant: letter to *The Times*, 20 December 1997. DASH (Doctors against Abuse from Steroidal sex Hormones) can be contacted at Coombe Heights, 20 Coombe Ridings, Kingston-upon-Thames, Surrey.

190   H. P. Schneider, 'Cross national study of women's use of hormone replacement therapy in Europe', *International Journal of Fertility and Women's Medicine* 42, Supplement 2 (1997), pp. 365–75.

191   *Science* 259 (1993), also following issue. Also E. Marshall; O. P. Judson, *Nature* 365 (1993).
        HRT and thrombo–embolic disorders: J. P. Vandenbrouke and F. M. Helmerhorst, 'Risk of venous thrombosis with hormone replacement therapy', *Lancet*, 348 (1996), p. 972.

testosterone

194   Lesley, Silverfish: Lucy O'Brien, *She Bop* (London, Penguin Books, 1995), p. 170.
195   Paul Kozminsky: *Guardian*, 24 February, 1997.
        Janet 'Texas' Scanlon: *Now* magazine, 3 July 1997, p. 27.
196   hyenas: Natalie Angier, 'Hyenas hormone flow puts females in charge', *New York Times*, 1 September 1992.
197–8   John Money: 'Commentary: current status of sex research', *Journal of Psychology and Human Sexuality* 1 (1988) 1, cf. 5–15.
198   Susie Orbach, 'Shrink Wrap'. *Guardian Weekend*, 19 July 1997.
        Guy Browning, 'Office Politics', *Guardian Weekend*, 4 April 1998.
200   J. C. Herz, *Joystick Nation: how video games gobbled our money, won our hearts and rewired our minds* (London, Abacus, 1997) p. 172.
201   'Lovers in for the kill or in for the thrill', *Guardian*, 21 December 1996.
        Sandra: *Cosmopolitan*, January 1997.
202   declining sperm count: see p. 269 and n.
203   David Thomas, *Not Guilty: in defence of modern man* (London, Weidenfeld and Nicholson, 1993).
        Warren Farrell, *The Myth of Male Power: why men are the disposable sex* (London, Fourth Estate, 1994).
203–4   The British Crime Survey: the latest survey, 1996, is based on interviews with 16,500 individuals over sixteen years of age.
204–5   Jason Humble: *Guardian*, 31 March and 3 April 1998.
205   Professor John Groeger: *Guardian*, 4 April 1998.

soldiers

206–7   US Defense Department's Breast Cancer Research Programme: *Chronicle of Higher Education*, 19 December 1997.
209   Kamlesh Bahl: *Guardian*, 7 February 1998.
        Tamil Tiger: 'Arms to fight; arms to protect. Women speak out about conflict', *Everywoman*, September, 1995.
210–1   Bruce Fleming, 'Gay Poets, Women and Other Threats to Group Loyalty at the Naval Academy', *Chronicle of Higher Education*, 30 January 30, 1998.

213   Tamil Tiger: 'Tiger, Tiger, burning bright', *Everywoman*, July 1996. Claire Alcock: press, 28 January 1998.

213–4 US Navy: Peter J. Boyer, 'Admiral Boorda's War', *New Yorker*, 1996.
       See also Sarah Ruddick, *Maternal Thinking: toward a politics of peace* (Boston, Bacon Press, 1989).

sorrow

220–1 'Things are different': *Everywoman*, May 1995.

223   Jane Ussher, *Women's madness: misogyny or mental illness* (Hemel Hempstead, Harvester Wheatsheaf, 1991) p. 234.224

224   'A woman who is unhappy . . .': Ussher, pp. 103–4.

sex

229   Betty Dodson, *Sex for One: the joys of self-loving* and Susan Bakos, *Sexational Secrets*, quoted by Jonathan Franzen in 'Anti-climax. No sex please, we're readers', *New Yorker*, 21 April 1997, p. 92.

230   Cecil Lewis: obituary, *Guardian*, 1997.

231   Philip Larkin: Andrew Motion, *Philip Larkin: a writer's life* (London, Faber & Faber, 1993), pp. 222, 234, 266–7, 307.

233   the Anne Summers Party Plan: *Everywoman*, September 1995, pp. 28–9.

234   US porn industry: Aliz Sharkey, 'The land of the free' *Guardian Weekend*, 22 November 1977.

235   Sally Potter interviewed by Beverley D'Silva, *Guardian*, 27 October 1997.
       Alan Paul Barlow: see press reports of Operation Starburst, 26 July 1995.
       an English priest: press, 13 November 1996.

236   Colin Laskey, Roland Jaggard and Anthony Brown: *The Times* Law Report, 20 February 1997, Laskey, Jaggard and Brown vs UK.

237–8 Orlan: see p. 47 and n.

239   Luce Irigaray: 'This sex which is not one', originally published as 'Le Sexe qui n'en est pas un' in *Cahiers du Grif* No 5, and in Elaine Marks and Isabelle de Courtivron, eds, *New French Feminisms* and again in Sneja Gunew, ed., *A Reader in Feminist Knowledge* (London and New York, 1991), p. 208.

240   Lucretia Stewart: *Punch*, 6 September, 1996.

241   Ava Cadell: 'Hollywood Sex', Sky TV, April 1998.

love
mothers

247   Leigh Bowery: Hilton Als, 'Life as a Look', *New Yorker*, 30 March 1998.

250   Melissa Benn, *Madonna and Child: towards a new politics of motherhood* (London, Jonathan Cape, 1998); Kate Figes, *Life after Birth: what even your friends won't tell you about motherhood* (London, Viking, 1998); and Rozsika Parker, *Torn in Two: the experience of maternal ambivalence* (London, Virago, 1995).

        See also Sharon Hays, *The Cultural Contradictions of Motherhood* (Newhaven and London, Yale University Press, 1997) and D. Richardson, *Women, Motherhood and Caring* (London, Macmillan, 1993).

        Patricia Beer, 'The Lost Woman' in Linda France, ed., *Women Poets* (Newcastle upon Tyne, Bloodaxe Books, 1993), p. 52.

251   Marni Jackson, *The Mother Zone: love, sex and laundry in the modern family* (Toronto, MacFarlane, Walter and Ross, 1992), p. 4.

253   Adrienne Rich, *Of Woman Born: motherhood as experience and institution* (London, Virago, 1977), p. 21.

254   See Laura M. Purdy, *Reproducing Persons: issues in feminist bio-ethics* (New York, Cornell University Press, 1997).

254–5   Sally Bevan: *Guardian*, 4 September 1996.

255   Fay Weldon, quoted by Larry Elliott, in 'Women's Sterile Choice at Work', *Guardian*, 17 November 1997.

        Jane Gregory quoted from *Woman's Weekly*, 21 January 1997.

256   Grace Nichols, 'Because she has come', France, op. cit., p. 211.

257   The General Household Survey (London, Office of Population, Censuses and Surveys, 1997).

        Evelyn Shaw and Joan Darling, *Female Strategies* (New York, Walker and Co., 1985), p. 146.

258   Deborah Benady: *Guardian*, 18 February 1998.

259   children in poverty: Barnardo's, *The Facts of Life 1997*.

        Marni Jackson, as above.

fathers

267   Adrienne Burgess: *Guardian*, 9 April 1998. See also *Fatherhood Reclaimed: the making of the modern father* (London, Vermilion, 1997), *passim*.

268   *Fathers and Fatherhood in Britain* (London, Family Policy Studies Centre, 1997).

269   the validating father: Barbara Goulter and Joan Minninger, Ph.D., *The Father–Daughter Dance* (New York, Putnam's, 1993), p. 214.

270   ibid. See also Lynda E. Brose and Betty S. Flowers, eds, *Daughters and Fathers* (Baltimore, Johns Hopkins University Press, 1989) and Thomas Laqueur, 'The Facts of Fatherhood', in M. Hirsch and E. Fox Keller, eds, *Conflicts in Feminism* (New York and London, Routledge, 1990), pp. 205–221.

271   Vidal Sassoon: 'I wish my children had suffered more', *Now* magazine, 23 April 1998.

daughters

273   For the feminist account of incest, see, for example, Louise Armstrong, *Kiss Daddy Goodnight: ten years later* (New York, Pocket Books, 1987) and *Rocking the Cradle of Sexual Politics: what happened when women said incest* (London, Women's Press, 1996).

273–4   women abusers: Linda Grant, 'Beyond Belief', *Guardian Weekend*, 14 September 1996.

275   Martin Amis: *Guardian*, 16 April 1997.
         'It is probably fruitless': Beryl Anderson-White, 'Thanks for the memories', *Everywoman*, February 1996, p. 15.

276   Jeremy Irons defending *Lolita*, press, May 1998.

276–9   Blake Morrison, *As If* (London, Granta Books, 1997), pp. 180–3.

283–4   'In the shop window': Anderson-White, as above.

sisters

286   old girl networks: Evelyn Shaw and Joan Darling, *Female Strategies* (New York, Walker and Co., 1985) p. 145.
         McLintock and Stern: *Nature*, 12 March 1998.

286–7   Matt Ridley, *The Origins of Virtue* (London, Viking, 1996).

287   Christina Rossetti, *Goblin Market*, first published in 1862, ll. 562–7.

288   Susan J. Douglas, *Where the Girls Are, growing up female with the mass media in America* (London, Penguin Books, 1995), p. 224.

291   Michele Roberts, 'Magnificat' in Linda France, ed., *Women Poets* (Newcastle upon Tyne, Bloodaxe Books, 1993), p. 232.

292   Brigid McConville, *Sisters: love and conflict within the life-long bond* (London, Pan Books, 1985).

the love of women

297   Judith Butler, *Gender Trouble: feminism and the subversion of identity* (New York and London, Routledge, 1990), p. 17.

300   Adrienne Rich, *On Lies, Secrets and Silence* (London, Virago, 1979), p. 12, quoted by Celia Kitzinger and Sue Wilkinson in 'Transitions from heterosexuality to lesbianism: the discursive production of les-

bian identities', *Women, Men and Gender: ongoing debates*, ed. M. Roth Walsh (New Haven and London, Yale University Press, 1997), p. 197.

301   Julie Burchill: *Guardian* , 5 March 1998.

302   Alice Fisher, *Esquire*, April 1998, p. 80.

           D. McFadden and E. G. Pasanen, *Proceedings of the National Academy of the Sciences*, 3 March 1998.

303   S. Le Vay, 'A difference in hypothalamic structure between heterosexual and homosexual men', *Science*, 253, pp. 1034–1037.

           L. S. Allen and R. A. Gorski, 'Sexual orientation and the size of the anterior commissure of the human brain', *Proceedings of the National Academy of the Sciences*, 89, pp. 7199–7202. A good commentary on this kind of thinking is Chandler Burr, *A Separate Creation: the search for the biological origins of sexual orientation* (New York, Hyperion, 1996).

           Celia Kitzinger, *The Social Construction of Lesbianism* (London, Sage, 1993).

           Celia Kitzinger and R. Perkins, *Changing Our Minds: lesbian feminism and psychology* (New York, New York University Press, 1993).

305   Cherie Aitken: poem printed in girls' zine with dateline 'Oct. 1993'.

306–7   Dana International reported in *Minx*, April 1998.

308   Lilian Faderman, *Surpassing the Love of Men: romantic friendship and love between women from the Renaissance to the present* (London, Women's Press, 1985).

single

310   Charlotte Raven, *Guardian*, 21 January 1997.

316   Imogen Edwards Jones: *The Times*, August 1995.

318–9   statistics on single-person households from *Social Trends* (London, Office for National Statistics, 1997); *The General Household Survey* (London, Office for National Statistics, 1997).

319   Kuwait: *Guardian*, 17 December 1997.

wives

325   Denise Levertov, 'The Ache of Marriage', in Jeni Couzyn, ed., *The Bloodaxe Book of Contemporary Women Poets: Eleven British Writers* (Newcastle upon Tyne, Bloodaxe Books, 1985), p. 84.

328   Philip Larkin, 'To My Wife', *Collected Poems* (London and Boston, The Marvell Press and Faber & Faber, 1988), p. 54.

power
emasculation

337 Alexander Niccholes, *A Discourse of Marriage and Wiving* (1615), p. 152.

339 Susan Faludi, 'The Money Shot', *New Yorker*, 30 October 1995, pp. 64 ff.

340–1 Sister Biggins, *Woman's Own*, 27 April 1998.

345 declining sperm counts: the literature is vast. A useful overview of the controversy can be got from the editorial in the *Journal of Urology* for November 1997. A search on the Medline database under the words 'sperm' and 'count' will reveal at a glance the extraordinary range of the research that is being carried out in all the developed countries. See also Laurence Wright, 'Silent Sperm', *New Yorker*, 15 January 1996, pp. 42 ff., and Deborah Cadbury, *The Feminization of Nature: our future at risk* (London, Hamish Hamilton, 1997), *passim*.

fear

349 Dee Dee Glass, *All My Fault: why women don't leave abusive men* (London, Virago, 1997).

350 British homicide statistics: *Criminal Statistics for England and Wales 1993*, (London, Her Majesty's Stationery Office Statistical Service). FBI statistics: Nanci Koser Wilson, 'Gendered Interaction in Criminal Homicide', *Homicide: The Victim/Offender Connection*, ed. A. Victoria Wilson (Cincinnati OH, Anderson Publishing Co., 1993).

351 women's fear levels: Elizabeth Anne Stanko, 'Ordinary Fear: Women, Violence and Personal Safety', in *Violence against Women: the bloody footprints*, ed. Pauline B. Bart and Eileen Geil Moran (Newbury Park CA, Sage Publications, 1993), p. 154.

353 self-defence classes: Stanko, p. 156.
Jennifer Rankin, 'A man is following me', *Collected Poems*, ed. Judith Rodriguez (University of Queensland Press, St Lucia, 1990).

355 fear as social control: S. Riger and M. T. Gordon, 'The Fear of Rape: A Study in Social Control', *Journal of Social Issues*, 37:4 (1981) pp. 71–92; M. Warr, 'The Fear of Rape among Urban Women', *Social Problems*, 32 (1985), pp. 238–250; M. T. Gordon and S. Riger, *The Female Fear* (New York, Free Press, 1989).
rape as a sport: P. Reeves Sanday, *Fraternity Gang Rape: sex, brotherhood and privilege on campus* (New York, New York University Press, 1990).

356 Sandra McNeill, 'Flashing: Its Effect on Women', *Women, Violence and Social Control*, ed. Jalna Hanmer and Mary Maynard

(Basingstoke: Macmillan, 1987), pp. 100, 102, 104. See also Sheila Jeffreys, 'Indecent Exposure', *Women against Violence against Women*, ed. D. Rhodes and Sandra McNeill (London, Only Women Press, 1985), and Jalna Hanmer and Sheila Saunders, *Women, Violence and Crime Prevention: a West Yorkshire study* (Aldershot, Avebury, 1993), pp. 344–5.

357–8   Donna B. Schramm, 'Rape', in *The Victimisation of Women*, ed. Jane Roberts Chapman and Margaret Gates (Beverly Hills CA, Sage Publications, 1978) p. 5.

loathing

359–60   the Golightly case: from press reports of the trial at Newcastle Crown Court where Golightly was sentenced on 16 January 1998.

360   Jacqueline Newton: from press reports of her husband's trial at Nottingham Crown Court, e.g. *Daily Telegraph*, 29 January 1998.

360–1   Milton Brown: *The Times*, 6 November and 6 December 1997.

362   Ralston Edwards: press, 24 August 1996.
Japanese student: press, 7 September 1996.

363   Dennis Altman from *Defying Gravity: a political life* (Sydney, Allen and Unwin, 1997).
David Daniels: press, 28 November 1997. See also the *Sunday Times*, 30 November 1997.

364   O. J. Simpson: interview with Celia Farber, *Esquire*, April 1998.

365   James Smith: press, 20 November 1997.

366   'Sometimes boys say . . .': *Shout* magazine, 13–26 March 1998.

367   *Domestic violence: a health issue* (London, British Medical Association, 1998); Kamran Abbasi, 'Obstetricians must ask about domestic violence', *British Medical Journal*, 316:7.

masculinity

369   Bertrand de Jouvenel, *Power: the natural history of its growth* (London, Batchworth Press, 1952), p. 122.

370   J. Scourfield, P. McGuffin and A. Thapar, 'Genes and social skills', *Bioessays*, 19:12 (December 1997), pp. 1125–7.

371   Katie Roiphe on Clinton: *Sunday Times*, 9 February 1997.

372   Nina Simone, *Guardian Weekend*, 6 December 1997.

373   'Strange Teachers: Cane and Unable', *loaded* magazine, March 1997, p. 74.

374   Jonah Lomu: Bill Borrows, 'You think I'm big? You should see my tackle', *loaded* magazine, March 1997, p. 95.

375   Nick Green: *Guardian*, 13 April 1998.

376   US naval officer: *The Times,* July 1989.

377   Wall Street: *FIASCO: blood in the water on Wall Street* (London, Profile Books, 1997).

378   'In the Company of Women', Ken Auletta, *New Yorker,* 20 April 1998.

See also Rowena Chapman and Jonathan Rutherford, *Male Order; unwrapping masculinity* (London, Laurence and Wishart, 1988).

equality

380   Christine Hoff Sommers, *Who Stole Feminism?: how women have betrayed women* (New York and London, Simon and Schuster, 1994).

382   Nick Varley on Jane Couch: *Guardian,* May 1995.

382–3   Dr Whiteson: press, November 1996.

383   Emily Sheffield: *Guardian,* 31 June 1997.

390   anonymous policewoman: quoted Rebecca Fowler and Patricia Wynn-Davies, *Independent,* 22 May 1996.

391   Catherine McKinnon, 'Legal perspectives on sexual difference' in Deborah L. Rhode, ed., *Theoretical Perspectives on Sexual Difference* (New Haven, Yale University Press, 1990), p. 215.

Cydena Fleming: press, October 1996, March 1997.

393   secretary survey: *Guardian,* 16 March 1998.

395–6   Women's pay: A. Zabalza and Z. Tzannatus, *Women and Equal Pay: the effects of legislation on female employment and wages* (Cambridge, Cambridge University Press, 1985), also Labour Market Trends, 104 (March 1996), p. 91, and Catherine Hakim, *Key Issues in Women's Employment* (Athlone, 1996) p. 166.

396   Country Joe McDonald: Robyn Archer and Diana Simmonds, *A Star is Torn* (London, Virago, 1986), p. 190.

396–7   nurses: see the reports of the study commissioned from Stephen Pudney and Michael Shields of the University of Leicester by the Policy Studies Institute for the Department of Health, press, 13 April 1998.

397   Patricia Pearson: *When She Was Bad: violent women and the myth of innocence* (New York, Viking, 1997).

girlpower

400   Courtney Love: see above p. 44 and n.

Drew Barrymore displayed her breasts to the millions of Americans who watch the David Letterman show.

Björk's attack on television journalist Julie Kaufman was seen world-wide on television news, 20–21 February 1996.

401   Björk quoted in *Everywoman*, August 1995, p. 10.
        Sugar, February 1997, pp. 28, 33, 75.
403   Michael Hogan: 'Grrrl power – one lad's had enough!', *Looks* maga-
        zine, February 1997, p. 99.
        Kidscape: press, 29 March 1998.
405   *Riot Grrrl* : Simon Reynolds and Joy Press, *The Sex Revolts: gender,
        rebellion and rock 'n' roll* (London, Serpent's Tail, 1995), pp. 323–1.
        Sassy: *Ms.* magazine, January/February 1997.
407   'The Ultimate Shag', *Looks* magazine, February 1997.
        Paul Stanley: *Kerrang!*, 18 January 1997, p. 62.
408   Angela Neustatter on *The Girlie Show*: *Guardian*, 9 December 1996.
        Clare Gorham: *Guardian*, 9 December 1996.
409   Charlotte Raven: *Guardian*, 3 December 1996.
        Kathy Acker: *Guardian Weekend*, 3 May 1997.
        International conference on children's oral culture, Sheffield
        University, April 1998.
410   Serena Rees: *Guardian*, 7 December 1996.
        See also Lyn Mikel Brown, *Raising their Voices: the politics of girls'
        anger* (Harvard University Press, 1998) and *Feminism and Youth
        Cultures*, special issue of *Signs: a journal of women in culture and
        society*, 23:1 (Spring 1998), *passim*.

liberation

412   Debbie Taylor, *My Children My Gold: Meetings with women of the
        fourth world* (London, Virago, 1994), p. 4 and *passim*.
413   Guerilla Girls: conversation with Suzi Gablik, Women's Art 60
        (September–October 1994), pp. 6–11, also printed in Gablik,
        Conversations Before the End of Time (London, Thames and Hudson,
        1995) and *Confessions of the Guerilla Girls* (London, Harper Collins,
        1997) as well as the Guerilla Girls' newsletter *Hotflashes* and their
        website www.guerillagirls&voyagerco.com.
414   Nicaraguan women: J. A. Reichert, L. W. Nagel, N. S. Solberg,
        'Sterilization for family planning in a third-world country',
        Minneapolis Medicine 80:17 (July 1997), pp. 27–30.
416   Alice Echols is here encapsulating the arguments of cultural
        feminism as adumbrated in Jane Alpert, 'Mother Right', first
        published in *Ms* magazine in 1973; quoted by Ann Snitow, 'A
        Gender Diary', *Conflicts in Feminism*, ed. Marianne Hirsch and
        Evelyn Fox Keller (New York and London, Routledge, 1990), p. 15.
        Mona Hatoum: 'Corps étranger', Guy Brett, *Mona Hatoum: the
        monologue* (London, Phaidon Press, n. d.).

417   Judith Lorber, *Paradoxes of Gender* (New Haven and London, Yale University Press, 1994), pp. 20–1.

418   Donna Haraway, *Simians, Cyborgs and Women: the reinvention of nature* (London, Free Association Books, 1991), p. 181, quoted by Lorber, p. 302.

419   Andrew Clements: *Guardian,* 16 April 1998.

420   Penelope Fitzgerald: *Guardian*, 13 April 1998.

421   Professor Keefe: conference in Maryland on gender and pain, reported in the *Guardian*, 10 April 1998.

422   Françoise Parturier is a popular French feminist whose works are not translated into English.

425   the wrong side: David Conway, *Free-market Feminism* (London, the Institute of Economic Affairs, 1997).

acknowledgements

Acknowledgement is made for kind permission to reprint material from the following copyright sources: Hilton Als, 'Life as a Look', *New Yorker*, 30 March 1998, by permission of the author; Dennis Altman, *Defying Gravity: A Political Life* (Allen & Unwin Pty Ltd, Sydney, 1997), by permission of the publishers and Curtis Brown, Australia, on behalf of the author; Martin Amis: 'Road Rage and Me', first published in the *Guardian*, 7 March 1998, © Martin Amis 1998, by permission of the Wylie Agency (UK) Ltd; Leland Bardwell, 'Husbands' in *Dostoevsky's Grave* (Dedalus Press, 1991), by permission of the publisher; Patricia Beer, 'The Lost Woman' from *Collected Poems* (Carcanet Press, 1988) by permission of the publisher; *Bliss* magazine (published by Emap Elan), by permission of the Editor; *British Medical Journal* article, 18 January 1997, by permission of the *BMJ*; Judith Butler, from *Gender Trouble*, copyright © Judith Butler 1989, by permission of Routledge Inc; Helene Cixous, 'The Laugh of Medusa' in Elaine Marks and Isabelle de Courtviron (eds): *New French Feminisms* (Harvester, 1991), by permission of Prentice Hall Europe; Lawrence Cohen, 'The pleasures of castration: the post-operative status of hijras, jankhas and academics', Pinkerton & Abramson (eds), *Sexual Nature, Sexual Culture* (University of Chicago Press, 1956), by permission of the publisher; *Company* magazine, March 1997, by permission of the National Magazine Company; Wendy Cope, 'My Lover' in *Making Cocoa for Kingsley Amis* (1986), by permission of the publishers, Faber & Faber Ltd; *Cosmopolitan*, February 1997, by permission of the National Magazine Company; D. Denny, *Gender Dysphoria* (Garland Publishing Inc., 1994), by permission of the publishers; Maureen Dowd article, *New York Times*, 7 July 1997, © 1997 by the New York Times,

29 January 1998, by permission of the author; Jennifer Rankin, 'A man is following me', from *Collected Poems*, ed. Judith Rodriguez (University of Queensland Press, St Lucia, 1990), by permission of the publisher; Janice Raymond, from *The Transsexual Empire: the making of the she-male* (Beacon Press, 1979), by permission of the publisher; Simon Reynolds and Joy Press, *The Sex Revolts: gender, rebellion and rock 'n' roll* (Serpent's Tail, 1995), by permission of the publisher; Adrienne Rich, *Of Woman Born: motherhood as experience and institution* (Virago, 1977), by permission of the publishers; Michèle Roberts, lines from 'Magnificat' from *The Mirror of the Mother* (Methuen, 1986), © 1986 Michèle Roberts, by permission of Gillon Aitken Associates Ltd; *Shout* magazine, by permission of the publishers, D. C. Thomson & Co Ltd, Dundee; Polly Toynbee, 'Comment', *Guardian*, 22 April 1998, by permission of the author; Jane Ussher, *Women's Madness: misogyny or mental illness* (Harvester, 1991), by permission of Prentice Hall Europe; John Walsh, Elizabeth Davis: *Heart and Hands*, © 1997 by Elizabeth Davis, by permission of Celestial Arts, California; Naomi Wolf, *Fire with Fire: the new female power and how it will change the twenty-first century* (Chatto & Windus, 1993), by permission of Random House UK Ltd and Random House, Inc; Carl Wood and Alan Trounson, *Clinical in Vitro Fertilization* (Berlin, Springer Verlag, 1989), by permission of the publisher; *Woman*, and *Woman's Own*, by permission of Rex Features; *Women's Art Magazine*, now retitled *make – the magazine of women's art*: Guerilla Girls in conversation with Suzi Gablik in *Women's Art Magazine* 60, September–October 1994; 'In my Gash' by Josepha Grieve from 'Screen Bodies: the body and computer technology in contemporary Australian Art', *Women's Art Magazine* 63, March–April 1995; Orlan, 'I do not want to look like ...' in *Women's Art Magazine* 64, May–June 1995; Martina Abramovic interview with Guy Hilton, *make* 73, December 1996–January 1997, all by permission of the publishers, Women's Art Library, London; Iris Marion Young, 'Throwing Like a Girl', *Women's Studies International Forum*, 8:3, © 1985, by permission of Elsevier Science.

We have made every attempt to identify and contact copyright holders correctly. If oversights or inaccuracies remain we will rectify the situation at the earliest opportunity.

My special thanks go to Vique Martin, jen angel, Jane Shag Stamp and the many anonymous contributors to the zines, *Simba*, *Scars and Bruises*, *Girlfrenzy*, among many, for inspiration and encouragement as well as the texts quoted, to Pamela Pickton and B. Anderson White, contributors to the now defunct feminist periodical *Everywoman*, whom I have been unable to contact, and to Carol Horne for unfailing grace under pressure, to Emma

Parry of Gillon Aitken Associates for her sensitive but firm dealing with many vicissitudes, and above all to my students from whom I learn much more than I presume to teach.